MULTI-DISCIPLINARY APPROACHES TO ROMANY STUDIES

T0346431

MULTI-DISCIPLINARY APPROACHES TO ROMANY STUDIES

edited by
MICHAEL STEWART and MÁRTON RÖVID

© 2011 by Central European University
Linguistic revision © 2011 by Christopher Ryan
Cover designed by Anca and Sorin Gog
Photo of the front cover was taken by Concetta Smedile
Photo of the back cover was provided by the Hungarian Museum of Photography
Copyedited and typesetted by Andrea T. Kulcsár

Published in 2011 by
CEU Summer University, Central European University
Október 6. utca 12, H-1051 Budapest, Hungary
E-mail: summeru@ceu.hu

Distributed by
Central European University Press

An imprint of the
Central European University Limited Company
Nádor utca 11, H-1051 Budapest, Hungary
Tel: +36-1-327-3138 or 327-3000
Fax: +36-1-327-3183
E-mail: ceupress@ceu.hu
Website: www.ceupress.com

400 West 59th Street, New York NY 10019, USA
Tel: +1-212-547-6932
Fax: +1-646-557-2416
E-mail: mgreenwald@sorosny.org

ISBN 978-615-5053-16-0

MARIE CURIE **ACTIONS**

This book is one of the products of the training program entitled *"Multi-Disciplinary and Cross-National Approaches to Romany Studies – A Model for Europe" (2070–2010)*, which was financed by the European Union Marie Curie Conferences and Training Courses "Romany Studies" – MSCF-CT-2006-045799.

Library of Congress Cataloging in Publication Data

Multi disciplinary approaches to Romany studies / edited by Michael Stewart
and Márton Rövid.
p. cm.
Includes bibliographical references.
ISBN 978 6155053160 (pbk.)
1. Romanies—Study and teaching. I. Stewart, Michael, 1959– II. Rövid, Márton.
DX115.M78 2011
305.891'497—dc23
2011016717

Printed in the USA

CONTENTS

ANTI-ROMANY RACISMS

History and Memory

Contemporary Manifestations

Romany Responses

Michael Stewart

INTRODUCTION

Challenges for Scholarship in the Field of Romany Studies

Listen to the Mayor of a poor, north Hungarian village who is quoted by Judit Durst in this volume saying the following:

> I just don't understand this question about who is a Gypsy. It is quite clear, isn't it? Everyone who is a Gypsy is a Gypsy. You can smell them from a kilometre. There is no definition for this—I can't find one. You have to accept that a person who was born a Gypsy has a different temperament; they live differently and behave differently. I grew up among Gypsy children. Everyone who is a Gypsy has remained a Gypsy. It makes no difference if they have a bath every night, the smell remains, just like with horses. There is a specific Gypsy smell. And they can smell the smell of Peasants on us.

This claim from an elected public official—the tone of which will not surprise anyone familiar with the current political climate in some parts of Hungary—brings clearly into view the broader political and social context in which we publish this collection of studies by senior scholars and their students. Across eastern Europe, and to some extent in other countries of Europe where 'anti-Gypsyism' has political currency—either at a local level as in the United Kingdom, or at a national level, as in Italy—Gypsies are a population about whom it has until recently remained acceptable to be unapologetically racist.

This is a point I will return to below, but I am also struck by the fact that the Mayor's claim gains its full meaning only if we acknowledge the degree of rhetorical hyperbole in play here. Far from it being 'quite clear' in Hungary or most parts of Europe 'who the Roma are,' they are in fact what sociologists and demographers refer to as a 'hard to see minority.' Indeed, some years back the sociologists János Ladányi and Iván Szelényi conclusively demonstrated that observers systematically disagreed over whether to classify any given third party as 'Roma' or not. In a cunningly devised experiment the sociologists demonstrated that in Hungary, in 35% of instances a second interviewer classified a person previously labelled as Roma, as non-Roma and this interviewer was uncertain as to the classification in a further 16% of cases. The same figures for Romania were 28% and 34% respectively—indicating that in every other instance observers, in these countries at least, do not 'know' if an unfamiliar person is 'Roma' (Ladányi and Szelényi, 2001, p. 85).

1

This is not to make an absurd social constructivist claim that 'the Roma do not exist.' As the Romany activist and International civil servant, Andrzej Mirga, is fond of saying, 'you may not know who we are, but we do'—a stance that reflects a political commitment to openness to engage with anyone who thinks of themselves as Roma or 'like the Roma' and is not to be confused with the name-calling 'realism' of the village Mayor. Rather, it is to note that in the absence of state institutions that might clearly define the Roma, in the way citizenship regimes, educational institutions, passports etc. determine state affiliations, the Roma will never possess the kind of clearly demarcated 'group' boundaries and 'distinctive features' that those gathered within nation-state categories have acquired.

This much has recently been acknowledged from a completely different political stance in a recent statement by the European Commission, which published its first policy communication on the subject of Roma inclusion on 8th April 2010. Here is how the Commission defines the subject of their intervention:

> The Commission uses "Roma" as an umbrella term that includes groups of people who share similar cultural characteristics and a history of segregation in European societies, such as the Roma (who mainly live in Central and Eastern Europe and the Balkans), Sinti, Travellers, Kalé etc.. The Commission is aware that the extension of the term "Roma" to all these groups is contentious, and it has no intention to "assimilate" the members of these other groups to the Roma themselves in cultural terms.

No 'once a Roma, always a Roma' rhetoric there.

To put this another way, one of the recurring themes of the papers in this volume is how the all-pervasive methodological nationalism of anthropological and other social scientific approaches produces false and misleading accounts of Romany lives in Europe today; and how, therefore, rich and honest analysis of Romany lives demands that authors transcend the 'ethnic' frame of reference. Katalin Kovalcsik notes how the real history of the development of Romany musical forms in Hungary was both misunderstood by folklorists at the time, keen to discover 'pure, national' traditions and is now misrepresented by academics keen to establish the political power of this form in modern identity politics. It is only by the most careful and attentive listening to what the 'actors' say on the ground and by remaining resolutely faithful to the actual idioms used that we can begin to work with the complexity of the ways Roma make sense of the world they live in.

But this is not all. Our notions of 'culture,' of 'ethnic group' or 'people' are so utterly rooted in the schemas derived from practices of nation states (which are, or at least strive to be, homogeneous, neatly bounded entities) that Romany communities appear as an anomaly. A theoretical rigour is therefore demanded of analysts in this field—as Picker, for instance, demonstrates with his subtle and careful search for the traces of nationalist politics in the apparently neutral policy constructions of two Italian towns.

Indeed, the stance of the racist mayor mentioned above may in one sense be best seen as an effort to create a type of rhetorical order where there is no such clear demarcation of distinct populations in reality—as the EU statement also quoted above acknowledges. But the problem exists not just for the racists and xenophobes who seek to identify 'foreign or alien elements' in the nation who can be blamed for national decline. It is equally an issue for those who would defend Roma or promote the well being of communities known as Roma.

A striking example of this came in late 2009 from the offices of two of Hungary's Ombudsmen responsible for minority rights and data protection. Concerned with the treatment of 'ethnic data' by public and private institutions and the de jure repudiation of all such data in Hungarian public life, Dr.s András Jóri and Ernő Kállai were concerned with two contradictory phenomena. On the one hand, Hungarian state policy ensures that ethnic identification can only be made on the basis of voluntary self-identification and, being highly sensitive 'private' data, is subject to especially strong data protection rules. As a result, official institutions systematically claim that they do not have 'ethnic data' to hand concerning the impact of their policies. At the same time most Hungarian Gypsies experience systematic 'racial' discrimination and state officials, when questioned off-the-record and informally, will openly admit that they know 'exactly who and how many the Roma are' in particular areas, or social categories (illiterate, convicted of robbery, unemployed etc.)—rather like the Mayor quoted above.

Faced with the systematic nature of racial classification by the authorities and others the Ombudsmen have tried to define clear criteria by which such classifications can be recognized and then treated as aspects of racist practice. This is of course no simple matter, particularly in the case of a 'hard to recognize minority' (unlike say members of the Afro-Caribbean minority in the UK or the west African minority in France).

And in one way or another all of the papers in this volume address this question. Or rather, they demonstrate that in order to address the range of social phenomena involved here, the best approach is to rephrase the questions being asked today. In the chapters by Alexey Pamporov and Judit Durst it transpires that the term 'ethnic' is in effect semantically empty. If we follow Stefan Benedik in his analysis of changing interpretations of the phenomenon of beggars on the streets of Graz, we see a complex politics and strategy of interpretation and labelling that reveals how meaningless it would be to label the social phenomenon of 'begging' as a matter of a clearly identifiable, 'ethnic' population in Graz.

A Model for Romany Studies

The scholarly field of Romany Studies is trapped by the history of the Roma in a unique and peculiar position in Europe. The investigation of Roma was in the past marginal to academic concerns because most of its practitioners were amateur folklorists interested in treating the Roma as paragons of a lost world and not citizens of modern nation states. Today this field is hemmed in by two contrastive forces: the emotionally understandable if intellectually debilitating concern to turn the plight of the Roma into a matter of 'human rights' and the difficulty academics have of dealing with a people who are not a people in the sense that nation states constitute and make people (as illustrated by Eugene Weber's original, academic and Richard Robb's more recent and populist studies of the formation of a French nation during the 19th century).

One aim of this volume, along with a second text that we hope to produce later this year, is to chart a course away from these constraining and rather ideologised approaches. We have drawn on the work of senior scholars and their pupils who have been engaged in a unique collaborative project based in Budapest.

Over the past ten years Central European University has tried to bring together all those who wish to work for an understanding of Romany concerns in the academy. This particular volume is the result of the latest series of summer schools organised by myself at the Universities of Central Europe in Budapest and Babeş-Bolyai in Cluj, Romania. These took place, thanks to generous support from the Marie Curie Programme of the European Union, over three years, from 2006-2009, with the defining feature that the best students of the first two years became organisers and teachers of the school—with a new generation of students—in the third year.

It reflects both the enduring concerns of our teachers and students and responses to the, for the most part rather scary, developments in the position of Roma in Europe in the past few years adopting and adapting work from a number of different disciplines to refine understanding of the particular position of Roma.

In order to illustrate the interpretive difficulties faced by scholars in this field the book is organised to reflect a number of analytically distinct challenges. The first two deal with the vexed issue of 'ethnicity.' I say 'vexed' because ethnicity is commonly used as a 'holder' term, that is as a word that means utterly different things in different contexts and so allows its fundamental function to operate: enabling speakers not to define clearly what they are talking about. On the one hand, in folk speech 'ethnicity' is commonly used to refer to what used to be called race but can, for obvious and good reasons, no longer be so named. Hence you will find texts saying things like 'ethnically speaking the Roma are descendants of north Indian tribes'.... (concealing, let it be said, the strong possibility that Roma have succeeded historically as a European population by incorporating many, many non-Roma into their midst). For academic scholars, 'ethnicity' tends to be used to mean 'linguistic and cultural group'—a group sharing a historically formed traditional culture, but in that sense, of course, there is no 'Roma ethnic group'... rather perhaps a community of communities—as activists like Mirga understand.

The concealed 'racial' thinking behind ethnicity can be seen clearly in the widespread sense that members of visible minorities (like say Caribbean blacks in the UK, or Roma in the Czech Republic) who are entirely assimilated members of the national citizenry are still somehow 'ethnically distinct' even if they share all characteristic 'traits' of the majority population in the citizenry. Why else can a British black actor not play a 'white' character in, say, Shakespeare, without comment being made on his 'ethnicity' when no one comments on a white American actor doing the same?

Faced with this concealed racism, the authors in this volume come at the problem from new angles. Our opening section, *Operationalising ethnicity as a theoretical term*, contains four papers that demonstrate the dangers of accepting the notion of 'ethnic group' as a term of analysis. Judit Durst takes the issue head on, demonstrating that—contrary to a widespread and apparently unshakeable popular belief—it is not the ethnic label you live under but the history of your family's and community's integration into the local social order that determines the number of children you have. Judith Okely, who pioneered a sophisticated, modern approach to issues of Romany cultural differentiation back in the 1970s—in opposition to the amateur folklorists mentioned above—returns to the central issue of the nature of cultural creativity and the burden of nationalist fantasies of 'unique', 'self-generating' cultural schemes. Benedik, one of our 'new' students from 2009, illustrates how notions of ethnicity seep from one zone of analysis and action to another and demonstrates the utter incoherence of the culturalisation of begging in an Austrian city. This beautifully crafted paper speaks to profound issues in the transmission and epidemiology of cultural representations—providing a micro study of the spread and re-interpretation of cultural themes in a micro-social setting. Naturally, gender, religion, local history and the situation of this town in regional, transnational political history all play a role in the highly peculiar history of response to the emergence of different Slovakian and ex-Yugoslav beggars in this town. Katalin Kovalcsik, long the subtlest observer of Romany cultural production in Eastern Europe, develops Okely's line of argumentation a step further with an illustration of how the noxious notion of 'ethnicity' confuses the writing of the history of Romany artistic work.

Kovalcsik's ethno-history of the most famous Romany music group of the past twenty years presages a transition to a consideration of how Roma themselves are constrained to *operationalise ethnicity in practice*. Perhaps it is far from accidental that these reports from the front line come from three of our students. Yasar Abu Ghosh (an alumnus of an earlier CEU summer school) offers a subtle and deeply touching study of the moralities and practicalities of monetary exchange in a mixed Czech-Roma village demonstrating the power of de-ethnicisation of economic issues in intimate, day-to-day relations in a village. Cili Kovai and Kata Horvath, the most brilliant young Hungarian anthropologists to have emerged in the past ten years, provide two contrastive studies, one focussing on the child as a key figure in Romany kinship and the other on the parallels and overlaps and contrasts between representation of difference in sexual orientation and 'ethnic' identification.

We then move away from the intimate observation of everyday life to a series of studies that deal, in one way or another, with the way Roma are classified as 'ethnic or racial' others. My own paper deals with the specificity of the persecution of Roma by the Nazis and the way in which biologised social policy, rather than strict racial persecution, provided the idiom within which the Nazi assault on the Roma emerged. Huub van Baar provides a reflection on the ways in which Romany organisations and their allies then deal with the commemoration of those events. Zsuzsa Vidra concludes this section of the book with an archaeology of a central theme in Romany oral history—the parallel nature of Jewish and Romany experience.

Vidra's sensitive and sharp ear leads her to provide a rich account of Romany sensibilities and she rightly draws a strong contrast between the way Roma view the years of World War II and the way their Hungarian neighbours do. Roma who went on living alongside people who were implicated or involved in the persecutions or merely stood by passively, and watched how other Hungarian citizens systematically denied or ignored the lessons of that period, have developed specific sensibilities in this field.

The specificity of Romany history over the past one hundred and fifty years lies, as the French historian Henriette Asseo has long argued, in its divergence from the fate of the Jewish people over the same time. Whereas in early modern Europe Jews and Gypsies constituted the two largest, linguistically and culturally distinctive populations distributed across the whole continent, the rise of the nation state has fundamentally divided their fates: the institution of citizenship brought emancipation for the Jews and—the horrors of 1930-1945 notwithstanding—integration into modern European life; the same period has seen the gradual marginalisation, the criminalisation and immiseration of the great mass of Europe's Gypsies. And then, the fact that the persecution of the Roma by the Nazis and their allies has never been locally acknowledged, in dramatic contrast to the ever greater public and institutional acknowledgement of the genocide of the Jews, has further intensified the sense of utter abandonment. It is in this context, I believe, that Vidra's informants' stories should be read: the evocation of Jewish suffering in their stories acts as a way to demand attention for their own, unheard, suffering.

Much of the great tradition of Eastern European sociological writing about Roma in Eastern Europe has stressed the sheer oppression, the radical inequalities suffered and the misery of Romany lives in ghettos. Without in any way wishing to sideline or obscure these realities, van Baar and Vidra demonstrate the deeply meaningful ways in which the history of suffering is constructed by Roma today and the ways in which Roma, like other humans, find resources in the world they happen to live in to construct more or less coherent accounts of their fate.

I said at the outset that the Mayor of our author's field site who rhetorically claimed he could 'smell' a Roma might be allowed to stand here for a frightening rise in anti-Romany racism. This worrying, continental, trend is discussed in two papers both of which use Italian material to expose issues that can be found in any country of the EU. Both Giovanni Picker, writing on multiculturalism and the rise of Italian anti-Gypsyism and Tommaso Vitale and Enrico Claps, discussing regional patterns in anti-Gypsyism and Romany responses to them, come at this issue from work in one of Europe's old democracies. It has become fashionable to label 'new Europe' as the bearers of 'bad old habits' in the European Union. Picker, Vitale, and Claps demonstrate that in reality 'old Europe' never grew out of these vile habits and indeed provides fresh support and nourishment for the new forms of populist anti-Gypsy rhetoric that is so audible in many countries of the former Warsaw pact.

Finally, and with the help of the work of our students we return to 'the front line' where the lives of Roma are jostled up against the lives of the non-Roma in what is often an increasingly stressed social field. As I have argued here, Romany worlds cannot be understood if we do not recognise the central social processes by which meanings are constructed, challenged, transformed and transmitted among social actors. In the closing section of the volume Marcello Frediani, Johannes Ries and Hana Synková look at ways Roma have responded to and tried to make sense of the rapidly changing environments in which they find themselves. All too often commentators on the Roma attempt to put their own preconceptions, concerns and, to be frank, prejudices into the mouths of the Roma, confident, in effect, that these marginal persons will never have the chance to speak out for themselves. The tentative studies published here demonstrate a willingness in the younger generation of scholars to step away from the stale and, all too often, crudely politicised stances of an earlier generation of scholar-activists. They are to be admired for their courage.

Overall the organisation of the volume aims to establish two fundamentally important points that emerged from the experience of the summer schools. First, while the language of 'ethnicity' and 'ethnic relations' is as popular as ever in social scientific explanations as in the folk management of social conflict, labelling a phenomenon as 'ethnic' or as a matter of 'ethnic relations' adds precisely nothing to social analysis since the meaning of 'ethnic' is internally contradictory. The function of the term in everyday life is to obscure its own meaning and role—it is foolish, therefore for social scientists to adopt it, however convenient it appears as a term of shorthand. Our texts demonstrate the often dangerous consequences in particular circumstances of this incoherence.

Second, even though 'ethnicity' means nothing, the kind of phenomena that have traditionally been labelled 'cultural' do matter immensely. Humans live in worlds that are meaningful to them, full of deep and rich meanings that matter intensely to those implicated in them. Almost all the social phenomena under discussion in this book involve matters of cultural differentiation, signification and the historically shaped allocation of meaning and value to acts the motivation for which cannot be reduced to the rational strategising of interested social actors. And therefore many of the concerns discussed in academic analysis over the past thirty years under the rubric of 'ethnic relations' cannot be ignored even if the rubric itself should be abandoned.

A beautiful example of this can be found in Abu Ghosh's chapter which also provides one of the few opportunities for readers to see that hostility, opposition and miscomprehension are not structurally implied, not ordained in the order of things, but are also the expression of particular political choices. In Abu Ghosh's village the choices of a Czech couple to run a shop where Roma will be treated as equal citizens leads to the construction of a series of new and highly potent cultural representations. The story is not at all without its tragic miscomprehensions and unintended consequences. The hope it brings, however, derives from the ability of its principal protagonists—the two shopkeepers—to step, through an act of profound imaginative identification with social 'others', outside of the tired categories of conventional thinking and to take a risk, in more sense than one, with a fresh interpretation of the meaning and significance of the apparently irrational behaviour of people who are for the most part condemned as self-destructive fools. This is an appropriate place to come to a rest with a reminder that the kind of scholarly endeavour represented here has its counterpart outside of the academy. It is time for these two worlds to be brought together in more productive interaction and for the dynamism of anti-Gypsy politics with its counsel of despair, exclusion and rejection to be confronted with an equally lively politics of hope, integration and collaboration.

I noted at the outset of this introduction that anti-Roma speech has a political legitimacy that should cause disquiet. In fact, there are some recent and significant signs of changes in this respect. In September 2009, a different Hungarian Mayor, Oszkár Molnár, claimed that Romany women were inducing deformities in their children to increase the welfare payments they would be entitled to once the children were born. In March this year, before the national elections, his conservative political party, The Federation of Young Democrats or FIDESZ, expelled him for these remarks and replaced him with an alternative candidate. That is the encouraging part of the story. The more disquieting part is that, standing as an independent on a strong nationalist, anti-Roma and anti-Semitic platform, Molnár narrowly managed to beat his former party's official candidate in the second round of the election and entered the Hungarian parliament as an independent—drawing on explicit support from the far right and the concealed support of former supporters of the socialist party. Signs can be found here of political baselines changing in both an encouraging and a disturbing direction.

I trust that our essays will provide the reader with some guidelines to understand these contradictory and sometimes hard to read runes of a rapidly changing social world.

Bibliography

Ladányi, János and Iván Szelényi (2001). "The Social Construction of Roma Ethnicity in Bulgaria, Romania and Hungary during Market Transition." *Review of Sociology* 7, no. 2 (2001):79–89. Available at http://www.akademiai.com/content/v262584626015v13/?p= 90343eb4677d4917aa944ee385a9ce6f&pi=4, 22 July 2005.

OPERATIONALISING "ETHNICITY" AS A THEORETICAL TERM

Judit Durst

"WHAT MAKES US GYPSIES, WHO KNOWS...?!":
Ethnicity and Reproduction[1]

Anthropologists working in the field of ethnicity and ethnic groups tend to emphasise that the conceptual confusion surrounding ethnic phenomena largely springs from the fact that there is basically no consensus as to what the concept of ethnicity signifies (Hutchinson and Smith, 1996; Banks, 1996).

In the light of the above, it is surprising to see the self-assurance with which some demographers involved in this subject area (who are not many, let us note) handle the concept of ethnicity, without much acknowledgement of the conceptual uncertainty which surrounds it (cf. Hirschman, 2004).

This paper consists of three parts. In the first, I attempt to show how in most cases (with a few exceptions, e.g. Ladányi and Szelényi, 2000) the trust which demography has vested in 'statistical realism' (Labbe, 2000) and the construction of the 'ethnic categories' of demographic survey-type data collection has led to people ignoring the latest findings of social sciences. Even when they try to question the changing content of ethnicity, in the framework of a survey-type investigation, they ignore the idea that the content is not permanent but changes over time and space (Okamura, 1981). The second part of the paper describes the kinds of consequences that this has had for studies of the reproductive practices of different ethnic groups. In the third part, I hope to demonstrate how much a so-called 'cultural' or 'anthropological demographic' or 'microscopic' approach can enrich our understanding of the reproductive practices of various ethnic groups.

I shall present two case studies based on ethnographic research carried out in two Roma[2] communities in Northern Hungary, in the villages of Lápos and Palóca, aiming to show that ethnicity cannot be seen as a 'culture-bearing unit', as an ethnic group 'sharing of a common culture' (Barth, 1969). Instead it should be perceived as a

1 Thanks to Iván Szelényi and Sara Randall for their valuable comments and for the János Bolyai Postdoctoral Research Fellowship which enabled me to carry on with my research.

2 The literature on this minority group, the most numerous in Hungary, treats the terms Gypsy/Roma as interchangeable. I do the same, since although political correctness would have us use the term Roma, in the settlements where I have done my fieldwork, practically all Hungarian Gypsies are Hungarian speakers (in other words Romungro) who call themselves Gypsies (*cigány*) and use the term 'peasant' (and sometimes 'Hungarian') to refer to non-Gypsies. I adhere to this local terminology in my case studies.

relational variable (Eriksen, 1993) which is not only the result of the interplay between a number of different factors (social status characteristics and cultural practices) but is also deeply embedded in the social context which defines the location of the ethnic groups examined within the interethnic tissue of the society to which they belong.

The Concept of the Ethnic Variable:
the 'Statistical Realism' of Demography

The researcher analysing ethnic differences in fertility behaviour faces some difficulty in deciding who should be regarded as subjects for the survey: people who declare themselves members of the minority group in question or those whom other people consider as members. The two definitions may lead to very different results in the case of the Hungarian Roma (Ladányi and Szelényi, 2004; Durst, 2006).

A further difficulty arises from a characteristic shared by many systems of categorisation, namely that they tend to handle ethnic categories as 'discrete, sharply demarcated units which are internally homogenous and closed to the outside' (Brubaker, 2001, p. 58), while in fact such 'groupism' is by no means characteristic of these categories. To stick to my own subject, the comparison of two North Hungarian Gypsy communities, in line with the results of other Hungarian community studies (see e.g. Szuhay, 2004; Fleck, Orsós, and Virág, 2000; Feischmidt, 2008), has shown that Gypsies cannot be considered a homogenous ethnic group. They are rather to be seen as highly divergent 'life style groups' (Kemény, 1976) in Hungary.

In the light of the above we cannot interpret ethnic categories as groups which embody collective contents or 'prototypical behaviour' (Johnson-Hanks, 2003). At the same time, this is precisely the approach which we find, in more or less explicit forms and to a varying degree, in the background of most questionnaire-based data collection serving the analysis of the demographic behaviour of ethnic 'groups'.

One such distinguished source in demography is census data. The 'philosophy' of the census, if we can speak of such a thing, is commonly based on the belief that ethnic (or racial or national, these three categories often being conflated) identity can be objectively defined on the basis of origin. Statisticians who create the ethnic categories of various censuses share a tendency to take for granted the objective existence of these categories and treat them similarly to 'objective markers' such as, for instance, age. This kind of 'statistical realism' (Labbe, 2000) assumes that the ethnic category of the census, where membership is determined by the respondent, has a constant essence or objective content which is independent of time and space, or more precisely, of situation and context. If we review the ethnic and national categories of Hungarian (Durst, 2006) and Czech (Kalibova, 2000) censuses, with special attention to the category of Roma/Gypsies, we find that census data on minority groups cannot really be seen as the outcome of 'objective' surveying.

This is well illustrated by an example from my fieldwork. During the first couple of weeks of my stay in one of the studied villages, Paloca, I had come to realise that the official census data regarding the number of the Gypsy (Roma) population of the settlement had nothing to do with 'capturing the true reality'. The trouble with the census is not only that it is 'unreliable' (Kalibova, 2000; Havas, Kertesi, and Kemény, 2000; Kertesi and Kézdi, 1998), in the sense that the numbers of interviewees who declare themselves as Roma have been changing across time and that this change cannot be explained by demographic processes but rather by the changing political situation of this minority group. There is a more serious problem with the census, which is that its allegedly 'objective' ethnic categorisation—supposedly based on self-identification by the subjects—is sometimes rather a *construction of the enumerators themselves.* In Paloca, according to the census data in 1990, less than half of the local population was Gypsy ('reported' themselves as Gypsy), but by the next census in 2001, their number had increased to 60 percent. The difference between the respective sizes of the Gypsy population in the two censuses was not due to demographic processes but to the different attitudes of the two enumerators who had done the data collection. One of them, the local nurse, told me herself that she *"didn't let them mess her around"* [in other words, she did not take their self-identification for granted], but *"took those as Gypsy"*, of whom she knew that *"their mother or grandmother was a Gypsy, even if they wanted to deny their origins."* At the next census, ten years later, the other enumerator (another local bureaucrat) was *"much softer and regarded only those as Gypsies who admitted to being Gypsy."*[3]

In the light of the above, censuses, like the ethnic categories of other questionnaire-based statistical surveys, should be considered not as a 'reflection of reality' but much more as 'a practice of social naming' (Bulmer, 1980), as one of the 'discourses' on minorities, or as 'cultural construction' (cf. Kertzer and Arel, 2002).

Ethnic Differences in Fertility Patterns?

In multi-ethnic societies, demographers have long noted a phenomenon whereby women belonging to different racial or ethnic groups are often characterised by reproductive behaviour and family structures divergent from those of the majority society.

American researchers have been mostly interested in the differential fertility patterns of the Afro-American and white American populations. There has been a

---

3   Regarding the question of the census of 1990, interviewees were asked to identify their primary 'ethnic minority' affiliation. Scholars have already argued that this formulation of the ethnic/minority group question is not capable of 'capturing the reality' in the most common dual identity (Hungarian and Roma) of the Gypsies living in Hungary (Kertesi and Kézdi, 1998). Although in the 2001 Census the ethnicity question allowed the choice of dual identity, the increase in the number of those who reported themselves as Gypsies was not due to the different formulation of the question, as we have seen in Paloca.

tendency in the United States for over a hundred years for Afro-Americans to have higher fertility rates than white Americans (Haines, 2002).[4] What lies behind such ethnically based differences in fertility has remained an open question despite the numerous research findings that have been published so far. The demographic literature on European and North American societies offers three rival hypotheses to explain ethnic differences in reproductive patterns.

One of them is the *social characteristics* thesis. This claims that the differences in fertility spring not from ethnicity or race itself but from the social composition of ethnic or racial groups, which differs from that of the majority.[5] In the case of Afro-Americans, ethnicity is a mere indicator of lower levels of education, lower income, a less promising position in the labour market and in itself has no influence whatsoever on fertility behaviour (Johnson, 1979).

A theory which offers alternative explanations to the hypothesis of social characteristics is the thesis of minority status advanced by Goldscheider and Uhlenberg (Goldscheider and Uhlenberg, 1969). These researchers concluded that being in a minority position is something that has an independent effect on decisions regarding reproduction. They found that differences in fertility behaviour between the black and the white populations did not disappear after controlling for social and economic characteristics: Afro-Americans of higher status have significantly fewer children than white Americans of a similar status. What Goldscheider and Uhlenberg offer is actually a social psychological explanation which is based on the central idea that being in a minority position has an aspect independent of social status which affects fertility behaviour and this is the sense of *insecurity* stemming from the minority position itself.

The third explanation, referred to as the *cultural hypothesis*, claims that the truly important factor about diverging patterns of reproductive behaviour across ethnicities is the subculture of the minority group—a pro-natal value system which favours the

---

4   From the perspective of examining the demographic behaviour of the Roma, this is particularly interesting as it is customary to refer to Gypsies as 'the blacks of Europe' (Kligman, 2001), while their social standing is often compared to that of Afro-Americans living in the slums of metropolitan USA (see Ladányi and Szelényi, 2004).

5   Researchers in the subject tend to be rather inconsistent in their use of the categories that serve to designate various minority groups, speaking of them alternately as races or as ethnicities. Some seem to equate the two terms, or at least attribute little importance to the differences in meaning between these two categories (see e. g. Forste and Tienda, 1996; Johnson, 1979). In this work I consistently use the term 'ethnic group', indicating that an approach which perceives race in an essentialist sense emphasising the biological differences among different peoples is unacceptable to me. Instead, both race and ethnicity will be seen as social constructs, in other words as categories which are construed by members of the society. (For more on this see, for instance, Barth, 1969; Banks, 1996; Eriksen, 2002; Ladányi and Szelényi, 2000).

willingness to have many children and build large families (cf. e.g. Boriszov, 1969; quoted by Andorka, 1987).

Several authors have tried to contextualise the effect which 'ethnicity' (perceived as belonging to a minority group) has on fertility. It has been found that minority status affects reproduction not directly but through the social milieu and social context (Ritchey, 1975; Tober et al., 2006) which surrounds the group or through the opportunity cost structure of the studied minority (Bean and Marcum, 1978; Bean and Swicegood, 1985).

Some anthropologists studying differential ethnic fertilities in African societies see ethnicity as a type of 'cultural variable', but here culture is perceived not in the old, rigid structuralist-functionalist sense as conceiving 'objectified cultural contents' (such as values or attitudes) (see Hammel, 1990) but as sets of coordinated social practices, aspirations and ways of thought (elements of the shared 'cultural repertoires' characteristic of the different groups, which change continually through social interaction (Johnson-Hanks, 2003).[6]

In this sense, an ethnic group may be seen as a 'community of practice'—a community which changes along with the modification of the economic environment and where members are characterised by shared aspirations, expectations, ways of thought and social practices.

In Johnson-Hanks's explanation the demographic variables characteristic of the specific ethnic communities, such as the (premarital) total fertility rate,[7] are the result of precisely such shared aspirations and expectations and the common repertoire of their practices rather than of social characteristics such as level of education.

The analysis of the relationship between social processes and demographic indices, which Johnson-Hanks addresses in the above-mentioned study, underlies other recent work in 'anthropological or cultural demography' (see Bledsoe, 2002; Greenhalgh, 1995; Johnson-Hanks, 2003; Johnson-Hanks, 2005; Coast, Hampshire, and Randall, 2007; Bernardi, 2003).

This relatively newly emerged discipline, at least in European demographic studies, is also the background to the piece of research I present below. Before I present my own research findings, however, I must briefly survey the most important results of demographic research on the Roma to date.

---

6   "*The ethnography of an earlier age called it simply 'culture'*", says Johnson-Hanks in an attempt to explain the very different demographic behaviour of two major ethnic groups living in Cameroon. '*Contemporary ethnographers nearly uniformly reject the concept of bound, discrete cultures, emphasizing the exchanges, adaptations and collaborative innovations that have occurred across culture boundaries*' (Johnson-Hanks, 2003, p. 56).

7   Total fertility rate (TFR) is one of the most important indicators of reproductive behaviour in demographic research. It is actually an estimate of complete fertility: it shows the number of children that women of a childbearing age are likely to have on average at a particular time, provided that their fertility patterns do not change.

Demographic Research on the Roma

The majority of demographic research on the Roma works with census data (Kalibova, 2000; Mészáros and Fóti, 2000; Hablicsek, 2007). Studies using the ethnic categories of censuses have to tackle the problems of this data source that we mentioned earlier.

While censuses use 'self-reported identity' as a marker for forming the category of ethnicity (or national minority), the other large branch of survey-type demographic research also works with a different type of definition: they consider a person Roma if their environment considers them Roma (this may be the expert environment, cf. Kertesi and Kézdi, 1998, or the interviewing research assistant, see Ladányi and Szelényi, 2004). Such surveys, working with a small number of aggregated data, all show ethnic differences in reproductive patterns: namely, that although the fertility rate of the Roma is drawing ever closer to that of the non-Roma, the former still have more children on average than the latter (Kemény, 2004; Kalibova, 2000; Martin, 2003).

The majority of these surveys explain high fertility rates among the Roma by reference to Gypsy 'culture' and within that to its pro-natal value system, which favours large families (Kalibova, 2000, p. 175) or try to trace it back to the social status of Gypsies in society, mostly to their unemployment (see Gyenei, 1998).

The majority of anthropological works have already proven that such 'cultural' explanations are untenable. Anthropologists practically all agree that it is wrong to view Gypsies as carriers of a 'common cultural content'; they should be seen rather as participants in a relation (Okely, 1983; Stewart, 1993). 'Gypsyness' is not an inborn 'primordial bond' (see Geertz, 1996) which determines behaviour but is more something that is shaped in the context of the interethnic relation. "In the meaning of Gypsy there are the Gypsies themselves, and there are we, the Non-Gypsies, too, there are their realities and our imaginations about this reality, their being and our behaviour towards them, there is the whole history of our interethnic relations" (Williams, 2000, p. 69; quoted by Horváth, 2005).

In other words, when we try to understand how the category of 'being a Gypsy' affects the demographic behaviour of 'Gypsies', we are probably on the wrong track if we think that the ethnic group 'Gypsies' can be conceived as a variable marking prototypical behaviour forms, a unique value system or set of attitudes. The approach proposed by Eriksen appears far more promising—in this approach ethnicity is nothing else than "an aspect of social relationship between agents who consider themselves as culturally distinctive from members of other groups with whom they have a minimum of regular interaction" (Eriksen, 2002, p. 12).

With some exaggeration we might say that *the category of the Gypsy is itself a mere empty category[8] which only acquires any sort of meaning through contact with non-Gypsies. If we can clearly see the character of this relationship, it becomes far easier to understand the differential reproductive practices of (some groups) of Gypsies from non-Gypsies than if we simply try to identify the 'distinctive cultural trait' which could explain the differences in the demographic behaviour of Gypsies and non-Gypsies.*

If, however, we do not work with survey-type data but carry out microscopic, micro-demographic investigations, it becomes quite obvious that 'the ethnic variable' does not in itself affect reproductive behaviour. One cannot claim that 'the Roma' as a homogeneous group have more children than the non-Roma since, as we shall see below, the different Roma communities themselves may well also be characterised by divergent reproductive practices and certain groups have completely identical family planning strategies to those of non-Roma of the same social status. The following section of the paper presents the components of these strategies.

Two Roma Case Studies:
What Is behind the 'Ethnic Differences' in Reproduction Strategies?

Lápos and Palóca are two small villages in a region of Hungary consisting largely of small villages and affected by regional segregation (Virág, 2003).[9] It is one of the most backward parts of the country both in terms of the level of education among the population and their economic opportunities. The unemployment rate in villages in the region has been around 20% on average, with minor variations, since 1994 (G. Fekete, 2005).

Today, we could fairly term Lápos and Palóca as Gypsy villages. Of the 120 families of the former, 10 are non-Gypsy, while in the latter the proportion of non-Gypsies is around 10%.

These two villages, similarly to the poorly educated Roma population of the whole region, are characterised by large scale unemployment: differences occur only in the duration of it. Starting from the condition of almost 'full employment' characteristic of the 1970's (Kemény, Janky, and Lengyel, 2004), the population of Lápos had shifted by the mid- to late 1980's to a state of 'full unemployment' which has proved to be a long-lasting condition even now, 20 years after the post-communist transition.

---

8   "Whether I think of myself as a Gypsy? I do. What makes us Gypsies? Who knows, 'cause I'm sure I don't. 'Cause… this is what we were born. .. 'Cause these are the names we were given, peasant and Gypsy." (This extract comes from an interview with a young Gypsy woman from Lápos.)

9   In 2003, the national Gypsy survey found that by that time one third of the country's entire Gypsy population was living in this region (Kemény and Janky, 2003).

At Palóca, by contrast, unemployment affects a lower ratio of the population and for shorter periods of time, although it is still a chronic condition. (Social characteristics of the inhabitants of the two villages are shown in Table 1 in the Appendix). A major difference is that the men of this latter village, thanks to relatives living in Budapest, have been travelling to the capital on a seasonal basis—mostly working on building sites from Spring to Autumn.

A shared characteristic of the society of the two villages is that neither of them have what we could call a homogenous Gypsy community. The Roma community of Lápos contains at least three separate strata, even though, since the village is quite small, contact between them is inevitable. At the same time, members of each of the strata, when speaking of those 'below' them, make statements like "I don't mix with that lot..."

At one end of the social spectrum we find those who have 'risen'—these Roma families are referred to by the locals as 'gone proper' or 'assimilated'. They tend to change their names for a Hungarian name or enter a mixed marriage in order to indicate to the outside world that they no longer consider themselves Gypsies.[10] An important element of their mobility strategy is to make sure they send their children away from the village in order to rescue their future from a place which they see as having 'no future' and heading inevitably towards becoming a ghetto.

The reproduction strategy of these people is also strongly motivated by the desire for mobility and their ambition to emulate the lifestyle of the peasant population of the village. Usually they plan on having two children, although a third one often 'slips in', in order to make sure they will be well provided for in all respects. One of them aptly stated the opinion of the group,

> Where they have more than three children everything goes wild, it's no good any more. ... What do they want more children for? For poverty? To me it's important to give each of my children a proper education. It's important that they should study and learn a trade and marry decently. What do I mean by decently? Well, that they marry educated boys who have studied... It's hard enough to provide well for three... You should buy each of them a house, open a bank account for them so that they have something to start out with when they get to be eighteen.

Of the first generation who have 'risen', hardly any are still left in the village. Most of them moved away at the earliest possible opportunity, in the still 'prosperous' 1970's. They saw the early signs of the village turning into a slum and followed the mobility route of the peasants of Lápos (their important reference group), to the more well-to-do

---

10 "How could I be a Gypsy when we live in such a big house?" one of them, a fourteen-year-old girl, exclaimed when a new teacher, ignorant of the complex stratification of the local society, termed her a Gypsy purely on the basis of her skin colour. The children of Gypsy women who have 'risen', usually by way of a mixed marriage, are not seen as 'proper Gypsies' by their Hungarian companions.

areas of the country. These Gypsy women, now in their sixties or seventies, used various more or less modern methods of birth control, as early as the 1970's, since they saw restricting the number of children as the only way toward social mobility. They broke out of the abject poverty faced by their parents by seeking employment themselves and by their husbands working as miners and drawing regular monthly wages. A few of them even managed to find a place in the formal labour market, mostly working as cleaners and thereby encountering non-Roma people. Thus the workplace came to act as a space for socialisation, where the Gypsy people could establish 'weak ties' (Granovetter, 1991), develop a heterogeneous social network and absorb the influences of the majority society, which also affected their demographic behaviour.[11]

Similarly to local farmers of the same age group, this upwardly mobile Gypsy group tended to marry around 18–19. The women had their first child usually around the age of 21–22 and had a maximum of 3–4 children (see Tables 2 and 3 in the Appendix). Members of the next generation, mostly in their forties today, restricted their fertility even further and delayed the birth of their first child. In fact there is not one among them who became a mother before the age of 18, unlike their parents or the segregated Gypsies of the village.

The second group within Lápos society, let us call them the group 'hoping for mobility', are characterised by very different work experience and educational ambitions. Women in this group, most of them mothers of 4–5 children, still have some experience of the formal labour market. Indeed, most of them have spent a few months working at the nearby forestry commission, once a large employer in the region, some time in the 1980's before the birth of their first child. It is also true of most of them that their fathers were permanently employed for several decades in one of the nearby mines. Most of their husbands, however, had been unemployed for over fifteen years now. In the past year, however, many of them had been 'found' by Gypsy entrepreneurs—who provide them with occasional labour opportunities for a few months each year and thus offer a fleeting hope of stabilising their position or, as they put it, of 'moving from one to two.'

---

11 The powerful effect of social networks, which has also influenced the thinking of these assimilated Gypsies, is shown by the following quote from an interview. "I was already taking Ovidon [one of the most popular contraceptive pills of the 1970's] when no one else in this village had even heard of it. My relatives in Budapest and the women at work had told me to take it because it would be good... because, they said, lots of children meant great poverty."

Schools and education play an ambivalent role in the life of this group.[12] On the one hand they consider (or would consider) it important to have their children educated, the more so as education in Hungary is compulsory until the age of 18 and not fulfilling this obligation means the family losing entitlement to child benefits.

"In God's name, I thought to myself, I won't deprive my child of the chance to learn, and get to know the world so that at least she can have a better life", said the mother of 15-year-old Szabi when I was trying to find out whether the girl, who had been wandering around the village with her boyfriend during school time for the past week, was now going to drop irrevocably out of secondary school or not.

From the mother's reply below, given to my question, "Why is Szabi not in school", I might have thought that she was determined to have her daughter educated and was merely experiencing temporary financial difficulties. "Her boots have a hole in them, and I don't even have money for food just now, so I don't want her to go for a while until I get the benefit, 'cause I don't want the others to laugh at her."

I soon found out, however, that Szabi's family are far from sure whether their daughter will have a better life if she finishes school. The main reason for this is that practically the only school available to the Roma of Lápos is a technical school in S., 50 kilometres from the village, which trains social nurses. This institution, practically a depository for young, school age Gypsy people, has very low standards according to parents and the qualification it provides is barely marketable in Hungary today. This is proven by experience. There is only one girl in the village who completed this secondary school but she has been unable to find work for more than a year. "Look at Angi, she has done all her schooling, she went for eleven years and what good has it done her? She just sits here in the village all day and then in the evenings she goes over to Sz. [the neighbouring village – editor's note] to play on the slot machines and waste all her father's money. ... Is that why I should kill myself [forcing her to study]? Gypsies get no work round here anyway...".

The low standard of the school at S. and the appalling boarding conditions deter the boys of Lápos even more than the girls—they usually drop out after the first year. This in turn makes girls uncertain about carrying on. During the summer holidays Szabi's mother was feeling ambivalent about whether her daughter should carry on with her studies the following year. "You know, I'm not sure I mind if she doesn't go back. She and her boyfriend are getting on so well. He intends to stay at home, as he

---

12 I fully agree with Johnson-Hanks that the relevant question for a demographic examination is not only why educated women have fewer children almost all over the world than those who have had less schooling (this is one of the recurring questions of demography). It is equally important to ask what sort of a place getting an education occupies amongst the ambitions, expectations, life plans of the social actors of different (ethnic) communities. (Cf. Kovai, 2008; Durst, 2006). This latter at least partially explains why the childbearing strategies of women in different (ethnic) communities differ (if at all) (Johnson-Hanks, 2003).

can't bear the dormitory any longer, and if this is the case, Szabi would worry that they won't see each other all week, as she can only come home for the week-end. And then who can tell whether the boy will wait for her or not?"

Apart from feeling that the time and money invested in learning might not bring the expected returns, the very institution of the school is seen by the Roma of Lápos as an alien place that belongs the world of the *gadjo* (the teachers are all *gadjo, non-Roma*) where you have to worry about your child's welfare. Beyond their own ambivalent feelings, Szabi's family also had to tackle the disapproval of the local Gypsy community when their daughter started school at S. The mother summed this up at the time by saying,

> The other Gypsies are funny about us... they laugh at as... they say, "What do you think she'll become? Some sort of a great teacher or something? A junky and a prostitute, that's what she'll become!" ... But I always say to Szabi, "Mother and Father trust you, and you should look after yourself, too, you know you're not at Lápos..." I pray so hard that the good Lord will not allow them to get lost...

Despite all of their conflicting emotions, we may discern the hope for mobility in the background of the demographic behaviour of this stratum of the Gypsies of Lápos and their attitude towards having children. Women usually 'marry' around the age of 16–17 (if by marriage we mean what the given community means by it; cf. e.g. Bledsoe, 1999) and have their first child rather young, at 16–18 (see Table 3 in the Appendix). The main influence in this respect is usually their peer group in the village[13] the 'fashion' or, as the literature calls it, 'contagion' (cf. Bernardi, 2003).[14] Even though the first baby comes early, members of this group usually stop after their fourth or fifth child.

For these women, birth control serves not as a means of spacing but to terminate childbirth. This is when many of them start using the Depo Provera injection, despite its numerous unhealthy side-effects.[15] "At least you now have this injection... Yes, it

---

13 "We had only just got married, I was 16, and Zsolti was already worrying about why we haven't got a baby. All his mates had got babies by that time and they could boast in the pub saying 'I'm gonna be a father'... Here the Gypsies envy each other and bully each other into having a baby ... if there is a couple who don't have a baby, they say, 'what's wrong with you, if you can't have babies, you should go and see a doctor."

14 "It was Móni who started it, she ran away with Ati when she was 14. You know, we were all one gang. And then there were others who left with their man, so there was just me and my friend, the only two girls left behind here, so what were we supposed to wait for? ... Our friends all had a baby to look after by that time so it felt really bad that we did not have one..."

15 Depo Provera became popular among Gypsy women of Lápos because it was what they found cheapest of all the available options. It is also quite easy to administer, it requires no special attention: all one has to do is go and see a doctor every three months to receive the injection.

does give me a headache, sometimes so bad it almost drives me crazy. And it makes me put on weight, too, but I don't care, I don't want to have any more kids, because it is not worth it. Tell me, how can you get on with so many children in this poverty?" When the injection fails to prevent pregnancy, they use *post factum* birth control—this is the group which the hospital view as notorious abortion clients. "They said to me in the hospital, 'Mrs Cs is that you again?' They said they would tie a knot in my husband's thingy... So I told them it's better I'm here.... So they aborted the baby for 1500 Forints [6 EUR – editor's note] because I'm poor. Why have a baby in this filth? In filth and poverty?"

The third and the most numerous group of the local Roma population consists of people that even the local Gypsies tend to call 'slum-dwellers'. They have only recently been relocated into the main street of the village from the previous slum (as part of the latest social housing policy intended to integrate the Gypsy population into Hungarian society), which caused a great deal of tension. In contrast to those hoping for mobility, for these very poor Gypsy families school plays practically no part in their life and acquiring any sort of qualifications is not seen as being of any particular value. This is mainly because they do not believe that having their children educated would lead to any significant improvement in their lives as regards work or 'a better life'. "I have had eight years at school and where has it got me? ... There are no jobs at all anywhere around. This is a national problem. But even if there happens to be something they are sure not to give it to a Gypsy." The lack of ambition to get educated is also reflected in the attitude which most of the Gypsy community hold and which was voiced here by a mother of six children from the slum. "Why should I have studied? I wouldn't have become anybody anyway. Most Gypsies don't become anything. They aren't like the Hungarians who get themselves schooled, although I don't really know what they study for, either. If you're not at home you'd worry that your husband would cheat on you. A woman's job is to cook for the children, keep them clean, look after them. What else should I worry about? My children and my husband and the life they have..."

Long term unemployment is characteristic of practically all men and women within this stratum. Besides social welfare and child benefit they live on occasional sources of income from work such as picking mushrooms, gathering herbs, collecting scrap metal or, most recently 'hunting'. Thus it is hardly surprising if their social life and everyday practice are characterised by what is called a 'present-oriented' attitude.[16] (Cf. Stewart, 2003). Understanding this will allow us to explain the majority of their social behaviour, including their attitude to school. One of their central traits in this respect is that they will not let their children go to school unless the family has enough money (for clothes and a pack of elevenses) and if the child has enough time to study. In these large families, which often number 8–10, the help of older children is extremely valuable: when the mother goes out to collect mushrooms, she leaves the older girls and boys in charge of the younger children. During the mushroom season

---

16   For more detail on this see Durst, 2006.

it is hard to find a Gypsy child from Lápos in the district primary school—which the teachers accept as an 'unalterable fact'.

Such a present-oriented attitude, springing from the sheer need to make a living, is also discernible behind the birth control practices of these people. The following example is typical within this sphere. M, aged 39 and already the mother of 10 children, received special aid from the local Mayor for the abortion of an unplanned child who would have faced serious health hazards according to the doctors. After much deliberation M. reluctantly went into the hospital but the very next day, before the operation, she ran away from the ward to return to her home. The money meant for the doctor could be put to better use at home. "Was I supposed to take that tiny bit of money away from the hungry mouths of the children?" she asked me a few days after her return. "She's kept both the money and the baby", as the Major commented on her case later.

Practically the entire group display uniform demographic behaviour: they marry for life, start having children early (usually around 16) and carry on for many years, with a total fertility rate of around six children (Table 4 in the Appendix) and live in large extended families. This group are characterised by long-term unemployment. They live permanently below the poverty line, and draw what little positive identity they can build (as opposed to the non-Gypsies, 'the peasants') from having children. This is particularly true of the women. "Having twelve children by the age of 32, that's something, isn't it? The peasants can't do that, I bet! They only have one or two children, because they are selfish, they want everything. Gypsies are used to having little. Where there is enough for ten to eat, there'll be enough for the eleventh." At Lápos, the love of large families and the family-centred attitude are important elements of Gypsy identity. One of them recently expressed this by saying, "Making mud bricks, playing music and bringing up children come from the Gypsies. This is what we brought along with us, this is what we are proud of."

For Roma women (and men) who have practically no 'capital' or means of enhancing their prestige, children, offspring of their own, are the only source of the 'symbolic capital' (Bourdieu, 1988) which provides them with self-esteem, a possible source of distinction within the egalitarian community of the Roma of Lápos (cf. Kelly, 1998). To use micro-economic terms, the 'gain' from having children is considerable for those Gypsies of Lápos who have dropped out of the channels of mobility (education, the formal labour market), while the 'cost' of bringing up children is not considerable. Such potential costs are reduced by the fact that the parents have low welfare aspirations, thanks to structural reasons and socialisation, with respect to both themselves and their children. The social structure of the Roma of Lápos also helps reduce these costs—the system of extended family networks helps share the burden of child care. Finally, the low opportunity cost of having children (cf. Bean and Marcum, 1978) also acts in the same direction: most women at Lápos have only completed six years of primary education and this, coupled with discrimination in the formal labour market, leaves them with little hope of finding employment. Because of this they need not worry about the costs of having children (loss of position or income) which persuade highly qualified woman to put off having even the intended number of children.

Finally, and complementing the above, the example of the other Roma community we examined, that of Palóca, also directs our attention to the importance of the networks of ethnic groups and within that to the 'density and intensity of ethnic relations' (Bean and Marcum, 1978) shaping reproductive decisions.

The Roma community of Palóca is also highly structured and may be divided into three main groups. The group called 'white Gypsies' by the locals corresponds to the assimilated Gypsies in Lápos. Their reproduction strategies are also similar. Secondly, the group customarily referred to as 'the filthy' consists of the poorly educated, jobless Gypsy families who have come into the village over the past few years from the neighbouring settlements. Their demographic behaviour is similar to the poor Roma of Lápos with some minor differences. Finally, the group we are presently focusing on is that of relatively mobile Roma who have completed at least eight years of primary school education and are different from the other Gypsy groups at Palóca in that they make their living from relatively regular occasional work.

In contrast to the 'the filthy' group in the village and the segregated Roma of Lápos, these 'mobile' Gypsies of Palóca have a social network which is relatively open, ethnic relations are less dense and there are 'weak ties' (Granovetter, 1991) with the better-off non-Roma as well. This has a considerable effect on their reproductive decisions. The primary factor here is not that through these weak ties they have come into possession of new information regarding modern and affordable means of contraception, as is held by diffusion theory in demography. The main influence is that these networks shape their thinking and mobilise new desires and ambitions (cf. Pollack and Watkins, 1993).

Several of the 'mobile' Gypsies of Palóca have relatives living in Budapest. It is with the help of such family members that many of the young men find seasonal employment in the capital, and later on help each other to establish employment links. As the good weather sets in, from Spring to Autumn, they only visit home for one week-end a month. In almost all cases, although these young men work together in a group, they have a much better chance of encountering role models different from those seen in their village and to adopt their behaviour. This is partly the reason why, unlike their counterparts at Lápos, the young members of this group do not start their families early: first they would like to 'live', as they put it, before taking on the burdens inherent in family life. One of them, a young man in his mid-20s, said, "it's no good having a baby at sixteen. How do you support your family? There are enough stupid people at Lápos... Customs are different in every village. At Palóca this is not the fashion... When do I want a child? It would be too early now. Maybe when I am thirty... two children... until then I have to live my young life..."

The difference in networks and the divergences in attitude coming from different types of social networks partly explains why the rate of teenage mothers and the average number of children per family are far lower at Palóca than at Lápos (see Table 2 in the Appendix).

Summary

At the beginning of this paper I raised the question of what lies behind the different demographic behaviour of ethnic (minority) groups. By the end I found that if we do 'microdemography' we notice that the reproductive behaviour of Gypsies does not always diverge in all cases from that of the majority group. Even in the case of Roma groups where family planning strategies differ significantly from the non-Roma population (e.g. the Gypsies of Lápos) it is difficult to claim that 'Gypsyness' (Gypsy identity or 'Gypsy social and cultural practices') is the factor that explains the differences.

The results of my fieldwork in Romungro (Hungarian Gypsy) communities may also be read as a kind of criticism of the approach which sees ethnicity in terms of homogeneous communities and assumes them to be 'communities of shared social practices'. (cf. Johnson-Hanks, 2003; Pollack and Watkins, 1993).

Through the examples of the Gypsy communities I examined, my aim was to demonstrate that ethnic groups, at least in the case of the Gypsies who are in a minority in every country where they live, cannot be interpreted as 'culture-bearing units' (Barth, 1969).

Instead, the 'Gypsyness' of the people of Lápos consists of a combination of several factors such as life-long 'marriage', which is at present a general practice among them, the protective network of large extended families, a very homogeneous, dense ethnic network, lacking "bridging (weak) ties" with different social status groups, low levels of education and the lack of opportunities for mobility. However, not one of these is an ethnic characteristic and they do not characterise all Gypsies as an ethnic category. As we have seen, being a Gypsy is something totally different for the assimilated stratum from Lápos, for the 'slum-dwellers' of the same village or for the Roma inhabitants of Palóca.

One of the things that my case studies have shown is that ethnicity should be viewed not as 'a variable similar to culture' (cf. Andorka, 1987) but much more as a *relational variable* which is not only the sum total of a number of other factors (social status characteristics and cultural practices) but is at the same time embedded in the social context which determines the place of the examined ethnic group within the tissue of the interethnic relations of the surrounding society. To put it slightly differently: the category of 'Gypsy' is in itself a hollow category which only acquires its genuine meaning through the relationship with non-Gypsies. It is probably through understanding this relationship that we can also understand the reproductive practices of certain Gypsy groups which differ from those of non-Gypsies.

In the light of all of this we can state that being a Roma affects the practices of child-bearing not through the characteristics of 'Roma culture' (since there is no such thing as a unified Roma culture, for the various subgroups can be characterised by divergent social practises, cf. Stewart, 2003), nor through the 'collective social identity' of the Roma.[17] If such ethnic membership affects these behaviours at all, this emerges insofar as 'being a Roma' means an unfavourable, stigmatised social position, a double disadvantage (Eidheim, 1969) in today's Hungary and in most of Central and Eastern Europe as well.

The above statement applies particularly to the contemporary social context of Hungary, loaded as it is with ethnically charged conflicts. Today one can come across videos on the internet where ethnic communities (namely the Gypsies) are judged to be 'demographically dangerous' (seen as excessive particularly when contrasted with a shrinking Hungarian population).

In the light of all of this it may not sound surprising if we conclude that just as it is not worth talking about 'Roma culture', there is no real point in speaking about 'Roma demography' or 'Roma reproductive behaviour' either (cf. Neményi, 2000). By doing so, we would only be doing a favour to the 'groupism' described by Brubaker and would be contributing to the 'social naming practice' of data sources which hypothesise homogeneous categories in their attempt to grasp minority groups—even though such homogeneity does not exist in reality.

In fact the Roma living in our region vary widely in terms of lifestyle, social characteristics, everyday practices and have only one shared characteristic: they are all affected by the anti-Gypsyism of the surrounding societies.

Bibliography

Andorka, Rudolf (1987). *Gyermekszám a fejlett országokban* (Number of children in the developed countries). Budapest: Gondolat.

Arel, Dominik (2002). "Language Categories in Censuses: Backward- or forward Looking?" in *Census and Identity*, eds. Kertzer, David and Dominik Arel. Cambridge: Cambridge University Press.

Banks, Marcus (1996). *Ethnicity: Anthropological Constructions*. Routledge: London and New York.

Barth, Fredrik (1969). "Introduction" in *Ethnic Groups and Boundaries. The Social Organization of Culture Difference*, ed. Barth, Fredrik. Boston: Little, Brown and Company, pp. 9–38.

---

17 "What makes a Gypsy a Gypsy? Well, that they have brown skin. People can tell straight away, just by looking at them. They can tell from the way you speak, too. The way you dress. How shall I put it? I am not as polite as you, I don't have the same vocabulary as a Hungarian... If a Gypsy starts speaking, people can tell straight away that he is a Gypsy, even if he has white skin ..." This quote is from a middle-aged Gypsy lady from Lápos.

Bean, Frank D. and John P. Marcum (1978). "Differential Fertility and the Minority Group Status Hypothesis: An Assessment and Review" in *The Demography of Racial and Ethnic Groups*, eds. Bean, Frank D. and W. Parker Frisbie. New York: Academic Press, pp. 189–209.

Bean, Frank D. and Gray Swicegood (1985). *Mexican American Fertility Patterns*. Austin: University of Texas Press.

Bernardi, Laura (2003). "Channels of Social Influence on Reproduction." *Population Research and Policy Review* 22 (2003): 527–55.

Bledsoe, Caroline (2002). *Contingent Lives: Fertility, Time and Aging in West Africa*. Chicago: University of Chicago Press.

Bodnár, Lóránt (1981). "A cigány nők terhességeinek társadalmi, demográfiai jellemzői Szabolcs-Szatmár megyében. IV. A szociális-gazdasági tényezők szerepe" (The social and demographic characteristics of Gypsy mothers-to-be in Szabolcs-Szatmár county. IV. The social-economic factors). *Népegészségügy* 62 (1981): 308–14.

Bourdieu, Pierre (1988). *A társadalmi egyenlőtlenségek újratermelődése* (The reproduction of social inequalities). Budapest: Gondolat.

Brubaker, Rogers (2001). "Csoportok nélküli etnicitás" (Ethnicity without groups). *Beszélő*, no. 7–8 (2001): 60–66.

Bulmer, Martin (1980). "On the Feasibility of Identifying 'Race' and 'Ethnicity' in Censuses and Surveys." *New Community* 8 (1980): 3–16.

Coast, Ernestina, Katherine Hampshire, and Sara K-Randall (2007). "Disciplining Anthropological Demography." *Demographic Research* 16, no. 16 (2007): 493–518.

Csalog, Zsolt (1973). "Etnikum? Faj? Réteg? Adalékok a 'cigányság' fogalmához" (Ethnicity? Race? Strata? Notes on the terms of "Gypsyness"). *Világosság* 13, no. 1 (1973) 38–44.

Csepeli, György, Antal Örkény, and Mária Székelyi (1997). "Szertelen módszerek" (Extravagant methods) in *Szöveggyűjtemény a kisebbségi ügyek rendőrségi kezelésének tanulmányozásához* (Reader on the studies of how the police deal with minority issues). Budapest: COLPI, pp. 130–72.

Durst, Judit (2002). "Fertility and Childbearing Practices among Poor Gypsy Women in Hungary: The Intersections of Class, Race and Gender." *Communist and Post-Communist Studies* no. 35 (2002): 457–74.

Durst, Judit (2005). "'Csak a pénzre hajtik mind'?: Az antropológiai megközelítés haszna a demográfiában" (Do they "all go for money"? The use of anthropology in demography). *Tabula* 8, no. 2 (2005): 283–310.

Durst. Judit (2006). *Kirekesztettség és gyermekvállalás* (Social exclusion and reproduction). PhD Thesis. Manuscript.

Eidheim, Harald (1969). "When Ethnic Identity is a Social Stigma" in *Ethnic Groups and Boundaries. The Social Organization of Culture Difference*, ed. Barth, Fredrik. Boston: Little, Brown and Company, pp. 39–57.

Eriksen, Thomas Hylland (2002). *Ethnicity and Nationalism: Anthropological Perspectives*. London: Pluto Press.

Feischmidt, Margit (2008). "A boldogulók identitásküzdelmei – Sikeres cigányszármazásúak két aprófaluból" (Identity struggles of successful Gypsies in two Hungarian villages). *Beszélő*, no. 11–12 (2008): 96–114.

Fleck, Gábor, János Orsós, and Tünde Virág (2000). "Élet a Bodza utcában" (Life in Bodza street) in *Romák/cigányok és a láthatatlan gazdaság* (Roma/Gypsies and the invisible economy), ed. Kemény, István. Budapest: Osiris and MTA Kisebbségkutató Műhely, pp. 80–138.

Forste, Renata and Marta Tienda (1996). "What's behind Racial and Ethnic Fertility Differentials?" in *Population and Development Review* 22, no. 3 (1996): 109–33.

G. Fekete, Éva (2005). "Cigányok a Cserehát–Hernád–Bódva vidéken. Tájegységi jellemzés" (Gypsies in the Cserehát–Hernád–Bódva territory. Characterisation of the region) in *Roma szegregációs folyamatok a csereháti és dél-baranyai kistérségekben* (Roma segregation processes in the Cserehát and South-Baranya areas), ed. Baranyi, Béla. Budapest: Gondolat Kiadó and MTA Etnikai-Nemzeti Kisebbségkutató Intézet, pp. 53–83.

Geertz, Clifford (1996). "Primordial Ties" in *Ethnicity*, eds. Hutchinson, John and Anthony Smith. Oxford and New York: Oxford University Press, pp. 40–45.

Goldscheider, Calvin and Peter Uhlenberg (1969). "Minority Group Status and Fertility." *The American Journal of Sociology,* 74 (1969): 361–72.

Granovetter, Mark (1991). "A gyenge kötések ereje. A hálózatelmélet felülvizsgálata" (The strength of weak ties. The review of network theory) in *Társadalmak rejtett hálózata* (Hidden network of societies), eds. Angelusz, Róbert and Róbert Tardos. Budapest: Magyar Közvéleménykutató Intézet, pp. 371–400.

Greenhalgh, Susan (1995). "Anthropology Theorizes Reproduction: Integrating Practice, Political Economic, and Feminist Perspectives" in *Situating Fertility*, ed. Greenhalgh, Susan. Cambridge: Cambridge University Press.

Gyenei, Márta (1998). "A 'stratégiai gyerek'" (The "strategic child"). *Népszabadság,* November 14.

Hablicsek, László (2007). "Kísérleti számítások a roma lakosság területi jellemzőinek alakulására és 2021-ig történő előrebecslésére" (Projection of the number and regional characteristics of the Roma population by 2021). *Demográfia* 50, no. 1 (2007): 7–54.

Haines, Michael R. (2002). "Ethnic Differences in Demographic Behavior in the United States: Has There Been Convergence?" *NBER Working Paper,* No. 9042, July.

Hammel, Eugene (1990). "A Theory of Culture for Demography." *Population and Development Review* 16, no. 3 (1990): 455–85.

Hannerz, Ulf (2004). *Soulside. Inquiries into Ghetto Culture and Community.* Chicago: The University of Chicago Press.

Havas, Gábor (1996). *A megélhetési módok és a többségi társadalomhoz fűződő viszony változásai a magyarországi cigányok különböző csoportjaiban* (Strategies of making a living and the changes of interethnic relations in different groups of Gypsies in Hungary). Doctoral thesis. Budapest.

Havas, Gábor, István Kemény, and Gábor Kertesi (2000). "A relatív cigány a klasszifikációs küzdőtéren" (The relative Gypsy in the battle for classification) in *Cigánynak születni. Tanulmányok, dokumentumok* (Being born as a Gypsy. Studies, documents), eds. Horváth, Ágota, Edit Landau, and Júlia Szalai. Budapest: Új Mandátum Kiadó, pp. 193–201.

Hirschman, Charles (2004). "The Origins and Demise of the Concept of Race." *Population and Development Review* 30, no. 3(2004): 385–415.

Horváth, Kata (2005). "Sose voltak modernek? (A 'cigányok' és a kulturális antropológia)" (They never used to be modern?: "Gypsies" and cultural anthropology). *Anthropolis* 2, no. 1–2 (2005): 94–104.

Hutchinson, John and Anthony D. Smith, eds. (1996). *Ethnicity.* Oxford and New York: Oxford University Press.

Janky, Béla (2005). "A cigány nők társadalmi helyzete és termékenysége (Social position and fertility of Gypsy women) in *Szerepváltozások. Jelentés a nők és férfiak helyzetéről* (Changing roles. Report on the situation of women and men), eds. Nagy, Ildikó, Tiborné Pongrácz, and István György Tóth. Budapest: SZCSEM and Tárki, pp. 136–48.

Janky, Béla (2007). "A korai gyermekvállalást meghatározó tényezők a cigány nők körében" (Early childbearing among Gypsy women). *Demográfia* 50, no. 1 (2007): 55–73.

Johnson, Nan E. (1979). "Minority-Group Status and the Fertility of Black Americans: A New Look." *American Journal of Sociology* 48, no 6 (1979): 1386–400.

Johnson-Hanks, Jennifer (2003). "Education, Ethnicity, and Reproduction Practice in Cameroon." *Population–E* 58, no. 2 (2003): 153–80.

Johnson-Hanks, Jennifer (2005). *Uncertain Honor: Modern Motherhood in an African Crisis.* Chicago: University of Chicago Press.

Kalibova, Kveta (2000). "The Demographic Characteristics of Roma/Gypsies in Selected Countries in Central and Eastern Europe" in *The Demographic Characteristics of National Minorities in Certain European States.* Vol. 2, eds. Haug, Werner, Paul Compton, and Youssef Courbage. Strasbourg: Council of Europe, pp. 169–206.

Kapitány, Balázs and Zsolt Spéder (2004). *Szegénység és depriváció. Életünk fordulópontjai* (Poverty and deprivation. Turning points of our lives). Budapest: KSH – Népességtudományi Kutatóintézet.

Kapitány Balázs and Zsolt Spéder (2009). *Életünk fordulópontjai* (Turning points of our lives). Budapest: KSH – Népességtudományi Kutatóintézet.

Kelly, M. Patricia Fernandey (1998). "Társadalmi és kulturális tőke a városi gettóban: következmények a bevándorlás gazdaságszociológiájára" (Social and cultural capital of the urban ghetto: consequences on the economic sociology of the immigration) in *Tőkefajták*, eds. Lengyel, György and Zoltán Szántó. Budapest: Aula Kiadó, pp. 239–80.

Kemény, István, ed. (1976). *Beszámoló a magyarországi cigányok helyzetével foglalkozó, 1971-ben végzett kutatásról* (Report on the 1971 study about the situation of the Gypsies in Hungary). Budapest: MTA Szociológiai Kutató Intézet.

Kemény, István and Béla Janky (2003). "A 2003. évi cigány felmérésről – Népesedési, nyelvhasználati és nemzetiségi adatok" (On the 2003 Gypsy Survey: Data on population numbers, use of language and nationality). *Beszélő* 8, no. 10 (2003): 64–76.

Kemény, István, Béla Janky, and Gabriella Lengyel (2004). *A magyarországi cigányság 1971–2003* (The Gypsies in Hungary 1971–2003) Budapest: Gondolat Kiadó.

Kemény, István (2004). "A magyarországi cigány népesség demográfiája" (Demography of the Gypsy population in Hungary). *Demográfia* 47, no. 3–4 (2004): 335–46.

Kertesi, Gábor and Gábor Kézdi (1998). *A cigány népesség Magyarországon* (The Gypsy population in Hungary). Budapest: Socio-Typo.

Kertesi, Gábor (2005). *A társadalom peremén* (On the outskirts of society) Budapest: Osiris.

Kertzer, David and Dominik Arel, eds. (2002). *Census and Identity.* Cambridge: Cambridge University Press.

Kligman, Gail (2001). "A 'másság' társadalmi felépítése: A 'Roma' azonosítása a posztszocialista közösségekben" (The social structure of the "otherness": the identification of "Roma" in post-socialist communities). *Szociológiai Szemle* 4 (2001): 66–84.

Kovai, Cecília (2008). "Az iskola és a család. Kizáró és megengedő viszonyok" (The school and the family). *Beszélő* 13, no. 5 (2008): 80–86.

Labbe, Morgane (2000). *Censuses, Plebiscites and the Categorizations of Identities.* Conference on "Whose Self-Determination? Agency and Amnesia in the Disintegration of Yugoslavia". Watson Institute and Brown University, 4–5 February 2000. Recorded lecture.

Ladányi, János and Iván Szelényi (2000). "Ki a cigány?" (Who is the Gypsy?) in *Cigánynak születni. Tanulmányok, dokumentumok* (Being born as a Gypsy. Studies, documents), eds. Horváth, Ágota, Edit Landau, and Júlia Szalai. Budapest: Új Mandátum, pp. 179–91.

Ladányi, János and Iván Szelényi (2004). *A kirekesztettség változó formái* (Different forms of exclusion). Budapest: Napvilág Kiadó.

Martin, Elisa (2003). "A Note on the Demographic Structure of Spanish Gypsies" in *Ethnic Identities in Dynamic Perspective. Proceedings of the 2002 Annual Meeting of the Gypsy Lore Society*, eds. Salo, Sheila and Csaba Prónai. Gondolat: Budapest.

Mészáros, Árpád and János Fóti (2000). "A cigány népesség jellemzői Magyarországon" (Characteristics of the Gypsy population in Hungary) in *Cigánynak születni. Tanulmányok, dokumentumok* (Being born as a Gypsy. Studies, documents), eds. Horváth, Ágota, Edit Landau, and Júlia Szalai. Budapest: Új Mandátum Kiadó, pp. 285–312.

Miklósi, Miklós and Zoltán Nagy (1983). "Termékenységi és születésszabályozási vizsgálat Alsószentmárton cigányközségben" (Fertility and birth control study in a Gypsy community in Alsószentmárton). *Egészségnevelés* 24 (1983): 256–58.

Neményi, Mária (2000). "Kis roma demográfia" (Little Roma demography) in *Cigánynak születni. Tanulmányok, dokumentumok* (Being born as a Gypsy. Studies, documents), eds. Horváth, Ágota, Edit Landau, and Júlia Szalai. Budapest: Új Mandátum Kiadó, pp. 277–82.

Okamura, Jonathan (1981). "Situational Ethnicity." *Ethnic and Racial Studies* 4, no. 4 (1981): 452–65.

Okely, Judith (1983). *The Traveller-Gypsies.* Cambridge: Cambridge University Press.

Pollack, Robert A. and Susan Scotts Watkins (1993). "Cultural and Economic Approaches to Fertility: Proper Marriage or Mésalliance?" *Population and Development Review* 19, no. 3 (1993): 467–94.

Ritchey, P. Neal (1975). "The Effect of Minority Group Status on Fertility: Reexamination of Concepts." *Population Studies* 29, no. 2 (1975): 249–57.

Spéder, Zsolt (2004). "Gyermekvállalás és a párkapcsolatok alakulása" (Childbearing and partnership) in *Társadalmi riport*, eds. Kolosi, Tamás, István György Tóth, and György Vukovich. Budapest: TÁRKI, pp. 137–51.

Stewart, Michael (1993). "Daltestvérek" (Brothers in song). Budapest: T-Twins Kiadó, MTA Szociológiai Intézet, and Max Weber Alapítvány.

Stewart, Michael (2003). *Discrimination, Politics and Culture: Divergent Perspectives on the Reproduction of Deprivation among Roma in CEE.* Manuscript.

Szalai, Júlia (2003). "Az elismerés politikája" (The policy of recognition). *HOLMI,* 12, no. 7–8 (2003): 779–94; 988–1005.

Szuhay, Péter (2004). "A társadalmi együttműködés megteremtése és optimalizálása cigányok és magyarok között Szendrőládon" (Establishment and optimalisation of social cooperation between Gypsies and Hungarians in Szendrőlád) In *Új Holnap*, no. 3 (2004): 156–70.

Tober, Diane M., Mohammad-Hosseinn Taghdisi, and Mohammad Jalali (2006). "'Fewer Children, Better Life' or 'As Many as God Wants'?" *Medical Anthropology Quarterly* 20, no. 1(2006): 50–71.

Virág, Tünde (2003). "Kirekesztve" (Being excluded). *Kritika* 32, no. 4 (2003): 10–13.

Virág, Tünde (2008). "Változó gazdasági-társadalmi kapcsolatok egy cigányok lakta faluban" (Changing social relationships in a Gypsy village). *Szociológiai Szemle* 19, no. 1 (2008): 60–77.

Weinreb, Alexander A. (2001). "First Politics, Then Culture: Accounting for Ethnic Differences in Demographic Behavior in Kenya." *Population and Development Review* 27, no. 3 (2001): 437–67.

Williams, Patrick (2000). "A helyszínen és a korban" in Cigányok Európában I. Nyugat-Európa" (Gypsies in Europe. Vol. 1. Western Europe), ed. Prónai, Csaba. Budapest: Új Mandátum Kiadó.

Appendix

Table 1. Social characteristics of the populations of Lápos and Palóca, 2004

Social characteristics	'Segregated' Gypsies at Lápos (N=85)	Assimilated Gypsies at Lápos (N=17)	Non-Gypsies at Lápos (N=32)	Gypsies at Palóca (N=119)
Per capita monthly income	HUF 20,750 (83 EUR)	HUF 33,594 (134.4 EUR)	HUF 49,213 (196.9 EUR)	HUF 19,875 (79.5 EUR)
(The minimum old age pension in 2004 was HUF 23,200 [92.8 EUR])				
Rate of unemployed fathers	97,5%	70,0%	10,0%	89%
Average length of unemployment of the head of family (in years)	11,5	4,1	7,3	7,6
Rate of mothers dropping out of primary school	75,0%	–	8,0%	41%

Source: Data collection by the author in autumn 2004.

Table 2. Average number of children at Lápos and Palóca according to the mother's age and ethnicity, 2004

Mother's year of birth	Segregated Gypsies at Lápos	Assimilated Gypsies at Lápos	Non-Gypsies at Lápos	Gypsies at Palóca
–1950	7,6 (N=10)	3,5 (N=8)	2,5 (N=21)	5,0 (N=20)
1951–1969	5,8 (N=37)	2,9 (N=7)	2,4 (N=11)	3,6 (N=55)
1970–1989	2,9 (N=44)	1,5 (N=2)	1,5 (N=2)	2,4 (N=52)

Source: Data collection by the author in autumn 2004.

Table 3. Average age of women at Lápos at the birth of their first child according to the mother's age and ethnicity, 2004

Mother's year of birth	Segregated Gypsies	Assimilated Gypsies	Non-Gypsies
–1950	20.1 (N=10)	21.7 (N=8)	23.3 (N=21)
1951–1969	19.2 (N=37)	20.6 (N=7)	21.5 (N=11)
1970–1979	18.6 (N=22)	24.0 (N=2)	23.5 (N = 2)
1980–	17.6 (N=22)	–	–

Table 4. Total fertility rate amongst the total population,
the Hungarian Gypsy population and the segregated Gypsies of Lápos (1999–2004)

Mother's age group	Total population (1999–2002)	Hungarian Gypsy population[1] (1999–2002)	Segregated Gypsies at Lápos (2001–2004)[2]
15–19 years	22,6	120,8	250,1
20–24 years	67,1	218,1	266,4
25–29 years	92,6	133,7	112,2
30–34 years	55,9	64,1	333,5
35–39 years	20,0	48,6	166,2
40–49 years	1,4	6,7	17,8
Total fertility rate (TFR)	1,3	3,0	5,7

Source:
1: Data on the total population and the Gypsy population: Janky, 2005.
2: Data on the Gypsy population of Lápos may be treated as estimates and come from two sources: the number of Gypsy women in each particular age group from the author's record of practically all households while the number of live births comes from the pregnant women's files kept by the district nurse. The TFR was calculated, for methodological reasons, for the average of four years: 2001, 2002, 2003 and 2004 in order to prevent distortion coming from the annual fluctuation of live births. I also take this occasion to thank Ildikó Husz for her assistance in calculating the TFR.

Figure 1. Distribution of mothers at Lápos
according to age at the time of the birth of first child (2004)

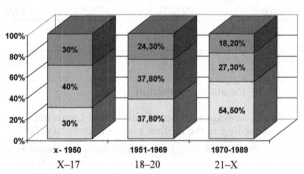

Figure 2. Distribution of Gypsy mothers at Palóca
according to age at the time of the birth of first child, 2004

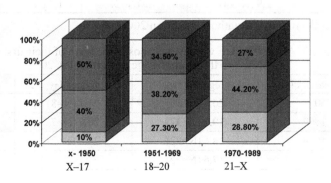

Judith Okely

CONSTRUCTING CULTURE THROUGH
SHARED LOCATION, BRICOLAGE AND EXCHANGE:
the Case of Gypsies and Roma

This article addresses the vexed link between place and culture and the age old presumption that cultural authenticity depends on a spatial as well as bounded isolate. As a student of anthropology, I recall world maps being placed on a board with marked places for peoples and their cultures. This may have had the intention of expanding horizons, but it rooted culture, implying that it was defined by geographical location. While presented as the ideal, yet this is rarely what the anthropologist encountered in practice, although s/he may have felt obliged to invent and create cultural isolation in the field locality. Malinowski is an early example. His Diary (Malinowski, 1967) revealed his daily encounters with non-indigenous traders, administrators and the influence of missionaries (Okely, 1996). Yet such persons and cultural, political and economic influences were rendered near invisible or marginalised in his final public texts.

Despite the presumptive ideal of cultural and geographical isolation and fieldwork in a bounded location, many later anthropologists reveal leakages and problems of boundaries. Indeed both Leach (Leach, 1954) and later Barth (Barth, 1969) confronted and explored the creation of cultural boundaries where geographical isolation is not the causal explanation for separation and cultural distinctness.

While raising interesting questions about location, Gupta and Ferguson rest their iconoclastic arguments on a caricature of most previous fieldwork (Gupta and Ferguson, 1997). They seem to suggest that, long after Malinowski and well into the mid 1990s, anthropologists stayed in their one enclave presenting the ethnography as geographical isolate to the neglect of movement, migration and transnational changes. This straw or mud hut version has long been inappropriate. The fixed link between geographical place and culture is being increasingly questioned even for sedentarised peoples (Fog Olwig and Hastrup, 1996). Those most likely not to have fallen into the spatial trap were anthropologists studying Europe, and other native anthropologists studying their own localities. They have had to confront the cultural variability and instability of culture(s) in place. Europeanist anthropologists, like minorities, have long ago lived the paradoxes of inhabiting geographically familiar but socially, unfamiliar contexts. The boundaries and divisions are lived and recognised as constructed.

Gypsies are a case study of the new interest in hybrid, border cultures. The focus on a minority in a Western context confronts the presumption of isolation as explanation for authenticity of culture. I, for one, hit the field a few miles from London in the 1970s and occupied a caravan in the arc lights of major motorways (Okely, 1987; 1996, Chapter 1). Fieldwork among the Gypsies was never a physically let alone culturally bounded place. Even the camps were open to non-Gypsy intrusion. They were demarcated insofar as only I and the Gypsies slept there.

'One site near houses and major road where the author lived' (Anon).

Fieldwork consisted as much of routes traversed by everyone else and in public non-Gypsy places such as house dwellers' doorsteps, government offices and courthouses. When the subject of Gypsies appeared on TV, word went round the camp and companions turned on their generator-driven sets in their trailers. They were thus open to and knowledgeable of the cultural representations of themselves as other in the non-Gypsy controlled mass media.

The 'field' for the anthropologist was also a mental, imagined locale created by the people she was with and that included non-Gypsies. It could not become a permanent encultured space. The next week the patch of land could be abandoned, then fenced off, piled with council rubble or turned over by diggers. The field as place could thus be dug up, dumped upon and obliterated. Thus Gypsy culture for stigmatised and persecuted nomads was created from contrast and difference, if not conflict.

'Former stopping place rendered officially inaccessible by ditch and posts' (H. Turner).

Gupta and Ferguson should, nevertheless, be applauded for assisting in destabilising the classical linkage between place and culture, recognising that "anthropology appears determined to give up its old ideas of territorially fixed communities and stable, localised cultures, and to apprehend an interconnected world in which people, objects and ideas are rapidly shifting and refuse to stay in place" (Gupta and Ferguson, 1997, p. 4).

For centuries, the Gypsies have been economically and politically intertwined with a wider sedentary economy and polity (Okely, 1983, pp. 49–65). They provide a special example of culture as created in shared territory and which involves daily, ubiquitous encounters with non-Gypsies and their powerful representatives. In the last resort it is the non-Gypsies who hold the power, with potential for persecution.

At the same time, non-anthropologists, especially linguists concerned with Gypsies, or Gypsiologists, held fast to the sedentarist mythical charter which privileged an Indian origin going back to 10,000 AD (Okely, 1997, pp. 224–43). They have sought to legitimate Gypsies in the light of a primordial, self sufficient and bounded whole. This freezes them in a mythical past as well as place. It colludes with rather than challenges the politically dominant non-Gypsy ideal of culture as place and geographical isolate. It also continues an orientalist tradition which privileges exoticism from which modern transformations are seen as dilutions and even contamination. The implication is that everything after the alleged departure from the mysterious and still contested exact Indian region is a loss of purity of culture.

The Gypsies refer to non-Gypsies or their 'Other' as *gadjes* or *gorgios*. Silverman discusses how Roma musicians have themselves responded to the largely *gadje* interpretation of Roma/Gypsy by constructing for *gadje* consumption an Indian origin and alleged linear trail of similar orientalised "Gypsy" music, regardless of the obvious dissimilarities. This was influenced by the film *Latcho Drom* (1993) a "staged documentary which traces the musical diaspora from India to Spain" (Silverman, 2007, p. 339). This has in turn encouraged promoters to make their Gypsy performers re-enact such presumptions and conceal any musical instruments, costume or music which do not fit the *gadje* exoticised and presumed commercial potential.

The renewed focus on India parallels the burgeoning investment by displaced persons in imagined places and homelands. Some Roma representatives approached institutions such as UNESCO emphasising Indian migration although regrettably Gypsies or Roma are likely to be more recently and regularly displaced as nomads in localities closer to their current abodes. I suggest the greater problem is the Gypsies' contemporary displacements rather than any centuries old and mythical displacement from an alleged, unremembered ancient one homeland. Here also the Indianists have proclaimed a once isolated cultural homogeneity.

The questions raised by research on Gypsies lock into what have now been recognised as mainstream concerns. Phillips and Steiner (Phillips and Steiner, 1999) have drawn attention in subtle degrees to the problematisation of hybridity in the discussion and collection of art and artefacts from non-Western cultures and locations. There is the notion of pure and unadulterated object but indigenous creativity and ingenuity in confrontation with new forms and mass reproduction and external market demands. Their discussion of non-Western peoples and production focus on cultures, peoples and groups which nonetheless are presumed self-contained before colonial/ capitalist encounter. There is less discussion of the interrelationship between adjoining non-Western cultures.

Clifford notes: "It is increasingly clear... that the concrete activity of representing a culture, subculture, or indeed any coherent domain of collective activity is always strategic and selective. The world's societies are too systematically interconnected to permit any easy isolation of a separate or independently functioning system. The increased pace of historical change... forces a new self-consciousness about the way cultural wholes and boundaries are constructed and translated... What is hybrid or 'historical' in an emergent sense has been less commonly collected and presented as a system of authenticity" (Clifford, 1988, p. 231).

Phillips and Steiner explore this in relation to art (Phillips and Steiner, 1999). The contributors to Gupta and Ferguson's *Culture Power and Place* trace "ways in which dominant cultural forms may be picked up and used—and significantly transformed— in the midst of the field of power relations" (Gupta and Ferguson, 1997, p. 5). They emphasise the "sometimes ironic political processes through which cultural forms are imposed, invented, reworked, and transformed... Rather than simply a domain of sharing and commonality, culture figures here more as site of difference and contestation" (Gupta and Ferguson, 1997, p. 5).

Ortner suggests that rather than "banishing the concept of culture... the issue is one of reconfiguring this enormously productive concept for a changing world" (Ortner, 1999, p. 8).

One imperative is to "welcome the ethnographies and histories of "borderlands" of zones of friction (or worse) between "cultures" in which the clash of power and meaning and identities is the stuff of change and transformation" (Ortner, 1999). A second imperative is to "emphasise the issue of meaning-making" (Ortner, 1999). "...Even if as many thinkers now claim, there are fewer and fewer in the way of distinct and recognisable "cultures" in the contemporary world... the fundamental assumption that people are trying to make sense of their lives, always weaving fabrics of meaning, however fragile and fragmentary, still holds" (Ortner, 1999, p. 9).

In fact we already have in the Gypsies or the Roma a centuries-old tradition of interlocking cultures between the Gypsies and non-Gypsies. Rather than being confronted with a sudden change, Gypsies have changed all along, through time and space. They are both an example of culture with "distinct and recognisable" aspects (Ortner, 1999, p. 9) in the borderlands and an example of continuous meaning-making in the face of a dominant encircling system with the greater political and economic power. This is inevitable, given that the Gypsies have not inhabited a separate place or geographical location, let alone a bounded political entity for centuries, if ever.

Instead, we should look at Gypsy, Traveller or Roma cultures as a complex and pioneering form from which refugees, migrants and emergent minorities might themselves seek to devise creative strategies. Gypsy culture inhabits and constructs its internal coherence alongside or in opposition to other dominating cultures; in the same geographical and political space. For example, the Gypsies' animal classification which deems some ritually polluted such as the cat and others special, such as the hedgehog, is constructed in part on the Gypsies' recognition that *gadje*s or non-Gypsies value the former and ridicule or ignore the latter (Okely, 1983, pp. 91–104). Their case has long destabilised the classical notion of culture as a geographically bounded entity grounded in place as isolate.

Michael Stewart, studying the Vlach Gypsies in Hungary (Stewart, 1997), suggests how, instead of a culture located in a mythical homeland of Indian origin, the Gypsies create an alternative and imagined autonomous space in song, horse dealing activities, communality, commensuality and speech. Anthropologists are increasingly alert to the ways in which the colonised have mimicked their colonisers. Previously, it was thought that this was mere deference, when in fact it was defiant reinterpretation, and subversion (Taussig, 1993). Gypsy culture inhabits and constructs its internal coherence alongside or in opposition to other dominating cultures; in the same space. Gypsies have created their own semi-autonomous cultural space. There may be correspondences between what both Gypsies and non-Gypsies each see as their own culture(s). It should not be concluded that these have the same meaning for the different groups of Gypsies, Travellers and non-Gypsies.

The Gypsies have been creative bricoleurs (Lévi-Strauss, 1966; Okely, 1983); selecting from wider surrounding systems and inverting the meaning in line with their own interpretation. The apparent similarities are neither simplistic copying nor merely a result of influence by the majority systems on a supposedly passive minority. The Gypsies have both rejected and selected with finesse and aesthetic sensibility. Out of this creative process Gypsies have in turn given back and added new form to the surrounding dominant or other cultures. Gypsy, Traveller and Romany culture(s) take on semi-autonomous coherence. They are not archaic remnants disappearing under the hegemony of non-Gypsy systems which forever confronts the ethnic minority.

I contend that Gypsies have for centuries provided a pioneering example of cultural coherence with continuing insider appropriations and constructions. These are then redefined on their own terms. Such reconfigurations at the same time have been dismissed as mere hybrid or passive imitation. Gypsies have continuously created and recreated their cultural autonomy with notions of authenticity in the midst of others' space and cultures. Authenticity does not lie in an imagined sedentarist place but in the Gypsies' historic ingenuity and inventive originality in the shadow of the ever-present dominant other.

Gypsy culture is created through contact, sometimes conflict and specific exchange. Gypsy culture is one emerging from ever-present and changing culture contact rather than a former isolate allegedly undermined by contact. Theirs is a culture created from and through difference.

Musical Examples of Hybridity

In Kertesz-Wilkinson's study (Kertesz-Wilkinson, 1997, pp. 97–126), she argues that the Vlach Gypsies in Hungary make their own culture by dancing to a Hungarian tune and style, yet with "Romanised steps and movements." On a broader level it could be said that the Gypsies dancing to the non-Gypsies' tune, yet on their own terms, symbolises exactly the Gypsies' cultural and social predicament. The Gypsies subvert the dominant form in novel ways often invisible to non-Gypsies looking for "pure" and "authentic", untouched cultural forms.

In a project I have overseen on Romungro Gypsy music-making in Hungary with Kertesz-Wilkinson as the researcher, it is illuminating that she initially found it considerably more difficult to gain access to the Romungro as opposed to the Vlachs. The former only speak Hungarian whereas the Vlach also speak Romanes, a Gypsy language. The presumption among many outsiders and doubtless some anthropologists was that it would be easier to gain access to a group not marked by a separate language. Yet the absence of a separate language points to the greater need for a group to create less obvious and constructed boundaries and barriers. The shared language between the Romungro and the non-Gypsy researcher, a native Hungarian speaker, was no proof of greater cultural assimilation as might have been the presumed belief. In fact a shared language was all the more deceptive. The cultural boundaries were more subtle (Okely, 2002).

Similarly Carol Silverman (Silverman, 2007) has exposed how Balkan Roma on tour, especially in the USA, create exotic so-called "Gypsy" music in line with the expectations of the non-Gypsy marketing priorities and the stereotyped expectations of the audiences.

Exchange and Transformation of Objects with Opposing Authenticity

Gypsies also create difference through objects which cross the borderlands. Some are sold or exchanged by Gypsies for non-Gypsy consumption. Others are selected, commissioned and purchased from non-Gypsies for Gypsy internal cultural elaboration. The former are used by Gypsies to enhance their exotic difference from non-Gypsies and to make financial profit from the transaction. The latter, through financial purchase from non-Gypsies, are used to create and affirm an autonomous cultural space for Gypsies. Thus a form of 'Gypsy culture' for non-Gypsies is invented partly through objects. This verges on pastiche. At the same time, but for different purposes, an *alternative* Gypsy validated culture, separate from non-Gypsies and often unknown to them, is created by Gypsies. I explore how this is enacted through objects that Gypsies select and acquire but of which they then *transform the meaning* from that associated with or understood by the dominant society.

The circulation of goods and practices between Gypsy and non-Gypsy is highly significant but highly selective. As a group with nomadic non-sedentarist traditions, they make few material objects among themselves. Granted, nomadic pastoralists of the Middle East have made their own tents and weave carpets from their animals' wool. Unlike other nomads, whether hunters and gatherers or pastoralists, there can never be even the semblance of economic self-sufficiency for Gypsies. Engaged continuously in relations with others who have the economic infrastructure to produce goods, Gypsies have made use of those objects on their *own* terms rather than hand made them themselves. There are some goods or objects which they select and acquire because they have the potential to be transformed into expressions of their own values. It is no matter that these are made by the 'enemy' and who interpret them for their own purposes.

Trivia

There is renewed interest in material culture, at least after an extended lull in British social anthropology. Museums established their own separate traditions of dealing with objects. Paradoxically, Malinowski's famous monograph *The Argonauts of the Western Pacific* (Malinowski, 1922) was devoted almost entirely to the circulation of two types of objects. Malinowski was keen to explore the wider context in which to Western eyes some apparently banal armbands and necklaces were exchanged across islands and after hazardous sea journeys, all without barter-like value. He emphasised how these precious objects were utterly useless although highly prized and the subject of endless myth-making through individual histories.

More recently ethnological museums have confronted in creative ways the problems of display and interpretation of seemingly dead things. They have begun to problematise the very choices and acts of display for different viewers (Phillips and Steiner, 1999). Similarly the display of so-called 'Gypsy cultural objects' identified in the same 'home' territory as the museum and curators raises problems about the criteria and contradictions in collections usually brought from afar (O'Hanlon and Welsch, 2000; Gosden and Knowles, 2001; Hendry, 2005; Junghaus and Szekely, 2007).

Here the Gypsies pose intriguing questions. On a number of occasions in talking to art connoisseurs and others, I have been informed that one major proof that Gypsies have 'no culture' is that they have no distinct material objects of their own. Non-Gypsy collectors cannot seek out and accumulate things like carpets for which other nomads are celebrated. There are some collections of Gypsy caravans and the occasional and rare museum, e.g. in Bristol, England and in Poland. But the records do not suggest that the waggons were always made by Gypsies. Instead, they were commissioned from non-Gypsy specialists, with the paint work completed by some Gypsy artists, but also by non-Gypsies. David Smith, a non-Gypsy art teacher, was often asked by Gypsies to paint their waggons.

Faced with this lack of exotic, museum-collectable objects, over the years, I have found myself collecting apparently banal or trivial objects from my encounters with Gypsies. At the same time, these could not be placed in glass cases as aesthetic or immediately exotic objects. They could in no way act as trophies as researchers are increasingly depicting 19th century collections by Western explorers (O'Hanlon and Welsch, 2000). I have always been impressed when visiting some Norwegian anthropologists' homes where each had their illuminated glass cabinet in the living room displaying as proof of their 'having been there' (Clifford and Marcus, 1986) beautiful objects from either South East Asia or South America. I could not do quite the same. But intellectual history moves on: seemingly banal if not trivial objects and detritus have come into their own.

Attfield is indicative of this growing interest in what she calls "the material culture of everyday life" (Attfield, 2000). "In spite of the all embracing attempts to integrate 'commercial art' and industrially mass-produced products in the 'new art history' of the eighties, its subsequent re-categorisation as visual culture failed to consider its materiality and the most distinctive qualities which make design different from art in its relationship to the everyday, the ordinary and the banal" (Attfield, 2000, p. 3).

She regrets that "The model of design history.... disregards the social life of things that unfolds beyond the initial commodity stage" (Attfield, 2000, p. 5). In addressing "the physical embodiment of culture" she discusses the notion of authenticity and originality. The latter is a concept foreign to trade practices which depend on repetition (Attfield, 2000, p. 5). Yet she argues for the "role of domestic things in materialising the construction of self-identity" (Attfield, 2000, p. 7).

Similarly, I argue that in the case of the Gypsies, we find some mass-produced objects which in several contrasting ways embody forms of identity; either the perceived identity of Gypsies among non-Gypsies or the Gypsies' own usually hidden self identity. It is not so much that the objects can necessarily be restricted to everyday life: they take on meaning in the very exchange across the cultural and ethnic divide. That is, they take on an exotic form in the transaction. They may be seen by the Gypsies as trivia in their own circles but with potential for transformation when exoticised by them for non-Gypsy consumption. On the other side, non-Gypsy manufacturers or salespersons may not know the ethnic significance and transformation of objects which they themselves sell to Gypsies.

While considering objects as embodiments of culture and identity, Attfield does not consider ethnic identity and exchange *across* boundaries. The exchange between Gypsy and non-Gypsy is crucially concerned with ethnic contrast. This is also different from the Trobriand *kula* circulation of objects. Although the *kula* takes place between potentially hostile islands, there is a *shared and agreed* value placed on the necklaces and armbands. This contrasts with the differing and often *unshared* values placed in the objects exchanged between Gypsy and non-Gypsy.

Material Objects in Gypsy–*Gadje* Exchange as Contrasting Categories of Culture

Those presented and imaginatively transformed in transactions initiated by Gypsies and sold to *gadje*s. They are often used as mediators for the act of fortune telling. Such objects may be partly hand-made by Gypsies or mass-manufactured in *gadje* factories, but transformed by presentation into exotic goods for *gadje* eyes and beliefs. Such objects may not in fact be considered 'real' or meaningful goods in terms of the Gypsies' own ethnic less visible values.

Secondly, those goods which the Gypsies select or commission and purchase or acquire from *gadje*s and which they transform as signals of their *own* ethnic values, especially in relation to pollution beliefs and daily *habitus* (Bourdieu, 1982).

1. Objects created as 'real' Gypsy for *gadje*, not Gypsy, consumption
   – 'Hand made' objects
   In the earlier folklore writing and still in popularist texts it is asserted that 'traditional' Gypsy occupations were based often on their handicraft skills. Gypsies have hand made wooden clothes pegs. I encountered only one such person who did this as long ago as the 1970s and I was sold some of them in the 1990s in Hull. Other objects sold on the doorstep which approximate to the authentically hand-made are wooden or paper flowers (Adams, Okely *et al.*, 1975, pp. 217, 248). I have examples of wooden chrysanthemums carved skilfully from sticks and then dyed, which I acquired in the 1970s. But I have not seen any since.

Then there were the wax flowers: made of melted wax in a rose-like shape placed on sticks. I was taught by a fellow Gypsy hawker how to make such objects when I went 'calling' at houses with her. When I asked my Gypsy fellow hawker "Surely those privet leaves on the sticks will die?" she answered "It won't matter, we'll be gone". She, as a Traveller on the move, had little interest in the long-term life of such transient objects. When we had some left over, these were never used as display within her or her neighbours' trailers. These hand-made objects had no value for the Gypsies' own display and consumption.

Since my earlier fieldwork, when accompanying the Gypsies, and now as anthropologist at the receiving end as house dweller, I have been sold paper flowers made from either lavatory paper or paper handkerchiefs. They were wired to freshly cut privet with healthy green leaves. I have retained these objects, but cannot display them in a lit cabinet like my Norwegian anthropologist friends as trophies of my professional authenticity. Long since, the leaves have died and droop, as in fact we would expect real flowers to do. I suggest that, in contrast to the wax flowers I once made with my Gypsy work partners, there is an added irony in the paper flowers. Made from lavatory paper for unmentionable bodily cleansing, they have been re-presented by Gypsies as ornaments and objects of beauty for *gadje*s, but not for Gypsy interior space.

The Gypsies recognised the importance of presenting objects to *gadje*s as the product of a specialised craft. One Gypsy woman described how when she went hawking, a major item was lace: "We say we made it ourselves but we get it by the yard in Noggingham" (i.e. Nottingham).

Years before tourism privileged the cultural authenticity of 'native' hand-made crafted cultural objects, the Gypsies were aware of the advantages of selling authenticity in the guise of ethnic products. Now mass global tourism exploits and indeed recreates or invents the notion of 'local' and 'indigenous' authenticity for the sale of items to outsiders. The following example presents the ultimate paradox of an Asian woman assisting Europeans in the production and sale of local European authenticity.

For example, in 2001 in Bruges, which sells its image as home of a special lace, I discovered that the bulk of this is imported from Taiwan and recycled as the 'authentic locally hand made' product from this iconically beautiful European town. Thus lace, like culture, was authentic if associated with 'traditional' place, although in practice it is now bogus.

The creation of indigenous authenticity for external consumption has indeed a longer history than mass tourism. Daniel Miller also describes how image construction has operated in the Oriental style of cloth. Researchers at London's Victoria and Albert Museum at first presumed that some distinctive textile was "made in the original style of a group of people" (Miller, 1987, p. 123) but in fact it evolved over time in response to the taste of the British at that time. "There emerged a style embodying an image of what the European consumers thought the Indian manufacturers ought to be making" (Miller, 1987, p. 123). Thus *Orientalism* was objectified (Said, 1978).

Similarly, the Gypsies through trial and error have evolved their own exoticism to please the *gadje*s who also have their own idea of what a 'true' Gypsy embodies. The objects usually play on a specific contrast. As Miller suggests "the object may lend itself equally to the expression of difference, indicating the separate domains to which people or aspects of people belong" (Miller, 1987, p. 130).

– Fortune-telling and 'gold' charms

Lace selling and hawking for Gypsy women are often an entrée for fortune telling. For the latter, one Gypsy woman who did not indeed tell fortunes explained to me: "You have to look Gypsified; put on gold earrings and say 'Cross my palm with silver or paper money nowadays'". Thus she was fully aware that being exotic entailed a performance.

In *Own or Other Culture* (Okely, 1996) I have explored how fortune-telling, like the selling of ostensibly hand-made lace to the *gadje*, is asymmetrical in knowledge. Generally, the Gypsies do not believe in the supernatural powers accredited to them, although they recognise that character reading skills and long-term experience are required. The Gypsies are in effect giving good psychotherapy. But they do not engage in fortune-telling among themselves. It is the *gadje* who credits supernatural powers to Gypsies. A sedentarist society sees the geographically and occupationally mobile as both threatening and mysterious, therefore with potential if not 'real' magical power. Thus a people seen as placeless are constructed as having magical powers. They are 'here today and gone tomorrow'.

The so-called 'gold' charms which Gypsies sell as intermediaries between household utilities and the opportunity for fortune-telling are made of the cheapest metal. But they are sold to the *gadjes* for a relatively high price to the Gypsies' advantage. Like the lace, such objects are bought in bulk from long established *gadje* contacts. They are brass trinkets then sold back to other *gadjes* for perhaps £5 apiece or more if calculated for the money earned in the fortune telling session. Such objects, in this face-to-face encounter, are performatively imbued by the Gypsy with a special power to bring good fortune to the non-Gypsy recipient. Gypsies or Roma throughout Europe and in North America prize and recognise real gold, which they would never mix up with fake gold, but it seems the *gadjes* will accept such goods. The fake gold *gadje*-made objects are thus transformed into 'true' Gypsy items when sold back in the circular cultural exchange. The Gypsies, it seems, have the Midas touch.

In my earlier analysis of fortune-telling (Okely, 1996), I described how, despite my awareness of the Gypsies' scepticism about fortune-telling for themselves, I found myself having mine told. A Gypsy woman had spotted my anxiety when walking in Durham market place. It proved to be excellent ethnography. But the final irony was that the charm which she then sold me was a small plastic elephant. And it was white. In Britain the 'white elephant' is a powerful metaphor. A dictionary definition is: "anything which gives more trouble than its worth… an unwanted possession, often given away at a jumble sale: something which proves to be useless" (Chambers, 1983, p. 404). Thus the Gypsy has the last ironic laugh at the property-accumulating *gadje*.

Classically, the Gypsy fortune-teller has been associated with another distinct material object which acted as a vital mediating and transitional object; namely the crystal ball. The paintings by Laura Knight give excellent portrayals of Gypsy women advancing their objects for the *gadje* gaze.[1] The crystal ball exemplifies all the potential ambiguity in objects. The Gypsy can claim to see here what is appropriate for the *gadje* client. Again by trial and error, through exploratory statements and assertions, she can give what the client wants—for a fee. As already noted, such an encounter is also used to ascertain the house-dweller's openness to fortune-telling. That is when the charms come out. They may be sold 'just for luck' without further moves to fortune-telling.

– Others' manufactured goods for *gadjes*

From my examination of the literature, it seems that Gypsies, up to the 1950s or later, peddled manufactured goods often in rural areas where the goods might not have been so easily available. There are other manufactured items which have no exotic pretensions but which convey other meanings; not the promise of good fortune but cleanliness. Here the sale of goods from Gypsy to *gadje* reveals the contrasting beliefs among Gypsies that non-Gypsies are dirty, especially inside their houses (Okely, 1983, pp. 77–104). I noted through my home-based 'fieldwork' in the 1990s, Gypsies acting as door to door salespersons selling common household goods such as dusters, brushes, tea towels, mass produced clothes pegs and car cleaning cloths to us *gadjes*. All such items are associated with washing and cleaning.

The circulation of goods manufactured by *gadjes* or, in a few cases, hand crafted by Gypsies and then transformed as Gypsy items sold to *gadjes*, reveals aspects of the relations between the ethnic minority and the representatives of the non-Gypsy majority. In the Gypsies' case, the recycled, selected items are moments when the transaction reverses the usual asymmetrical power relationship between the dominant sedentarist political and economic majority and the vulnerable, often mobile ethnic minority.

2. *Gadje* objects selected or commissioned for Gypsy consumption and their cultural validation

– Waggons

The classical or 'traditional' horse drawn waggons were generally commissioned from sedentary *gadje* craftsmen, with some exceptional Gypsies engaging in their construction. The skills and artistic talents of the few specialised Gypsy waggon painters can be examined for creativity in selective imitation and recreation transferred to new contexts.

In the 1930s, one English Gypsy spent hours looking at shop window displays of carpets whose overlapping designs influenced his style (Smith, 1997, pp. 7–15). Here is an example of the Gypsy as artistic bricoleur; taking something from the dominant system and giving it new meaning in the Gypsy context, simultaneously subverting other's cultural hegemony. After the era of horse drawn transport, waggons remained a repository of new decorative traditions. Over time, the painting designs were greatly elaborated and cultural differences were explicitly amplified.

---

1   See image (figure 5.1) in Okely, 1996, p. 96.

– Motor drawn trailers

From the late 1960s, the wealthy Travellers or Gypsies commissioned from non-Gypsy manufacturers special motor drawn, not horse drawn trailers as they call them. These are heavily beaded with stainless steel and their interiors are noted for their ornately designed mirrors (Okely, 1983, p. 29). In accord with Gypsy pollution beliefs, such trailers have neither internal lavatories nor sinks (Okely, 1983, pp. 77–104), and are thus unlike caravans designed for dirty *gadjes*. By the late 1990s, the main firm which constructed these went out of business. At the same time, the Gypsies no longer commission such elaborate, easily identifiable exteriors. The reasons are not fully clear. One may be that they did not want to appear too conspicuous, another is that the trailers are very heavy, causing high fuel consumption for the towing vehicle. Nonetheless, the increasing number of Travellers who now use the internet enjoy a special website devoted to images of these authentic cultural objects made Gypsy by non-Gypsies. Thus new traditions were created to make sense of and fit in with a changed context. Additionally, a new generation of semi-settled Gypsy individuals, educated at art school, have taken such objects and re-presented them in photographs and other framed forms as art pieces, for example the artist Daniel Baker (Baker, 2007, pp. 14–15, 43–49). Such re-presentations of Gypsy material culture are again transformed for a *gadje* metropolitan consumption, namely the Venice Biennale.

While becoming less functional as day to day living abodes, the earlier painted wooden waggons, sometimes with canvas roofs, have been elevated to an even more powerful symbol of authentic Gypsy identity and past history. I have a miniature example of a 'traditional' horse drawn Gypsy waggon made by a Gypsy. It is largely materially accurate in its mechanics. But it was not made on a Gypsy site as some traditional activity. It was indeed made by someone who was a camp neighbour of mine during fieldwork. But it was made some time later, during a lengthy spell in Wandsworth gaol. It does indeed bear the hallmarks of innovation in that it is meticulously constructed from material at hand, namely matchsticks. It shows inside knowledge of how the cart can be pivoted.

'Miniature waggon made of matchsticks' (Judith Okely).

But this was made in *gadje* dictated space far from the Gypsy community. Given that I know that the specific Gypsy craftsman had been ostracised by the Gypsy community for his crime of rape, albeit of a *gadje* woman, it may be that the exotic artefact helped to restore his dignity where, in prison, he would also be vulnerable to other prisoners as a sex offender. He sold the item to a sympathetic solicitor.

– Crockery for Gypsy and *gadje*

Other specially significant objects acquired from non-Gypsy manufacturers are: antique china (Okely, 1983, p. 87), cut glass vases, stainless steel washing up bowls and water containers. Selected, usually Crown Derby china, is displayed on upper shelves or in glass cabinets (Okely, 1983, p. 82). It is rarely if ever used but is a celebration of purity and the value of objects associated with unpolluted cooking, cleaning and eating. This antique crockery is also a storage of value. Some designs are favoured over others and can in emergencies be sold to either *gadje* or Gypsy.

On occasion, Gypsies acquire crockery with paintings of Gypsy caravans and similar motifs. I only rarely saw such items on display. They were put away in the cupboards. Ironically some could be sold back to *gadje*s who were recognised as sympathetic if not sentimental about Gypsies. I was sold such a set by a Gypsy woman, with ethnically near-stereotyped images of long skirted Gypsies with horse and waggons.

Later, a Finnish Gypsy visiting my house (Okely, 1983, p. 54, figure 3.2) was fascinated by such items and wept when I gave her one of the cups. This was a tiny and insignificant repayment for what Gypsies in general have given me in hospitality and shared knowledge. In July 2006 a Bulgarian Roma student whose Masters dissertation I supervised

'Barnsley water jugs commissioned by Gypsies' (Homer Sykes).

graduated. Her parents attended the ceremony in Oxford. I gave the remaining 'Gypsy' cup and saucer to the Roma mother. She has, I am informed, put it in on display back home. Thus the anthropologist entered the Maussian circulation of Gypsy cultural objects (Mauss, 1967).

Gold jewellery is greatly valued and perfectly suited to a travelling group which carries only portable wealth. Acquired from non-Gypsies, it takes on its own intense cultural significance. Women wear earrings, men rings. The designs are highly specific, i.e. although made by the 'enemy', only certain kinds are favoured. Earrings are ornate and circular. Men's rings ideally have jagged edges: lethal in fist fights.

'Trailer Interior reflections through ornate mirrors and showing owner's china and gold' (*Echo and Post*).

Gadje Objects for Gypsy Death Rituals

While Gypsies select and appropriate specific objects for their own cultural significance, it cannot be presumed that such objects are held in perpetuity. Ideally, all property of a deceased person should be destroyed. The traditional waggons and modern caravans are burned. It is said that not only the clothes and personal possessions of the dead are burned but also their valuables. In practice this may be left ambiguous. A smaller trailer may be burned and the more expensive one, worth thousands of pounds, may be transported and resold across the country where is owner was not known to the purchaser. At the elaborate funerals for the dead, wreaths are made in the form of replicas of the most prized items of the dead, e.g. a miniature lorry, a pepsi-cola bottle and a pony or a chair as a symbol of sedentarisation in death (Okely, 1983, p. 220).

'Horse wreath commissioned from *Gadje*s for Gypsy funeral'

These floral items are commissioned from and made by non-Gypsies who in these instances are creating transient items as pastiche of the original items for the Gypsies. This is a reverse activity and the *gadje*s are lucratively rewarded for their handcrafted labour. Like the wax and paper flowers sold by Gypsies to non-Gypsies, these material objects are degradable. But in this case they are more elaborate and costly. Headstones, also commissioned from non-Gypsies, are long-lasting material objects and the only long-term monuments but final resting place for this historically nomadic peoples (Okely, 2003, pp. 151–64). Whatever the Gypsies' skills at flower design, they do not put them into practice in death rituals. Like other aspects of mortuary rites, it is the task of *gadje*s to deal with the pollution of Gypsy death and the consequent transformation of individual Gypsy identity (Okely, 1983, pp. 215–30).

'Headstones and chair wreaths commissioned by *Gadjes* for Gypsy burial' (Herts Advertiser).

To Conclude

The Gypsies or Travellers have been deeply involved in the recycling of non-Gypsy waste, broken down into different parts and resold back to the non-Gypsy. As with the waste material which they recycle, so they recycle other manufactured objects re-presented as their unique 'handmade objects', as Gypsy exotic culture for non-Gypsy consumption. They also salvage, select and commission objects from non-Gypsies. These objects 'found', within the non-Gypsy manufacturing process, are then symbolically transformed into material embodiments of their own separate Gypsy ethnicity. Thus both the culture and exchange of material objects can only take this form where there is overlapping geographical place and national polity between different peoples rather than any claims to cultural and regional isolation and separation.

There are some informative parallels between the transformations enacted by Gypsies and the work of the Cubists and Duchamp.[2] Like Duchamp, they elevate 'ready-mades' into aesthetic creations, although specifically into symbols of cultural separateness. What has been dismissed as mere 'copying' or practicality is subtle re-formation. Although economic and political inter-dependence is inescapable, the Gypsies yet strive for economic autonomy by exploiting exoticism in others' desires and longings, while simultaneously constructing cultural difference through an alternative aesthetic. Gypsy cultural identity is constructed through opposition, not isolation.

Bibliography

Adams, Barbara, Judith Okely *et al.* (1975). *Gypsies and Government Policy in England.* London: Heinemann Educational Books.

Attfield, Judy (2000). *Wild Things: the Material Culture of Everyday Life.* Oxford: Berg.

Baker, Daniel (2007). "Art Images" in *Paradise Lost. The First Roma Pavilion*, eds. Junghaus, Timea and Katalin Szekely. Venezia: Open Society Institute.

Barth, Frederik (1969). Introduction to *Ethnic Groups and Boundaries.* London: Allen and Unwin.

Bourdieu, Pierre (1982). *Outline of a Theory of Practice.* Cambridge: Cambridge University Press.

Chambers (1983). *Chambers 20th Century Dictionary.* Edinburgh: Chambers.

Clifford, James (1988). *The Predicament of Culture.* Cambridge, M.A.: Harvard University Press.

Clifford, James and George Marcus, eds. (1986). *Writing Culture: The Poetics and Politics of Ethnography.* Berkeley: University of California Press.

Fog Olwig, Karen and Kirsten Hastrup, eds. (1996). *Siting Culture: the Shifting Anthropological Object.* London: Routledge.

Gosden, Chris and Chantal Knowles (2001). *Collecting Colonialism, Material Culture and Colonial Change.* Oxford: Berg.

Gupta, Akhil and James Ferguson, eds. (1997). *Culture Power and Place, Explorations in Critical Anthropology.* Durham: Duke University Press.

Hendry, Joy (2005). *Reclaiming Culture: Indigenous People and Self-Representation.* New York: Palgrave Macmillan.

Junghaus, Timea and Katalin Szekely, eds. (2007). *Paradise Lost. The First Roma Pavilion.* La Biennale Di Venezia: Open Society Institute.

---

2   "In making collages and assemblages, Picasso and Braque seized upon discarded materials transforming the detritus of urban life into art. Sculptures too were constructed from found objects. In its most radical form, this introduction of everyday items into the elevated realm of culture became 'ready made'-a mass produced article displayed as a work of art." (Tate Modern 10th Gallery.)

Kertesz-Wilkinson, Iren (1997). "Song Performance: a Model for Social Interaction among Vlach Gypsies in South-Eastern Hungary" in *Romany Culture and Gypsy Identity*, eds. Acton, Thomas and Gary Mundy. Hertford: University of Hertfordshire Press, pp. 97–126.

Leach, Edmund (1954). *Systems of Highland Burma*. London: G. Bell and sons.

Lévi-Strauss, Claude (1966). *The Savage Mind*. London: Weidenfeld.

Malinowski, Bronislaw (1922). *The Argonauts of the Western Pacific*. London: Routledge and Kegan Paul.

Malinowski, Bronislaw (1967). *A Diary in the Strict Sense of the Term*. London: Routledge and Kegan Paul.

Mauss, Marcel (1967). *The Gift*. New York: Norton.

Miller, Daniel (1987). *Material Culture and Mass Consumption*. Oxford: Blackwell.

O'Hanlon, Michael and Robert L. Welsch, eds. (2000). *Hunting the Gatherers: Ethnographic Collectors, Agents and Agency in Melanesia, 1870s–1930s*. Oxford: Berghahn.

Okely, Judith (1975). "Gypsy Women: Models in Conflict" in *Perceiving Women*, ed. Ardener, Shirley. London: Malaby, pp. 55–86; reprinted in Okely, Judith (1996). *Own or Other Culture*. London: Routledge.

Okely, Judith (1983). *The Traveller-Gypsies*. Cambridge: Cambridge University Press.

Okely, Judith (1987). "Fieldwork up the M1: Policy and Political Aspects" in *Anthropology at Home*, ed. Jackson, Anthony. London: Tavistock, pp. 55–73.

Okely, Judith (1996). *Own or Other Culture*. London: Routledge.

Okely, Judith (1997). "Some Political Consequences of Theories of Gypsy Identity: The Place of the Intellectual" in *After Writing Culture*, eds. James, Allison, Jennifer Hockey and Andrew Dawson. London: Routledge.

Okely, Judith (2002). "Music as Roma Cultural Performance: the Magyar Gypsies in Hungary." *Leverhulme Final Report* F/00181/C.

Okely, Judith (2003). "Deterritorialised and Spatially Unbounded Cultures within Other Regimes." *Anthropological Quarterly* 76, no 1 (Winter 2003): 151–164.

Ortner, Sherry, ed. (1999). *The Fate of "Culture": Geertz and beyond*. Los Angeles: University of California Press.

Phillips, Ruth and Christopher B. Steiner, eds. (1999). *Unpacking Culture: Art and Commodity in Colonial and Postcolonial Worlds*. Los Angeles: University of California Press.

Said, Edward (1978). *Orientalism*. New York: Pantheon Books.

Silverman, Carol (2007). "Trafficking in the Exotic with 'Gypsy' Music: Balkan Roma, Cosmopolitanism, and 'World Music' Festivals" in *Balkan Popular Culture and the Ottoman Ecumene: Music, Image and Regional Political Discourse*, ed. Buchanan, Donna. Lanham, M.D.: Scarecrow Press.

Smith, David (1997). "Gypsy Aesthetics, Identity and Creativity: the Painted Wagon" in *Romany Culture and Gypsy identity*, eds. Acton, Thomas and Garry Mundy. Hertford: University of Hertfordshire Press.

Stewart, Michael (1997). *The Time of the Gypsies*. Oxford: Westview Press.

Tate Modern 10th Gallery, London.

Taussig, Michael (1993). *Mimesis and Alterity: a Particular History of the Senses*. London: Routledge.

Katalin Kovalcsik

THE ROMANI MUSICIANS
ON THE STAGE OF PLURI-CULTURALISM:
the Case of the Kalyi Jag Group in Hungary

T here is today a touch of apology in recollections from the 1970s, when the Roma began to express their drive at emancipation through traditional music. Speaking of the French Romani film director Tony Gatlif's *Latcho Drom* (Gatlif, 1993), which is a musical journey following the legendary migration route of the Roma from India to Spain, identifying the Roma with their traditional music-making, Anikó Imre notes that "despite *Latcho Drom*'s positive reassessment of Roma hybridity and mobility, some unspoken claim to musical and ethnic authenticity lingers, inseparable from the film's high modernist aesthetic" (Imre, 2008, p. 332). She therefore hails today's Romani *hip hop* singers, whose activity has shifted from an attitude of degradation in music-making to a youthfully cool, flexible and profitable approach. She regards traditional Romani music-making for a living as outdated, claiming that "Eurocentric national education and high cultural sophistication" is the only way to achieve equality in Europe (Imre, 2008, p. 336). As this reveals, the musical activity of the Roma, its assessment and the expectations towards the Roma have undergone rapid changes in the past few decades. In the majority—minority discourse Romani musicians adapted themselves to the changing requirements, while they gradually acquired skills in most existing musical genres. At the time of the political change in Eastern Europe, which approximately coincided with *Latcho Drom*, it would probably have elicited fierce protests among the Roma to call their culture hybrid and mobile. At that time it was the stress on sedentary life and the conservation of folk traditions modelled upon peasant culture that could bring them closer to being accepted in the countries where they settled. Hybridity and mobility as values began to be noticed in Eastern Europe in the 1980s; concerning the Roma, they appeared parallel with the spread of anthropological literature and the upswing of world music in general, but they only became more widely prevalent after the mid-1990s. (The hybridity of international popular music receives little attention in this region, for it is the rural musical tradition that is concentrated on as a value.) It is therefore highly instructive to examine how some Romani musicians reached the decision to represent a peasant-type culture, and how they were capable of moulding it to adapt to the expanding possibilities without a break. The best example in Hungary is the career of Kalyi Jag, a group which perfectly ruled the "Romani" musical space (of the poli-cultural scene known at that time as multiculturalism) around the time of the political turn, and whose activities were,

for over a decade, a compulsory model for all who wished to show the wider public the music of the Roma as an ethnic group. First we will examine the aesthetic-ideological space in which Kalyi Jag emerged, then move on to a discussion of how they adapted to, and altered, this space. In the chapter "After Kalyi Jag" we shall investigate the options that the Roma have today to make music. This discussion is framed by the assessment of Romani music-making by the rest of society.

The cover sheet of the Kalyi Jag group's CD "O suno", 1992. From left to right: József Nagy, Ágnes Künstler, József Balogh, Gusztáv Varga. © Hungaroton Classic.

The Traditional Evaluation of Romani Music-making in Hungary

The historical chronology of Romani music-making is a product of the 20th century. The "heyday" of professional Romani musicians was placed in the first half of the 19th century (Sárosi, 1978) when as performers of the repertoire of the newly emerging Hungarian urban music, known as *verbunkos* (a Hungarian instrumental music genre) and later of the *magyar nóta* (popular Hungarian song) they became the repository of Hungarian musical culture. This music was first called "Magyar", "Magyar song" and only later, because of the performers, did it begin to be called "Gypsy music" both abroad and in Hungary. Though performing music offered some musicians the possibility of integration and a stable middle-class existence, much of society still kept aloof from the musicians and the acceptance of their music in no way entailed acceptance of the Roma pursuing other occupations. Most recently Levente Szabó cited an article from the December 12th 1858 issue of *Vasárnapi Újság* in which a "correspondent" complained about the participation of some writers from the capital in the wedding of a famous Romani band leader, Ferkó Patikárus. "The great majority was shocked to hear that in honour of the wedding the writers from Pest did a performance. The little theatre was packed with people but they left dissatisfied—why? I don't know; but I know that I love Gypsy music: when I have it played, I pay for it—and the friendship ends there" (Szabó, 2003, p. 269).

A few months after the *Vasárnapi Újság* article, the Paris-based composer Ferenc [Franz] Liszt published his notorious book on Hungarian Gypsy music, in which he stated that not only the performers but the musical material itself were of Romani origin.[1] The general uproar that the "eviction" of Hungarian music caused in a country which had recently fought—and lost—a war of independence not only raised the possibility of questioning the correctness of performance by Romani musicians but also directed attention to the question of origin.[2] Towards the end of the 19th century Romani musicians began to be blamed for the gradual decline of the genre. Roma researcher Antal Herrmann (1851–1926) summed up his ideas about the musical activity of Romani musicians in five points in the supplement entitled *Gypsies* to the Pallas Great Encyclopaedia (Herrmann, 1893, pp. xxxiii–xxxix). He also expounded them to the recently established *Gypsy Lore Society* at the London folklore conference in 1891 (Bódi, 1999, p. 83) where they were accepted, in the absence of other musical specialists. Two statements by Herrmann are relevant to our theme. One is the allegation that the Roma "corrupted and falsified" the "aboriginal" Hungarian music. The notion of Roma "bad taste" had already appeared in the work of a pioneer of Romani research, Grellmann, and was later cited by Liszt in his book (Liszt, 1861, p. 130). The view that the Roma "corrupt" any music which they get hold of is related to the colonialist attitude (Szabó, 2003, p. 260), which holds that the Roma as "natural" and "primitive" or at least peripheral people obviously do not have sophisticated tastes similar to those of the host peoples.

Another observation by Herrmann, based on his collections in Romani communities, states that the Roma do not play their own songs on instruments but perform them vocally, and that the melodies are borrowed from the neighbouring peoples, then tinted with certain "Gypsy" peculiarities of performance. This thesis of nation-state thinking—notably, that each nation has specific products of an indigenous folk culture that are only typical of that nation—was particularly disadvantageous for the Roma. It was a bias that prevented their music and other cultural products (tales, dances, etc.) which are closely connected to those of the host nations from being seen

---

1   In French: Liszt, 1859; in Hungarian: Liszt, 1861.

2   Liszt's reputation was not improved by the fact that the greater part or even the whole of the book was probably not written by the composer but by his companion, princess Carolyne de Sayn-Wittgenstein, as some of his contemporaries already guessed and as seems to have been confirmed at the end of the 20th century, see Sárosi, 1978, p. 141; Hamburger, 2000, pp. 20–25; Hamburger, 2001, pp. 11–17.

as expressions of an integrative attitude or from being judged positively even in the 20th century. At the same time, it was discovered through systematic folklore collection in the 20th century that rural Romani communities used among themselves the forgotten or abandoned traditions of surrounding peasant communities. This somewhat improved the evaluation of the Roma as "preservers" of the culture of surrounding peoples, but their servicing role remained or became more widespread. The folk revival initiative known as the "dance-house" movement that started in Hungary in 1972 (Frigyesi, 1996, pp. 54–75), which popularises Hungarian instrumental musical folk traditions and the allegedly "authentic" performing style chiefly of rural Romani musicians, invites and sometimes hires rural Romani musicians, mainly Transylvanian, as teachers. It is not suggested in this context that these musicians "corrupted" the Hungarian peasant tradition. Since, however, the aim of the movement is to integrate cultural products into the national tradition and performing practice via the training of the younger, so-far predominantly non-Roma generations of musicians, there is reason to fear that the Romani musicians will be relegated to the background.

Beginnings of the Romani Folklore Movement

In the decades of socialism, one of the state's objectives was to provide adequate housing, health care and education for the Roma (Kállai, 2002). Compulsory employment should also have contributed to the social rise of the Roma in a supportive environment. However, the Roma were invisible in the cultural sphere (with the exception of Gypsy music) and usually encountered forbidding obstacles if they strove to rise above semi-skilled or skilled labour. Anthropologist Tamás Hofer pointed out—following historian István Bibó—that "for lack of adequate agencies of representation—or their limited–obstructed functioning, several political, human rights, etc. efforts find their expression in the cultural sphere, including literature, in East-Central Europe" (Hofer, 1991, p. 8). The deep silence enveloping the Roma was first broken by the explosive success of a 17-year-old secondary school pupil, Károly Bari, whose first book of verse was published in 1970 (*Holtak arca fölé* [Above the face of the dead]) (Bari, 1970). Mature and cultured, the expressive poems shed new light on the life of the Roma and elicited broad solidarity. The next cultural harbinger of Romani problems was Ágnes Daróczi. She recited poems—also at the age of 17—in both Hungarian and Romani in a televised talent-spotting competition "Who knows what?" (*Ki mit tud?*) in 1972. The Romani folklore movement, the last musical movement of socialism, was initiated and organised by Ágnes Daróczi, who obtained a university degree in the meantime, and her lawyer husband János Bársony.[3] A folk music movement was launched in

---

3   In addition to her performing and folklore group organising activity, Daróczi also built a forum for the emerging Romani fine arts labelled "naive" Romani art, see Daróczi and Karsai, 1979; Daróczi and Kerékgyártó, 1989.

Hungary in 1969 with the name *Pávamozgalom* [Peacock Movement] (Frigyesi, 1996, p. 72) after an emblematic Hungarian folksong expressing the desire for freedom (*Röpülj, páva, röpülj* / Fly, peacock, fly), initiated by professional ethnomusicologists to encourage folksong singing among the rural population. The initiative led to the foundation of several "women's choirs" for whom occasional performances in the vicinity and sometimes on television and on the radio provided great motivation. The Daróczi-Bársony couple organised groups of rural, mostly Vlach Romani families, who traditionally did not play instruments, and had them debut at the *First Meeting of Gypsy Tradition-Preserving Groups* in the Transdanubian town of Tata in 1981. By then the couple had attracted the support of folk dance researchers, first of all György Martin, who initiated the Hungarian dance-house movement. Martin's activity, which had a European perspective, laid the firm scientific foundations for ethnochoreology in Hungary. He and his research team had started to systematically film Romani folk dances back in the 1950s (Martin, 2005). The dance-house movement forged an important link with the majority culture and its movements, since it was a basic principle that the dance-house movement had incorporated in its repertoire the traditions of other ethnicities from the very beginning.[4] The involvement of the Roma probably appeared expedient not only because the positive stereotype of their musical talent could be relied upon but also because, despite its low social prestige, professional music-making was still a desired occupation among the Roma and there was now an opportunity for several new groups to try their hands at it. The emergence of the Hungarian dance-house movement also determined the course of Romani musical culture as an ethnic movement. While earlier some Romani musicians (including Gusztáv Varga and József Balogh, later members of Kalyi Jag) had played rock music or joined rock groups, this line faded. Martin and a few other folk dance specialists (Tibor Erdélyi, László Vásárhelyi) first supported two young Romani folk dancers from the same north-eastern Hungarian village, Nagyecsed: Béla Balogh (1957–1995) and Gusztáv Balázs. Then the Nagyecsed relatives of the two dancers began to appear in the academic sphere, first as informers and later as potential members of a folklore ensemble. In the meantime Balázs graduated in ethnography and did active cultural political work among folklore groups.

However, from the very start the Romani folklore groups refused to adopt the purist idea, voiced by Hungarian specialists, that village traditions should be put on stage unaltered. In the 1980s, when Romani folklore ensembles had more and more opportunities to perform in rural and urban programs, the movement soon liberated itself and immediately turned towards professional venues.

---

4   Dance-house musician and later musicologist Ferenc Sebő recalled that the dance-house movement regarded the traditions of other ethnicities "as variants of a common European language of local colour, representing different ages" (Sebő, 1994, p. 90).

The Appearance of Kalyi Jag

From the 1950s onwards, compulsory employment forced large masses of the Roma to take to the road. Especially the Romani villagers of north-eastern Hungary were forced to take jobs in large towns or the capital, mainly as unskilled labourers on building sites, for there were no jobs for them in local agriculture. Living in workers' hostels during the week and commuting home for the weekend by what was called the "black train" because of the crowds of Roma, the young people made music in their free time, which transformed the rural Romani traditions. The appearance of Anglo-American rock and pop music—the beat movement—popularised the use of the guitar (hardly known earlier). In performances by young Romani people the earlier vocal tunes, once sung without instrumental accompaniment, were changed so that they could be accompanied, using motifs borrowed from rock and pop music. When the time came to present rural traditions on stage, the character of folk music had changed massively, adjusted to the surrounding popular musical world.

The first truly successful, stage-ready ensemble was Kalyi Jag (Black Fire) rallying young men from north-eastern Hungary living in workers' hostels, who took their name from a poem in Károly Bari's second book of verse *Elfelejtett tüzek* [Forgotten Fires] (Bari, 1973).[5] Although the group was awarded the title "Young Masters of Folk Art" as early as 1979, they had to wait eight years before a record could be released, as socialist cultural policy was very slow to thaw. The leader Gusztáv Varga commented on the start in an interview when they had been awarded the Europe Prize:

> The group was perhaps six months old when ... we played to the folk dance researchers. They were perplexed and couldn't decide if it was Gypsy folklore and if we deserved it [the Young Masters prize]. They were surprised hearing us sing in our mother tongue. In the '70s it was forbidden to sing in Gypsy because the Gypsies 'droned' *(gajdolnak)* ..., they said. Then we realized that this culture was not a thing only to be cultivated among ourselves and on the trains. When we were commuting on the night black train, we would sing and dance all the way. Many people gathered around us and listened, sympathizing with the Gypsies. I think what startled the committee, the jury, was that there

---

5   The phrase is from the introductory poem of the book, written in Hungarian with a line in Romani: "Kiszolgáltatva hitemnek / haláltalan szavakkal szólok, / ande muro jílo káli jag phabol, [szívemben fekete tűz ég, transl. K. K.] / kimondom nektek az éjszakát." [Exposed to my faith / I speak with deathless words / ande muro jílo káli jag phabol [a black fire is burning in my heart] / I am telling you the night.]. As the group leader Gusztáv Varga noted, "*black* [italics B.M. throughout] denoted the people's frame of mind full of fear and anxiety, while *fire* symbolises destructive power. The black fire overcomes, defeats fear and the resultant prejudice. I feel that the activity of Kalyi Jag is a destructive force in Hungary and all over the world that abolishes prejudice." (Blaha, 1992, p. 13).

was a group of young men in jeans and sandals who spoke of folklore and folk music. What seemed really strange to me was that even folklorists were afraid to openly declare that there was a Gypsy folklore (Gábor, 1995).

Based on interviews with Gusztáv Varga and another group leader, János Balogh, Barbara Rose Lange also writes that speaking and singing in Romani was stigmatised by the rest of society. It was forbidden to speak Romani at school. Villagers labelled Romani singing as "droning" and warned them to stop singing in public places, regarding it as a sign of *műveletlenség* (lack of education).[6] In Lange's view singing in Romani was a prerequisite for ethnic legitimacy. However, they changed the style of their singing, bringing it closer to artistic singing so as to generate sympathy towards themselves and through them towards the Roma; to rework "the relationship between Roma and Hungarians in mainstream society" (Lange, 1997, p. 7). In the interview Varga mentions jeans and sandals, which came into fashion with the beat movement and were kept by the dance-house movement. That would mean identification with the values of the dance-house movement. It worth noting that while Varga refers to the urban life of labourers by mentioning the black train, he states that researchers failed to admit that there was "Gypsy folklore". The definition of the music of small Romani communities as workers' folklore was an interesting transitional attempt, made towards the end of socialism. The idea came from musicologist János Maróthy (Maróthy, 1981, pp. 15–25), the patron of a group called *Monszun* (of mostly non-Romani members, also including János Bársony) in the early 1970s, who adapted Romani folksongs as well.[7] The fact that researchers did not regard Romani folklore as autonomous on the basis of its musical features appears as secret information about the existence of folklore in Varga's interpretation. His version thus presents the researchers as victims of the system, who were not to blame for not being allowed to speak openly about Romani culture. In the report, recalling events sixteen years earlier, the group leader presented a harmonious picture: the aim of the movement (getting the Roma accepted through the Romani language and culture) and the gradual attainment of that goal via the persuasion of the professionals and the group's international successes. In this way Varga and the Romani folklore movement consummated a discourse which had started in the 19th century, doing so at a time—the end of the 20th century—when in the ecstasy of freedom and democracy it would have been insulting to question the truth of the statement.

---

6   Lange translates the Hungarian word correctly as "without culture", but it is used to refer to uneducated, uncivilised, ill-mannered people. According to "commonsense opinion" only people who have no manners would speak and sing in a language the majority cannot understand.

7   Lange described the history of the group but was not aware of Maróthy's role (Lange, 1997).

The Activity of Kalyi Jag

The members of Kalyi Jag, which was formed in 1978, began making music at workers' hostels in Budapest, and eventually reached the great stages of the world, receiving several important awards and becoming the most widely known representatives of Hungarian Romani folklore. They worked out their style from their own folklore traditions and their attraction to pop music, as well as from the recommendations of Gusztáv Balázs and the helpful Hungarian folk dance specialists and researchers. Their first record (1987) sold thirty thousand copies in a month, becoming a gold disc in 1989 (see Kalyi Jag, 1997). The members of the group at that time were Gusztáv Varga (Nagyecsed), József Balogh (Újfehértó), Balogh's wife Ágnes Künstler, a non-Roma from Budapest and the dancer Béla Balogh (Nagyecsed). The great success made Hungaroton—the only record company in Hungary before the political change—release another three records (1989, 1992, 1993). In the nineties they toured the world and also performed frequently at home in clubs and also for Romani families who invited them to play at christening or wedding ceremonies. From the second record onwards, Béla Balogh was replaced by József Nagy in the rhythm section.

An important milestone in the development of their music and dance on stage was their involvement in the German-Austrian "superproduction" *Magnetenshow*, starting in 1993, to which professional Romani groups had been invited from India and Europe. The basic concept was the virtuosity of the Roma in music and dance (the show appeared at the same time as Tony Gatlif made *Latcho Drom*. We can see that in that period the emancipatory efforts of the Roma were supported by the positive stereotype of their talent for music-making). Kalyi Jag performed Romani solo, couple and stick-dance choreographies in addition to folk music. In six months they did 138 concerts in Austria, Germany and Switzerland. This gave them a stage experience that few other groups could compete with. Their involvement in the show brought them an invitation to the *World Music Festival* where they won the title of *World Music Megastar*.

They were awarded the Europe Prize by the European Youth Parliament and One World Group and Music Television in 1994. In the same year Gusztáv Varga started the Kalyi Jag minority school in Budapest, relying on the *Kalyi Jag Roma-Art Association*. The school teaches the Romani language and culture (first of all music and dance). Originally a special school with a two-year programme, it has evolved into a four-year vocational secondary school, with two subsidiary schools in provincial towns (Kalyi Jag Roma Nemzetiségi Szakiskola és Szakközépiskola, 2009). In 1996 the group received a state award. In their next two records (1998, 2002) a cautious orientation towards the new fashionable trend of the '90s, *ethnomusic* (a term often used by Hungarians to refer to the folkloristic lineage of world music) can also be sensed through the invited instrumentalists. This recording involved a new member, a somewhat younger relative from Nagyecsed, Zsolt Farkas. József Balogh and Ágnes Künstler formed separate groups from 2003 (first called Ethnix, then EtnoRom), also making records (Ethnix, 2003; EtnoRom, 2006). Gusztáv Varga kept the Kalyi Jag name, first releasing a CD of Hungarian Christmas and pilgrimage songs tinged with rock elements (Kalyi Jag, 2004), then converting the group into a music theatre which usually performs his rock opera *Romani Legend*. This is an adaptation of the mythical history of the Roma, employing the story of the Indian epic Ramayana as if the people of King Rama were the Roma, which premiered in 2005. Another premier in 2005 was József Balogh's musical play—*Nomadic Passion. Snake Ballad*—based on a Romani folk ballad and performed by a professional folk dance ensemble, Honvéd. *Romani Legend* returns to Gatlif's treatment of myth, approaching the legend from a different angle, which now arouses moderate interest. *Nomadic Passion* is quality entertainment, intended for the habitual audience of folk dance productions; it may contribute to the development of Romani folk dance motifs into standards for broader use.[8]

During their meteoric career Kalyi Jag managed to work out, preserve and improve their unique style. Towards the end of the fashion wave, the two successor groups returned to the favourite genre of their youth, rock music, drawing on it, and experimenting with it. Thanks to the school, Kalyi Jag is not only registered by music history as the representative of a more or less dated musical fashion, for the school—as will be seen later—is one of the springboards for young Roma's successes in fashionable international popular genres.

After Kalyi Jag

With their first record of 1987 (Kalyi Jag, 1987), which had a revelatory effect on the Romani population of the country, Kalyi Jag set an example and launched a fashion among folklore groups, but the changes of this fashion was not dictated by them. True, the group also adapted foreign Romani folk and folk-like materials, showing Romani culture as transnational, which nourished the ideas of other ensembles. In the folklore movement of the first half of the '90s there were three waves of fashion which followed each other in quick succession: Russian, Balkan and Spanish. These relied mainly on the respective "Gypsy music" i.e. local urban, folky musical styles, expanding the frames of "folklore" in this way. Kalyi Jag played only a few of these pieces, sticking to the style they had elaborated in the early '90s. As a result, they were deemed conservative by young Hungarian Roma, who were more strongly attracted to international pop music. On the international stage they remained popular because

---

8   Demand for it is illustrated by the performance of a finalist in the televised talent-spotting competition A Star is Born: Szabolcs Csikó's performance of virtuoso Romani folk dance routines provided the basis for modern thematic choreographies (TV2, 12 and 19 December 2009, *Csillag születik*).

they were recognised as the most "traditional" Romani folklore group. There were no initiatives like Hungary's dance-house movement in the neighbouring countries, which is why the Romani groups there had a more popular sound and repertoire than the Kalyi Jag.

The Romani folklore groups—though set on the road by the dance-house movement—failed to strike roots in it because they rejected its purist aesthetic approach. Interestingly, the dance-house movement also created its own version of Romani folk music with the *Parno Graszt* (White Horse) group. This consists of members of a large rural Romani family, who were kneaded into a professional folklore ensemble by Hungarian folk and ethno publisher, Fonó Records. The vocalists of *Parno Graszt* use all they have learnt from Kalyi Jag and other professionalized Romani folklore performers, but their singing is accompanied by a professional folk instrumental ensemble that makes it seem more archaic than it really is (Parno Graszt, 2002). Fonó Records occasionally issues CD's by folklore ensembles living in Budapest, but the Romani participants in the major annual dance-house event, the Dance-House Meetings in Budapest, are mostly members of rural families. The problem here is that the rest of the participants do not appear socially handicapped. The ambiguity of the purist approach was painfully obvious at a representative folklore program around 2005 in the new National Theatre, to which an inexperienced Romani group, who rarely performed, was also invited in the name of democracy. Apart from the embarrassment caused by the glittering environment of the National Theatre, the village Roma's clothing, in notable contrast to the rest of the performers, elicited pity in some of the audience and politely concealed rejection in the rest. The Romani folklore performers were right to take an independent course at the beginning, for choosing purism implied the danger of conserving the social hierarchy.

Until the mid-'90s Kalyi Jag had no rivals in the sense that it was acknowledged as the most professionally expert group. Its style of adaptation was the starting point for other groups, who defined themselves in reference to it. Though *Ando Drom* (On the Road) emerged as a rival to Kalyi Jag, its breakthrough came only after 1997, when almost all its earlier members had been replaced and it had worked out an *ethnomusical* style of its own (Ando Drom, 1997). The second half of the 1990s witnessed a great upswing. Graduates of the Kalyi Jag school formed not only the *Ternipe* (Youth) group playing traditional music but also the *Fekete vonat* [Black Train] rap group, modifying the representation of the Roma as a transnational ethnic group into that of a colourful minority. The first CD of the latter group met with great success (Fekete Vonat, 1998), galvanising young Hungarians also through its youthful vigour and political texts based on Afro-American *hip-hop*. Since then, the gap between Romani music in the capital and Romani music in the countryside has widened. The capital became the venue for the debut of newer and newer young Romani performers in diverse genres. The folk music range is chiefly represented in the capital by *Váradi*

Roma Café, originally a Romungro light-music orchestra lacking the others' village background, who developed a kind of folk style in the early 21st century by adopting the style of Romanian Romani singers (first of all Nicolae Guṭă) and by remoulding Romani folksongs in a jazzy–Latinate manner (Váradi Roma Café, 2002; Váradi Roma Café, 2006; Váradi Café, 2004). The surviving or newly formed groups in the capital converted into world music groups with good instrumental qualities (such as *Romano Drom, Karavan Familia* and *Khamoro,* the group led by Zsolt Farkas). Their popularity among the Roma of Hungary is, however, nowhere near that of *Váradi Roma Café.* They earn their living mainly by playing in exclusive clubs abroad and in Budapest, instead of performing for a broader Romani public. It is still typical of the Hungarian media that folk groups are rarely, if ever, broadcast, while the arena of popular music is more open to the Roma, for popular music has a far broader audience. This explains why *Romantic,* a group playing a popular melodic music style named *dance,* earned great popularity at the beginning of the new millennium, followed by the success of Romani competitors in the talent-spotting TV show *Megastar* from 2004. In the countryside, the Romani variant of *lakodalmas* [wedding] *rock* prevails among the Roma. The first successful performer of this genre, *Nagyecsedi Fekete Szemek* [Black Eyes of Nagyecsed]—which existed in the 1980s as a folklore group as well—was introduced by the country by Lajos Galambos, better known as Lagzi Lajcsi [Lou of the Weddings] in his TV show *Dáridó* [carousal] from 2002 and *Új Szuperbuli* [new super-party] later.

Wedding rock, the leading genre in rural balls including weddings, is the main territory of the modernisation of Hungarian folk-oriented popular music, and is consequently stigmatised by intellectuals (Lange, 1996).[9] The intellectuals, for whom folk music is a valuable heritage, do not regard *Magyar nóta* [Hungarian popular song] as something of value, whereas *Magyar nóta,* especially in its rock and disco variants, is much loved by the rural population and is actually the organic continuation of Hungarian rural culture. Most of the performers of Hungarian *wedding rock* (called later wedding, carousing music) are non-Roma, but the performers of the Romani variant to Romani audiences are mostly Roma. Some performers of today's Romani wedding music (called Gypsy or Romani song by the Roma: *Cigány nóta, Roma nóta*) were folklore musicians in the 1990s who switched over to this rugged path to make a living or for other reasons (Kovalcsik, 1999). These Romani ball-room musicians are the most defenceless stratum of the musical community today, trying to make ends meet by entertaining low-income Roma. This is in striking contrast to the well-being of CD-releasing pros in the capital, such as *Nagyecsedi Fekete Szemek.* The aversion for the Hungarian variant has also been transferred to the Romani version, and thus the Romani intellectuals of the capital condemn it in the same way as the

---

9   Hungarian *wedding rock* belongs to an Eastern and Southern European group of genres, on which see Silverman, 2000, pp. 270–293.

majority intellectuals do, failing to understand its role. As we can see, "bad taste" and the "corruption" of music are not characteristics of the Roma alone. According to the definition of Christopher Washburne and Maiken Derno, "bad music is first and foremost a social construct" (Washburne, 2004, p. 2), and "it can be loosely understood along contextualist lines to be music that is somehow unwanted, played in the wrong contexts for the wrong reasons" (Washburne and Derno, 2004, p. 1). The context of wedding music is a rural environment of which the urban elite know nothing.

Romani small-community folklore lives on in this group of genres which will survive, adjusted to the changing times, as long as there is a demand for it among the Roma masses. It feeds the self-awareness of the rural Roma that they have a micromusic acknowledged by their environment, too, that the hits of their favourite groups can be found in the juke box in every village pub and they can listen to them in public whenever they want to. On the basis of my research in Transdanubian villages[10] I have found that the rural population have accepted this music—though some aesthetic reservations may sometimes be expressed behind the back of the Roma—and the most recent hits of the *Nagyecsedi Fekete Szemek* are part of the repertoire of village balls, the scenes of rural pluri-culturalism, as are pieces from the music of other minorities (Germans, South Slavs) living in the area. As regards the traditional occupation of music-making, Gypsy music and its performers are sources of nostalgia today, especially because this kind of musician had come from the stratum of poor peasants even before World War II. Performing in the village today is not a degrading occupation; the musicians are usually skilled workers or artisans who eke out their wages by playing music. The greater instrumental competence of the Roma is acknowledged by them and by the youngsters playing fashionable pop music as a pastime.

As far as Romani music making in general is concerned, it is not yet a thing of the past, for Romani musicians have not reached the limits of their possibilities. The great success of Romani jazz musicians and a growing number of virtuoso classical musicians show that they still have plenty of potential for knowledge and development. As for the Roma involved in low-prestige musical genres and entertainment programs, the paradoxical situation is that although the intellectuals of the capital regard them—sometimes with disdain, sometimes with indignation—as showbiz-manipulated performers, they fail to realise that the Roma must gain experience in these venues as well. From this observation I cannot help concluding that the depreciation of Romani musicians will prevail until Romani music-making stops being considered in stereotypes and a healthier attitude to musical genres, free from political ideologies, can evolve.

---

10   The research was supported between 2008 and 2010 by the Hungarian Scientific Research Fund (OTKA), (76875).

The Szilvási Gipsy Folk Band, a Romani folklore group. Pécs, 7 May 1999.
Photo: Katalin Kovalcsik (NZ 15693 in the Photo Archive of the Institute of Musicology, HAS).

István Szilvási, the leader of the Szilvási Gipsy Folk Band dancing with a little girl.
Pécs, 7 May 1999. Photo: Katalin Kovalcsik
(NZ 15719 in the Photo Archive of the Institute of Musicology, HAS).

Bibliography

Bari, Károly (1970). *Holtak arca fölé* (Above the face of the dead). Budapest: Szépirodalmi Könyvkiadó.
Bari, Károly (1973). *Elfelejtett tüzek* (Forgotten fires). Budapest: Szépirodalmi Könyvkiadó.
Blaha, Márta (1992). "A szívet melengető Fekete Tűz. Beszélgetés Varga Gusztávval, a Kalyi Jag együttes vezetőjével" (The heart-warming Black Fire. Interview with Gusztáv Varga, leader of the Kalyi Jag group). *Amaro Drom* 2 (1992): 13.
Bódi, Zsuzsanna (1999). "Antal Herrmann and Gypsy research in Hungary" in *Tanulmányok Herrmann Antal emlékére* (Studies in Memory of Antal Herrmann), ed. Bódi, Zsuzsanna. Budapest: Magyar Néprajzi Társaság, 82–86.
Daróczi, Ágnes and István Kerékgyártó, eds. (1989) *Autodidakta Cigány Képzőművészek II. Országos Kiállítása* (2nd National Exhibition of Self-taught Romani Artists). Catalogue. Budapest Magyar Művelődési Intézet.
Daróczi, Ágnes and Zsigmond Karsai, eds. (1979). *Autodidakta Cigány Képzőművészek Országos Kiállítása* (National Exhibition of Self-taught Romani Artists). Catalogue. Budapest: Népművelési Intézet.
Frigyesi, Judit (1996). "The Aesthetic of the Hungarian Revival Movement" in *Retuning Culture. Musical Changes in Central and Eastern Europe*, ed. Slobin, Mark. Durham and London: Duke University Press, pp. 54–75.
Gábor, Péter (1995). *A cigány kultúra közelről* (Close-up of Romani culture). Budapest: MTV, documentary film.
Gatlif, Tony (1993). *Latcho Drom.* KG Production, La Bande Son, and Virgin France S.A.
Hamburger, Klára (2000). "Liszt cigánykönyvének magyarországi fogadtatása. Első rész. 1859–1861" (The Hungarian reception of Liszt's book on Gypsy music. Part 1. 1859–1861). *Muzsika* 40, no. 12 (2000): 20–25.
Hamburger, Klára (2001). "Liszt cigánykönyvének magyarországi fogadtatása. Második rész. 1881–1886" (The Hungarian reception of Liszt's book on Gypsy music. Part 2. 1881–1886). *Muzsika* 41, no. 1 (2001): 11–17.
Herrmann, Antal (1893). "A cigányok népköltészete és zenéje" (The folk poetry and music of the Gypsies) in *A Pallas Nagy Lexikona*. IV. kötet. „Cigányok" (Pallas' Great Encyclopaedia. Vol. IV. Roma). Budapest, Pallas, xxxiii–xxxix.
Hofer, Tamás (1991). "A 'népi kultúra' örökségének megszerkesztése Magyarországon (Vázlat egy kutató vállalkozásról)" (Editing the legacy of "folk culture" in Hungary (Outline of a research venture)) in *Népi kultúra és nemzettudat. Tanulmánygyűjtemény* (Folk culture and national consciousness. Collection of studies), ed. Hofer, Tamás. Budapest: Magyarságkutató Intézet, pp. 7–13.
Imre, Anikó (2008). "Roma Music and Transnational Homelessness." *Third Text* 22, no. 3 (2008): 325–336.
Kállai, Ernő, ed. (2002) *The Gypsies/The Roma in Hungarian Society.* Budapest: Teleki László Foundation.
Kalyi Jag (1997). *The Kalyi Jag Group (1978–1997).* Information sheet.

Kalyi Jag Roma Nemzetiségi Szakiskola és Szakközépiskola (2009). *1994–2009. Kalyi Jag.* Budapest: Kalyi Jag Roma Nemzetiségi Szakiskola és Szakközépiskola.

Kovalcsik, Katalin (1999). "Folklore Musicians, Traditionalists and 'Electronic Gypsies'" in ESEM Proceedings of the XV European Seminar in Ethnomusicology. London: SOAS. Published as a CD-Rom and part of the book: Giuriati, Giovanni, ed. (2003). *World Music, Globalizzazione, Identitá Musicali, Diritti, Profitti.* Rome: *EM* Rivista Degli Archivi De Ethnomusicologia, Accademia Nazionale Di Santa Cecilia.

Lange, Barbara Rose (1996). "*Lakodalmas* Rock and the Rejection of Popular Culture in Post-Socialist Hungary" in *Retuning Culture. Musical Changes in Central and Eastern Europe*, ed. Slobin, Mark. Durham and London: Duke University Press, 76–91.

Lange, Barbara Rose (1997). "Hungarian Rom (Gypsy) Political Activism and the Development of *Folklór* Ensemble Music." *The World of Music* 39, no. 3 (1997): 5–30.

Liszt, Ferenc (1861). *A czigányokról és a czigány zenéről Magyarországon* (About Gypsies and Gypsy music in Hungary). Pest: [Haeckenast].

Liszt, Franz (1859). *Des Bohémiens et de leur musique en Hongrie.* Paris: Librairie Nouvelle and Bourdilliat.

Maróthy, János (1981). "A Music of Your Own" in *Popular Music* 1, eds. Middleton, Richard and David Horn. Cambridge: Cambridge University Press, 15–25.

Martin, György (2005). *The Music of the Stick Dance*, eds. Kovalcsik, Katalin and Zsuzsa Kubinyi. Budapest: Institute for Musicology of the Hungarian Academy of Sciences – House of Tradition.

Sárosi, Bálint (1978). *Gypsy music.* Budapest: Corvina.

Sebő, Ferenc (1994). *Népzenei olvasókönyv* (A folk music reader). Budapest: Magyar Művelődési Intézet.

Silverman, Carol (2000). "Rom (Gypsy) Music" in *The Garland Encyclopedia of World Music*, Vol. 8, eds. Rice, Timothy, James Porter, and Chris Goertzen. New York and London: Garland Publishing Inc., 270–293.

Szabó, Levente (2003). "Csupán zene? Liszt Ferenc *A cigányokról és a cigány zenéről Magyarországon* című könyve és kontextusai" (Only music? Ferenc Liszt's book "About Gypsies and Gypsy music in Hungary" and its contexts) in *Antropológia és irodalom. Egy új paradigma útkeresése* (Anthropology and literature. Reflection of a new paradigm), eds. Biczó, Gábor and Noémi Kiss. Debrecen: Csokonai Kiadó, 252–269.

Washburne, Christopher J. and Maiken Derno (2004). "Introduction" in *Bad Music. The Music We Love to Hate*, eds. Washburne, Christopher J. and Maiken Derno. New York and London: Routledge, 1–14.

Discography

Ando Drom (1997). *Phari mamo.* Frankfurt: Network. MK/CD.

Ethnix (2003). *Hívd a Zenét. Call the Music. Gipsy Pop–Folk Music.* Budapest: Künstler Kft. MK/CD

EtnoRom (2006). *Rományi Luma. Szá szá szá. Cigány Világ* (Gipsy world). Budapest: Fonó Budai Zeneház – Fonó Music Hall.

Fekete Vonat (1998). *Fekete vonat* (Black Train). Budapest: EMI-QUINT. MK/CD.

Kalyi Jag (1987). *Gypsy Folk Songs from Hungary.* SLPX/MK/HCD 18132. Budapest: Hungaroton. LP/MK/CD.

Kalyi Jag (1989). *Lungoj o drom angla mande Gipsy Folk Songs from Hungary.* Budapest: Hungaroton. LP/MK/CD.

Kalyi Jag (1992). *Karingszo me phirav. Amerre én járok. Gypsy Folk Songs from Hungary.* Budapest: Hungaroton. LP/MK/CD.

Kalyi Jag (1993). *Cigányszerelem. Gypsy Love. Romano Kamipo.* Budapest: Authors' edition. MK/CD[CD-ROM].

Kalyi Jag (1993). *O suno. The Dream. Az álom.* Budapest: Hungaroton and Fonofolk. LP/MK/CD.

Kalyi Jag (2002). *Köszöntünk titeket. Naisaras tumen. Greating* (sic!) *for you.* Budapest: Kalyi Jag Roma Művészeti Egyesület and G+A Production. MK/CD.

Kalyi Jag (2004). *Minden dalom a Tiéd. All My Songs Are Yours. Tjirej le Gilja.* Budapest: Kalyi Jag, A Production, and RTL Zeneklub. MK/CD.

Parno Graszt (2002). *Autentikus cigány népzene* (Authentic Gypsy folk music). Budapest: Fonó Records. CD.

Váradi Café (2004). *Szeress még!* (Love me more). Budapest: BMG Hungary. MK/CD.

Váradi Roma Café (2002). *Járok-kelek a világban* (I walk all around the world). Budapest: BMG Hungary. MK/CD.

Váradi Roma Café (2006). *Isten hozott a családban!* (Welcome to the family!). Budapest: Sony BMG. CD.

Stefan Benedik

HARMING "CULTURAL FEELINGS":
Images and Categorisation of Temporary Romani Migrants to Graz/Austria[1]

For about fifteen years Roma and Romnija[2] have been migrating temporarily to the city of Graz in the southern part of Austria.[3] Despite public perceptions, these include not only Hungarian speaking people from the south-eastern Slovak town of Hostice-Gesztete, but migrants from almost all the Central and Eastern European countries. Unknown before 1989, these Roma and Romnija have since then become part of everyday life in Graz—mostly as beggars. As such they have aroused both sympathy and racist sentiments. Repeatedly, beggars in general become the targets of local media campaigns and individual attacks. Whilst mayors and city councils have tried to contain mendicancy by a creatively executed anti-begging act, which has been enthusiastically acclaimed by shopkeepers and a significant part of the public, some organisations have emerged in support of certain groups among these people, focussing specifically on those from the village of Hostice-Gesztete. The following paper sums up the development of discourses on these Romani migrants by analysing the press coverage of the assumed "begging problem" in Graz.

Background and Basic Features

Since the fall of the Iron Curtain a new type of migration has emerged within the reconstructed Central European regions, clearly shaped by the framework of transregional socio-economic and other disadvantages. Some work has already been done on Romani migrations caused by this, which covers issues such as asylum-seeking (Cahn and Vermeersch, 2000) or classical labour migration (which has a much

---

1   This article is based on results from my study done in the framework of the "Research Group Migration" on the University of Graz—chaired by Heidrun Zettelbauer, generously funded by the federal-state-foundation "Zukunftsfonds Steiermark". My current team-colleagues Barbara Tiefenbacher and Wolfgang Göderle helped me to develop my arguments and contributed to this paper with some of their thoughts and perspectives.

2   Although I prefer to operate with the phrase *Romani men and women*, I use *Roma and Romnija* here to highlight the fact that speaking about "Roma" only would mean referring exclusively to male persons.

3   Graz is the second-largest city of Austria (some 290,000 inhabitants), situated in the South, near to Hungary and Slovenia.

longer tradition (Halwachs, 2004)), reviewing the causes and features of movements away from a given "homeland" and the circumstances of a possible "integration" into a "receiving society".[4] The common ground of these concepts is the assumption of a long-term or permanent change of place.[5] Thus, reflections on short-term migration are not necessarily included, unless they are fitted into a teleological push-pull-model. This paper follows a broader conceptualisation of (Romani) migration, focussing on the example of a network which was established through flexible movements within a relatively small region and communication in two directions. In the last 15 years or so, activities between the two central European localities of Graz (Austria) and Hostice-Gesztete (Slovakia) are an example of one of these networks.

The results of those processes are well-established and complex structures of economic, physical and cultural exchange. Calling this connection a means of exchange and a network of communication does not necessarily mean that those ways are used for forms of "positive" exchange only (e.g. support, aid and encouragement): they have also given a place for openly hostile and/or actively harmful messages and actions. The majority of discussions in question here are actions or messages which may result in both advantages and disadvantages for the Roma and Romnija involved. This is related to the fact that these exchanges are not taking place on an equal level. In fact, they are shaped by striking economic dissimilarities and commonly superseded by the assumption of a "beggar problem". After 1997 a huge infrastructure project (involving housing, official bureaucracy and even a factory) proved this strong, but unequal connection between "rich" Graz and "poor" Hostice-Gesztete. In this context, the latter is referred to as a village, which is defined (from the Graz p.o.v.) as a Roma/Romnija-only-settlement, even represented by a Romani mayor. The associated Romani identity is described by all forms of discourse which are analysed here as an imagined otherness, as a "foreign culture". Voices from inside Romani communities have not had and still do not have any influence on the invented narratives and other actions. Nevertheless they have become rather pervasive and exert significant influence within political, legal and cultural contexts in the specific regions.

---

4   Central European Romani Migrations have aroused interest especially in recent months, e.g. in the conference "Romani mobilities in Europe: multidisciplinary perspectives" at the University of Oxford. In recent years several publications have presented case studies on this region, hardly ever discussing migration within Central Europe. See: Crowe, 2003; Guy, 2004; Homoláč, 2006; Matter, 2003; Sobotka, 2003; Szép, 2003; Uherek, 2007; Weinerová, 2003.

5   Forms of more flexible movement have aroused academic interest more recently. For one example see Canek, 2006.

Discourses on Romani Beggars from Hostice-Gesztete in Graz, Their Production and Their Consequences

1. The Contexts of Discourses on Roma Begging in Graz:
Circumstances of Image-production

It was precisely 1989 that beggars began to feature in the newspapers, raising the issue of "problems" on the streets of Graz. Twenty years later, local media reports no longer discuss a seemingly sudden and inexplicable emergence but rather a "problem" to which everybody is only too accustomed. This shift in perception from exception to normality happened in 1996, when the beggars in this city dominated local coverage and political activity. In this context it is of the greatest importance to note that it is counter-productive to distinguish between abstract "discourse" and concrete "actions" (Singer, 2005, p. 17). As the example of reactions to these begging Romani people proves, all forms of activity, from the publication of an opinion to the negotiation and execution of a law or the simple act of donating or refusing to donate, contribute to a huge and rather complex discourse (in the broadest sense of the word). With respect to sources, this paper will primarily focus on debates which have taken place in newspapers and magazines, especially analysing the production and development of images.

Finally it seems to be necessary to sum up who were the main protagonists in the creation and negotiation of images and what their motivations/backgrounds may have been. Here, a classification into three main groups seems to be reasonable. Generally and regarding of the vast majority of those involved, it is crucial to acknowledge that the production of ideas in the mass media has clearly been dominated by people who are not journalists in the classical sense of the word. This is highly relevant as the discourse was created and formed by newspapers and magazines only—especially in the first few years. Nevertheless, knowledge about the begging Roma in Graz and the "problems" their presence and work supposedly caused was mainly generated by people who were not professionally involved in media work: firstly, people who were involved in politics and were responsible for the creation of new legislation, secondly representatives or lobbyists of charity organisations and thirdly (and possibly most important) "committed" citizens without professional interests in the topic. These people were active in a wide range of different forms of media, including the classical mass media (newspapers, magazines and audiovisual media) as well as in more limited ways (bulk-mail, flyers, posters and graffiti). As this paper draws less attention on the latter, two examples for the language of this media will be given here briefly: a poster which was placed on the door of the headquarters of the Vinzi-Organisation (the main charity organisation for the Roma from Hostice-Gesztete) demanded: "Roma ins

Gas" ("Roma to the gas chambers"), elsewhere in the city comments such as "Roma-Bastards, we are going to kill you!" were visible.[6]

2. Categorising the Beggars: Problems and Results of Definitions

Talking about stereotypes, one might suppose that prejudices and negative images are generally caused by scanty knowledge, which creates a space for the emergence of vague suppositions. Quite to the contrary, this case shows that knowledge which is highly developed and differentiated, as well as being widely spread, may also be the basis for the spreading of new—but possibly even more harmful—stereotypes. The perception of beggars in Graz has changed over time especially in terms of specificity, always creating more detailed information. But surprisingly, these processes lead directly to a creation of "new" and seemingly more accurate negative images.

To go back to the emergence of extensive discussions about beggars in Graz, one of the most interesting aspects is the fact that at this stage (1989–1996) it remained totally unclear who the people begging were. Furthermore, it was not usual in those days to define them as Roma. This was not only true for silent beggars—mostly men—from Slovakia, but also for a number of Romnija from Ex-Yugoslavia who preceded them, who were less easy to ignore. Initially, the basic problem seemed to be that the people did not fit into existing categories. Thus, one of the primary tasks of the discussion was to create categories which would suit the people and create terms that would allow generally understandable debates and arguments. These processes of definition and categorisation can be divided into five successive steps:

First Step: Differentiation
At the beginning of the discussion of "problematic situations" on the streets in the first district of Graz, statements and information did not distinguish between "beggars", "dossers" and other "troublemakers". Consequently, "punks" and "vagrants" as well as "youths" or "social cases" generally featured on the list of people endangering the security and proper condition of the old town. Stereotypes and threatening images were very hazy, forming around diffuse and highly generalised assumptions. Understandably, the first step towards a more complex discussion was to differentiate between the groups involved: The category "beggar" was invented and linked to certain features. One of these features was extra information about the background of these people and the placement of the category: it became common to talk about "beggars from abroad". Although the term "abroad" ("Ausland") was not explicitly defined it was obvious that it implicitly denoted "poor" countries and thus the European "East".

---

6   Both mentioned posters/graffiti are recorded in the private archive of Wolfgang Pucher, a priest and head of the catholic Vinzi-Association, who devotes himself especially to the Roma from Hostice-Gesztete. For a biographical approach see: Krebs and Pucher, 2009.

From then on various countries were mentioned as possible homelands. The important aspect within this lack of distinction is that with regard to images it did not make any difference whether one talked about Romanians, Czechs or even people from neighbouring Slovenia or Hungary. Thus already the first differentiation opened the way not only for more concrete information, but also for more concrete—in this case: chauvinist—stereotypes and attacks that could refer to common nationalist images.

Second Step: Ethnisation

In late November 1996 Father Wolfgang Pucher, the head of the Catholic "Vinzi community" NGO, was the first to define the beggars in Graz publicly as Roma: "They were the well known, begging Roma" (Pucher, 1996a; Pucher, 1996b). The intentions behind this ethnisation seem to be clearly revealed by the following sentence, which was a reference to the suffering of this people (with an implicit, but impossible to ignore, focus on the crimes committed by the national socialist regime). This is of interest also insofar as just a few months preceding this definition a bomb-attack on a Romani settlement in eastern Austria aroused broad public awareness of the Romani minority and the issue of its "integration" (Rieger, 2003). The subsequent discussions formed a very wide-ranging debate on the problems which the minority was facing, and the authorities monitored right-wing activities comparatively harshly. Hence the ethnisation could be seen as an attempt at gaining support and especially at stopping strict policies. Giving the beggars this specific name should have illustrated their problems and should have integrated narratives of suffering into the discussion.

Although the identification (beggar = Rom) was extremely successful, the ethnicisation as victimisation turned out to be not only helpful but also damaging. The specification in the definition made it possible for more specific—in this case: racist—stereotypes to emerge, along with the link to negative images. Additionally, the populist tabloid press used this to (re)turn to older denominations enhancing the usage of "Zigeuner", which is clearly associated with racist concepts (e.g. Gnam, 1996). The use of this terminology itself was only possible for a very short period of time, before even this kind of newspaper had to switch (via the transitory double terms "Zigeuner-Roma", "Zigeuner (Roma)" or others) to the term "Roma".

Third Step: Gender Definition

It seems remarkable that the third step towards a more concrete picture of the people in question was a definition regarding the gender of the beggars. Before talking about countries of origin, attention was drawn to discussion how Roma behave differently from Romnija. Closely connected to the discussion of the threat coming from the migrants was the question of who begged in an "acceptable" or "unacceptable" way. It becomes clear at the very first glance on which criteria this separation was based: the first—tolerable—group consisted of young men (from Slovakia), the second—inappropriately behaving—group consisted of women and their children (from an undefined area

Images of begging people in Graz were mostly
depicting women in the very beginning
(*Steirerkrone*, 7 July 1999, anonymous photographer).

in Ex-Yugoslavia). This differentiation resulted from the discussion of "aggressive" begging which was framed by highly gendered concepts: only women (and children, also supposedly powerless and passive) were accused of "intrusive begging". At that time there was even a special begging-act passed for the city of Graz, banning activities defined by this term. From that point onwards the construction and re-invention of negative images of Romani migrants in Austria has constantly focussed on the gender of the beggars and thus established again more differentiated and harmful stereotypes, proposing that Romani culture lacks "healthy" or "normal" gender relations.

Erste Ausweisungsbescheide gegen zwei

Die Polizei greift

Ob bei den Exekutivorganen Freude aufkommt oder auch nicht – die von der Stadtpolitik geforderten rechtlichen Schritte gegen die Bettler in Graz werden jetzt von der Fremdenpolizei angewendet. Zwei Ausweisungsbescheide wurden bereits ausgestellt. Pfarrer Pucher geht unterdessen das Geld für sein Projekt aus.

Zuletzt gab's wieder Bettler in Graz – jetzt gibt's Ausweisungen

"There have been beggars again lately. Now they are expelled." Women as central focus of the discourse and the official action (*Steirerkrone*, 22 January 2000, anonymous photographer).

Von 800 Dorfbewohnern haben nur zehn eine Arbeit

Hunger und Arbeitslosigkeit treiben Angehörige der ungarischen Minderheit von der Slowakei in den Goldenen Westen bis nach Österreich.

■ VON PETER FILZWIESER

„Da stehen Männer vorm Geschäft, die haben Hunger und frieren. Bitte schau, was da los ist, die tun mir so leid!" Aufgeregt und voll Sorge erzählte die elfjährige Ilona Anfang Oktober ihrem Vater, was sie soeben gesehen hatte und brachte damit eine Lawine der Hilfsbereitschaft ins Rollen.

Der Vater – Kurt Nemetz –, ein Judenburger Unternehmer und Obmann des Vereins „Hilfsforum", nahm sich der Sache an und fand folgendes heraus: Die jungen Bettler gehören der ungarischen Minderheit im Südosten der Slowakei an. Nach der Trennung von Tschechien sind viele arbeitslos geworden. Die meisten stammen aus dem kleinen Dorf Uzovska Panica; von 800 Einwohnern haben nur zehn eine Arbeit. Ihre letzte Hoffnung: Sie fahren mit ihren alten, schrottreifen Autos in den Westen und hoffen, soviel Geld zusammenzubetteln, daß sie ihre Familien am Leben erhalten können. Wie berichtet, sind auch in Graz einige dieser Männer in letzter Zeit aufgetaucht, andere haben sich bis Linz und Salzburg durchgeschlagen.

Der Verein Hilfsforum hat bisher 28 der verarmten Menschen aufgegriffen, verköstigt, eingekleidet und mit Lebensmitteln, Geld und Geschenken wieder zu ihren Familien nach Hause geschickt. Die Belegschaft der Firma Nemetz verzichtete auf eine Weihnachtsfeier und Geschenke und hat für die notleidenden Slowaken bisher rund 40.000 Schilling gespendet. Im Jänner soll der erste Lebensmittel- und Hilfstransport in die Slowakei geschickt werden.

Weil das Judenburger Hilfsforum (✆ 0 35 72/85 4 85-302) das Problem aber jetzt nicht mehr alleine lösen kann, appelliert es an die Bevölkerung, die ärgste Not der ungarischen Minderheit in der Slowakei lindern zu helfen. Außerdem wurden die Caritas, der Bundespräsident und die Europäische Union alarmiert.

„Wir dürfen keinen Bogen um die

Bettler in Graz: Die ungarische Minderheit sucht ihr Heil im Westen   FOTO: BINDER

Armut machen", meint Kurt Nemetz, der weiß, daß „viele Österreicher zwar viel tun, aber viele andere noch viel zuwenig". „Diese Leute leben in bitterster Armut und sind fix und fertig. Für eine Tageslosung von rund 70 Schilling sitzen sie den ganzen Tag in der Kälte", hat Nemetz in vielen Gesprächen erfahren. Der Unternehmer ist überzeugt, daß das Problem nur alle europäischen Länder gemeinsam – mit Arbeitsplätzen in der Slowakei – lösen könnten, bis dahin gelte es aber, „schnell und unbürokratisch zu helfen."

Damit dann immer mehr hilfesuchende Slowaken nach Österreich kommen?

„Ja", zuckt Nemetz die Achseln, „im Krieg hat es in unserer Gegend einen Bauern gegeben, der uns hungrigen Kindern Milch gegeben hat. Da sind wir natürlich alle hingelaufen. Zuletzt waren wir Dutzende. Aber das haben viele schon vergessen."

„ÖVP und FPÖ gefährden den sozialen Frieden und das friedliche Miteinander. Damit diese beiden Faktoren auch weiterhin einen hohen Stellenwert besitzen, wähle ich am 17. Dezember die SPÖ."

Hannes Bammer

Wir stehen zu Euch.

Peter Schachner   SPÖ

Not all localisation turned out to be successful: Attempt of labelling the beggars as Hungarian Slovaks in a local newspaper (*Kleine Zeitung*, 10 December 1995. Photographer: Binder).

Fourth Step: Localisation

Focussing on the short period of time around the end of 1996, it seems that the labelling of the begging migrants in Austria as Roma was not immediately successful. Independently, theories of homelands became more and more important at the same time. Among these there was also an attempt to identify the beggars as part of the Hungarian minority in Slovakia. However, the labelling of the migrants as Slovakian was much more successful, although in the long run it survived only in combination with the ethnicisation as Roma and Romnija, to which it was subordinated. This success of the ethnic label may also be explained by some specific features of the local situation: In the Graz-context, "Roma" automatically defines somebody as foreign.

As the most important step towards a concrete localisation, the Catholic priest mentioned above labelled the beggars of Graz as inhabitants of only one Slovakian village, called Hostice-Gesztete. This was a crucial chapter for all charity activities as it was then possible to check the situation in the "genuine" village of origin and thus prove the "authenticity" of poverty. On the other hand, this turned out to be a rather weak argument against people who would refuse to accept this concrete localisation. For those approaches, "Hostice" became a synonym for the "East" with

"The beggar-saint" local clergy-man Wolfgang Pucher
in Hostice, which public discourse defined in accordance with him as the only home-village
of all beggars (*profil*, 26 July 1999, anonymous photographer).

all the blurring and the connotations discussed above. Summing up the reactions it becomes obvious that this differentiation did not make it more difficult to develop new negative images. For instance, the localisation in a Slovak village was paradoxically the reason for frequent attacks on the Czech Republic, eight years after the separation of the two neighbouring countries: "When members of the Eastern Bloc (!) such as the 'Tschechei' (a pejorative term for Czech Republic) have enough money to join NATO, then they should take care of their own people" (Jauernig, 1999).

Moreover, the assumption that all beggars must come from Hostice-Gesztete was publicly doubted. The critics were mostly as superficial as the generalisation they were attacking, suggesting that none of the beggars actually hailed from Slovakia: If the "East" is something vague and indefinite, a localisation within the "East" is no warranty at all. Even one of the attachés of the Austrian Embassy in Bratislava suggested that the beggars in Graz might possibly come from Romania (Schneider, 1998). Besides that, this localisation was merely a more concrete definition which did not challenge the ethnic term.

Fifth Step: Concentration

Recapitulating these processes, it is apparent that the label "Roma", or more specifically "Roma from Hostice", became the central term in these discourses. It is therefore interesting that this denomination has become a synonym for any beggars in Graz. The definition is applied to all of them, whatever their national provenance and their ethnic self-affiliation, using the term not only to mark but also to discriminate against them. It has proved effective irrespective of circumstances, as for example even men who are legally Austrian citizens face a very stable labelling as Roma from abroad. How strong this connection has been, and still is, may be illustrated by a statement made by the official representative of the Romani minority in Austria, in which he was not declaring that Roma are not only beggars. Despite such suppositions, he felt forced to point out that "not only Roma are begging."

It was not only this identification that made it much easier to talk about beggars. At the turn of the millennium it became possible to use the mere word "Hostice" as a marker in newspaper headlines to refer to people begging in Graz (Hecke, 1999). Nevertheless, this certainly does not imply that it was more complicated to attack Roma and Romnija, beggars or Romani migrants. A quite illustrative example for the new reservoir of negative images is the following (published in a high-quality newspaper): "We know where those people come from, now we know why they are coming... The Slovakian Majority knows that Roma are work-shy" (Thanei, 1999). Thus not only did more, and specific, support and differentiated debates become possible, but also more concrete (and effective) stereotypes were invented.

Die organisierten Bettler in der Grazer Innenstadt sorgen seit Jahren für große Aufregung unter der Bevölkerung.

Picture in the most popular Austrian newspaper, showing an "organised beggar",
thus a Rom from abroad, indeed depicting a Graz-native
(*Steirerkrone*, 18 June 2006, anonymous photographer).

Menschen in Hostice im „wunschlosen Unglück"

Grazer Pfarren betreuen 40 Roma im Monat. Nun fehlt aber das Geld.

"Hostice in sorrow beyond dreams" (*Kleine Zeitung*, 17 July 1999). The name of the Slovak village became a synonym for the "beggar-problem", for misery, poverty and the "East" in general.

3. Racism Needs the Fiction of Threat: Analytical Approaches

The basic framework for all these discussions—no matter which label is applied—is the imagining of a specific danger or a series of hazards threatening the city of Graz and its inhabitants. Since the very beginning of the debate, various laws have been discussed that would prevent some or all forms of begging. Although in these legal negotiations (as well as in the final act) "race" and "ethnicity" were never explicitly applied as categories or even mentioned as terms, it is obvious from the context that the targets of the regulations are begging Roma. More specifically, the acts were in fact especially used to expel Romnija from the streets and consequently from the city, although gender was not referred to in the act. On the contrary, begging by children, which is explicitly prohibited, was not as extensively discussed in the first place.

However, it is not only legal regulations that rely on the power of imagined menaces. Fictional hazards are crucial for the development of any racist or xenophobic image. In the following, I will describe finally three of the most important threatening images and sketch some rough ideas for possible analytical approaches.

A Quick Introduction to the Foreign Culture:
The Public Presence of the Powerless is an Attack

It has already been mentioned that in the perception of beggars there is a notable difference between those coming from Hostice-Gesztete and especially migrants from Ex-Yugoslavia. This is closely connected to the differentiation of the discourse according to the gender of the beggars, consequently forming NGO-policies and the legal framework: when the city council of Graz passed an act on "intrusive begging and begging with children" in December 1996, it was responding to imagined menaces which focussed on women, who were described as being unfairly exploited on the one hand and as aggressive on the other. The presence of the thus-described Romnija was discussed broadly and included among other things the following accusations referring to the second description: women as well as their children were begging aggressively, i.e. they attacked pedestrians and spat at them, they refused to accept food which was given to them, they robbed people who refused to donate money and they acted aggressively towards people who were just passing by (*Steirerkrone*, 1996; *Der Standard*, 1996). The media were very quick to provide reasons for this, favouring one argument: all these forms of inappropriate behaviour could be defined as part of a foreign culture. From this perspective, the refusal to adapt to the culture of the receiving country leads naturally to such manners. A member of the city council at the time formulated it thus: the "cultural feelings of the people of Graz" are violated (Miedl, 1996).

The question that remains is why exactly the term "culture" was so strongly emphasised in these statements and why it was not enough simply to highlight the assumed exploitation as problematic. Evidently these arguments operated with the idea of this constellation as a very basic, "essential" structure.[7] The core of these narratives was the presentation of the begging women and children not as exceptions, but as the rule of the "foreign" culture of the Roma and Romnija. The specific feature of the "other" culture (women visibly begging on the street) served as a basis for alienation

---

7   What is visible here is again the function of culturalisation as essentialisation, which is the most important step towards the perception of a group as "nationally" homogeneous. (Blom, 1996, p. 318.) For essentialised Romani Identities see Vermeersch, 2005; Picker, 2010.

and for ethnicisation. This link between practice and culture made two assumptions possible and successful: Firstly this practice was defined as radically different and deviant from "our culture" and thus "foreign", and secondly the whole "culture" which permits that sort of behaviour was defined as "foreign" and somehow "uncivilised". To emphasise this difference, all of these images of threat stressed the assumption that *only* women and children were begging. Obviously the construction of a threat regarding the gender of the beggars was very successful in shaping the perception and generalising the images of begging people: "It has hardly anything to do with poverty, when women with small children are sent to the streets" (Zankel, 1996)

However, it remains unclear why this essentialised practice and the whole imagined "culture" behind it was seen as threatening to the local culture. Notably, it was not the actual practice, but the "foreign culture" which formed a hazard towards "our own". (Women were begging in a way that was defined as legal—i.e. "not intrusively"—but were rigorously expelled by the police (Zankel, 1996).) The "own cultural" setting which was seen to be in danger was the gendered division of labour and the gender order in general: in "our" way, men are in charge of the public sphere, women are responsible for the private/invisible spaces, men own (and control) the aggression, women are passive and caring (E.g. Zettelbauer, 2005).[8] Hence, the reason for imagining this as a serious threat lies in the perception of a highly problematic perversion of the gender order, which is inseparably linked with the appearance of the migrants. As in the classical narrative on viragos, this fantasy depicts the female as trying to obtain power through unjustified terror. The Romnija were present on the streets (where they didn't belong) and were actively asking for money (which contradicted the passiveness demanded of them). Thus the assumed menace may be summed up as being formed by an assumed gender disorder, which would question conventional spheres of action and duty. The underlying ethnicisation also explains why the described aggressive forms of behaviour are seen as so frightening: all of them not only affect good manners, but also question a much more basic, even constitutive element of "culture". Aggressive men violate good manners; aggressive women violate the basic gender order.

The Streets Are Paved with Gold: Trustful Donors Are Betrayed

Narratives of threats are not always coherent or logical. Especially in racist discourses, Roma and Romnija as beggars are depicted as degenerate, lazy, cowardly and irresponsible. Simultaneously these discourses develop persuasive stories of powerful men controlling many others in a special secret business. Thus one of the most important menaces to be publicly discussed in Graz was what was labelled "organised mendicancy" (Schneider, 1998). Basically, this implies that all the begging is organised as a business, controlled by a certain Mafia led by a small group of Roma (men only),

---

8   For a generalised and theorised discussion of gendered divisions see Iveković, 2005.

which directs and exploits the powerless beggars. Even in political discussions one could hear talk of suspicious men in the background controlling an anonymous crowd of helpless poor (Müller, 1996). To reinforce this impression, elements which are symbols of social and/or cultural capital are used quite persuasively in the narratives: the powerful Mafiosi drive Mercedes, they gamble in casinos and they are guilty of

"Enough! Beggars as gamblers!" A local newspaper claims to "reveal" the practices of the "so called poor". (*Graz im Bild*, 28 December 2008).

alcohol abuse. Although these elements seem to be quite normal for male behaviour in patriarchal circumstances, in these cases they provide convincing evidence for the argument of an unjust relationship. Further, this is also useful for the—contrary— assumption that those who seem to be poor are actually rich.

Generally, the focus is once again on the problem of an unbalanced basic cultural order: "Justly", those who work should generally get the power/money, or at least some of it. Some of the begging-narratives imagine the opposite situation: in the case of Romani beggars, there is much more power on one side and those who have the power do not work to obtain it. It seems noteworthy that this was not only seen as basically unfair, but again as dangerous for "our own culture". The supposed menace lies not only in the assumption that the donors are betrayed by the presentation of fake poverty (which operates with similar arguments in newer narratives on fake illnesses/ handicaps (Matzl, 2000) or street music as hidden begging (*Der Uhrturm*, 2004; Pech, 2004)). The main obstacle is the lack of balance, which again threatens one of the basic (cultural) orders. Facing these contexts it seems comprehensible that NGOs and private supporters of beggars in Graz in general emphasise the role of men as fathers who need to earn money for the whole family (e.g. Müller, 1997). The idea behind this counter-strategy is that a father as a beggar guarantees both the "genuineness" of the poverty and the "normality" of the underlying culture.

The Beauty and Its Polluters:
The Immaculate Attractiveness of the City Is Endangered

As a last example for the numerous narratives on beggars as a hazard, let us consider the symbolic relationship between city and beggars. In this case, the fictive threat is based on the image of a beautiful, unharmed city which is endangered by the simple presence of people begging. It is of great relevance to acknowledge that in this case the whole discourse applies to male Romani migrants only. Analytically, this means broaching the issue of Romani people as organised in large groups, appearing as whole collectives of beggars. In fact Romani migrants in Graz were shown as large families or big, somehow "natural" collectives which are flooding the city. These well-known images combined three classical racist narratives: in the first place the invasion of Romani beggars supported the perception of Romani people as savages, who appear only in tribes. Secondly, the Romani migrants were metaphorically shown as parasites which were attacking the city collectively and (as a basic image) sucking its blood (Müller, 1996a).[9] Thirdly, Romani beggars were considered as grubby, indolent and dirty people, who would harm the tidy and nicely reconstructed historical centre of the city. When analysing the last form of images it is important to recognise that this menace only emerged years after women were banned from begging (by the law

---

9   Parallels with anti-Semitic images are evident in this case (parasites), although I would be
     very generally wary of simple comparisons.

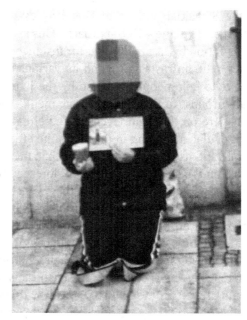

Serial images of anonymous, faceless individuals are the precondition
for the phantasies of "floodings" and "invasions" as well as for the
imaged "dirtiness" (*Graz im Bild*, 14 April 2006. Photographer: "GIB").

mentioned above). Beggars were then defined as causing a "disgusting picture" (Jauernig, 1999) or as a "defacement" of the city (Maget, 1998). The threat resulting from these images relied on perceptions of the city as "pure" and "untouched". Consequently, the pollution of this beauty by impure people was defined as a menace and as seriously harming the symbolic body of the city (Escher, 2004).

Conclusion: Talk about Romani Beggars Is not Logical, but Effective

This paper has dealt with discourses on Roma and Romnija who were/are temporarily migrating within Central and Eastern Europe towards the city of Graz. In emphasising the neutral term of discourses on these movements and with a focus on the mass media, it was my aim to offer some insights into the complexities and contradictions of these dynamics. Hence, I have tried to show that there are links between initiatives that claim to help and attempts to fight against Roma and Romnija. Beyond the dichotomous structure of "anti-Gypsyism" vs. NGO-activities lies a complex web of interdependent arguments, images and narratives.

With respect to the sustainability of these discourses, there remains no doubt that it was mainly NGOs and political actors which established the most stable and long lasting regimes in this context: An extremely strong network of economic exchange between the Slovakian village of Hostice-Gesztete and Graz is an example of the efforts and success of the NGO-approach. This exceeds classical perceptions of charity work on migration by far, including, for instance, a factory, facilities for housing and bureaucracy. This infrastructure and its various elements are not only driven by the simple desire to help people, but also by the intention to stop the migration or limit it to certain groups (in this specific case: men). Another example of the effect of the discourse—here on the legal level—is the already mentioned begging-law in Graz, which still regulates begging in the city quite effectively.

Generally, it has to be considered that the development of discourses is not teleological, and is thus impossible to foresee: Some statements may effectively support racism or prejudice even when they were honestly intended to do the opposite. A glance at the narratives of threats caused by Romani beggars has served to illustrate the complexity of arguments in the production of knowledge about migrants. In the given case, the ethnicisation of the people begging in Graz as Roma or Romnija was a clear attempt to establish a link with their experience of suffering as a people, with a clear reference to the specifically Austrian racist crimes (under National Socialism and in bomb attacks in the 1990s). However, this and other attempts to save Roma and Romnija through casting them as victims turned out to be not only problematic but actually counter-productive: Indeed, new and more precise racist stereotypes and images were the response.

Clearly ethnisised, radically de-individualised and victimised: Prototypical beggars in an artistic protest (*Kleine Zeitung*, 19 October 2001. Photographer: Ecke Herget).

Finally, I have tried in this paper to show once again how heterogeneous and diverse narratives are, even if they are aimed at essentialisation and thus homogenisation. The common basis for all the examples I have mentioned is the unequal treatment of Roma and Romnija. Quite to the contrary of the claim of one equal policy towards Romani people by the public, officials or NGOs are treating them quite unequally. This is also true for the public image of Romani migration: the more differentiated the discourses are, the more inequality there is likely to be in the way people are perceived and treated.

Bibliography

Blom, Ida (1996). "Das Zusammenwirken von Nationalismus und Feminismus um die Jahrhundertwende. Ein Versuch zur vergleichenden Geschlechtergeschichte" in *Geschichte und Vergleich. Ansätze und Ergebnisse international vergleichender Geschichtsschreibung.* Frankfurt and New York: Campus.

Cahn, Claude and Peter Vermeersch (2000). "The Group Expulsion of Slovak Roma by the Belgian Government. A Case Study of the Treatment of Romani Refugees in Western Countries." *Cambridge Review of International Affairs*, 13, no. 2 (2000): 71–82.

Canek, Marek *et al.* (2006). *Migration Processes in Central and Eastern Europe. Unpacking the Diversity.* Prague: Multicultural Centre.

Crowe, David M. (2003) "The International and Historical Dimensions of Romani Migration." *Nationalities Papers* 31, no. 1 (2003): 81–94.

Escher, Georg (2004). "Prager Femmes Fatales. Stadt, Geschlecht, Identität." *Kakanien revisited* 6–7 (2004): 1–8.

Gnam, Peter (1996). "Die SPÖ unter Druck: Schwärme von Bettlern suchten Graz heim," *Steirerkrone*, 5 December 1996.

Guy, Will, ed. (2004). *Roma Migration in Europe. Case Studies.* Hamburg: Lit.

Halwachs, Dieter W. (2004). *Roma and Romani in Austria.* Graz: University of Graz. Available at http://romani.uni-graz.at/romani/download/files/ling_rom_at_e.pdf [accessed 12 January 2010].

Hecke, Bernd (1999). "Menschen in Hostice im 'wunschlosen Unglück'," *Kleine Zeitung*, 17 July 1999.

Homoláč, Jiří (2006). "Diskurz o migraci Romů na příkladu internetových diskusí" (The discourse on the migration of Roma on the example of Internet discussions). *Sociologický časopis/Czech Sociological Review* 42, no. 2 (2006): 329–49.

Iveković, Rada (2005). "The Fiction of Gender Constructing the Fiction of Nation. On How Fictions Are Normative, and Norms Produce Exceptions." *Anthropological Yearbook of European Cultures* 14 (2005): 19–38.

Jauernig, Miss (1999). "Bettler wollen kein Essen," *Grazer Woche*, 7 April 1999.

Kotvánová, Alena and Attila Szép (2002). *Migration and the Roma. Historical, Social and Political Aspects.* Bratislava: Slovak Institute for International Studies.

Krebs, Cornelia and Wolfgang Pucher (2009). *Rebell der Nächstenliebe.* Vienna: Styria.

Maget, Wolfgang (1998). "'Bettlerjagd' FP blieb mit ihrem Antrag allein," *Neue Zeit*, 17 April 1998.

Matras, Yaron (2000). "Romani Migrations in the Post-Communist-Era." *Cambridge Review of International Affairs* 13, no. 2 (2000): 32–50.

Matter, Max (2003). "EU–Osterweiterung und 'ethnische Migration'. Zur Situation der Roma-Bevölkerung der Länder Zentral- und Osteuropas und deren Migrationsbereitschaft." *AWR-Bulletin* 41, no. 3–4 (2003): 149–57.

Matzl, Christoph (2000). "Bettler in Scharen nach Österreich!," *Steirerkrone*, 10 April 2000.

Miedl, Werner (1996). "Diese Bettler-Verordnung muß noch heuer kommen," *Kleine Zeitung*, 9 November 1996.

Müller, Walter (1996). "Sichere Stadt mit 'Hilfe' für die Sandler, Bettler, Zigeuner," *Steirerkrone*, 20 June 1996.

Müller, Walter (1997). "Keine Anzeichen organisierter Bettelei," *Der Standard*, 22/23 March 1997.

Nationalities Papers 31, no. 1 (2003) on Romani Migrations.

Pech, Michael (2004). "Verstimmte Töne gegen Kindermusiker," *Kleine Zeitung*, 5 May 2004.

Picker, Giovanni (2010). "Welcome 'in'. Romani Migrants and Left-wing Tuscany (1988–2007)." Available at http://romanimobilities.files.wordpress.com/2010/01/conference-proceedings1.pdf, 152–165.

Pucher, Wolfgang (1996a). "Offener Brief an den Bürgermeister," *Salzburger Nachrichten*, 28 November 1996.

Pucher, Wolfgang (1996b). "Wir verkraften Bettlerkinder," *Neue Zeit*, 26 November 1996.

Rieger, Barbara (2003). *Roma und Sinti in Österreich nach 1945. Die Ausgrenzung einer Minderheit als Prozeß*. Frankfurt: Lang.

Schneider, Viktor A. (1998). "Die perfekt organisierte Bettelei," *Die Presse*, 23/24 May 1998.

Singer, Mona (2005). *Geteilte Wahrheit. Feministische Epistemologie, Wissenssoziologie und Cultural Studies*. Vienna: Löcker.

Sobotka, Eva (2003). "Romani Migration in the 1990s—Perspectives on Dynamic, Interpretation and Policy." *Romani Studies* 13, no. 2 (2003): 79–221.

Der Standard (1996). Müller, Walter. "Aufdringlichkeit kostet 3000 Schilling." 7 December 1996.

Steirerkrone (1996). "Der Krone Detektiv," 13 December 1996.

Szép, Attila (2003). "Some Aspects of the Roma Migration from Slovakia" in *Social Networks in Movement*. Šamorín: Forum Minority Research Institute, pp. 185–90.

Thanei, Christoph (1998). "Die Roma gelten in der Slowakei als arbeitsscheu," *Die Presse*, 10 July 1999.

Der Uhrturm (2004). "Von der Kulturhauptstadt Europas zur Bettlerhauptstadt Österreichs," March 2004.

Uherek, Zdeněk (2007). "Roma Migration from Slovakia in the Context of European Migration Trends." *Sociologicky casopis/Czech Sociological Review* 43, no 4 (2007): 747–74.

Vermeersch, Peter (2005). "Marginality, Advocacy, and the Ambiguities of Multiculturalism: Notes on Romani Activism in Central Europe." *Identities: Global Studies in Culture and Power* 12 (2005): 451–78.

Weinerová, Renata (2003). "From East to West. The Roma Migration from Slovakia" in *Social Networks in Movement*. Šamorín: Forum Minority Research Institute, pp. 191–210.

Zankel, Erwin (1996). "Maßvoll," *Kleine Zeitung*, 7 December 1996.

Zettelbauer, Heidrun (2005). *'Die Liebe sei euer Heldentum' Geschlecht und Nation in völkischen Vereinen der Habsburgermonarchie*. Frankfurt and New York: Campus.

OPERATIONALISING "ETHNICITY"
IN PRACTICE

Yasar Abu Ghosh

CREDITING RECOGNITION:
Monetary Transactions of Poor Roma in Tercov

In Tercov (South Bohemia) nearly all adult Roma have been long-term unemployed since the beginning of 1990s when the two main employers of local villagers, the cooperative farm and the sawmill, disintegrated.[1] Since then Roma[2] have depended on social benefits as their only regular source of income. Housed in two decaying apartment blocks in a village where public transport operates only sporadically, so that their social life is usually limited to interaction among themselves and with the few local non-Roma, they experience what sociologists describe as social exclusion. This can hardly be regarded as an unusual situation for Roma in the Czech Republic: a government-commissioned report on the scale of social exclusion in the country, referred to as *Gabal's report* and published in 2006 (Gabal Analysis and Consulting, 2006), has revealed some three hundred similar communities affected by social and spatial exclusion comprising over eighty thousand Roma. Although the report has played a crucial political role in alerting the public to the extent and development of the phenomenon, it also diverted the attention to the factors of social exclusion rather than enhancing the comprehension of various patterns of inequality. Paradoxically, the publication of the report has had the effect of strengthening even further the existing discourse on Gypsiness in which poverty and identity constantly mingle in reshaping the social categorization of Roma: the magnitude of social exclusion is seen as corresponding to the social inadaptability of Roma.

---

1   The writing of this article was supported by the "*Specific research grant*" scheme of the Faculty of Humanities, Charles University in Prague. I wish to thank David B. Edwards, Jan Grill, Jakub Grygar and a number of other colleagues and friends who read and commented on the text at various stages of its preparation.

2   Most of the Roma in Tercov do not speak Romani and those who do, the elders, do so only in the company of other Romani speaking people which is consequently only a limited number of occasions. However, this brings about a kind of a diglosic language practice in which people use Romani words when speaking Czech. One of the examples is how they refer to themselves. Terms like *Rom* (pl. *Romové*) and *cikán* (pl. *cikáni*) are used indiscriminately. Interestingly, the Roma in Tercov also used some original terms, like *Romák* (pl. *Romáci*) combining the Romani term with the Czech colloquial suffix signifying group belonging like in *Pražák* (a Prager). I use the term Roma and Romani in a generic way. Although it is not always consistent with how the people under study referred to themselves, it allows me to distinguish between their self-perception and the various discourses of Gypsiness imposed on them. The term Gypsiness, however, does not have a real Czech equivalent (theoretically, this would be *cikánství*).

There is not enough space in this text to elaborate in detail on how pervasive the discourse of Gypsiness is and how it operates in various contexts. My concern is different. From one point of view, marginality is a type of non-attachment, which "implies a difficult and ambivalent relevance to the heart of things" (Green, 2005, p. 1). Can we then take heed of such a non-attachment? How does one cultivate difficulty or ambivalence? The peculiarity of a reflection on marginality lies, in my view, in this observation: while it seems apparent to the observer, confessing it is often so humiliating that those who are deemed marginal make enormous effort to conceal it through various kinds of passing. The history of marginality then becomes a history of its denial. And also, this is not only a history of impression management. If marginality is a relative category, if it really conveys what it suggests—distance from the centre (imagined or imposed, as an aspect of hegemony or counter-hegemonic resistance)— then there must be as many accounts of marginality as there are measures of distance and indeed as there are conceptions of relatedness to the centre. The idea of objective margins at which difference is constituted emanates from the understanding of social space as containing vectors inscribing the movements within it; at the same time this movement is seen as inherently centrifugal in that it creates the margins from the centre, never the other way around. So far, many of the accounts of the marginality of Roma in the Czech Republic have drawn on this view: their 'exclusion' (e.g. Gabal Analysis and Consulting, 2006), 'deprivation' (e.g. Sirovátka, 2003), or 'traditonality' (e.g. Jakoubek, 2006) is produced by an observing eye unquestionably located in the centre. My intention is different. I wish to contribute to this history of marginality denial as it is attempted by the Roma in Tercov.[3] Here non-attachment is reinvented as attachment precisely in order to test to what extent being attached, however temporarily, may bring about any change in redefining such central values as dignity and subjective recognition.

---

3   I am aware of the historical as well as contemporary records of the economic patterns of other rural Roma groups in Central and Eastern Europe which point to some mode of "economic complementarity" that has historically developed in spite of deeply rooted convictions about the exclusion of Roma (e.g. Horváthová, 1964; Hübschmannová, 1998; Stewart, 1994; Stewart, 1997; Engebrigtsen, 2007). However the reciprocity between Roma and non-Roma is culturally processed and whatever exchange form it takes (be it begging, barter, horse dealing or work), it seems it is always closely linked to the contested values of peasant life-style. In Tercov there are no peasants (there is one, to be precise) and since the disappearance of the common workplace after 1990 the space of potential interaction was limited to piddling and highly odd occasions.

The Attraction of the Poor

Martin came to Tercov in 1990 with two goals. His newborn son suffered from allergies caused by the polluted environment in North Bohemia cities where he lived with his family. The southern borderland region, with its large forest areas, was considered the least polluted. His other intention was to rear livestock on the grasslands abandoned after the collapse of local cooperative farming. His son soon recovered but his original business plan failed because by the time he arrived the state-owned pastures were already being farmed by a number of newly emerging large local farmers who profited from patronage networks established under socialism. In April 2002 he confided to me that he was planning to open a small convenience store (known as *večerka*), a small business that would provide a stable income for his family. I asked him how a small convenience store in a village of three hundred inhabitants could provide for such an income—in a village where almost half of the adults were either unemployed or retired and there was already a similar grocery store. At this point his business project was directed at a specific clientele. As he believed, the region and particularly the border area of which Tercov was the hub was destined to become a prosperous tourist attraction. Having observed increased numbers of cyclists touring the region *en masse* during the summer months, to which the underdeveloped region had not responded, Martin kept to his business plan and just before the summer season in of 2002 started, he invested much time and considerable resources in setting up his little shop.

During the firsts months of operation Martin realized that the just developing tourist business in conjunction with the sudden devastating floods of that year are not going to bring his family the economic tranquility he envisaged. Martin began to stock the shop with more and more goods so that after a few weeks, to my surprise, the wares on offer in his convenience store were very varied indeed, and were becoming less and less of the kind designed for convenient consumption by tourists: he now offered canned processed food, frozen poultry, milk, all the basic household staples like sugar, salt and flour, detergents and other sanitary products, even dog food and certainly a large variety of cheap alcohol, cigarettes and tobacco. Tourists passing by may have appreciated the offer of cold drinks, ice-cream and candy, but they were apparently no longer the chief target of his business. Soon after the *večerka* opened, I started to see Romani kids coming in to spend their change on candies, time and time again followed by Romani housewives replenishing their stocks with missing goods or seeking last-minute ingredients for their daily meals. And Martin, apparently happy at the prospect of having a stable clientele, turned to me and made sure the gathering heard him say: "You see it's different here; I'm not picky about my customers. It's cheaper here than in the grocery store. And people like to come here because we treat everybody the same way. We don't play on prejudices… As long as people can pay we don't care." Martin here revealed one of his recurrent poses: that of the entrepreneur. This, indeed, was his favourite one. It fitted into the discursive battle that he was engaged in with denizen villagers—a battle which in his eyes opposed him as the agent of new post-socialist libertarian ethos against the benighted attitude of the established village elite. The prejudices alluded to in his utterance and allegedly echoed in the treatment of Roma in the village grocery store delineated the separation of the established residents from the rest, i.e. from Roma and newcomers. Martin was exhibiting his entrepreneurial morale in a consciously chosen framework of inter-ethnic relations. This consisted in obliterating any pertinent divide between him and Roma by invoking the ideal of equality embodied in exchange relations. In compliance with the logic of "Money is money…" Martin underscored the colour-blindness of his entrepreneurial ethos.

Patterns of Consumption

As I already mentioned above, as Martin's business evolved I noticed that his stock gradually responded to particular patterns of consumption. The business success of Martin's *večerka* was now closely tied to his ability to attract Roma customers, and this was manifest in the adjustment of his range of goods to their patterns of consumption. Brand-name products were generally absent from his inventory from the beginning, so that most of the items were represented by the cheapest brands. This was especially evident regarding alcohol and tobacco products. The one or two international brands of cigarettes sought by tourists and only occasionally by local residents gave place to cheaper Czech brands preferred most by all Roma regardless of age or gender.[4] The same went for beer and liquors. Cheaper, locally produced mild beers were especially prized by Roma (mild Czech Budweiser) as well as wine in cartons and traditional liquors (especially fake vodka-style liquors). During the first weeks that the shop was open Martin's wife, Nadia, kept a little book where she regularly noted the preferences of Romani kids for sweets and lemonades. She often noted with concern that Romani kids asked for the sweetest products, the most seductive tastes and the products specially designated by big suppliers for child consumption. And because Romani kids enjoy almost complete liberty in the choice of how to spend money on candies, Nadia was able to adjust the stock according to her notes with quite a high degree of accuracy. However, the range of goods was not limited in kind. To a large extent, the *večerka* offered the Roma all that they usually needed. If fresh meat was not on offer, it had a worthy substitute. A huge freezer standing at the back of the room contained

---

4   Moreover, the *večerka* was the only store that offered pipe tobacco. For Roma, the much cheaper pipe tobacco, which they rolled in cigarette papers (and sometimes in a shred of newspaper), often represented the last resort in times of money shortage, despite the pipe tobacco's extremely unpleasant taste and its horribly irritating effect on the throat acknowledged by everyone.

predominantly frozen poultry, which is basically the most frequent meal ingredient for Roma[5] (at the grocery store, in contrast, one could find frozen vegetables, pasta, fish, and processed pastry, all typical products of Czech cuisine).

There was also a more striking, though less visible demonstration of Martin's adjustment to Romani patterns of consumption. This consisted in the overall character of the convenience store as a counterpoint to the other grocery store in the village. The grocery store was run by Janyš and his wife, long-standing residents of the village. The building itself was the property of the community council. It had been constructed in the mid 80s as a cooperative enterprise run by village inhabitants.[6] Thus the community council rented the property out to Janyš, but at the same time retained the responsibility for its maintenance. Given this context, the grocery store was somehow perceived as a communal service which served the demands of local residents.[7] It was common, for example, to place orders for anniversary cakes or banquet snacks for private or public events at the grocery store, which then arranged the order with an external supplier. The opening hours were publicly authorized, as they were spelled out in the contract of lease. Moreover, the economic payoff for the council budget was

---

5   This should be understood in contrast to "Gypsy food" (*cikánský jídlo*) which often contains meat, such as for example roasted pork fatback or the greatest delicacy, *pašváre* (roasted or cooked pork spare-ribs) or even *halušky* (home-made flour gnocchi most often served with lard and curd but also with chicken and tomatoes). The attitude of the Roma in Tercov towards "Gypsy food" was ambivalent. On the one hand they were pleased when visitors praised their cuisine; on the other preparing a "Gypsy food" was a sign of backwardness. If I asked about this ambivalence in the appreciation of "Gypsy food," I was told that chicken meat is simply the most common and ordinary ingredient which may be combined with a variety of side dishes (pasta, potatoes, and rice). Its universality and frequency led to ironic remarks, as when Šafrán said, "We'll all be flying one day." I might add that the biggest advantage of chicken consists in its easy preparation, either in the oven or in a boiling paprika or cream sauce which can feed the entire household at once. The preference for chicken over other meat was thus argued in terms of economic and practical advantages. However, if we operate on the symbolic level, the distinction marked the separation between a new and an abandoned life-style.

6   This was under the notorious *Akce Z* (Action Z) scheme with *Z* standing for *zvelebování*, "improvement." Under this scheme the socialist economy sought to respond to communal needs which the central and local authorities were not able to handle. Officially it was defined by a governmental decree (14/1959, § 27 art. 1) as work performed for free by citizens for the good of their community. Originally the "improvement" involved cleaning up communal property. Later it was to develop into institutionalized investment plans with steering committees, guidelines and a centrally allocated budget.

7   This was further confirmed when the extension of the lease was put on the agenda of the community council. The issue was barely discussed and the extension was accorded unanimously within a few minutes—not least because Janyš is also an elected member of the community council.

nil. Quite the contrary, in the long term the maintenance costs seemed to exceed the revenues from the lease. All this added up to the common perception, shared by non-Roma denizens, that this was their *sámoška* (a colloquial diminutive for *samoobsluha*, a small grocery store). The contrasting characters of the two shops thus reflected two different attitudes towards Roma in the village. On the one hand there was an attitude that limited contact, on the other an intensified effort to socialize.

"Gypsies have money"

Martin's interaction with the Roma in Tercov preceded the opening of his *večerka*: either he would hire some Romani boys as temporary help on the contracted woodworking jobs he used to carry out for a local lumbering company or he would provide Roma with various services (most often transporting people or things for them and charging excessive prices). He also once invoked the image so familiar in the region, an image of a Gypsy car packed to the roof with foodstuffs just purchased in a supermarket, something that was frequently to be seen the day they received welfare cheques. In conjunction with his generally critical attitude toward the generosity of the welfare state Martin shared the conviction that "Gypsies have money." The only question, then, was how to prosper by attracting Romani customers and the *večerka* was simply a way how to tap into the circulation of money issuing from welfare benefits. In view of the existing patterns of consumption, by which Roma spent the largest portion of the benefits on big purchases at retail centres in nearby towns on the day they received them (or within a few days thereafter), the attraction of the poor for a small shopkeeper consisted in securing the rest of the meagre resources they might have had.[8] Martin's adjustment of his inventory to Romani patterns of consumption was the direct result of this calculation. However, in order to assure that the Roma would really opt for spending their money in his *večerka* Martin had to offer a comparative advantage that would bind Romani customers to him and at the same time guarantee the connection's longevity. This advantage consisted in the practice of granting informal credit.

The Social Meaning of Informal Credit

Anthropologists have recorded informal credit in Central and Eastern Europe in the past (Sampson, 1986) and present (Verdery, 1995). For the latter the accounts referred to contexts in which informal credit helped to reconcile the scarcity of money on the part of people without access to financial resources with household economies

---

8   I assume that even the following abstract calculation that one may make in advance is quite convincing: If there are some 100 people in 16 households and if each of the households spent an average of EUR 70 a month, i.e., approximately 1/4 of the average income per household, it would result in some EUR 1120 a month in sales revenues.

during the post-socialist economic transformation. However, informal credit in the Czech Republic never reached the scale observed in other transforming economies, where it might have represented "a facet of the transformation from shortage economy [...] to what could be regarded as *delayed payment economy*" (Chelcea, 2002; italics in original).[9] The case in question was rather exceptional.[10] The exception consisted precisely in the fact that both parties involved, the shopkeeper and the customers, were compelled to engage in a system of informal credit: the shopkeeper to retain his business and the customers to secure their subsistence. In this it closely resembled the case from rural Southwest Romania where retailers kept customers "hooked up" (*agai*) on consumer goods and at the same time themselves became enmeshed in a situation which forced them to continue to sell to their customers on credit (Chelcea, 2002). This mutual dependence forced both parties to frame their interactions in accordance with values of trust and cooperation. However, and this is also the difference from the economically "innocent" practice of informal credit in other south Bohemian areas that did not involve Roma, these values of trust and cooperation had to be negotiated and repeatedly tested. Thus as a framework for action and in the context of daily interactions, the practice of informal credit in the *večerka* created an arena where questions pertaining to subjective integrity and household sustenance came into play.

Given the context in which the *večerka* started operating, the practice of informal credit was somehow logical. There was not a particular moment at which Martin announced his willingness to sell on credit. It arose from ordinary interaction: Martin was aware that social benefits came on more or less fixed dates and that the Roma were always short of cash for a couple of weeks before payday. I suggest that there are three main features of informal credit as I encountered it in the *večerka*. Firstly, the credit establishes an informal relationship between creditor and debtor in the sense that the validity of credit depends solely on its mutual recognition by the parties. Although Nadia kept a book of debts, this was only for her personal use as a memory aid. Debtors didn't know what was written in the book; neither did they refer to it when they wanted clarification about their balances. Secondly, the range of products that

---

9   In structural terms the post-socialist Czech Republic economic transformation after 1989 bore similar characteristics where indebtedness among firms was a major feature (see Altshuler, 2001, for an account of "tunnelling", an original Czech form of high-level corruption based on an elaborate system of juggling liabilities).

10 I randomly investigated the practice of informal credit in other villages in South Bohemia. Although regularly present in many of them, in economic terms it was mostly a very innocent practice. Both customers and shopkeepers considered it more as part of usual everyday service that facilitates shopping. For example, on their way home people would pass by the local grocery store and grab some missing goods without paying for them because they did not have enough cash on them. It was not an economic necessity for either of the parties; it was just a convenient way of shopping and paying for everything at the same time once every one or two weeks.

could be purchased on credit depended on the debtor's credit history. I will provide some examples later, but for the moment it will suffice to say that this feature is essential to the quality of relations established through informal credit. The creditor at this moment works as a credit analyst who questions the capacity of the debtor to pay up his debt. In particular, the credit analysis is directed at household expenditures and thus introduces into the monetary transaction implicit judgments about a debtor's life-style. In this feature informal credit resembles market credit, something which is further confirmed by the inclination of the creditor to formalize credit repayments in cases of notorious debtors with a low willingness to pay up. At the same time it cancels out, to some extent, the original imbalance in handling the risk of informal credit, which rests entirely on the shoulders of the creditor. This, then, is the third feature of informal credit in the *večerka*: Martin is the only one who might be sanctioned by the fiscal authorities for irregularities on his balance sheet or in his account book.[11] However, this eventuality was never really taken into consideration either by Martin or by his customers, as if possible consequences were largely compensated for in advance by the arrangement itself.

Gaining Dignity through Credit

Martin and his wife established a series of individual relationships with each of their debtors in which they set the terms of the creditor/debtor relation. To accentuate his colour-blind entrepreneur attitude, Martin took an individualist approach and meticulously upheld the conviction that everybody should be treated accordingly. It was this ideal of equal and individual treatment[12] which made informal credits noteworthy in the eyes of Roma. It matched their desire not to be seen through an essentialising prism which would equate Gypsy-like behaviour with gregariousness. Once established, this ideal depended upon how each Rom negotiated the credit with Martin or his wife. The overwhelming majority of the cases where money was lent were never placed in doubt. Every Rom actually believed that he or she could buy on credit and they all did. Indeed, there was not a single family, household or person who did not use the opportunity, and all did so regularly. Informal credit could thus be understood as a rehearsal of the ideal of equal treatment. And, since credit history is

11 See Chelcea, 2002, for a different definition of the contrast between informal credit and proper market credit practices.

12 Understandably there are also some "general" rules. For example, the credit extended to a given household should not have exceeded a tolerable rate, this being fixed between 500 and 1000 CZK depending on the circumstances. However, there was always a certain amount of leeway. For example, shortly before receipt of welfare checks Martin's attitude tended to be rather lax. The same applied if there was a special occasion, for example a birthday party.

at the same time the history of mutual trust, informal credit is a framework whereby every Rom could ideally establish him/herself as an individual entity with its own dignity.

Crack in the Mirror

This notwithstanding, the individualized approach became untenable when informal credit became regular and routine. With the passage of time, Nadia was increasingly faced with the necessity of consolidating the list of debts. Keeping track of dozens of individual credit lines was no longer possible. Owing to the fact that social benefits are perforce defined as household income that obliges recipients to spend the bulk of their resources on common needs, the debts predominantly involved expenditures on household goods. Nadia's originally individual entries in the debt list were consequently regrouped into more general categories representing households. Interestingly enough, these were not headed by a single name—let's say the father or family name—but by the two names of the partners or spouses. This signalled a shift in credit negotiation in that a given household credit history was introduced into the originally individual evaluation of the debtor. Thus, paradoxically, the fact that the money was obtained from welfare benefits marked the practice of informal credit in a way that favoured households over individual customer/debtors and had a significant effect on the relations established by informal credit.

Take the example of Šafrán. He had the reputation of "running on beer" (*jede na pivo*), the beer was his fuel. Especially in the summer months when Šafrán was looking for seasonal work, the beer was a necessity. Thanks to his talkative nature Šafrán would often be able to negotiate another beer on credit. However, over a two-week period a few beers every day would come to represent a sizable budget item. After a few weeks into the month Nadia would stop giving him more. The reason would be that taken together with household purchases his credit balance would exceed the agreed-upon credit limit. The expectancy for repayment depended either on the income level from welfare benefits, which differed according to the size of families, or on the status of the debtor (a retired person with a regular pension, for example). Clearly, Šafrán always knew about his household purchases so there was no question of his challenging Nadia's accounts. However, for him the beer was something personal that he had to procure on his own. At times like this it was evident how values of trust in fact meant something different to the creditor and the debtor. Nadia and Martin believed that Roma could repay their debts for most of the year only from welfare benefits. When they refused to accord Šafrán another beer on credit, they also imposed their ideas about responsibility for the household on him. They would not accept, at least rhetorically, a further debt burden on the grounds that household needs should be given preference over individual whims. In the *večerka* Šafrán would not question this logic as such. His success in negotiating credit to buy beer would be framed in terms of trust in his personal ability to cover his own personal needs. The negotiation of credit thus often opened up a discursive field in which the creditor and the debtor staked out the subjective characteristics of the customer. As a result, in critical situations Šafrán's otherwise entertaining and well-liked personality came to represent a symptom of intemperance which caused him to be perceived as truly Gypsy. In a condensed résumé such as this one, this may give the impression of a linear and causal story. In reality this was never the case. Martin, Nadia, Šafrán and his wife continuously attempted to regain each other's trust. Nonetheless, the experience of being turned down as well as of being duped left its mark and the ideal relationship promised by informal credit was never again achieved. On the part of Martin and Nadia, this sometimes meant being cautious, sometimes being formalistic when dealing with Šafrán. From Šafrán's point of view, on the other hand, it strengthened his conviction about their greed.

Drawing on this example and many others of the same kind, I assume that the fact that Nadia opted to record the credit line of a given household under the name of both spouses reflected her confusion about the organization of Romani households. She might have simply put the family name (though to tell the truth, this would have caused some confusion since some of the family names are shared by several households), but she opted for a more concrete entry as if she was expressing uncertainty about competencies and hierarchies in the household. The confusion is not groundless, as Biba and Šafrán's case demonstrates. No matter how much welfare benefits obliged recipients to spend on common needs, Nadia could never definitively assess the "quality" of the money handed over to her. This is precisely the distinction Šafrán referred to when he insisted on meeting his personal needs: debts accrued for household consumption should not be confused with credit he requested for his own personal consumption. What Šafrán was asking for and what caused confusion on the part of Nadia was the differentiation of money according to their differing trajectories. Šafrán was asking Nadia to accept him as a sovereign economic actor regardless of his social status as a recipient of welfare benefits. Money assessed as household income should go on covering household needs, but this should also allow the assumption that there is money other than that derived from welfare benefits. Throughout the year Šafrán was always earning some money from various activities, even if they were very irregular (like scrap-collecting). It was precisely this conviction—that he could always find a way to earn money for his personal consumption—that he was trying to advocate in negotiating credit. This did not mean that he always bought his beer from the money he earned. Nonetheless, his sheer potential for acquiring outside income legitimated, in his eyes, the claim to an individualized approach and to being perceived without reference to household obligations. However, this differentiation of money according to its origin eluded the purview of the creditor, who was assessing the overall indebtedness of the given household. The names of spouses in the debts list then capture the experience of the creditor of the two voices speaking from within the household. Though Nadia attempted to merge the voices by placing them under the same credit line while retaining the distinction between spouses, for the Roma it opened up a potential for subverting the credit plan in its function as a control mechanism over their pattern of consumption. Biba could thus, depending on the availability of resources, sometimes decide to repay the credit opened by her husband and sometimes not, by referring to the "quality" of the money at hand.

Other examples reveal a more profound impact of credit negotiation on the delineation of customers' subjectivities. Despite her natural politeness, Nadia sometimes questioned the selection of articles for purchase. After a long day of collecting birch foliage Laci and Dáša needed a quick meal. Because they had not yet cashed in their harvest, they came to the *večerka* to buy a few things on credit to prepare a dinner for their family. They ordered three cans of processed Bolognese tomato sauce and two packages of pasta. They also ordered sausages, bread, lemonade and a variety of candies. The price of the purchase was approximately 300 CZK. They already had some credit due, which caught Nadia's attention while they were making the order. It turned out that they were well over the credit limit. Moreover, two days earlier a similar situation had arisen. Nadia thus ventured to question the necessity of the purchase. According to her Laci and Dáša had spent 700 CZK in three days and, more importantly, they had been left with nothing to eat the day after, so it could only be presumed that the situation would get worse. With that kind of money, she continued, it should be possible to keep them fed for much longer. Instead of buying expensive canned food at the end of the day, Nadia suggested, she would have bought cheaper fresh food in bigger quantities and prepared it in advance. Nadia thus unwittingly acknowledged that the manner of consumption to which the *večerka* had adjusted its inventory (remember, it offers no fresh meat) had in fact contributed to the creation of continual indebtedness. As she was talking, Laci and Dáša started to sort out some of the articles and give them back. In the end they reduced their purchase to 100 CZK and ate sausages for dinner. At home Dáša said: "We bought on credit, we got even more into debt and we still wind up eating sausages. And all that because she doesn't like canned food?" The situation grew even more disconcerting when other Roma mocked Laci and Dáša's for having been forced to eat a dinner of sausages and bread just like the poor do.

The Agency of the Creditor

One of the peculiarities of informal credit arrangement consists in the shopkeeper consciously risking potential legal sanctions because of possible discrepancies in the balance sheet. In fiscal terms, when a shopkeeper sells on informal credit, there is bound to be a discrepancy between inventory and the cash book. Martin and Nadia never actually mentioned the legal fragility of the arrangement while negotiating a credit. Nonetheless, the threat of a fiscal inspection was theoretically present. In the absence of legal norms to constrain or support his creditor claims when dealing with customers, Martin was left to his performative skills to collect outstanding debts. This created a situation where Martin, as the owner who was not in continual contact with customers in the same way as his wife behind the counter, was obliged to conduct transactions more sternly and on the basis of explicit agreements. Because he was not always present in the *večerka*, he did not actually negotiate every credit himself. It was predominantly Nadia who listened to the demands and pleas of her customers. In consequence Nadia moved within a different context than Martin. Her very accommodating personality invited the Roma to speak openly about their situation. Not only did they disclose the details of their financial situation, they also expressed their worries. Hence the positions of Martin and Nadia constituted two differing natures of interaction which consequently gave rise to different responses to the exigencies of trust. Agreements concluded with Martin were more similar to a formalized credit arrangement in that Martin demanded their punctual settlement and sanctioned breaches with a temporary suspension of the credit line. Nadia, on the other hand, found herself in a more complex situation in which economic considerations, values of household reproduction and human worth came into conflict with one another.

There were, for example, numerous situations when somebody waited for the moment when he or she would be left alone with Nadia in the shop so that they could launch a more private conversation about their distress. Nadia thus often had a unique access to stories of suffering. She was particularly sensitive to the predicaments of children and women. Unlike Martin, whose preoccupation was more with the rationality of the requests, Nadia's insights allowed her to reflect on the "sociology of poverty."

In her interactions with Roma in the *večerka* Nadia arrived at the conclusion that they were living in a vicious circle of poverty which prevented them from undertaking any long-term planning of resources. She often listened to stories which emphasized the helplessness of women vis-à-vis their deeply felt need to ensure household subsistence. Hence she was very sympathetic to individual attempts to reverse this habitual course of events. Quite instructive in this regard was her support for Marko and Margita's efforts to establish their household on principles of self-sustenance and independence.

Breaking away

After Margita's parents left Tercov she was able to move with her boyfriend Marko into a one-bedroom apartment in Block Three that her parents had left behind. Until then, Marko and Margita occupied one room in Marko's parents' two-bedroom apartment, where they spent almost two years after the birth of their first daughter. Although they cohabited in one apartment with Marko's parents and three brothers, legally they constituted a separate household. As such they were eligible for welfare support for low-income families. This consisted of a child and parental allowance and a variable sum of money guaranteeing the minimum household subsistence level, which in their case amounted to about 7000 CZK a month. Had they "really" been a separate household they would have been eligible for an additional housing allowance, which in this case accrued only to Marko's parents as the official tenants of the apartment.

Marko and Margita's attempt to separate from his parents and to establish a genuine household on their own was for a long time a story of failed efforts. Under the existing circumstances they had to be resourceful and accept the fact that such a separation could be only partially achieved. Hence they tried to construct a household within a household both spatially and economically. They restored an annexed room from the abandoned apartment next door and made it into a kitchen. The symbolic separation culminated in Marko's hanging a door in the doorframe from the outside of the corridor to mark the main entry to their part of the apartment. The fantasy of an independent household was almost complete when they bought a small refrigerator and a stove, the signs of independent sustenance. However, the ideal repeatedly collided with details which eventually ruled out real independence. Regardless of the original parental endorsement of their decision to found a family, in practice it gave rise to a series of difficulties which revealed the generally constraining conditions impinging upon social welfare recipients.

Because their little "apartment" did not have any functioning sanitary facilities they were obliged to use the bathroom in the parent's space. The newly installed kitchen did not have its own water supply either; water had to be carried in buckets from the main part of the apartment. Consequently, their household budget was locked into the budget of Marko's parents by contributions to electricity, water and other bills. And even this did not take place on equal terms: they paid half of every bill, although in number they didn't constitute half of the occupants of the apartment, and their contribution was not measured against their real consumption. This yearning for an autonomous source of income applied no less to Margita. Before their first daughter was born, while Margita was still a minor (17 years old), and since the couple has been living out of wedlock, her parents' social benefits were officially still calculated as if she were part of their household. The additional welfare support which adjusts household incomes to the level of minimum subsistence is calculated after all benefits received by the household have been added together. Thus when Margita left to live with Marko, she took her social benefit cheque with her, which was intended for a dependent and which was issued in her name. However, her parents kept receiving welfare support as if her benefits were still part of the household income. Her parents thus insisted that they were entitled to her welfare money and kept claiming it. Caught in the middle of disputes between parents from both sides, Margita had to balance the claims of both families every month. And since there wasn't any particular rule or reason which would favour one over the other—both were legitimate[13]—Margita and Marko were constantly badgered by both sides for their lack of attachment and loyalty.

Later, after the birth of their daughter, Marko and Margita started being confronted with yet another pressure: to merge their income from social benefits with those of Marko's family. This they resisted with varying degrees of success. To amass the largest possible resources needed to carry out collective bulk spending within a given period of time is the chief survival strategy of the long-term unemployed who depend on social benefits. In the case in question, pressure was exerted on Marko and Margita to contribute significant sums to household subsistence. For Marko and Margita, yielding to this pressure would have meant giving up any semblance of self-sustenance and independence. Typically, they would start the month as they wished: refill their stocks, contribute to the bills, and put some money aside for the rest of the month (as Marco said, "I would always have 'a thousander' in my pocket to buy cigarettes or drinks for myself. At that time, I believe, I was the only Gypsy (cikán) who had any 'spare dough' (volný prachy)"). As the end of the month approached and their parents' reserves ran out, Marko and Margita would be compelled first to lend them money and later to share the remainder of their own reserves with the rest of the family. Naturally the reserves corresponding to their needs as a small household would be insufficient to provide for a household that was three times larger for any length of time. As a result, Marko and Margita started to suffer shortages much earlier in the month than they had planned.

For Nadia their plight was the axiomatic expression of how poverty reproduces itself. In her eyes, the young couple had broken away from their parents' untenable way of life by consolidating their patterns of spending and by setting up their priorities according to common family values. Marko never declared his wish to "break with the Gypsy way" (po cikánsku) openly in public as he did to the anthropologist. Instead, he expressed aversion for what he considered to be various expressions of this life-style.

---

13 In Tercov both patterns of residence, patrilocality and matrilocality, are represented (4/3). Although rhetorically patrilocality is considered as the preferred option, due to the shortage of housing it is often compromised. In the case under discussion the fact of patrilocal residence did not therefore in itself justify claims to money from welfare benefits.

In contrast to the "Gypsy way" he sought a life without malnutrition, to be independent of the exigencies of sharing with his larger family and to escape the communal life devoid of privacy that was typical of Gypsy settlements. For Nadia Marko and Margita's failure to follow their chosen way of life was caused solely by their social environment, for which the principles of long-term household consolidation were not a priority. Her approach towards the couple was thus often marked by a patronizing ethos symbolized, for example, by unexpected gifts of clothes for their child. If they found themselves in critical circumstances, Marko and Margita could rely on Nadia's willingness to give them credit. Paradoxically, Nadia's sympathies for their attempt to break away out of the vicious circle of poverty meant allowing them easier access to credit (often without the knowledge of Nadia's husband) which was, after all, a practice tailored to the economy of the poor. Eventually, her caring attitude towards the couple was incorporated as a strategy of contouring the exigencies of trust: as soon as the parents of both Marko and Margita found out about their children's favourable position in obtaining credit, they started demanding that they take on credit for them after they had reached their own limit. Although Nadia never found out about it, Marko and Margita's disposition to repay their debts was no longer in their own hands.

To complete the picture we need to go back to the different relationship that Martin established with his customers. Whereas Nadia responded to the complexity of circumstances of her customers by adopting various attitudes resulting from differentiated apprehensions of their situation, Martin's attitude was driven by the logic of standard agreements which erased all traces of the special circumstances in which his customers found themselves. However, this attitude was constantly at odds with the exigencies of the day to day life that his customers often maintained. The attempt to fix a date for paying off debts was manifestly dependent on Martin's capacity to assess the right moment to do so. As he gradually got to know the dates when people cashed their benefits or pensions (welfare checks are received on the 23rd of each month, pensions arrive around the 7th), this moment became firmly fixed in time. The problem was that it reduced the time span between cashing the cheques and spending the money in bulk to between one and three days. Even when Martin attempted to keep tabs on what went on in this short time span (as, for example, when he went to the post office and waited at the entrance for indebted recipients of social benefits to cash their checks), it was much easier for his notoriously indebted customers to avoid repayment by going to cash their checks elsewhere. It is not surprising, then, that Nadia was much more successful in recovering debts than Martin was.

Conclusion: the "Take-over" of the Večerka

As soon as Martin had adjusted to his customers and their tastes, the Roma initiated a concomitant take-over of the *večerka*, which very soon gained the reputation of a "Gypsy store," signalled not only by the regular presence of a cluster of Roma outside and inside it but also by its unorthodox organization and animated atmosphere. The *večerka* was almost never visited by those who could not bear the idea of sharing a space where the hierarchy they were used to was not respected (and there were even a few people who publicly expressed disgust at the idea of sharing the space physically with Roma). Throughout my fieldwork, the customers of the *večerka* were predominantly the same people. Besides Roma, these were also non-Roma villagers who in some way resembled Roma. They were equally marginalized in the social order of the village. They were either long-term unemployed or unskilled labourers who worked seasonally as loggers. Although informal credit was designed uniquely for Romani customers, the non-Roma villagers who came regularly to the *večerka* were often in a similar economic situation to the Roma. However, neither Martin nor the villagers thought of the practice of informal credit as an option for them. For Standa, a young man in his twenties who worked as logger, it was acceptable to borrow money from a Romani friend but he would never take part in the informal credit system. And this was very typical of all the villagers who were in close contact with the *večerka*: they were all very careful about keeping a public distance from informal credit. Through informal credit the *večerka* developed into an imaginative space where village social divisions materialized. The reluctance to be associated with informal credit would sometimes lead to absurd situations. When Standa was temporarily broke he would ask his Romani friend to buy for him on credit. A Romani friend helping Standa to avoid association with Gypsiness reveals the fragility of the existing categories that associate poverty with Roma. At the same time it highlighted the fact that from the point of view of the Roma the *večerka* often offered a temporary context in which they had the upper hand. What seems to me important here is the fact that the Roma integrated the *večerka*'s system of informal credit into their range of possible actions to such an extent that using the *večerka* became a regular strategy in their economic behaviour. What their more respectable and fortunate neighbours considered shameful and humiliating, the Roma turned it into an economic device which allowed them to juggle the meagre resources they had in a way that it made them central to the functioning of exchange. The examples of how credit negotiations prompted actors to draw on a repertoire of character roles would be infinite. But most importantly, in conjunction with this economic strategy, the *večerka* produced situations in which Roma restated their relations with their "significant others." Besides the *večerka's* role as a site of exchange, its genuine contribution to social life consisted in the practice of informal credit as a new framework within which actors could claim a subjectivity denied to them outside of this framework: those without money (the poor), by becoming moneyed (customers) reinvent the meaningless (being recipients of social benefits) as meaningful (objects of attraction).

Bibliography

Altshuler, David (2001). "Tunnelling Towards Capitalism in the Czech Republic." *Ethnography* 2, no 1 (2001): 115–38.

Chelcea, Liviu (2002). *Informal Credit, Money and Time in the Romanian Countryside*. Paper presented at the Fourth Nordic Conference on the Anthropology of Post-Socialism, Copenhagen, April 2002. Available at http://www.anthrobase.com/Txt/C/Chelcea_L_01. html [accessed 25 September 2004].

Engebrigtsen, Ada I. (2007). *Exploring Gypsiness: Power, Exchange and Interdependence in a Transylvanian Village*. London: Berghahn.

Gabal Analysis and Consulting (2006). *Analýza sociálně vyloučených romských lokalit a komunit v České republice a absorpční kapacity subjektů působících v této oblasti* (Analysis of the localities and communities marked by Romani social exclusion in the Czech Republic and of the absorption capacity of actors operating in this field). Prague: MPSV.

Green, Sarah F. (2005). *Notes from the Balkans*. Princeton: Princeton University Press, p. 1.

Horváthová, Emília (1964). *Cigáni na Slovensku* (Gypsies in Slovakia). Bratislava: Slovenská akadémia vied.

Hübschmannová, Milena (1998). "Economic Stratification and Interaction: Roma, an Ethnic Jati in East Slovakia" in *Gypsies: An Interdisciplinary Reader*, ed. Tong, Diane. New York and London: Garland, pp. 133–267.

Jakoubek, Marek (2006). "Přemyšlení 'Romů'"(The rethinking of „Roma") in „*Romové" v osidlech sociálního vyloučení*, eds. Hirt, Tomáš and Marek Jakoubek. Plzeň: Vydavatelství a nakladatelství Aleš Čeněk, pp. 322–400.

Sampson, Steven (1986). "The Informal Sector in Eastern Europe." *Telos* 66 (1986):44–66.

Sirovátka, Tomáš (2003). "Exkluze Romů na trhu práce a šance na jejich inkluzi" (Romani exclusion in the labour market: is inclusion possible?). *Sociální studia* 10 (2003): 11–34.

Sirovátka, Tomáš and Petr Mareš (2006). "Chudoba, deprivace, sociální vyloučení: nezaměstnaní a pracující chudí" (Poverty, deprivation, social exclusion: unemployed and the working poor) *Sociologický časopis/Czech Sociological Review* 42, no 4 (2006): 627–55.

Stewart, Michael (1994). "Fils du marché: les maquignons tsiganes et le modèle anthropologique." *Études Tsiganes* 2 (1994): 105–26.

Stewart, Michael (1997). *Time of the Gypsies*. Boulder: Westview Press.

Verdery, Katherine (1995). "Faith, Hope and Caritas in the Land of the Pyramids: Romania, 1990 to 1994." *Comparative Studies in Society and History* 37, no 4 (1995): 625–69.

Cecília Kovai

ON THE BORDERS OF GENDER
Marriage and the Role of the "Child" amongst Hungarian Gypsies[1]

This paper is about gender relationships among Hungarian Gypsies. First of all, I wish to examine the relationship between gender and power. I argue that in most cases, the presence or absence of power is not identical with the boundaries between genders, as field experiences show. I argue that power comes from the "most important" (in this field) gender relationship, which is marriage, and that gender issues are strongly defined by the question of kinship. In the field 'the common child', as a new relative, plays a very important role in gender relations, therefore the 'child' will be placed in the centre of gender relationships.

A Few Thoughts about Gender and Power

In 2000, together with my classmate Kata Horváth, I spent three months in a Gypsy settlement in Gömbalja. Gömbalja is inhabited by Hungarian Gypsies, who make up 15% of the village population. Apart from one or two exceptions, they all live in one of four Gypsy settlements. In the winter of 1999 we visited one of them. At that time I was a second-year university student, convinced that I would base the next few years of my professional career on the experiences of these three months. Three months was all I had to collect everything: 'opinions', 'customs', 'events', 'stories'. In this situation, nothing makes one happier than when the Gypsies start to talk about themselves, saying for example what they think about sex and gender. I devoted my time to hunting for such remarks and opinions.

I just listened to what the Gypsies said among themselves, and watched how from one situation to the next my carefully collected statements lost their coherence. I was positively upset when a woman declared one moment that she "wouldn't want her daughter running around with half her pussy showing, so that everyone even in the Pirittyó would be talkin' bout who fucked her", and the next moment stated with equal conviction "let the young ones dress as they please". All statements gained from such speech were 'depreciated', for the "the category of lies exists only in retrospect, the truth-value of a statement can only be raised by the next speech-act. At the time of its utterance everything is true, and has to be reacted to as such" (Horváth, 2002, p. 243).

---

1   I call the people "Gypsies" instead of Roma because they refer to themselves as "cigány".

Yet I still expected the woman to be 'consistent', and not pull the rug from under my would-be concepts, which were built precisely on her previous remarks. I felt she shouldn't change her opinion from one minute to the next, as if nothing tied her to her earlier statements. Then moment by moment was replaced by situation to situation, the participants and the relationships between them. This was what the words of the woman were genuinely connected to, without which Gömbalja speech would constantly trip itself up in the struggle to reach 'genuine opinions'. The situational dependency of 'Gypsy-speech' seems to pre-empt all other questions, for these are the "places" where the statements so desperately searched for are born, and where their absolute validity crumbles. It was in the characteristics of this speech that I started to try to establish what the seemingly volatile opinions of these women really were.

During the five years that have passed since 2000 our relationship with the Gypsies of Gömbalja has become a process, both personally and as far writing is concerned. From the perspective of opinions, throughout the years the process has consisted of going from statement to question, for a question always emerged from behind every single statement: how and for what purpose does the speakers use his/her statements? This text carries paragraphs from the whole span of my last five years, though at this point they are gathered in service of one train of thought.

Among the Gypsies of Gömbalja the difference between the two sexes and the behavioural forms related to them are not determined by male or female characteristics fixed in gender roles, but rather by varying speech- and life-situations. I would find it difficult to write about the men and women of Gömbalja as Paloma Y Blasco does of the Gypsies living around Madrid, who in a nice 'essentialist' manner view sexuality as the undivided essence of personality as it manifests itself in the body (Blasco, 1997, pp. 523–33). Of course there are sentiments in Gömbalja according to which men who do the cleaning, or women who frequent pubs are 'csira' (homosexuals). But these opinions can be either softened by "let 'em do it, if it makes them feel good" arguments, or be made into everlasting truths if the situation so demands: for example if the "homely" man has others problems as well with his wife. This was the case with Laji[2] Balogh, who was a constant source of worry to the Balogh 'brothers' who observed how Laji became the "slave of the Bodárs" (his wife's family) while he "ignored his own". Even if they only saw Laji hanging clothes out to dry once, it was enough to shape the general opinion: "This Laji is becoming a real csira with these folk, what a csira! A man, and he does the laundry!?" This view of manly behaviour is used by the Balogh brothers to prove to the other Gypsies that by ignoring his family Laji is not only becoming 'subservient' to the Bodárs, but is surrendering his manliness as well.

Views concerning manly and womanly behaviour do not usually emerge on their own, but are embedded in a specific context, where certain types of relationships are prevalent. Thus the statement above can hardly be understood without a certain

---

2   In this paper the people's names are not their real names.

familiarity with kinship relations. Since the meaning of certain claims is always dependent on concrete relations within a situation, it is quite rare, indeed almost unheard of, for people to refer to statements born in previous situations as having an intrinsic truth value. So as Kata Horváth writes: "The credibility of an account never comes from the assumed factuality of an event, that is through a referent that is outside of the speech-act, but is created within the act itself" (Horváth, 2002, p. 6). Because of this it would be unwise to forget about the characteristics of 'Gypsy-speech', and thus overemphasize related claims concerning gender roles independently of the contexts that generate their meaning. I would then be referring to elements of speech which cannot really be referred to. So I think that in trying to understand such opinions, it is best to look at how they come to be, and how, as the context that brings them to life changes, so statements concerning manly and womanly behaviour can emerge or indeed disappear. In Gömbalja every stated opinion is at the same time a strategy as well, it is a form of public orientation for a Gypsy or non-Gypsy group in which they manoeuvre and maintain their own position. When the Gypsies discussing the case of Laji Balogh expound, at length, on the fact that a man should not "abase himself" with womanly chores, what is really being discussed is the struggle of the Balogh family, in which they wish to protect themselves from 'outsiders', and not some ideological concept on which one can base a scholarly monograph dealing with the division of labour between the sexes. If I were to do this, I would be mistakenly using the statements emerging from 'Gypsy speech' in a context that is foreign to it. In other words, I would be putting a full stop at the end of a sentence, the characteristic feature of which is that while the Gypsies are together there is never a full stop, for the situations and positions are constantly changing.

"Contemporary reinterpretations of gender dismiss concepts concerning hidden roles, and wish to gain a deeper understanding of the development and maintenance of gender differences within speech. In my opinion, gender should be considered a system of culturally constructed power relations, which are constantly created and recreated in the interactions between men and women" (Gal, 2001, p. 164). There is a long-standing tradition in gender studies which contextualizes relations between the sexes within certain power relations. Opinions on gender are thus seen as a kind of ideology, which maintains these power relations. The feminist critique holds this point, just as do those works which are criticized by them. See Evelyn Reed's critique of Levi-Strauss, which is a typical example of how critique becomes ideology, how it loses its edge, triggering the angry criticism of newer and newer groups (Reed, 1998). Pierre Bourdieu's *On male domination* is also a part of this tradition. He reminds us not to confuse our examination of gender with our epistemological categories, that is categories used as devices for understanding, rather than the subjects of understanding, warning against letting the categories and presuppositions deeply embedded in the "objective social structures and subjective mental structures" guide us blindly towards a confirmation of themselves (Bourdieu, 1994).

Anthropological Roma studies are partly in line with this tradition. Aparna Rao, for example, occasionally makes generalisations which seem to resemble the logic of a Hollywood movie on Islam: "In practice however a Gypsy woman is subordinated to her father, her husband or her brothers", that is to any male relative she might have (Rao, 1996, p. 73). She then reaches the so-called 'universal cultural categories': "Gypsy women within their own societies reinforce what Ortner postulates as universal cultural categories: As a female being women are categorized by men as belonging in society to the realm of nature" (Rao, 1996, p. 74).

Judith Okely also found a "male dominated Gypsy society" in England, but she places a strong emphasis on the "female perspective", decisively breaking with the anthropological tradition, which is centred on the interpretational perspective of males. Indeed, she places the Gypsy woman in a very honorific position on the boundary between two 'ethnic groups' (Gypsies and *Gadjos*), where 'Gypsy women' are defined by how they make or break contact with the "other" (Okely, 1996, pp. 76–91).

In anthropological Roma-studies the question of sex and gender is—as in Okely—always interpreted as a question of boundaries; indeed, it often appears as the metaphor of borders, the meanings of which animate relations between such concepts as "ethnicity", especially in the writings of Okely, or 'power', as in Stewart, 'body' and 'identity' in Stewart, Okely, Sutherland, Miller, Silverman and Blasco. These texts operate with strong concepts of boundaries, which is understandable since their fundamental questions are directed to how various worlds can be sustained.

However, these texts deal mostly with the cultural systems of Vlach Gypsies, and interpret gender roles within this context. Though my personal field experience very rarely correlated with these writings (for example the often-cited concept of purity among the Vlach Gypsies is virtually absent among the Magyar Gypsies), the conceptual framework used in these works can be utilized here as well. In these studies the issues of sex and gender are usually addressed in relation to their concepts of purity and impurity, in a classification system where gender itself becomes a category. Within these categories crossing borders results in becoming morally impure, for both men and women. Some scholars, like Michael Stewart, claim that this is a fundamentally male-dominated society, while others—and I found reading them more fruitful, even if they did basically agree with the above claim—place a greater emphasis on the diversity of perspectives, going deeper into the situation and strategies of women, and how they participate in the lives of their communities. The latter group includes Okely, Sutherland, Miller etc.

However, the above texts all agree that questions relating to sex and gender are mainly concerned with limits and borders. I myself raise these questions when I focus on the sexual relations of the Gömbalja Gypsies. Looking at Gömbalja, however, the power discourse mentioned above becomes even more dire, at least for me personally. Almost from the very start of my fieldwork I became involved with the problem of gender-boundaries, since I myself preferred the company of men to that of women. I preferred to fetch water or wood, rather than to cook or do the dishes, and was more interested in the conversations of half-drunk men in pubs, than in the talk of women. Possibly the anthropological tradition just renounced by Judith Okely got the better of me, and I too felt that the male-interpretations were more important. I don't know. In any case, I tried to be as permeable as possible, relaxing these boundaries as much as I could. It is quite possible that this paper is also a part of this project, for here I endeavour to show that my questions do not necessarily have to be concerned with the boundaries and what lies behind them, they do not necessarily have to address the process of delimitation in which the aspect of power comes between the sexes. Our questions can be directed at situations where men and women find themselves together with the other, constantly keeping in motion limits such as kinship, power or the ownership of the body. In the field this relationship was called "marriage". In this relationship, the boundaries are not between the man and the woman, but rather they are generated by this relationship.

We often hear or read about ideologies concerning the sexes as something necessary for 'delimitation' (Csabai, 2003, p. 238). That is something that can be used to enforce other categories. Judith Okely explains that the English Gypsies' concepts of impurity (which as pointed out above in relation to Stewart and Sutherland are about the boundaries between the sexes) lower-upper, and outer-inner body serve to separate the Gypsies from the *gadjo*s, to express and sustain ethnic borders. But let's not dwell on Gypsies, and return to Márta Csabai, who in her review of Laqueur's book often cites Ludmilla Jordanova's study on sexuality in 18–20th century medical depictions, in which Jordanova "claims that traditional dichotomies—nature/culture, health/illness, public/private etc.—are so vague and ambivalent, that there is a need for a sexual dichotomy as a form of 'delimitation'" (Csabai, 2003, p. 238). In the case of the Gömbalja Gypsies, I would rather speak of the "modification" of limits, which is ongoing in their speech, thus constantly redefining who belongs to whom, if need be with the help of ideologies relating to the sexes, as in the case of Laji Balogh. However, in order for this question to arise a certain type of relationship is necessary: the relationship between a man and a woman: that is, a couple such as Laji and Melinda, man and wife.[3] This is the perspective from which the relationship between Laji and his children can be brought into question, while his bond with Melinda remains unquestionable. From this point of view very few relationships differ so profoundly as that between "married couples" and that between mere dating couples.

---

3   In the Gypsy framework of categories, wedded means that a man and a woman live together and have children.

Marriage and Other Relationships

When I entered the scene in the spring of 2000, Laji and Melinda already had a small boy, and were expecting a new baby within a few weeks, so they were well past the stage when a teenage couple can be preoccupied with their own relationship, battling with the forces that want to separate them. There are very few situations which are determined by the love affair of a young boy and girl, where the relations are constructed around them. When for example teenagers spend their time in gangs, boys leave little room for their girlfriends to express their belonging. These get-togethers are usually permeated by sexual comments and gestures, in which a girl has difficulty finding her place, especially if and when she herself becomes one of the targets of speech. It is difficult to come out of such a situation well. Recently I too had difficulties in a similar situation. Gathering in the Katalin pub the boys started playing a game in which one of them stood next to me, then, accompanied by the licentious glances of the others, gradually moved closer and closer until our shoulders nearly touched. At first I pretended not to even notice and stepped aside a bit, but the guy kept coming after me. Though I was in no way emotionally attached to any of the boys I still felt very uncomfortable, and from then on felt strong empathy towards Anita, as she wondered helplessly around the room, trying to fix a date with her boyfriend for the next day. The boy either took absolutely no notice of her, or just said: "What!?! All right then, I'll see you later...!". On our way home the girls talked about Anita and her friend Feri and of course the topic that had been a matter of concern for those close to the couple also came up: "What a sap that girl is—ranted Zita, Anita's cousin—Feri is just playing cool in front of the others,—the other day we were just standing in the square, and Feri says into Anita's face, right in front of us and Adél and Kálmán and the others, and Feri says that Jeni gave him a blow-job out in the Pirittyó, and Anita was just giggling at it, what a sap!" Similar stories are thrown in daily among couples going out together, spiced up by the perpetrator adding that he/she wasn't in love with his/her girl/boyfriend for even a minute. Then they start talking about these stories everywhere, using all sorts of variations, to the point when there is not a single speech-act in which the love of the couple is treated as a fact. Such periods do not necessarily lead to break ups, and even if they do, within a short time, when the topic takes another direction, the youngsters link up once again. Most couples experience such periods more than once. Feri and Anita, for example, are together today. There is a very popular, often cited wise saying among Gypsies according to which "nothing is as strong as first love; that never leaves your heart". The question is, which love is seen as the first one. Many times I have listened to the long stories of husbands and wives, now with many children, recounting the rough road—similar to Anita's story—that led to their marriage, a road filled with other lovers, with jealousy and difficulties, but all of these stories end with the same lesson learned "I wouldn't give up my man/wife for anyone". I'm curious whether in five years Feri too will close his story with a similar ending.

I spent a lot a time wondering whether that thing really happened out in the Pirittyó, and whether Jeni was really the kind of girl the others suggested. It was especially difficult to accept because at that time Anita insisted that Jeni was her best friend: she was the closest to her among the cousins, and they often strolled through the town hand-in-hand. Unlike Anita, Jeni had many different links with Feri. Firstly they were relatives, (though not by blood), second they lived in the same place, the Gypsy camp called the Pirityó. "My sis Jeni tells me everything …" Anita used to say, meaning everything she, Anita, would be left out of because she didn't have those links, all of the stories about Feri's affairs and emotions. For Anita, 'ownership' of Feri was achieved through controlling other relationships. She herself will become the source of all information, when she shares the intimately detailed stories of her time with Feri with Jeni and all the others, thus ensuring that all talk about her will herald the fact that they are an inseparable couple.

However, the little story about Jeni and Feri was just the opposite, and wherever she went, Anita heard it. Indeed it was at home that she had to listen to it most often as told by her mother while doing the laundry, cooking or cleaning: "I have to put it this way, the girl is just crazy for a dick, all the Gypsies know about it; are you the only one who doesn't notice? That little Jeni is with Feri!? And he's only using you, takes you to bed, but that's all he needs you for, but he goes everywhere with little Zsani, when he comes out here little Zsani comes too, and then they leave together, only you don't see this!?" Anita was left totally on her own with the conviction that Feri and she belonged together; the story of Jeni and Feri's oral romance virtually destroyed all her relationships. "I'm just all nerves, nerves all day—she repeated to me—they jump on my nerves, and I don't know what I'll do one day …! Only, when I put my head on Feri's chest, and he pulls me to him, only then… then my nerves calm down, that's the only time I can relax somehow." It seemed that Anita's feelings towards Feri had no other place than in Feri's arms, their fleeting moments were spent making love, a situation in which there was no room to question their emotions. Physical encounters, the disappearance of the bodily limits, were the only rebuttal of the speech described above, of the constant reminder of the distance between Feri and Anita. The use of the body is similar to the strategies of speech, both shaping the nature of relations.

It is as if making love was the only way for the teenage couple to be together without external relations and the speech born out of these getting in their way. With the painful experience of being thus separated, this seems to be the only moment of certainty. A large part of the time spent together by teenage couples is about bodily contact; when young people talk about their love-relations among their friends, most of the attention again focuses on bodily relations. On the contrary, in the case of adults living together in 'marriage', concrete sexual experiences are considered to be private affairs.[4] Stories like the one about Jeni are much rarer, and have a very different focus. It becomes much more important who is behind the rumour, and why they are spreading it. Do they have their eyes on the husband or the wife? If they do, how is the couple coping with this? Does the husband 'fear for' his wife, the wife for the husband? These things are discussed by the Gypsies: careful attention is given to how far such rumours challenge the trust between the couples. But who would question two people being together, who share their bed every night, the result of which, sooner or later, is two or three children. Nowadays Anita is constantly playing with the idea of being pregnant ...

Before living together and having children or vice-versa—for often pregnancy comes first—they are not present together in the web of relations, which is an important question, for as Patrick Williams writes "the social identity of the individual corresponds to their place in the web of relations" (Williams, 2000, p. 274). In the same study Williams writes of the Kalderash Gypsies that the identity of individuals is determined by the marriage of their parents, the conditions of which were ironed out by their grandparents. The old relations in which the grandparents sought to gain the best positions through a strategy of 'endowment' are still present on the level of individual identity, or rather in the flexibility of identity, for this is what creates the space in which one can manoeuvre: "The 'flexibility' of identity cannot change the system of relations, the maneuvering room remains within the system. The rules are still those that were laid down by the grandparents, when they wedded their children" (Williams, 2000, p. 281). Though in Gömbalja the past does not enter into the present in such a direct way, and the endowment of children is no longer such an important strategy in the struggle to gain positions, the relation between identity and such strategies is still very strong. The "who am I" question is identical with the position from which I speak, whether I'm a sibling or an in-law, someone's daughter or son-in-law. But all of these relations originate from marriage. Someone always belongs to someone. If a Gypsy speaks well, he/she always recognizes the position within the web of relations from which his/her words have power, from where he/she can give direction to the speech of others. The security created by such a position is thus what empowers them.

In Gömbalja things happen within speech, they happen due to it, speech is a tool for everyone to try to control the interpretation of events in a way that best suits them at that moment. "The internal speech (among the Gypsies) never has an end, it can always be taken up, and the same events can appear with ever differing aims" (Horváth, 2002, p. 243) The 'aims' change relative to the speech-acts, in which relations are constantly reshuffled, creating newer and newer positions for the speakers, from where they try to control the ongoing events. These positions however are usually

---

4 Although sex is a frequent topic, it is mostly a theme for jokes; indeed it is included in virtually all forms of jesting, though these are not about personal experiences, but serve as metaphors for various relationships.

based on marital relations. The "Who is who relative to the other?"-type questions are framed by marriage. If the proper position is not found, it can result in the loss of word-control, creating a situation where a person is no longer protected by his/her place in the web of relations.

Husbands and wives, as the Gypsies say, always 'side with each other', they always stand together, demonstrating the certainty of their marriage, constantly reinforcing the power of their speech-acts through their positions. If one of them speaks as a husband or a wife, for example, disagreeing with his/her siblings, through this they are not only fortifying their marital status, but all of the other relations as well, which are derived from this. The strength of marriage lies in the fact that it is the foundation of other types of ties, always presenting an opportunity for the creation of new relationships.

In Gömbalja almost everything is overridden by efforts to keep a man and a woman together in a relationship. As if the sad facts of my own 'fleeting romance' had no effect here. When I tried—with little success—to recount the emotional life of some of my friends in Budapest, who they also knew, and explain their break-ups with the passing of passions, my host pondered this at length and sighed with relief "It's good that with us such passion never leaves". It is as if all situations in which a man is present as husband, a woman as wife, are sites for continuous reconnecting, thus guaranteeing that they will never lose each other.[5]

There are of course cases when one of them—usually the wife—tears themselves from the marriage in a drastic way. She decides to leave her 'master' and often her children behind and runs off. Usually she takes refuge at the home of one of her siblings, living in a nearby settlement. This indeed occurred at our host's house, where Savanyú[6] sheltered one of her sisters for several weeks. Anett, who in her haste left her three children behind, was completely unstrung when she arrived in Gömbalja, and with her horrible stories about her husband she quickly gained the sympathy of the locals. To the best of her ability, Savanyú took Anett under her wing, losing no opportunity to proclaim that her brother-in-law was an animal, and it was amazing that Anett had been able to last as long as this next to such a man. She denied her sister nothing, she cooked for her, shared her earnings with her, even provided her with a child to sleep with, thus lessening her motherly anguish. Savanyú's husband Rudi did not protest against this, he accepted that from then on there were not seven of them in house, but eight. However it seemed that because she stayed so long, the

---

5   Running away like this doesn't usually lead to divorce. Divorce is a rare form of problem solving, though it does occur. I never witnessed a train of events that led to this, but I do know two women and one man in Gömbalja whose marriages broke up. But there isn't a single case where I know both partners. It seems that for a divorce to be effective, one of the players has to disappear from the scene, in order for another person to be able to fully take their place. In all three cases, this is what happened.

6   The wife of our host, Rudi. Savanyú, which means "sour", was her nickname.

new member of the family stirred the emotions of Gömbalja residents, especially of the wives. Stories started to circulate of jealousy, of certain glances between Anett and some of the men, or of dubious rendezvous in strange places, where supposedly Anett was caught in the act with someone's husband. Savanyú's sibling ties were no longer sufficient to guarantee a place for her sister within the web of relations in Gömbalja. Perhaps to everyone's relief, after a few weeks Anett returned to her husband, and has since given birth to two more children.

In effect Gypsy speech is the act of continuously finding one's identity, constantly adapting to the relevant situation, and the relevant people, in a struggle to control that situation. Delicately adjusting and gliding through speech is usually the most effective strategy; pure debate is almost unknown, for that would require a permanent standpoint. Thus every contradiction is a signal, a message towards the Gypsies: the debater is openly taking the side of whoever he/she is defending. This is no less than announcing which family he/she belongs to, that of his/her siblings or that of his/her in-laws. In this way a Gypsy husband and wife, when they 'side with each other', give proof of their love, and their fidelity not only to each other, but to their siblings, in-laws and the whole Gypsy community. If they did not do so, especially in the case of younger couples without children, the—often not very kind—gossip of Gypsies, their continuous talk, would soon destroy the relationship. I know of situations in which a young man aroused the anger of his prospective mother- and father-in-law precisely because in an important situation he did not stand by his soon-to-be wife, but decided to hide behind his own family. "If he didn't stand by you now, girl, what will happen latter? This one will let the Gypsies take you apart"—said the mother.

The husband or wife who allows Gypsy-speech to go in whatever direction it pleases, blemishes his/her own reputation as a spouse, losing ground in the everlasting prestige-struggle of the Gypsies, for "what kind of man doesn't stand up for his wife"? Controlling speech is the joint task of the couple, it is their joint 'truth', which "only exists in a given speech situation, but there seems to be absolute" (Horváth, 2002, p. 246).

In speech, identity and strategy co-determine one another; speaking gives the chance of controlling speech in such a way that the speakers can continuously find themselves within the web of relations from which they gain their authority, which in the case of spouses, means each other.

Power does not serve to mark the limits of sex and gender, as we read in feminist literature, for the capacity to gain power for a Gypsy lies in the marital relationship. If the other is absent, both men and women risk losing their self-identity, for a person who belongs to no one, is virtually no one, and thus cannot be a benchmark for the other Gypsies when the true question is, "Who is who?", that is, "Who belongs to whom?"

Body and Ownership

The scholars mentioned above who mostly work with Vlach Gypsies follow Mary Douglas' symbolic anthropology, according to which the boundaries of the body recount the boundaries between various groups. In this case the body is a text, 'the microscopic image of society', in which the process of cultural self-creation can be identified (Douglas, 2003, p. 69–83). This hypothesis has been heavily used in anthropological Gypsy studies: Stewart, Sutherland, Okely and Blasco, just to mention those already referred to above, all base their formulations on this.

They all decode where boundaries are between the sexes via the partition of the body (lower-upper, or as with Okely's English Gypsies inner–outer body). The Gypsies of Gömbalja do not separate the lower and upper parts of the body along these lines into unclean and clean: we cannot find concepts of body and purity similar to those quoted above in relation to men and women, Gypsies and *gadjos*. Within these writings the body is a whole, it is an existing text, out of which one can understand the boundaries of a so-called culture, and in its meanings it expresses the subject-matter through which this culture talks about itself. Thus this body is like a sort of universe, the borders of which can only be imagined within itself. More precisely, these authors talk about 'the' body and not a multitude of bodies, thus they cannot interpret the boundary-modifications stemming from the relationships between them.

In the context of the Gömbalja Gypsies, however, just as with the categories of male and female, the body too can only be understood relative to the other. It is through the shifting of the boundaries between the bodies that they can experience the relationships that are very important to them, in which the people involved can almost 'belong to each other' in such a way that their bodily limits disappear. Ownership creates these relationships, the positions in which identity is formed. Paradoxically it is ownership that nullifies the border between bodies, between what is mine and what is yours. The intimate physical rapport between the Gypsy mother and the child during the first few years is often cited: Formoso explains this along the lines of the satisfaction of needs: "the Gypsy mother does not separate herself from the baby—in order to be able to satisfy her needs quickly" (Formoso, 2000, p. 80). In Gömbalja too, mothers have a strong physical attachment to their children: some are breastfed until their third or fourth birthdays. The children spend most of the day in their mother's arms and sleep next to her at night. The need, which is satisfied by the 'intimate union day and night between mother and child' is the mother herself. Through touch all young children have the privilege of becoming one with their mothers. The next time they will experience such intimacy will be when they themselves are married.

Every relationship is about ownership, and without a doubt marriage is the starkest form of this, where such ownership is not disturbed by other relationships. Even the sibling relationship cannot rival this: siblings might grumble because their own family is not being treated the way they would see fit, but I have never seen this cause the break-up of a marriage. The act of ownership does not split the couple into one who owns and the other who is owned; belonging to one another is not a passive state, as if the person was an 'object', who can be treated in whatever way the active participant wishes. There is no aspect of power in owning each other's bodies.

When the Gypsies identify someone with their body, they refer to him/her via their genitalia, in other words, one's identity is equated with one's sex (see Blasco, 1997, p. 530). All varieties of emotion between man and woman are described through this. "She's crazy for a cock" as Savanyú sums up her daughter's emotions; "sits next to the pussy of his woman", they say about a man whose other ties loosen because of his relationship with his wife; when someone is jealous they say she "fears for his cock", or he "fears for her pussy" The parents or relatives huddled around the newborn baby will always compliment the little one's genitalia "bless your pretty little hole" they say to the girls. The first question of the parents and close relatives to the baby immediately brings in the ownership of the body: "whose is your little cock?"—asked the mother of her few-month-old son, answering herself: "this little cock is your mother's, who else's would it be?!" Later it will belong to his wife, who when she has a quarrel with another woman can freely say "you wanna fool with my man's cock, come over here and I'll get him to bang you with it"—so goes a more heated argument. If the wives are quarrelling with men, then they will offer "my man's cock" to the other wives. At first, my fellow researcher Kata and I often joked with the women, pointing out how enthusiastic they were about offering to their enemies something that was otherwise so important to them, and asking what they would say, if their offer was actually accepted. The Gypsies laughed at this, for they were simply utilizing what was theirs, while the "here's my man's cock" type of angry statements were attributed to the fact that their enemies were quarrelling simply because they envied something that did not belong to them.

One afternoon I had a chance to witness a love-quarrel between a young teenage couple. This was nothing extraordinary, since teen couples don't really have any privacy during the day, so they live their love life pretty much in front of the family and relatives. That is how it happened that afternoon as well, when Feri and Vivien were lying in bed fully dressed, but very much intertwined. Feri persistently wanted to get a hold of Vivien's breasts, but she constantly pushed his hand away. "What, girl, whose are your tits?" he exclaimed, quickly answering his own question "Well, they're only mine!" "Well! Yours?! Sure, sure...! You're sure they're yours?" joshed the girl. "What, you've got another guy or something, and they're his?" said Feri apprehensively. "I haven't got any other man!"—said the girl reassuringly. There was a moment of silence as if he was searching for another solution, and then he found it: "Well? Your mother's then? No it ain't your mother's either, these here are mine," he said, announcing the final word. I found it really difficult not to comment, raising the possibility that a girl's breasts might in fact be her own property, but it seemed this version had not occurred to anyone else. The boundaries of their bodies disappear as they unite, inevitably creating something that will permanently bind them to one another, a child.

The sexes become whole through a third entity, the child, without whom in Gömbalja a man cannot become a husband, or a woman a wife. The relation between the sexes does not have two players, but three,[7] and all paradigms which take into account only two actors will—as far as Gömbalja is concerned—be incomplete, just as a man is incomplete without a woman, or vice-versa. It's worth pondering what the concept of 'child-centred' means, for it is something that so many writings on 'Gypsy culture' assume as one of its key characteristics (Formoso, 2000; Réger, 1990). In language sociology, for example, Gypsies are seen as belonging to this category. In Gömbalja you can hardly ever hear stories about a person's characteristics. Fathers and mothers rarely recount past events to dwell on the origins of their adult children's characters. It is not the 'personality' that is constructed in the stories, but rather the relationship. The child is indeed a central figure, not as an unfolding personality, but rather as someone relative to whom relations are formed: sisters become wives, strangers become in-laws, sons become sons-in-laws, always something different to what they were previously.

The power struggles that at times permeate these texts, and cause us to reread the 'classics' from Freud to Levi-Strauss, seem to go silent when examining Gömbalja. Recently I spent a long spring-break there, but not long enough to adjust to the rhythm of their daily schedule. Things quiet down around 10 PM, one can still sit with someone for a couple of hours, talk, settle in bed, or lull 'hyperactive' children, but then silence irrevocably sets in. I'll do some studying, I thought to myself. I had prepared some mandatory readings way in advance, and one night I was just reading Nancy Chodorow: "According to Mead, through identification with their mothers, girls begin to acquire their female identities from the moment they are born, whereas male identity only develops through a process of differentiation. Natural identification with the person who is closest to them, and who they depend on the most is, as far as cultural values are concerned, unnatural and detrimental to the stable male identity ...." (Chodorow, 2000, p. 36). At that moment I noticed that my host's son was still awake, lying on his stomach, watching TV. "Sanyi," I said to him, "Sanyi, you're still up." "Well! Yeah, I'm up," he answered. "I would like to ask you something," I said gingerly. "What?" With difficulty I started: "Look! There's a man and a woman. They're Magyars. They both say something else...", I then rather haphazardly summed up Freud's theory on 'penis-envy', comparing it to Margaret Mead's formulations, then proceeded to explain

---

7   In my train of thought I mould the multitude of children growing up in a nuclear family into an abstraction, for according to the claim above, it has no relevance how many children a couple has, what's important is: "the" child.

that both men and women define the other sex as lacking something that they have. When I got to the end of my monologue, I asked him: "So what do you think, are they right? Which one has it right?" "I don't know, maybe the man, but this is stupid," he answered. "But why?" I asked anxiously. "Well, well because both are stupid. Look, if a man has a cock, and a woman has a pussy, what good are they by themselves? No matter how big the guy's cock is, without a wife who would he be making children for? And it's the same with the woman; they both need each other, so that they can make kids."

If we follow Sanyi's suggestion, in other words, we place the third actor, the 'child' in the centre of gender relationships, we can get rid of the necessity to interpret them as power relations. At the same time, we are forced to place gender on the field of kinship, which is, however, no less shaky ground and no less compelling, since the question "Who belongs to whom?" always leads to the same answer: "to nobody". And this answer threatens to provoke disidentification. The question of gender is inseparable from kinship issues, as kinship raises the gender issue again and again, since "without a wife who would the man be making children for? And it's the same with the woman: they both need each other, so that they can make kids." It is the child who reifies the union of its parents, and in relation to whom kinship relationships make sense.

Bibliography

Bourdieu, Pierre (1994). "Férfiuralom" (Masculine domination) in *Férfiuralom* (Masculine domination), ed. Hadas, Miklós. Budapest: Replika Books, pp. 10–59.

Chodorow, Nancy J. (2000). "Férfi és női szocializáció kultúraközi összehasonlítása" (Being and doing: A cross-culture examination of socialization of males and females) in *A feminizmus és a pszichoanalitikus elmélet* (Feminism and the psychoanalytical theory). Budapest: Új Mandátum Kiadó, pp. 32–56.

Csabai, Márta (2003). "Szexpolitikai testtörténet" (Gender embodied). *Budapesti Könyvszemle* 15, no. 3 (2003): 234–39.

Douglas, Mary (2003). *Rejtett jelentések* (Hidden reports). Budapest: Osiris Kiadó, pp. 69–85.

Formoso, Bernard (2000). "Cigányok és letelepedettek" (Gypsies and the settled-downs) in *Cigányok Európában* 1. *Nyugat-Európa* (Gypsies in Europe. Vol. 1. Western Europe), ed. Prónai, Csaba. Budapest: Új Mandátum Kiadó.

Gal, Susan (2001). "Beszéd és hallgatás között" (Between the silence and the talking). *Replika* no. 3 (2001): 162–72.

Gay y Blasco, Paloma (1997). "A Different Body? Desire and Virginity among Gitanos." *Journal of Anthropology* no. 4. (April 1997): 523–33.

Horváth, Kata (2002). "Gyertek ki nálunk, hogy jobban megismerhessük egymást" (Come to us to become better acquainted with each other) in *Tér és terep* (Space and ground), eds. Szarka, László and Nóra Kovács. Budapest: Akadémiai Kiadó, pp. 275–354.

Miller, Carol (1988). "Girls Go Home: Status of the Machvanka Daughter-in-Law" in *Papers from the Eight and Ninth Annual Meetings*, ed. DeSilva, Cara and Joanne Grumet. New York: Gipsy Lore Society, pp. 95–104.

Okely, Judith (1996). "Gypsy Women. Models in Conflict" in *Own or Other Culture*. New York: Routledge, pp. 56–85.

Rao, Aparna (1996). "A nő a cigány kultúrában" (The women in the Gypsy culture). *Magyar Lettre Internationale* no. 21 (1996): 71–72.

Reed, Evelyn (1998). *Sétáló Agyak*. Budapest: Kijárat Kiadó.

Réger, Zita (1990). *Utak a nyelvhez. Nyelvi szocializáció, nyelvi hátrány* (Ways to the language. Linguistic socialisation, linguistic disadvantage). Budapest: Akadémiai Kiadó.

Silverman, Carol (1976). "Pollution and Power: Gipsy Women in America" in *American Kalderash: Gypsies in the New World*, ed. Salo, Matt T. Hackettstown: Gipsy Lore Society, pp. 70–86.

Stewart, Michael (1994). "A romnyiban lakó gádzsi" (The *gadje* living in Romny) in *Daltestvérek* (Brothers in singing). Budapest: T-twins Kiadó, MTA Szociológiai Intézet and Max Weber Alapítvány, pp. 207–33.

Sutherland, Anne (1978). "Gipsy Women, Gipsy Men" in *Papers from the Sixth and Seventh Annual Meeting of the Gipsy Lore Society*, ed. Grumet, Joana. New York: Gipsy Lore Society, 104–13.

Williams, Patrick (2000). "Struktúrák vagy stratégiák? Házasság a kalderás romáknál" (Structures or strategies? Wedding at the Kalderas Gypsies) in *Cigányok Európában 1. Nyugat-Európa* (Gypsies in Europe. Vol. 1. Western Europe), ed. Prónai, Csaba. Budapest: Új Mandátum Kiadó, 277–86.

Kata Horváth

"PASSING": REBEKA AND THE GAY PRIDE
On the Discursive Boundaries and Possibilities of Skin Colour

In this article I discuss the question of skin colour as a strong constraint in the construction of Gypsyness in rural Hungary. This constraint is fundamental when speaking about sexual, gender and family relationships in this field. My paper presents this constraint in an unusual, carnival-like situation where skin colour becomes not a limit upon femininity but, on the contrary, empowers the sexuality of a young Gypsy girl.

Rebeka is 21 years old, and lives with her mother, step-father and one of her siblings in a Gypsy settlement of a Hungarian village called Gömbalja. I became acquainted with her eight years ago, when together with my friend Cili Kovai we lived in the settlement as anthropologists.

We are now trying to redraw our experiences, with Cili working on gender-relations and sexuality (Kovai, 2006), while I try to examine the constructions of Gypsyness in everyday situations (Horváth, 2007). However, what seems to be interesting for both of us is how constraints concerning gender and race mutually and recursively construct and reconstruct one another, interacting with two other important aspects: the construction of differences in family belonging and wealth.

More specifically, I was interested in how through the discursive construction of skin colour the often self-binding and seemingly dangerous meanings of 'Gypsy' shift due to the fact that within the frame of skin colour, the differences associated with Gypsyness can be interwoven with difference-constructing aspects of sexuality and family belonging.

A no-doubt everyday situation within this context will serve to illustrate this. I am referring to what happens when, upon entering the room, the parents, siblings, relatives or visitors address a newborn baby in the following manner: "Let me suck your little black dick!"; "Let me eat your little black hole!". In other words, the baby is constructed and brought into the discourse not only through its sexuality (through of the affectionate naming of the genitals), but through (their) colour as well. Their sexuality is constructed via colour, colour via sexuality, and the baby itself at the point where these intersect. But these interpellations do not fix some sort of boyhood or girlhood, but rather introduce the aspects of differences, which manifest themselves via the other. Addressing the infant continues through the mobilization of another aspect of difference: "Whose is your little black dick?". The question of "Who do you belong to?" ("With whom will you...?", "Who do you give... to?", "Who do you consider...?", "Who do you side with?") permanently brings up fundamental questions of difference. The interpellation "Whose is your little black dick?" draws the body and sexuality into the realm of ownership, something that can be possessed, and thus given, which in certain situations can construct or reinforce fundamental relationships, and thus animate fundamental differences. The repetition of the interrogative "whose" involves the constant reformulation and animation of relations via the 'shuffling' of sexuality, kinship, and Gypsyness.

This arbitrary, but important example tries to explain how the discursive construction of skin colour articulates meanings of Gypsyness, gender and kinship through one another.

This article examines the same issues, through the interpretation of a concrete situation, where Rebeka and I 'got mixed up' with the Budapest Gay Pride March in the summer of 2004.

The aforementioned aspects of differences are decisive in the shaping of relations and fates. Nevertheless, there are very many ways in which these differences are articulated via one another in specific life-stories. But what can be said in general is that we are talking about a community where everyday teasing creates situations in which differences are constantly kept on the agenda, and are reformulated over and over again. Such teasing appears in the form of certain 'challenges', which function via the accusation of being different, and which necessitate the constant construction of, and negotiation about, differences. It is through the suggestion of being different that the challenged person is animated and given a chance to speak.

In the case of Rebeka, this is usually done via her darkness: "Hey Rebeka, you're here too? I didn't even notice you in the dark!" "Lay off it, Pepe, I didn't come here to see you!" (Imitating fastidious movements, she turns to me in a whiny voice). "You coming, Kati? I'm going to the solarium for a little tan!"

The difference created by the interpellation needs to be set in motion. A person who in a specific situation takes these differences upon himself, who accepts them as immutable—instead of animating them, or throwing them back—a person who considers himself to be the reference of such interpellations, and does not try to negotiate them, that person, in that specific situation is lost, or at least, temporarily defeated. The person who as a rule—and not just occasionally—accepts the designations of these interpellations, and acts as their reference will struggle with their brownness all their lives, or will be torn apart in the family-possession game ("Who do you side with?"). These people do not see the ball that has been thrown as something to play with or hit back, but as something that was thrown at them, and has even hurt them. They are the ones whose lives in this context follow a different (in general, more difficult) path. In my opinion Rebeka is one of these people. And although previously I quoted a situation where Rebeka mobilized her darkness, in most cases such a quip would cause her to run home, angry and devastated. Thus most people see Rebeka as someone who 'takes everything upon herself' and by this 'humiliates herself'. They say that "she is looking for trouble", and this is why "no boys want Rebeka". While, within this particular context darkness 'works' to dislocate certain 'dangerous' differentiations (specifically, aspects stigmatizing the Gypsies), Rebeka does not use darkness as a manoeuvring-ground, but allows it to become a cage, which determines her femininity and through this, her gender and family relations.

For example, in one of her stories about a failed rendezvous in the city of Eger, the expected 'gender-narrative' is completely overwritten by a 'skin colour story'. She says that in her opinion the 'showiness' of the boy was the reason why the date did not go well. Her account of a conversation between them explains this situation. She says: "So he asks me, 'do I wan' some ice-cream. Well—I says—if you invite me!' 'What' cha want?' 'What' cha think?' 'How should I know, chocolate?' 'You see, you can guess it'll be chocolate!'".

The reason why others find it hard to tolerate Rebeka is not because her way of life is unusual, or not going in the ideal manner. (Most of Rebeka's contemporaries, who from her early childhood on have been virtually her only points of reference, have been married, with children, for years...) What appears here is that Rebeka is realizing a rather dangerous interpretation of skin colour, when she portrays it not as an opportunity for a 'joint game', but as a 'personal trap'. In this way she is raising a question at the very centre of the construction of colour—the idea that it "becomes collective via its animation".

Once, when after a fight with her mother I was trying to console her, Rebeka turned to me with a serious face, and said: "I'm very dark, Kati, ain't I?".

If I remember correctly, it was in a similar post-argument situation that we agreed that she would move up to my Budapest flat for a few days. After long hours of doing our makeup in the morning, our days virtually consisted of parading our resulting femininity in the various streets of the capital. It was during one of these walks that we ran into the gay pride parade, a carnival-like situation in which the questions of otherness and likeness are primarily constructed within the discourse of gender and sexuality, and where Rebeka's skin colour was rearticulated through a type of 'sexualisation'. In this paper I will deal with this event, with the recursive joint rearticulation of colour and sexuality as manifested in this situation. My interpretation will be aided by the notion of 'passing'.

Passing

'Passing' is a key term in the interpretation of certain life-situations and fates where the individual appears as a result of some coercive norm which he tries to circumvent, deceive, conceal or simply 'cheat'. Specifically, I am referring to cases when, for example, an intersexual person raised as a male starts living a life as a woman (e.g.

Garfinkel, 1967, pp. 116–85), or when light-skinned 'half-blood' girls start appearing in certain situations (e.g. in their marriage) as white (e.g. Butler, 1993, pp.167–87), or when for the sake of a successful business transaction people make their Gypsyness 'disappear' (Williams, 1987, pp. 53–72). These three examples demonstrate three distinct traditions of 'passing'.

The notion first appears in a 1967 case study carried out by the ethno-methodologist Harold Garfinkel, concerning a woman known as Agnes who appeared at the Department of Psychiatrics at University of California in Los Angeles (UCLA). Agnes had been born with male genitals and raised as a boy, and was on the verge of a sex-change operation, which would enable her to become a woman physiologically, a transformation that she had already made in other parts of her life, including her exterior, a transformation that she longed for. Garfinkel described Agnes' whole life-strategy, that is the work done to enable her to function (speak, act) like a 'normal woman' in daily life, as 'passing'. Thus Agnes' 'passing' is the work through which the 19 year old girl "achieves and make secure her rights to live as a normal, natural female while having continually to provide for the possibility of detection and ruin" (Garfinkel, 1967, p. 137). In other words, passing is the performance of 'natural femininity', of 'normal sexuality', which tries to conceal the gap between the 'male biography' and the 'obtained vagina' by continuously presenting the possibilities of failure. Such 'crossing over' is not a free game with sexuality, nor is it a performance in this sense of the word ("Agnes was not a game-player"—says Garfinkel). It is a performance that is necessitated by the regulative norms of sexuality.

At the same time, passing is a particular type of performance, which through performing conceals the obviousness, or the naturalness of these norms, and shows that "hegemonic heterosexuality is itself a constant and repeated effort to imitate its own idealization". This is the claim made by Judith Butler when interpreting a drag party in Harlem (Butler, 1993, p. 125). According to Butler, the authenticity of the drag performance (the veracity of the role played, e.g. of white femininity) only means a performance that is in close proximity to an 'idea' ('white femininity'), which however can never actually be reached. In this sense the performance is the constant and competitive attempt to reach the idea of reality, which in turn demonstrates the 'idealness' of these norms. Thus, Butler's 'drag-performance' accomplishes the same thing as 'Agnes' daily performances'; they conceal how norms try to be natural, showing how heterosexuality seems to be natural.

But Butler's enquiry goes further, asking the question: "Does the denaturalization of the norm succeed in subverting the norm? Or is this a denaturalization in the service of perpetual reidealization?" (Butler, 1993, p. 129).

Let us not forget that the events we encountered in the streets of Budapest were very similar. Debate has raged for years about whether the gay pride parade does not in actuality serve merely to reinforce the hegemony of heterosexual norms, or whether the gay pride performance on the 'stage of its exclusion' could evoke some alternative interpretation of gender and sexuality.

But let us return to Rebeka's special presence at this event, and to another important aspect of the notion of passing introduced by Butler's interpretation of the drag ball. In these performances, sexual difference is not a primary or determining aspect. This is demonstrated by Butler via the tragic fate of a Latino transvestite prostitute, for whom appearing as a woman, and being successful as such, also involved the promise of being shielded from poverty and racism. In her case, 'sexuality' appears as the instrument of the imaginary transformation of 'race' and 'class'.

The notion of passing takes this even further. In Butler's interpretation and in the works inspired by her (Ginsberg, 1996; Ahmed, 1999; Rottenberg, 2003) the most important statement concerning 'passing' is that skin colour is articulated through sexuality. The interpretation is founded on late 19th and 20th century fictional stories from Afro-American literature (Ramsey 1976). These 'black life-stories' address how appearance can be rewritten through the concealment of skin colour, in cases where the masking of colour functions through a play with femininity. I am referring specifically to situations in which light-skinned, coloured women—through their sexual relations or even marriage—no longer appear to be 'black'.

Possibilities and Impossibilities of Passing

In the village where Rebeka lives such 'passing' would be unimaginable. Women there do not construct their skin colour via concealment, but rather rearticulate it through other possibilities of femininity.

Between spouses the construction of colour in most cases mobilizes the differences between kinship, since belonging to a man also means belonging to another extended family. This version of femininity—where one is simultaneously a 'young woman, a sister-in-law and a daughter-in-law'—can be constructed via skin colour. A woman who had married into Gömbalja years ago jokingly remarked: "I wasn't so black as a child. I only became this dark since I married into this family." Her husband quietly comments that "you ought to see the people in Sály (where his wife comes from)—the Gypsies there have become completely white," and that "you just have to look at her sisters, who are so nice and white". But the woman immediately reinforces her words: "True enough, damn it, I've become really dark amongst you folks!"

When a couple moves out of this frame, the construction of skin colour becomes an alternative formulation of the difference between Gypsy and non-Gypsy. In these cases, the tone of skin is the mark of the unconcealability, the reinforcement, the permanent presence of colour. The story of the girl who left the Gypsy-settlement with her non-Gypsy boy-friend is the following: "Cause that boy really loves her. He's crazy for her. He gives her everything she needs, and even things she doesn't, even that. And he doesn't even make her feel like that either. But in front of his relatives, it's a different story; they don't even visit them, they're always by themselves. 'Cause she may clean herself the way she wants, she may be wearing beautiful stuff, or gold, or whatever—her skin will remain brown. And that's how they see her."

Thus in this context, passing by skin colour cannot animate marital relations: this kind of 'crossing over' cannot take place. This shows the constraints of a context where skin colour designates and operates Gypsy-difference, something that cannot be dislocated or mobilized by the strategy of passing. But this is not to say that there are no couples where the differentiation between Gypsy and non-Gypsy appears. Young boys in the village who gain their first sexual experiences via some 'easy going' Gypsy girls; the married president of the city council who is having an affair with a divorced Gypsy woman; some kinless men who are in difficult situations and come to live in the settlement; a boy who falls in love with a Gypsy girl and is willing to take her away despite the family conflicts this causes—all animate this difference. But in all of these cases, the skin colour is the mark of the unconcealability, of the reinforcement, and of the permanent presence of the difference. 'Passing' would be inconceivable.

However, it is not the case that the strategy of 'passing' is absent in relationships, but only that it does not operate through skin colour, but much more through the concealment of poverty. At that time most of the inhabitants of this village lived in cave-dwellings (as did Rebeka's family) in a very impoverished environment. When the teenagers went out to the nearby towns, they went with their brand-name or seemingly brand-name clothes, their make-up, their hair-dos, their mobile phones. They wished to conceal their poverty (their mothers going around all day to get something to eat, their bare-footed little brothers and sisters, their father who went out to collect scrap-metal, or who just sat at home all day without any work).

"Kati, I love this girl so much!—says Ricsi—I don't know what would happen if I lost her." "And have you been together for long?" "Yeah, yeah, for a while now. But already, when we first met, we just started talking, and I wasn't posing, I told her frankly how we are, how we live. 'Cause from the way I was she wouldn't have noticed. But she didn't mind, she even said that that's what she liked about me, that I was straight with her. And now that we are getting the house, it'll be different, 'cause that the way it's been so far is that I didn't get into anything, 'cause I knew I couldn't take her home, you know, here…"

Rebeka's account of the failure of the date in the city via the story about the chocolate ice-cream is in my opinion an example of 'passing'. It should have functioned in such a way that her femininity could override and conceal her skin colour, along with the background from which she came. Conceal not just the place where she is constantly addressed and constructed via her skin colour, but where she has to pester her mother for days to go around and collect enough money to buy a single bus ticket to go to the city. The concealment of Rebeka's skin colour is, at the same time, the concealment of this whole background, which is necessary in her case, but which thus resulted in the cancelling of her femininity.

Gay Pride as Carnival of Skin Colour

The Budapest Gay pride parade, which Rebeka got involved in through our friendship, became a carnival-like situation for her, where the circumstances lessened the constraints and offered her new room for manoeuvre.

Walking up Andrássy Avenue (the main street in Budapest) we gradually crossed over from our own topics into the world of the parade: from discussing 'csira-ness' (a Gypsy word for homosexuality) to becoming immersed in the celebrations. The former (being 'csira') has a special place in Rebeka's story. Homosexuality is the point in Rebeka's life where her story 'deviates' from that of her peers. With her first boyfriend, after many months and years of dating, splitting up, cheating on each other, being jealous and so on, the end of the story wasn't marriage—as in the case of all her sisters and girlfriends—but separation, and since then Lóri (her boyfriend) has been living with another boy. "What a bummer if Lóri was here, that would be a real bummer," says Rebeka, while I stress her out by saying "look Rebeka, isn't that Lóri?" pointing to all sorts of strange characters. But while we are busy looking at how strange the participants in the parade are, others are watching our strangeness. Someone even takes our photograph, as Rebeka and I stroll hand in hand. And all of a sudden: "Where do you come from?" says a man from the crowd in English, kissing Rebeka's hand. Rebeka turned to me, puzzled: "Kati, what's he sayin'? And Rebeka is being looked at by more and more people as some sort of exotic beauty: More and more people are coming up to her, as she becomes increasingly comfortable with the situation. Finally, a consensus is formed about her origins and from then on, that is the game we are playing: namely that Rebeka has come from the distant land of Cuba. "Who knows, maybe I have a little of that in me too," she says—jokingly, I think.

Her brownness now appears as a form of exotic femininity. The eroticism of brownness conceals the brownness of being a Gypsy. Here it is no longer the usual "the brownest of them all", a difference that from the point of view of femininity is devastating, but just one of the many differences that are present here. A difference that emancipates sexuality.

Rebeka said that next time she wanted to come to Budapest on the very day of the gay pride parade. And just in case her girlfriends (her cousins) might want to come with her, we would organize it all secretly. I think this is more than just the usual rivalry, the threat that they might be more popular than she is; it is much more about the recognition that their presence would make Rebeka's performance impossible. Their presence would endanger her emancipation from 'Gypsy-brownness'. In an analysis of Nella Larsen's novel *Passing* Judith Butler also attributes the unmasking of the female 'performer' to such a presence. She writes "It is only on the condition of an association that conditions the naming, that the color become legible (...) If she associates with blacks, she becomes black where the sign of blackness is contracted through proximity. Where race itself is figured as a contagion transmissible through proximity" (Butler, 1993, p. 171).

Instead of Conclusion

However, next year the idea of Rebeka attending the gay pride parade did not even come up. Like many in her family, she became a born-again Christian, although even here her path was a bit more complicated, a bit more difficult. But that is another story, which would be difficult to tell within the present framework. Similarly to the brief and finite history of the Hungarian Gay Parade, of this carnival-like representation of sexuality, where, for a few hours, the blackness of Rebeka could become the performance of femininity.

Bibliography

Ahmed, Sara (1999). "She'll Wake up One of These Days and Find She's Turned into a Nigger." *Theory, Culture and Society* no. 16 (1999): 87–105.

Butler, Judith (1993). *Bodies that Matter. On the Discursive Limits of "Sex".* New York: Routlege.

Garfinkel, Harold (1967). "Passing and the Managed Achievement of Sex Status in an 'Intersexed' Person" in *Studies in Ethnomethodology*, ed. Garfinkel, Harold. Englewood Cliffs, N. J.: Prentice-Hall Inc, pp. 116–85.

Ginsberg, Elaine, ed. (1996). *Passing and the Fictions of Identity.* Durham: Duke University Press.

Horvath, Kata (2007). "Mire teszed magad? A cigányság diszkurziv konstrukciója a hétköznapi interakciókban" ("High and mighty? The discursive construction of Gypsyness in everyday interactions") in *A cigány nyelvek és kultúrák a Kárpát-medencében* (The Gypsy languages and cultures in the Kárpáthian Basin), ed. Bartha, Csilla. Budapest: Nemzeti Tankönyvkiadó, pp. 220–43.

Kovai, Cecília (2006). "Nemek határain" (On the borders of gender) in *Cigány világok Európában* (Gypsy worlds in Europe), ed. Prónai, Csaba. Budapest: Nyitott Műhely, pp. 196–209.

Ramsey, Priscilla (1976). "A Study of Black Identity in 'Passing' Novels of the Nineteenth and Early Twentieth Century." *Studies in Black Literature* no. 7 (1976): 1–7.

Rottenberg, Catherine (2003). "Passing, Race, Identification and Desire." *Criticism* 45, no. 4 (2003): 435–52.

Alexey Pamporov

THE EMPLOYMENT OF ROMA, TURKS AND BULGARIANS
A Comparative Report Based on the Outcome of the
Multipurpose Household Survey 2007[1]

The findings from the Multipurpose Household Survey in Bulgaria (MHSB[2]) show that in terms of employment the Roma are still the most vulnerable ethnic group in the country. Only 46.9% of working age Roma (18–65 years) have had jobs in the past week, whereas the relative proportions of employed persons in the two other ethnic groups are substantially higher: 71.3% for Bulgarians and 69.1% for Turks. However, a positive trend has emerged concerning Roma employment: previous representative surveys reported the proportion of employed Roma as 27.5% in 1994 (Tomova, 1995) and 41.2% in 2001 (Ivanov, 2002), indicating a steady increase through the years after the collapse of the socialist system.

The level of employment seems to be slightly higher in rural than in urban areas. The rural/urban difference is greatest among the Turkish population. Furthermore, employment status is clearly dependant on the respondents' major demographic characteristics: gender, age and education (table 1). Most visible in this respect is the so-called "genderfication", which emerges especially among the Roma population—the proportion of employed females is little more than half the proportion of employed males. Nevertheless, the absence of gender equity in employment is characteristic of all three ethnic groups.

As expected, employment among the Roma population is directly correlated with the level of education—the higher the level of education, the higher the employment rate. Bulgarians and Turks differ from this trend. Among Bulgarians, the level of employment is higher among persons with primary and lower education than among those with secondary education. Among Turks, the employment rate is much higher among persons with secondary education than among those with higher education.

1   I appreciate the data processing and assistance in statistical analysis provided by Dragomira Belcheva and Petya Braynova (both from Open Society Institute, Sofia). I acknowledge the peer review and comments of Boyan Zahariev (OSI-S) and Nikolay Tilkidzhiev (Sofia University). Finally, I would like to thank Valerie Evans (World Bank) for her extremely valuable language editing and remarks.

2   The survey was conducted in 2007 by BBSS Gallup by methodology and funding of the World Bank and Open Society Institute, Sofia. The main sample numbers 12,212 randomly chosen persons. There are additional booster samples of Roma N=2,564 and Turks N=1,921.

Table 1[3]
Percentage of Employed Bulgarians, Turks and Roma Aged 18–65
by Gender, Place of Residence, Age Group and Education

	Bulgarians	Turks	Roma
Total	71.3%	69.1%	46.9%
Male	77.8%	78.2%	60.1%
Female	65.2%	60.1%	34.4%
Urban	71.2%	65.1%	45.8%
Rural	71.9%	71.2%	48.5%
Age 18–30	63.1%	62.6%	45.8%
Age 31–45	85.5%	81.2%	54.0%
Age 46–60	76.7%	72.6%	43.9%
Age 61–65	34.0%	35.1%	25.6%
Higher	80.3%	67.1%	76.9%
Secondary	72.2%	76.8%	69.7%
Primary	50.5%	68.5%	48.3%
Elementary or lower	58.8%	49.8%	36.7%

Labour Status of the Employed Persons

The proportion of employed persons with higher education within the Turkish community is surprisingly low. One possible explanation for this phenomenon is the specificities of Turkish employment with regard to the labour status of the employed persons (table 2). Unlike Bulgarians and Roma, the Turkish community is characterised by a higher proportion of self-employed, a substantially lower proportion of employed persons and a significantly higher proportion of unpaid family workers. With respect to labour status Roma employment is not substantially different from Bulgarian employment and the existing minimum differences are within the tolerance for statistical error. Another interesting point is the smaller proportion of Roma employers compared to the self-employed, i.e. the proportions of "businesspeople" among Roma and Bulgarians are almost identical but most Roma businesses belong to the small category, of the "sole proprietor" type.

The general trend of urban-rural place of residence again is not markedly dependent on the ethnic group of the respondents (table 3). Paid labour is concentrated in urban areas whereas unpaid family workers are concentrated in rural areas—a fact which is conditioned by the forms and volumes of labour in urban and rural areas. Thus the

---

3   Source of the tables: Multipurpose Household Survey in Bulgaria, June 2007 – BBSS Gallup International/World Bank/Open Society Institute, Sofia.

higher proportion of unpaid family workers within the Turkish community can be easily accounted for by this minority's distribution across the country. The 2001 Population and Housing Census established that 37% of the Turks live in urban areas and 63% live in rural areas, whereas the respective proportions for Bulgarians are 73.5% and 26.5%. On the face of it, it seems strange that 53.8% of the Roma population should be distributed in urban areas and 46.2% in rural areas, but that does not influence the proportion of unpaid family workers. One possible explanation for this phenomenon is the fact that the majority of the Roma in rural areas do not own land and or necessary means of production (Tomova, 1995)—i.e. they would be practically excluded from typical rural labour if they did not lease land (Pamporov, 2006).

Table 2
Labour Status of Employed Bulgarians, Turks and Roma

	Bulgarians	Turks	Roma
Employer	2.9%	1.3%	0.9%
Self-employed	5.5%	9.2%	6.7%
Employee	80.0%	62.8%	78.2%
Paid family worker	1.6%	2.0%	2.4%
Unpaid family worker	10.1%	24.7%	11.8%

Table 3
Labour Status of Employed Bulgarians, Turks and Roma by Place of Residence

	Bulgarians		Turks		Roma	
	Urban	Rural	Urban	Rural	Urban	Rural
Employer	3.5%	1.4%	1.7%	1.2%	1.1%	0.6%
Self-employed	4.0%	8.4%	6.7%	10.2%	5.8%	7.1%
Employee	88.9%	69.5%	79.3%	59.2%	88.4%	68.3%
Paid family worker	1.6%	1.8%	1.7%	2.3%	1.9%	3.2%
Unpaid family worker	2.1%	18.9%	10.6%	27.1%	2.8%	20.7%

With regard to the respondents' labour status in terms of gender, there are substantial differences between the three ethnic groups. There is general gender equality among Bulgarians' labour status with the difference in the male-female values well within the survey's maximum tolerance for statistical error. Inequality is most prominent within the Turkish community but it is also considerable among the Roma population. In both the latter ethnic groups the proportion of employed males is higher than the proportion of employed females, and at the same time the proportion of female unpaid family workers is more then twice as high as the proportion of male unpaid family workers (table 4).

Table 4
Labour Status of Employed Bulgarians, Turks and Roma by Gender

	Bulgarians		Turks		Roma	
	Male	Female	Male	Female	Male	Female
Employer	3.5%	2.7%	1.8%	0.8%	1.0%	0.7%
Self-employed	5.3%	4.2%	9.0%	9.2%	7.3%	4.8%
Employee	85.3%	85.3%	72.7%	56.5%	83.5%	75.1%
Paid family worker	1.3%	1.9%	1.5%	2.9%	2.1%	3.1%
Unpaid family worker	4.6%	5.9%	14.9%	30.6%	6.0%	16.4%

Certain differences in labour status depending on the ethnic group of the respondents may also be observed at the level of education status (table 5). The employer status among Bulgarians is directly proportional to education: a higher level of education is correlates strongly with a larger number of persons in this category. No such correlation exists among Turks and Roma. Within these two ethnic groups the proportion of employers is highest among persons with secondary education. There are significant differences between Bulgarians, Turks and Roma in terms of self-employment. Among Bulgarians, the level of self-employed is highest among persons with primary and lower education. It is exactly the opposite among the Roma population—the proportion of self-employed persons is highest among the persons with higher education. While within the Turkish community the proportion of self-employed persons is lowest among those with higher education, the difference within the other is so negligible that it can be said that the status of self-employed persons among Turks does not correlate with the education of the respondents.

Nevertheless, there are certain similar trends between all three groups with regard to the level of education. The status of unpaid family worker is inversely proportional to education—the relative proportion of persons in this category increases sharply among persons with middle and primary education. At the same time, just the opposite process can be observed among employed persons—the relative proportion is directly proportional to the increase in the level of education.

With regard to age groups, there is no statistical dependence on the respondents' ethnic group and therefore the data will be presented only briefly. At a national level, the relative proportion of the employed persons is inversely proportional to age—the proportion decreases as age increases. With regard to labour status, the phenomenon is compensated in all three ethnic groups by a direct proportion between age and the relative proportion of unpaid family workers—the proportion of unpaid family workers increases with age. In other words, while young people take paid work, the elderly help in the family business and agriculture without any compensation.

Table 5
Labour Status of Employed Bulgarians, Turks and Roma by Level of Education

		Employer	Self-employed	Employee	Paid family worker	Unpaid family worker
Bulgarians	Higher	4.2%	4.1%	88.6%	1.4%	1.7%
	Secondary	3.0%	4.4%	86.6%	1.8%	4.2%
	Primary	0.3%	8.5%	68.1%	1.0%	22.0%
	Elementary or lower	0.0%	20.0%	56.7%	0.0%	23.3%
Turks	Higher	0.0%	6.1%	81.6%	2.0%	10.2%
	Secondary	2.7%	9.5%	75.3%	2.9%	9.6%
	Primary	0.4%	8.6%	60.3%	1.8%	28.8%
	Elementary or lower	0.8%	10.9%	44.5%	0	43.8%
Roma	Higher	0	10.0%	90.0%	0	0
	Secondary	2.5%	2.5%	89.2%	1.3%	4.4%
	Primary	0.5%	6.6%	82.2%	2.7%	7.9%
	Elementary or lower	0.4%	8.3%	71.3%	2.9%	17.1%

Legal Status of Paid Labour

Roma employment differs substantially from Bulgarian and Turkish employment with regard to formal agreements. Tables 6 and 9 below present the relative proportions of persons from the three major communities based on type and duration of contract. The proportion of Roma persons on employment contracts is considerably smaller than that of Turks and especially Bulgarians. The most conspicuous challenge in Roma employment is the fact that 23.5% of the employed persons have not been offered any form of agreement; in other words, they have been forced to work in the black economy without guaranteed social security. The proportions of such persons are considerably smaller among Bulgarians and Turks. Nevertheless, it is important to point out that a radical change has occurred with regard to the legal status of Roma employment over the past five years—the proportion of Roma on employment contracts has increased by 60% from the 10.5% registered by the UNDP in 2001 (Ivanov, 2002).

In view of the significant differences between the types of formal agreement about employment and their social importance, below we present the demographic characteristics of persons with employment contracts (table 7) and those working without contracts (table 8). The existence of an employment contract in all ethnic groups is strongly correlated with the level of education—the higher the level of education, the larger the number of persons working with employment contracts.

Table 6
Types of Labour Agreement of Employed Bulgarians, Turks and Roma

	Bulgarians	Turks	Roma
Labour contract	92.3%	84.0%	70.9%
Public servant	1.1%	0.6%	0.0%
Contract for services	2.2%	2.8%	3.2%
Other agreement	0.5%	1.0%	2.4%
No contract	3.8%	11.6%	23.5%

Among Bulgarians, gender makes little difference to whether or not an employed worker has a contract, but there is considerable genderfication within the Turkish community and to a certain extent among the Roma—the number of women with employment contracts is much larger than the number of men with employment contracts. The most significant differences between the three ethnic groups can be observed with regard to place of residence and especially the age of the respondents. While the place of residence is not a condition for signing an employment contract among the Turkish population, the relative proportion of Bulgarians and especially Roma with employment contracts is higher among those living in urban areas.

It should be noted that with regard to age the trends among the Bulgarian and Roma communities overlap despite having a different intensity. The relative proportion of the workers on employment contracts is lowest in the highest age group of the persons of working age. Just the opposite phenomenon is characteristic of the Turkish community. It is among the most elderly that the relative proportion of workers on employment contracts is the highest. However, it should be pointed out that within the Turkish minority in general there are much slighter differences between the separate age groups than among Bulgarians and Roma.

As expected, the persons working without contracts almost mirror the social characteristics of those hired on employment contracts. The average person employed without a contract is a male aged over 60 with primary or lower education living in a rural area if Bulgarian or Roma and in an urban area if from the Turkish community. In fact it should be highlighted that the number of male Turks working without contracts is eight times higher than that of females working without contracts. The proportion is only twice as high among the Roma population, but this is due to the large proportion of females employed without contracts. In practice the difference between female and male Roma and Turks working without contracts is also within the 13–14% range, whereas there is a much higher degree of equality by this indicator among Bulgarians. Within the Turkish community, age is definitely not a factor influencing whether a person will be employed with or without a contract.

Table 7

Relative Proportions of Bulgarians, Turks and Roma Working on Employment Contracts by Gender, Place of Residence, Age Group and Education

	Bulgarians	Turks	Roma
Total	92.3%	84.0%	70.9%
Male	91.7%	77.0%	66.3%
Female	93.1%	95.7%	79.1%
Urban	93.0%	83.2%	73.9%
Rural	88.5%	84.6%	64.9%
Age 18–30	89.0%	80.3%	66.4%
Age 31–45	93.1%	85.8%	71.8%
Age 46–60	95.1%	84.8%	78.5%
Age 61–65	74.8%	88.2%	46.2%
Higher	93.8%	90.0%	100.0%
Secondary	93.0%	86.5%	87.2%
Primary	83.7%	81.6%	69.0%
Elementary or lower	47.1%	77.2%	59.1%

Table 8

Relative Proportions of Bulgarians, Turks and Roma Working without Contracts by Gender, Place of Residence, Age Group and Education

	Bulgarians	Turks	Roma
Total	3.8%	11.6%	23.5%
Male	4.4%	16.9%	28.9%
Female	3.0%	2.8%	13.6%
Urban	3.0%	12.8%	20.2%
Rural	8.0%	10.9%	29.9%
Age 18–30	7.2%	12.3%	27.8%
Age 31–45	2.2%	11.1%	20.7%
Age 46–60	2.5%	11.7%	18.8%
Age 61–65	11.7%	11.8%	53.8%
Higher	0.9%	5.0%	0.0%
Secondary	3.8%	8.9%	9.2%
Primary	12.5%	14.1%	25.7%
Elementary or lower	41.2%	19.3%	32.7%

Table 9
Relative Proportions of Bulgarians, Turks and Roma Working with Contracts by
Gender, Place of Residence, Age Group, Education and Duration of Contract

	Bulgarians		Turks		Roma	
	Permanent	Temporary	Permanent	Temporary	Permanent	Temporary
Total	91.3%	8.7%	70.4%	29.6%	66.1%	33.9%
Male	91.2%	8.8%	68.4%	31.6%	67.0%	33.0%
Female	91.4%	8.6%	73.3%	26.7%	64.7%	35.3%
Urban	91.8%	8.2%	80.1%	19.9%	69.7%	30.3%
Rural	88.3%	11.7%	64.4%	35.6%	58.1%	41.9%
Age 18–30	86.2%	13.8%	63.1%	36.9%	65.8%	34.2%
Age 31–45	93.1%	6.9%	76.5%	23.5%	66.5%	33.5%
Age 46–60	93.6%	6.4%	70.8%	29.2%	65.8%	34.2%
Age 61–65	76.5%	23.5%	40.0%	60.0%	66.7%	33.3%
Higher	93.9%	6.1%	92.1%	7.9%	88.9%	11.1%
Secondary	91.0%	9.0%	76.7%	23.3%	85.2%	14.8%
Primary	83.5%	16.5%	61.3%	38.7%	63.2%	36.8%
Elementary or lower	70.0%	30.0%	67.4%	32.6%	48.7%	51.3%

The second major issue is that a larger proportion of Roma and Turks than Bulgarians are offered temporary employment contracts (table 9). The general trend for the country, which is reflected in all three ethnic groups, is for temporary contracts to be much commoner among the rural population than in urban areas—11.7% for Bulgarians, 35.6% for Turks and 41.9% for Roma. This fact can be easily explained with the seasonal characteristics of agriculture employment. The second general trend is that persons with higher education from all three ethnic groups are the least likely to be offered temporary employment contracts. Furthermore, it is safe to say that ethnic group is of almost no importance and the relative proportion of persons with higher education working on permanent contracts is similar for all communities—93.9% for Bulgarians, 92.1% for Turks and 88.9% for Roma. In fact among Bulgarians and Roma the level of education is directly proportionate to work on a permanent employment contract—the higher the level of education, the higher the relative proportion of persons with permanent contracts. This trend is partially true for the Turkish community as well but surprisingly there are more persons with primary and lower education working on permanent employment contracts than persons with middle education. Turks differ from Bulgarians and Roma also in the fact that more males (31.6%) than females (26.7%) work on temporary employment contracts. With regard to the duration of employment contracts, there are no significant differences between males and females within the Bulgarian and Turkish communities. However, Bulgarians and Turks are similar in terms of the higher proportion of permanent employment contracts in middle-aged groups and the significantly higher proportion of temporary contracts among young people and especially the most elderly. Within the Roma community, age group has no impact on the duration of the employment contract.

Employment by Sector of Activity

The three ethnic groups differ substantially by sectors of employment (table 10). Bulgarians are relatively widely distributed in all sectors of the labour market, with high numbers in the retail and catering industries (16.6%). Unlike Bulgarians, among Turks and Roma there is a considerable concentration of the workforce in some sectors and insufficient representation in others. The leading sectors for Turks are agriculture (37.6%) and construction work (16.4%), which combined employ more than half of the representatives of this community. These are also the leading sectors for the Roma community, with building and construction (22.4%) slightly more important than agriculture (20.1%). The third most important sector for the Roma population is community services (11.1%). The survey clearly shows the much smaller presence of Turks and Roma in the fields of healthcare, education and science and especially finance. The Roma are also considerably less well represented in administration and management, where Turks, however, occupy a relatively medium position.

Table 10
Participation of the Three Major Ethnic Groups
in the Various Sectors of the Labour Market

	Bulgarians	Turks	Roma
Public administration	6.2%	4.1%	2.5%
Healthcare	6.8%	2.0%	1.8%
Agriculture	10.0%	37.6%	20.1%
Community services	2.3%	4.2%	11.1%
Education & science	7.7%	2.2%	2.5%
Building & construction	10.2%	16.4%	22.4%
Heavy industry	5.3%	4.3%	5.7%
Transport & communications	7.6%	3.9%	2.5%
Retail & catering industry	16.6%	8.3%	8.7%
Craft & services	9.0%	3.2%	6.5%
Finances	4.7%	0.2%	0.3%
Food & drinks industry	3.0%	2.3%	4.4%
Other	10.6%	11.4%	11.8%
Total	100.0%	100.0%	100.0%

Among Bulgarians, employment in administration and management as well as healthcare is more characteristic of the urban population. For comparison, the proportion of Turks and Roma employed in administration and healthcare is higher in rural areas (table 11). The relative proportion of Bulgarians and Turks working in utilities is higher in rural areas than in urban areas, whereas the relative proportion of Roma employed in the sector is higher in urban areas. The service sector is generally more characteristic of urban Bulgarian and Roma populations, whereas it can be said that the place of residence does not influence the proportion among Turks. There are similar trends in all other employment sectors at a national level, and the relative proportions of the persons employed in urban and rural areas are conditioned by the specificities of the sector and not by the ethnic group of the employed.

Table 11
Participation of the Three Major Ethnic Groups
in the Labour Market Sectors by Place of Residence

Sector	Bulgarians		Turks		Roma	
	Urban	Rural	Urban	Rural	Urban	Rural
Public administration	6.5%	5.2%	3.2%	4.4%	2.2%	2.9%
Healthcare	7.1%	5.9%	1.5%	2.2%	1.5%	2.3%
Agriculture	4.6%	33.5%	19.0%	46.5%	7.8%	38.5%
Community services	2.1%	2.8%	3.0%	4.8%	11.9%	10.0%
Education & science	8.5%	4.4%	3.0%	1.8%	3.7%	0.6%
Building & construction	10.4%	9.3%	19.2%	15.1%	24.4%	19.4%
Heavy industry	5.5%	4.4%	7.8%	2.7%	6.3%	4.9%
Transport & communications	8.0%	5.9%	5.2%	3.3%	3.2%	1.3%
Retail & catering industry	17.8%	11.1%	12.1%	6.5%	10.6%	5.8%
Craft & services	9.8%	5.5%	3.4%	3.1%	9.5%	1.9%
Finances	5.6%	0.7%	0.6%	0.0%	0.2%	0.3%
Food & drinks industry	3.1%	2.5%	4.3%	1.3%	4.7%	3.9%
Other	11.0%	8.7%	17.7%	8.4%	14.2%	8.1%
Total	100.0%	100.0%	100.0%	100.0%	100.0%	100.0%

Public administration, agriculture and community services are the sectors with the widest differences between the three ethnic groups also in terms of gender of the respondents (table 12). Among Bulgarians, all three sectors are more characteristic of males than of females, whereas among Turks and Roma the relative proportion of females is higher in these sectors. For all other employment sectors the trends are similar at a national level and the relative proportions of employed males and females depend exclusively on the specifics of the sector and not on the ethnic group of the employed.

Table 12
Participation of the Three Major Ethnic Groups
in the Labour Market Sectors by Gender

Sector	Bulgarians		Turks		Roma	
	Male	Female	Male	Female	Male	Female
Public administration	6.8%	5.6%	3.9%	4.2%	2.1%	3.1%
Healthcare	2.9%	11.4%	0.6%	3.7%	0.2%	4.4%
Agriculture	10.4%	9.5%	32.3%	44.4%	15.8%	27.0%
Community services	3.1%	1.3%	3.1%	5.6%	9.6%	13.7%
Education & science	4.6%	11.3%	0.9%	3.9%	0.6%	5.5%
Building & construction	16.9%	2.6%	28.0%	1.3%	34.8%	2.0%
Heavy industry	6.9%	3.5%	6.0%	2.1%	6.3%	4.8%
Transport & communications	10.3%	4.5%	5.8%	1.4%	3.8%	0.3%
Retail & catering industry	11.3%	22.5%	6.8%	10.3%	7.1%	11.3%
Craft & services	11.3%	6.4%	3.9%	2.3%	7.1%	5.5%
Finances	3.4%	6.1%	0.1%	0.3%	0.2%	0.3%
Food & drinks industry	2.7%	3.3%	1.7%	3.1%	3.5%	5.8%
Other	9.4%	11.9%	6.8%	17.4%	9.0%	16.4%
Total	100.0%	100.0%	100.0%	100.0%	100.0%	100.0%

There are very significant differences between the three ethnic groups with respect to education as a factor for the sector of employment (table 13). In fact the only sectors with a common trend at a national level are public administration and agriculture. But while the level of education is directly proportional to administration and management, it is inversely proportional to agriculture. In fact the trend is not so strongly marked among the Roma holding a higher education degree employed in agriculture but this can be explained by the smaller proportion of Roma people in this education group in general. At the same time it is clear that the Roma with university degrees are employed in large numbers exclusively in two sectors—education (50%)

Table 13

Participation of the Three Major Ethnic Groups in the Labour Market Sectors by Education

	Bulgarians				Turks				Roma			
	Higher	Secondary	Primary	Elementary or lower	Higher	Secondary	Primary	Elementary or lower	Higher	Secondary	Primary	Elementary or lower
Public administration	10.0%	5.5%	0.5%	0.0%	16.3%	5.3%	2.7%	0.8%	30.0%	3.2%	1.9%	1.7%
Healthcare	15.2%	3.7%	3.4%	6.7%	14.3%	1.7%	1.6%	0.0%	0.0%	1.9%	1.4%	2.5%
Agriculture	3.3%	8.8%	35.2%	63.3%	18.4%	21.8%	48.0%	61.7%	10.0%	10.8%	18.6%	28.8%
Community services	1.4%	2.4%	3.9%	3.3%	4.1%	2.1%	5.8%	5.5%	0.0%	7.0%	9.9%	16.3%
Education & science	19.4%	3.6%	2.3%	0.0%	20.4%	0.9%	2.2%	0.8%	50.0%	0.6%	3.3%	0.4%
Building & construction	5.1%	12.0%	13.7%	6.7%	4.1%	20.4%	15.0%	10.2%	0.0%	19.6%	28.5%	15.8%
Heavy industry	3.0%	6.0%	7.0%	6.7%	4.1%	6.7%	3.1%	0.0%	0.0%	8.9%	5.5%	4.2%
Transport & communications	6.1%	8.7%	5.2%	0.0%	2.0%	6.9%	1.9%	1.6%	0.0%	7.6%	1.1%	1.3%
Retail & catering industry	11.2%	20.2%	8.0%	0.0%	6.1%	14.6%	4.2%	2.3%	10.0%	10.1%	9.6%	6.3%
Craft & services	7.5%	10.0%	7.0%	3.3%	2.0%	4.0%	2.4%	4.7%	0.0%	5.7%	4.7%	10.0%
Finances	11.5%	2.4%	0.3%	0.0%	2.0%	0.3%	0.0%	0.0%	0.0%	0.6%	0.3%	0.0%
Food & drinks industry	1.1%	3.6%	3.9%	6.7%	0.0%	2.2%	1.9%	5.5%	0.0%	7.0%	3.8%	3.8%
Other	5.2%	13.1%	9.6%	3.3%	6.1%	13.1%	11.1%	7.1%	0.0%	17.1%	11.5%	9.2%
Total	100.0%	100.0%	100.0%	100.0%	100.0%	100.0%	100.0%	100.0%	100.0%	100.0%	100.0%	100.0%

Table 14
Participation of the Three Major Ethnic Groups in the Labour Market Sectors by Age Groups

	Bulgarians				Turks				Roma			
	18-30	31-45	46-60	61-65	18-30	31-45	46-60	61-65	18-30	31-45	46-60	61-65
Public administration	5.6%	7.8%	5.6%	3.5%	4.0%	5.0%	3.5%	0.0%	2.3%	2.4%	3.0%	0.0%
Healthcare	3.8%	6.3%	9.3%	3.9%	1.7%	2.3%	1.8%	1.4%	0.4%	2.1%	3.0%	4.3%
Agriculture	4.6%	6.3%	10.8%	49.4%	23.9%	32.4%	47.5%	83.1%	15.2%	15.3%	29.3%	56.5%
Community services	1.3%	2.0%	3.1%	1.3%	2.6%	4.3%	4.9%	7.0%	8.3%	12.5%	12.1%	17.4%
Education & science	4.6%	7.8%	9.7%	5.2%	0.9%	1.6%	4.0%	1.4%	0.0%	4.5%	3.0%	0.0%
Building & construction	12.0%	9.4%	10.2%	8.7%	23.9%	15.2%	14.2%	2.8%	26.9%	22.9%	17.2%	8.7%
Heavy industry	4.7%	5.8%	5.4%	3.5%	5.4%	3.8%	4.7%	1.4%	5.7%	6.3%	5.6%	0.0%
Transport & communications	5.8%	8.9%	8.1%	1.7%	3.1%	5.7%	2.9%	0.0%	3.4%	2.1%	2.0%	0.0%
Retail & catering industry	26.9%	16.6%	12.1%	9.1%	14.5%	9.3%	3.3%	1.4%	10.6%	9.0%	6.1%	4.3%
Craft & services	11.5%	7.6%	9.1%	8.2%	3.4%	3.0%	3.8%	0.0%	6.4%	7.6%	5.1%	4.3%
Finances	5.5%	5.2%	4.2%	1.3%	0.0%	0.5%	0.0%	0.0%	0.4%	0.0%	0.0%	4.3%
Food & drinks industry	3.6%	3.2%	2.7%	1.7%	2.0%	3.4%	1.6%	0.0%	5.7%	3.5%	4.5%	0.0%
Other	10.0%	13.1%	9.7%	2.6%	14.5%	13.4%	8.0%	1.4%	14.8%	11.8%	9.1%	0.0%
Total	100.0%	100.0%	100.0%	100.0%	100.0%	100.0%	100.0%	100.0%	100.0%	100.0%	100.0%	100.0%

and public administration (30%). Turks with university degrees are mainly distributed in four sectors: education (20.4%), agriculture (18.4%), administration (16.3%) and healthcare (14.3%). Bulgarian university graduates are most widely spread across the different sectors, with the four largest employers of university graduates being education (19.4%), healthcare (15.2%), finance (11.5%) and trade (11.2%). Retail and catering are the sectors employing the largest number of Bulgarians with secondary education (20.2%). The Roma with secondary education are most strongly represented in the building and construction sector (19.6%), whereas Turks with secondary education are most represented in building and construction (20.4%), and agriculture (21.8%). Agriculture is a prominent sector in terms of the employment of Bulgarians and Turks in the two low education groups. It is also the biggest employer of the Roma with primary and lower education (28.8%) but the Roma with middle education are better represented in the construction industry (28.5%).

With regard to the age group of the respondents (table 14), a similar trend between all three ethnic groups may be observed in the sector of agriculture, where the relative proportion of the employed increases with age. Just the opposite trend is observed in the retail and catering sectors, where the relative proportion decreases as the age group increases. A similar indirect proportion exists in the construction sector, but while it is marked among Turks and Roma, the correlation can be only observed in the youngest and the most elderly age groups of Bulgarians.

Young Bulgarians are best represented in the retail and catering sector (26.9%). The largest numbers of young Roma are employed in construction (26.9%), whereas agriculture and construction are equally important for young Turks, each with 23.9%. The biggest employer of the most elderly in all three ethnic groups is agriculture. This sector employs nearly half of the members of the Bulgarian (49.4%) and Roma (56.5%) population and seems to be the only sector open to Turks aged between 61 and 65 years (83.1%).

Unemployment

This survey places a special emphasis on the analysis of unemployed persons and the reason why they do not seek work. The question, however, was asked without a filter (i.e. to all respondents and not only to those who said they were unemployed), which turned it into a hidden indicator of employment level and social status. It should be noted that by the principle of self-determination there is a certain overlap of the data about the employed persons and pensioners between the Multipurpose Household Survey and another survey conducted by the Open Society Institute,[4] which is representative of the segregated Roma neighbourhoods where the relative proportion of the employed Roma of working age is 42.9%, and the proportion of pensioners is 12.8% (Pamporov, 2008). This of course can be taken as verification of the data about this community.

---

4   The health status of Roma in Bulgaria survey, October 2007, N=1737.

As shown in table 15 below, there is a significantly high proportion of housewives among the unemployed representatives of the Roma community who have not looked for work. Within the Roma population the proportion is approximately four times higher than the share of Bulgarian housewives and twice as high as the share of housewives in the Turkish community. One negative phenomenon is the considerably lower proportion of students among the Roma population. The proportion is approximately three times lower than the respective proportion for Bulgarians and half that of the Turkish community. The most negative phenomenon with respect to labour integration, however, is the finding that the proportion of members of the Roma community not seeking jobs simply because they do not want to work (6.6%) is approximately six and a half times higher than for Bulgarians and three times higher than for Turks.

Table 15
Proportion of Respondents Aged 18–65 of the Three Major Ethnic Groups in Bulgaria
Who Have not Sought a Job by Reasons
Why They Have not Sought Job in the Past 4 Weeks

	Bulgarians	Turks	Roma
Already has a job	69.7%	59.5%	41.6%
Have a job that will start later	0.7%	0.7%	1.3%
Awaiting recall by employer	0.7%	0.9%	1.1%
Retired	15.4%	14.9%	12.8%
Student	5.5%	3.1%	1.3%
Housewife	3.6%	9.1%	17.7%
Illness (incl. disability)	1.9%	4.5%	7.2%
Do not want to work	1.0%	2.0%	6.6%
Other	1.3%	5.2%	10.3%

Since persons unwilling to work constitute a special risk group which requires targeted integration policies, table 16 below presents the social characteristics of the respondents from the three ethnic groups. Among the Bulgarian and Roma population, unwillingness to work is stronger among males whereas within the Turkish community it is more pronounced among females, although with a smaller intensity. The place of residence is not a factor for Bulgarians' and Turks' desire to work but the Roma living in urban areas are more willing to take jobs than those in rural areas. In fact the two major factors contributing to the desire for work (excluding ethnic group) are the age and the level of education of the respondents. Unwillingness to work is inversely proportional to both age and level of education. In other words, the desire for work decreases with age and/or the level of education. This is not a factor for unemployment for persons with higher education in any of the three ethnic groups.

Table 16
Relative Proportion of Respondents Aged 18–65 of the Three Major Ethnic Groups in Bulgaria Who Have not Sought a Job because They Do not Want to Work by Sex, Place of Residence, Age Group and Education

	Bulgarians	Turks	Roma
Total	1.0%	2.0%	6.6%
Male	1.3%	1.9%	7.6%
Female	0.7%	2.2%	5.7%
Urban	1.0%	2.0%	7.1%
Rural	1.0%	2.1%	5.7%
Age 18–30	1.7%	3.1%	9.1%
Age 31–45	1.0%	1.9%	6.2%
Age 46–60	0.7%	1.4%	5.2%
Age 61–65	0.3%	1.5%	0.0%
Higher	0.1%	0.0%	0.0%
Secondary	1.1%	1.7%	3.8%
Primary	1.4%	2.3%	7.9%
Elementary or lower	6.3%	2.8%	6.3%

In view of the difference in the relative proportions of employment between the levels of employment among Bulgarians (71.3%), Turks (69.1%) and Roma (46.9%) presented at the beginning of the survey and the levels of employment from the control question, a methodological clarification needs to be made. In addition to paid labour, the former set of figures also includes unpaid family workers, farmers and stockbreeders. In the latter, the respondents say whether, in their own judgment, they have a permanent job. The comparison between the answers to the two questions shows that the work they have had in the past week is the permanent job for 95.5% of Bulgarians, while 3.4% belong to the category of working pensioners. If the answers of Bulgarians who said "Yes" to the question "Have you worked in the past 7 days?" but did not chose the answer "I already have a job" to the question "Why haven't you looked for a job in the past 4 weeks?" are considered from the point of view of sector of employment, agriculture is much more prominent (81%) than retail and the service sector (with 4.5% each). The remaining 10% of the respondents are almost evenly distributed across the other sectors. Only 87.3% of the Turks declared they already had a job. The biggest proportions in this ethnic group are working pensioners (5.7%) and working housewives (3.7%). Agriculture is an even more prominent sector for Turks (90.1%). The other relatively important sector is the service sector (3.1%). Within the Roma community, the overlap between the persons who have worked in the past week and those who declare they have a permanent job is 93%. The two other important groups—although to a smaller extent than for Turks—are working pensioners (2.5%) and working housewives (1.4%). Also for this group, the most important sector of "unconscious" employment is agriculture (71.1%). Another conspicuous sector is utilities (8.9%), and there is a relatively considerable presence in administration and management, and the service sector (with 4.4% each).

Summary and Conclusions

The fieldwork for the Multipurpose Household Survey in Bulgaria was conducted from April to June. This is a period of high labour activity—not only in agriculture and construction but also in outdoor trade. It should be borne in mind that the data from such surveys always register increased indicators of employment, increased employment in the black economy and a higher proportion of temporary contracts. This clarification is extremely important especially in terms of the analysis of the data about the absence of a written employment agreement by sectors and ethnic groups (table 17). It is obvious that the two sectors employing the largest number of Turks and Roma—agriculture and construction—are also the sectors with the highest share of employment without any form of written agreement at a national level. In this case employment without contract is conditioned by sector and not by ethnic group. However, ethnicity may be a factor in retail for the Roma community and the craft and services sector for the Turkish and Roma communities. Unfortunately, the findings from the survey are insufficient to reveal the reason for this dependence. In other words, we cannot answer the question of whether the Turks and the Roma employed in these sectors prefer not to record their incomes and remain in the black economy, or whether they are offered discriminatory conditions of work by their employers.

The problem is very much the same with regard to the interdependence between the sectors of employment and the duration of employment contracts (table 18). Temporary employment contracts in agriculture, community services, retail and food service are sector-conditioned. In this respect a risky sector for Bulgarians is the craft and services sector, while for Turks it is administration, healthcare and the food industry. The most prominent sectors for the Roma are finance, administration and healthcare but Roma are generally in a risky situation in almost all sectors and therefore discriminatory attitudes on the part of employers can be assumed.

Table 17
Relative Proportions of Bulgarians, Turks and Roma
without Written Contract by Sector of Employment

	Bulgarians	Turks	Roma
Public administration	0.4%	0.0%	0.0%
Healthcare	0.4%	0.0%	0.0%
Agriculture	21.2%	26.3%	56.1%
Community services	0.0%	1.7%	7.0%
Education & science	0.9%	0.0%	0.0%
Building & construction	10.6%	26.6%	41.9%
Heavy industry	1.3%	1.6%	0.0%
Transport & communications	1.3%	1.8%	10.5%
Retail & catering industry	4.8%	6.8%	26.2%
Craft & services	5.3%	28.6%	44.2%
Finances	1.2%	0.0%	0.0%
Food & drinks industry	2.5%	0.0%	2.9%
Other	1.6%	0.6%	1.4%

Table 18
Relative Proportions of Bulgarians, Turks and Roma
on Temporary Employment Contract by Sector of Employment

	Bulgarians	Turks	Roma
Public administration	6.6%	45.8%	43.8%
Healthcare	4.4%	32.0%	38.5%
Agriculture	14.1%	26.8%	76.0%
Community services	12.6%	75.4%	62.9%
Education & science	3.8%	9.7%	15.8%
Building & construction	7.8%	36.9%	25.8%
Heavy industry	4.1%	19.7%	11.6%
Transport & communications	4.0%	9.6%	0.0%
Retail & catering industry	9.8%	15.8%	30.0%
Craft & services	9.6%	6.7%	26.1%
Finances	4.0%	0.0%	50.0%
Food & drinks industry	4.3%	27.3%	24.1%
Other	5.7%	11.8%	7.6%

To summarise the findings of the survey, there are several major characteristics of employment and unemployment with regard to the ethnic group of the respondents:

- The level of employment within the Roma community is substantially lower than within the other ethnic groups: 24.4%–28% lower than for Bulgarians and 17.9%–22.2% lower than for Turks.
- Employment "genderfication" is present in all three ethnic groups, but is especially marked among the Roma population, where the proportion of employed females is almost half that of the proportion of employed males.
- While for all three ethnic groups unemployment is generally much more characteristic of groups with low levels of education, among Turks there is a significantly high proportion of unemployed university graduates—32.9%. The proportions for Bulgarians and Roma are 19.7% and 23.1% respectively.
- Unlike the Bulgarian and Roma population, the Turkish community has a higher proportion of self-employed, a significantly lower proportion of employed persons and a significantly higher share of unpaid family workers. In this respect Bulgarian and Roma employment do not differ considerably.
- Although the proportions of employed persons among Bulgarians and Roma are approximately the same, the two ethnic groups differ significantly in terms of type of employment. The proportion of Roma employed without contracts is five times higher than the proportion of Bulgarians employed without contracts, and the proportion of Roma hired on temporary contracts is four times higher than the proportion of Bulgarians hired on temporary contracts.
- Level of education is the strongest factor for the existence of an employment contract for all three ethnic groups, and there is a marked direct proportion— the higher the level of education, the larger the proportion of persons with employment contracts. Furthermore, university graduates in all three groups are of the least likely to be working with temporary contracts. The relative proportion of university graduates working with permanent contracts is similar for all three communities—93.9% for Bulgarians, 92.1% for Turks and 88.9% for Roma.
- The three ethnic groups differ substantially in terms of sectors of employment. The largest employer of Bulgarians is the retail and catering service sector (16.6%). For Turks it is agriculture (37.6%), and for Roma it is building and construction (22.4%).
- There is an illusory correlation between Roma ethnicity and unwillingness to work as the reason for unemployment. In fact there is a general tendency at the national level across all three ethnic groups for the lowest desire for work to be found among younger age groups and persons with the lowest level of education. Given that the Roma ethnic group has the youngest age structure and the lowest level of education (Ivanov, 2002) unwillingness to work is naturally highest within this group.

Data from the Multipurpose Household Survey presented in this study shows that education is the most significant factor for the type and sector of employment as well as for the desire for work. If the government's policies aim at increased levels of employment, more legalisation on employment relations and a general increase in the desire for work, efforts should be focused on increasing the level of education of the population.

Bibliography

Ivanov, Andrey (2002). *Avoiding the Dependency Trap*. Bratislava: UNDP.
Pamporov, Alexey (2006). *Roma Everyday Life in Bulgaria*. Sofia: IMIR.
Pamporov, Alexey (2008). "Characteristics of Roma Employment in Bulgaria" in *Demographic Processes and Labour Force in Bulgaria*, eds. Mihova, Genoveva and Penka Naydenova. Sofia: Centre for Population Studies at BAS, pp. 144–61.
Tomova, Ilona (1995). *The Gypsies in the Transition Period*. Sofia: IMIR.

ANTI-ROMANY RACISMS
History and Memory

Huub van Baar

FROM 'TIME-BANDITRY' TO THE CHALLENGE OF ESTABLISHED HISTORIOGRAPHIES:
Romany Contributions to Old and New Images of the Holocaust

It has been argued that the Roma do not collectively remember and that they forget to endure and survive as a people (Fonseca, 1995; Clendinnen, 1999). It has also been argued that Romany minorities, their cultures, histories, and memories have persistently been denied a place in Europe (Trumpener, 1992). It has even been suggested that the denial of 'the time of the Gypsies' has been among the necessary conditions of possibility to develop modern European history, characterized by its supposed ability to be productive, innovative, and progressive at the same time (Trumpener, 1992).[1]

This chapter engages in these and other contemporary debates about the role of Romany histories and memories in European societies. I argue that we can maintain neither the thesis that the Roma collectively neglect their past, nor the thesis that Romany histories and memories are persistently denied a place in European cultures and societies. An increasing number of Romany agents are contributing to the current reshaping of memorial landscapes in Europe. Taking the example of how various Romany organizations have recently contributed to the establishment of the permanent exhibition on the Nazi genocide of the Roma in the Polish State Museum Auschwitz-Birkenau, I show that we can consider their contribution to 'memorial-making processes' as a present-day articulation of Romany memory and identity politics.

The Roma and 'the European Memory Problem'

In his reflection upon the increased attention paid to memory and its various instances since the 1980s, the American scholar Andreas Huyssen has suggested that the recent 'obsession' with memory could be considered as "a sign of the crisis of that structure of temporality that marked the age of modernity with its celebration of the new as utopian, as radically and irreducibly other" (Huyssen, 1995, p. 6). In the light of this

---

1   I use the term 'Roma' and its adjective 'Romany' to indicate those groups that are commonly referred to as 'Gypsies.' I use the term 'Gypsy' when I discuss specific, often stereotypical representations of Romany groups or individuals. Therefore, I usually set the term 'Gypsy' between quotation marks (unless I quote someone else who uses this term).

crisis we have also been able to observe a shift in scholarly analyses of how the past has been articulated in the present. This shift could be described as one from 'history' to 'memory' and this change represents "a welcome critique of compromised teleological notions of history rather than being simply anti-historical, relativistic, or subjective" (Huyssen, 1995, p. 6.).

Huyssen's observation is also relevant to how Romany memories have recently been mobilized to critique established historiographies of nation states, Europe, and the Holocaust. To explain the background of this argument, I want to engage in a contemporary debate on Romany history and memory. It has been argued that in the past, in the ages of Enlightenment, Romanticism, and literary modernism in particular, chroniclers, scholars, and various kinds of artists predominantly considered the 'Gypsies' as a people or group of wandering clans who were at odds with the modern structures of temporality and the paradigms of modernity more generally. They were often seen as a people who stood outside modern life, and the formation of the nation (state) in particular, and who were consequently relegated to the domain of pre-modern, traditional, natural, and 'history-less' societies. Particularly since the end of the eighteenth century, the 'Gypsies' also started to function as a trope of various kinds of escape routes, which led away from the modern socioeconomic, political, and cultural order towards a mythical or mystical realm of freedom and dissipation. From Johann Wolfgang Goethe's *Götz von Berlichingen* (1773) to Heinrich von Kleist's *Michael Kohlhaas* (1808), from Alexander Pushkin's *The Gypsies* (1824) to Charlotte Brontë's *Jane Eyre* (1847) and Emily Brontë's *Wuthering Heights* (1847), from Prosper Mérimée's and Georges Bizet's *Carmen* (1845/75) to Franz Liszt's *The Gypsies and Their Music in Hungary* (1859), from Thomas Mann's *Tonio Kröger* (1903) to Ezra Pound's "The Gipsy" (1912), and from Leoš Janáček's *The Diary of the One Who Disappeared* (1926) to Virginia Woolf's *Orlando* (1928) and "Gypsy, the Mongrel" (1939)—to mention but a few examples of a long history of Gypsy-related narratives—'Gypsies' were generally portrayed as representing either an escape from the order of modernity and its troubles or a serious threat to its maintenance and further development (Trumpener, 1992).[2] Whereas, in Von Kleist's *Michael Kohlhaas*, a Gypsy fortune-teller appears as a figure who lives outside of history to introduce "magical timelessness" (Trumpener, 1992, p. 869) into the main narrative, in Woolf's novel *Orlando* Gypsy men and women appear as almost indistinguishable and 'genderless' people during Orlando's gender transition from man into woman and liberation from a patriarchal world (Bardi, 2006). In both these narratives, as well as in many other ones, "the Gypsies are ... reduced to a textual effect" (Trumpener, 1992,

---

2   Various authors have reflected on how the 'Gypsies' were represented in various kinds of artworks during the nineteenth and early twentieth century processes of nation-state formation in East Central Europe (see, for instance, Solms and Strauss, 1995; Frigyesi, 1998; Trumpener, 2000; Cooper, 2001; Lajosi, 2008; Sokolova, 2008).

p. 869). Everywhere they appear in these narratives, they seemingly "begin to hold up ordinary life, inducing local amnesias or retrievals of cultural memory, and causing blackouts or flashbacks in textual, historical, and genre memory as well" (Trumpener, 1992, p. 869). In a thoughtful reflection upon the role of the 'Gypsies' as a trope in modern Western literature and art, Katie Trumpener has imaginatively suggested that the 'Gypsies' appear not only along the 'timeless' escape routes from the order of modernity, but also, and more particularly, as magical figures, in a sense, who ambivalently disrupt the structure of temporality of this modern order itself, as those whose main discursive job seems to be what she calls "time-banditry" (Trumpener, 1992, p. 869).[3]

The reduction of 'the Gypsies' to artistic effects is not limited to pre-Second World War narratives, as the selected list of works above may suggest. As various authors have analysed, in many ways the 'Gypsies' have continued to play this role in various post-war and contemporary works, including film, exhibitions, and popular culture (Tebbutt, 1998; van de Port, 1998; Gocić, 2001; Iordanova, 2001; Breger, 2004; Malvinni, 2004; Imre, 2006; Imre, 2007; Dobreva, 2007; Gay y Blasco and Iordanova, 2008; Hasdeu, 2008). In post-war policy documents, 'the Gypsies' and those who are usually associated with them also pop up as a people who have another sense of time and place and who apparently belong to another social order than that of the European majorities. A 1984 document of the European Parliament on 'education for children with parents who have no fixed abode,' for instance, represents 'caravan dwellers' as follows:

> [They] have a relatively casual attitude towards space and time. They live in the present and give little or no thought to the future. They do not live according to a fixed scheme of hours, days and weeks, etc. Work is integrated into the normal rhythm of the day so that there is no difference between work and leisure as such (EP, 1984, quoted from Simhandl, 2006, p. 106).

Back in 1984, the European Parliament suggested that the fact that the Roma live "in the present and give little or no thought to the future" resulted in their suffering from "educational backwardness." Living in a kind of eternal here and now and making no difference between work and leisure had apparently led to a situation in which their children were not "integrated in normal education" (EP, 1984, quoted from Danbakli, 2001, p. 30).

---

3 It could be argued that 'Gypsies' have also continued to play this role in Gilles Deleuze's and Felix Guattari's 'treatise on nomadology' in which 'becoming-Gypsy'—as well as 'becoming-Jewish,' 'becoming-woman,' and 'becoming-animal'—have been turned into semiotic figures. Despite the fact that Deleuze and Guattari have introduced these terms to avoid essentializing minorities, these concepts do semiotically function to interrupt or disrupt existing discursive and semiotic orders (Deleuze and Guattari, 1986 [1975]; Deleuze and Guattari, 2004 [1980]).

The ways in which timelessness has been repeatedly projected onto 'the Gypsies' have led Katie Trumpener to a general contemplation of the relationship between the continuous Western fascination with the 'Gypsies' and their lives on the one hand, and the formative moments of cultural traditions themselves, on the other:

> If in the course of the nineteenth century the Gypsies became increasingly stylized, exoticized, 'generic' figures of mystery, adventure, and romance, they also become intimately identified, on several different levels, with the formation of literary tradition itself, acting as figurative keys to an array of literary genres and to the relations between them ... If at the end of the nineteenth century, apparently disparate branches of literary production are thus peculiarly connected by their common fascination with Gypsies' 'primitive magic,' the longer list of authors and literary forms preoccupied with Gypsy life is ... virtually synonymous with the modern European literary canon—and is synonymous as well, if the many thousands of popular novels, poems, songs, operettas, paintings, and films featuring Gypsies are added to it, with European ... cultural literacy more generally. Over the last two hundred years, European literary and cultural mythology has repeatedly posed the Gypsy question as the key to the origin, the nature, the strength of cultural tradition itself. It could be argued, indeed, that *as the Gypsies become bearers, par excellence, of the European memory problem in its many manifestations, they simultaneously become a major epistemological testing ground for the European imaginary, black box, or limit case for successive literary styles, genres, and intellectual movements* (Trumpener, 1992, pp. 873–74, my emphasis).

In other words, Trumpener provocatively argues that the very formation and celebration of successive Western artistic traditions and intellectual movements as innovative, progressive, and radically and irreducibly other have only been made possible by the active, and in many ways effective reaction against the 'Gypsies' as the ultimate and universal representatives of a pre-modern, traditional, natural, and 'timeless' order. Consequently, the teleological time of modern, 'civilised' history, characterised by its supposed ability to be productive, innovative, and progressive at the same time, could only have been set in motion by immobilizing and bringing to a stop 'the time(s) of the Gypsies' and by perpetually instrumentalising correlated stereotypical representations of the Roma. The cultural uses and abuses of these kinds of Gypsy/Roma representations can thus be considered as a crucial condition of possibility of the temporal structures of modernity. Consistently following this argument and the reluctant tendency in Western thought to orientalise the Roma and deprive them of a time and place in modernity (Willems, 1997 [1995]; see also, more generally, Said, 1978; Fabian, 1983), Trumpener inherently relates 'the European memory problem' to the silent erasure of Romany memory from western canons and the impossibility for the Roma to effectively claim a representative space for their own memories and histories.

Finally, this leads Trumpener to pessimistically conclude that "those peoples who do not claim a history, are relegated to nature, without a voice in any political process, represented only in the glass case of the diorama, the dehumanizing legend of the photograph, the tableaux of the open-air museum" (Trumpener, 1992, p. 884).

Beyond 'the Art of Forgetting'

Trumpener wrote her article at the beginning of the 1990s, at the moment when Communism in Central and Eastern Europe fell and when Romany groups all over Europe began to increasingly challenge their neglect and invisibility in local, national, and European histories and memories. Twenty years later, therefore, it is high time to see whether we can maintain Trumpener's thesis and bleak image of the position of the Roma in European history and thought. I will argue that there are two reasons to challenge her analysis. My first reason is methodological and my second one has to do with the changed historical situation.

Firstly, Trumpener's thesis does not do sufficient justice to the internal ambivalences of the Gypsy/Roma representations of the literary and intellectual histories that she has interrogated. Indeed, we need to question to what extent Trumpener's own narrative does obscure a tension between history and memory in the traditions central to her analysis. Do the timeframes of her own narrative not have more in common with the modernist structure of temporality than she would probably admit? Apparently, she has been less interested in revealing the internal contradictions and ambiguities of the diverse artistic genres and intellectual movements that she has examined, than in putting forward their general and diachronic coherence. Ultimately, Trumpener's interpretation of historically distant attitudes towards 'the Gypsies' leads to a rather questionable reconciliation of diverse and heterogeneous traditions with the supposedly repeated and uninterrupted representation of 'the Gypsies' as 'a people without history' in 'the narratives' of 'the West.' I have set the terms of the title of Trumpener's article between quotation marks to emphasize that it is the generalized consideration of these terms that is part of the problem. A genealogical approach (Foucault, 1998 [1971]) of the Roma/Gypsy representations typical of the various genres, styles, and movements that Trumpener has discussed—from neoclassicism, romanticism, realism, and modernism to socialist and postcolonial fiction—would not only have led to a contestation of the internal coherences of each of these 'traditions,' but would also have challenged her central thesis that Romany voices are entirely absent from them. Recent scholarship confirms this methodological point of critique (see, for instance, Lemon, 2000; Finnan, 2004; Tebbutt, 2004; Tebbutt, 2005; Rosenhaft, 2008).

This brings me to my second point, which is related to the increased post-1989 Romany involvement in the development of current artistic and intellectual movements. This theme also connects with the outcomes of recent research. A number of scholars

(Lemon, 2000; Gay y Blasco, 2001; Stewart, 2004) have questioned the suggestion that Romany cultures are characterized by an 'art of forgetting.' In the 1970s, for instance, it was argued that the Roma's lack of interest in their past was the result of their temperament as a people (Quintana and Floyd, 1972). More recently, Isabel Fonseca, in her best-selling travel story *Bury Me Standing—The Gypsies and Their Journey*, has suggested something similar when, in a chapter on the Holocaust, she remarks that "the Jews have responded to persecution and dispersal with a monumental industry of remembrance. The Gypsies—with their peculiar mixture of fatalism and the spirit, or wit, to seize the day—have made an art of forgetting" (Fonseca, 1995, p. 276). Fonseca's theory of the Roma's 'art of forgetting' has been reworked more formally by Inge Clendinnen, who, in her influential academic study *Reading the Holocaust*, claims that the European Roma are an example of a people who have chosen "not to bother with history at all" and who "seek no meaning beyond those relevant to immediate survival" (Clendinnen, 1999, p. 8, quoted from Stewart, 2004, p. 568). Quintana and Floyd as well as Fonseca and Clendinnen have reversed cause and effect and turned the supposed absence of examples of Romany memorial practices into an argument that supports the reification of Romany cultures. The Roma would neglect their own pasts and not remember or would even actively and strategically forget to endure and survive as a people (see also Yoors, 1967; Yoors, 1971; Tucker, 2004). Put differently, these authors have neglected what could be considered as Trumpener's main argument, namely that European cultural traditions and movements have repeatedly considered Romany cultures as abject and reified ones that are located outside of European history, modernity, and civilization. What is more—and this argument also leads us beyond Trumpener's own thesis—Fonseca and Clendinnen have ignored how, particularly since the early 1980s, an increasing number of Romany agents have contributed to the development of current artistic and intellectual movements and challenged the trend to ignore Romany histories and memories, in particular in Holocaust-related historiographies (Seybold and Spitta, 1982; Seybold and Spitta, 1987; Hancock, 1987; Rose, 1987; Kapralski, 1997; Kapralski, 2004; Busurca, 2004; van Baar, 2005; van Baar, 2008b; van Baar, 2010b; van Baar, 2010c; Vermeersch, 2008).

More in general, in the contemporary age of the Europeanization of Roma representation (van Baar, 2008a; van Baar, 2008b; van Baar, 2010a), we need to interrogate how, and to what extent, diverse online and offline transnational Romany networks have influenced the debates about the place of Romany memory in various local, national, and even European histories, cultures, and societies.[4] The way in which

---

4   The focus on such transnational collaborations does not automatically presuppose that Romany memories have really or fully been 'transnationalized,' 'Europeanized,' or 'globalized.' Indeed, often "the *political* site of memory practices is still national, not postnational or global" (Huyssen, 2000, p. 26, his emphasis). Elsewhere, I have extensively illustrated this point by taking the example of Romany memory in the Czech Republic and the ways in which it has recently been discussed elsewhere in Europe (van Baar, 2008b).

Figure 1 and 2

Roma and Sinti commemorate the Nazi genocide on their minority in the former so-called 'Gypsy family camp' of Auschwitz-Birkenau, 2 August 2004. Photo: Huub van Baar.

various Romany and pro-Roma organizations and activists have recently enacted Romany Holocaust memories contributes to what Huyssen has called a "critique of compromised teleological notions of history" (Huyssen, 1995, p. 6). Indeed, the ways in which these Romany agencies have mobilized Romany Holocaust memories could also be understood as endeavours to address how Holocaust-related and national historiographies have largely ignored the histories and memories of Romany minorities in Europe.[5]

One of the ways in which Romany agents have recently tried to challenge the neglect of their histories and memories is by engaging in the politics of Holocaust remembrance that has been articulated at important sites of memory in Europe. Particularly since the fall of communism, we have been able to notice how an increasing number of former concentration and extermination camps, as well as other former sites of atrocities in Central and Eastern Europe (but also elsewhere), have been intensely reshaped and redesigned. Meanwhile, unremitting efforts of Romany and pro-Roma organizations and activists, including Romany acts of memory (see figure 1 and 2), have led to the inclusion of exhibitions and memorials on the Romany Holocaust in the museums that are situated or have recently been established at these sites of memory. Yet, these inclusions do not automatically characterize a shift from Sovietized, censored, pre-1989 Holocaust representations to adequate, post-Communist ones (see also van Baar, 2010b). We cannot easily suggest that we deal with the inclusion of 'adequate' Romany Holocaust representations in Holocaust-related memoryscapes in Europe. Alternatively, I propose to consider these memorials as some of the vital sites where the politics of Romany memory and identity has currently been articulated.

Taking the example of the entirely new permanent exhibition on the Nazi genocide of the Sinti and Roma in the Polish State Museum Auschwitz-Birkenau, I want to trace how the introduction of previously almost absent representations of this genocide to this museum has contributed to the revitalization of the debate about how the Romany Holocaust should be represented in the museum, and in Europe more generally.

Romany Memory and Identity Politics in the Auschwitz Museum

Established in 2001, the completely new permanent exhibition on the Nazi genocide of the European Sinti and Roma constitutes a unique part of the museum's multiple exhibitions. For the first time in its history, an exhibition has been dedicated to the suffering of the Roma. Since it was realized by various Sinti and Romany organizations and initiated by the Documentation and Cultural Centre of German Sinti and Roma in Heidelberg, the exhibition can be considered as one of the first opportunities for

---

5   But see, for instance, Kenrick and Puxon, 1972; Kenrick and Puxon, 1995; Kenrick, 1999; Kenrick, 2006; Hancock, 1989; Hancock, 1996; Rose, 1995; Fings, Heuss, and Sparing, 1997; Zimmermann, 1996; Zimmermann, 2007; Lewy, 2000; Margalit, 2002.

Romany self-representation at such an internationally important site of memories (Peritore and Reuter, 2006; van Baar, 2010c). The exhibition is located in one of the original barracks of the camp. Its content covers the immediate pre-war histories of the Roma, their wartime persecution, and their deportation from various European countries to concentration and extermination camps.

The exhibition has been made with great care, and conveys the suffering of the European Roma in an impressive manner. Yet some aspects of the exhibition invite us to rethink its representation of the Romany Holocaust. A large part of the exhibition is dedicated to the history of the Roma's persecution, resistance, and extermination in Auschwitz. The exhibition is roughly divided into two parts, a design that the exhibition's catalogue explains as follows:

> The central room, which stands for the persecuted people, does not blend in well with the existing architecture and also stands in contradiction to the original room in every respect: the axes of both rooms are not identical, here pleasant, safe forms, there hard and severe forms, here warm, earthy colors, there cold blue-white, here faces of people, laughter and family life, there typewritten documents of the captors. The wedge-shaped steel elements as symbols of persecution and violence dissect the central room, gliding more or less on the invisible axes of the original room and finally break it up completely (Reuter and Peritore, 2003, p. 317; see also figure 3).

Figure 3

A part of the central room of the permanent exhibition of the Nazi genocide on the Roma and Sinti in the Polish State Musem Auschwitz-Birkenau. Photo: Huub van Baar.

The pre-war past displayed in the exhibition's central room is almost exclusively represented by portraits and group photographs, e.g. of families, school classes, sports clubs, bands, and small orchestras. Few images show working Roma, and only very few shots are from Romany villages or caravan dwellers. Since the displayed photographs are mainly snapshots of members of Romany elites on their feast days, the exhibition shows peacefully living individuals and groups all over the European countries most of the time (cf. figure 4). Hence, the visitor passes by images from the pre-war period in which poverty, hard times, regional differences, and national forms of marginalization and persecution (apart from those instigated by Nazism) are practically excluded. In particular, the lack of these national forms of pre-war marginalization and persecution creates a radical contrast between the pre-war and the wartime period. Moreover, the exhibition ignores the way in which these pre-war measures and their local and national backgrounds, as well as the varying wartime collaborations with Nazi Germany throughout Europe, resulted in differently articulated forms of Roma persecution.

In fact, many European countries took restrictive measures with regard to their Romany populations, in particular in the interwar period. A Czechoslovakian law from 1927, for instance, "condemned the Roma as asocial citizens, limited their personal liberty, introduced Gypsy identity cards, and decreed that Romany children under 18 be placed in special institutions" (Barany, 2002, p. 99). A Hungarian law from 1928 "ordained semi-annual Gypsy police raids in order to weed out the criminal and parasitic elements from the Romany communities. As in Czechoslovakia, special regulations required the fingerprinting and registration of all Roma" (Barany, 2002, p. 100). From the 1920s onward, Ante Pavelić's Croatian Ustaše-movement increasingly endangered the position of Roma and Jews in the former Yugoslavia. During the Second World War, the pro-Nazi Ustaše-regime was responsible for the extermination of about 25,000 Roma (Acković, 1995; Dulić, 2006; Reinhartz, 2006). Many western European countries already took restrictive measures against Roma and Travelers during the migration waves at the end of the nineteenth and the beginning of the twentieth century (Lucassen, 1990; Gotovitch, 1998; Hubert, 1999). The under-representation of these national differences and of local anti-Roma measures in the exhibition creates the impression of a homogeneous European Romany people, which began to suffer as soon as, but not earlier than, the Nazi terror penetrated the occupied countries. This impression is intensified by the wedge-shaped steel elements that spear the central room as if the aggression against the Roma came merely from the outside (cf. figure 3). In this particular conception of Romany victimhood, possible aggressive elements against the Roma are excluded from the non-German national territory and history, and projected abroad.

Figure 4

Representation of Roma in prewar Hungary in the Romany exhibition
in the Auschwitz museum. Photo: Huub van Baar.

The representation of the wartime period is characterized by similar problems. By displaying the wartime period on steel elements, into which the related documents and photographs are entirely integrated—the pictures are not fixed, but reproduced on the panels—it seems that the memory of wartime is guaranteed 'forever' (cf. figure 5). Nazi documents and personal photographs of Roma that are inscribed with the numbers to which the Nazis reduced them mostly represent the wartime period. By carefully displaying many original documents, the exhibition attempts to provide "a literally 'documentary' past" (Hoskins, 2003, p. 10) and suggests that this past is really 'history.' However, by isolating the wartime experiences from both the pre-war and the post-war ones, history becomes conceptualized in terms of disjunctive periods. The war experiences seem to have neither predecessors nor successors, and the wartime period itself is represented as a 'distant past.'

Figure 5

Representation of the extermination of Roma in Auschwitz and other Nazi camps in the Romany exhibition in the Auschwitz museum. Photo: Huub van Baar.

However, when we consider post-war and current situations in many European countries, we can list several cases in which it is questionable whether the memory of the Roma's war history has been safeguarded at all. One of the most delicate examples is the neglect by the Czech authorities of the former Nazi concentration camps in Lety and Hodonín, camps that were used solely for the detention of Roma (van Baar, 2008b; van Baar, 2010a). At the sites of these former camps stand a pig farm and a cottage park respectively. The mass graves of both Roma and Jews in Transnistria, in today's Moldova, to which more than twenty thousand Romanian Roma were deported by the Antonescu regime, are still hushed up by local and national authorities (Kelso, 1999; Busurca, 2004). Last but not least, the Bosnian wars of the 1990s have radically disturbed the museum that was established in 1968 at the site of the former Jasenovac extermination camp, on the border of today's Croatia and Bosnia-Herzegovina. From 1991 to 1995, Serbian soldiers occupied this site. The area was mined and a part of the museum's collection 'removed' to Belgrade.

Concluding Remarks

The establishment of the Romany exhibition in the Auschwitz museum marks a historical opportunity for Romany self-representation at such an internationally crucial memorial site. Disappointed by the scarce attention paid to the Roma in the U.S. Holocaust Memorial Museum in Washington D.C., the Romany linguist Ian Hancock once expressed the hope that "we will eventually be moved out of the category of 'other victims' and fully recognized as the only population, together with the Jews, that was slated for eradication from the face of the earth" (Hancock, 1996, p. 59). To some extent, the opening of the Romany exhibition in Auschwitz shows that Hancock's hope was not in vain.[6] Yet, we need to interrogate the consequences of the specific way in which the Romany exhibition cultivates Romany victimhood and periodizes the history of Romany minorities in Europe. As I have also argued elsewhere (van Baar, 2010c), the particular way in which the Romany Holocaust has been represented in the exhibition may contribute to the loss of the specificity of various Romany groups

---

6   Once we arrive at the point of what has been called 'comparative genocide studies,' however, we also need to ask ourselves, as Edward Linenthal did with regard to the U.S. Holocaust Memorial Museum, to what extent groups that argue that they belong within the boundaries of the Holocaust define their position always "*in relation to the Jewish center*" (Linenthal, 1995, p. 249, original emphasis). When we consider the debates and studies that have been published on the genocide of the Roma, we indeed have to acknowledge the considerable effort that has been expended on the demonstration that the scale and the manner of the atrocities are (or are not) of the same kind as in the case of the Jews (see, for instance, Rose, 1995; Hancock, 1996; Zimmermann, 1996; Lewy, 2000). Elsewhere, I have discussed this theme in the context of the globalization of Holocaust discourses (van Baar, 2010c).

and their histories. By focusing on a conception of victimhood that excludes both the pre- and the post-war anti-Roma measures that were taken in most countries in the region, the treatment of the various Romany communities within the different local and national contexts becomes underrepresented. A better understanding of the ways in which Roma and non-Roma were historically related to each other at local and national levels, as well as a better contextualization of the ways in which the communist victimization of many of the inhabitants of the former Eastern Bloc is related to the suffering of the Roma, are of crucial importance to formulate a concept of victimhood beyond artificial polarizations.

Yet, Roma representations such as those included in the Auschwitz exhibition do not stand alone, but are part of the current remaking of European memorial cultures to which also other Romany agents have increasingly contributed (see, for instance, Kapralski, 2004; van Baar, 2008b; van Baar, 2010b). Therefore, my analysis of the Auschwitz exhibition about the Roma leads me to suggest that we need to revise the formulation of 'the European memory problem,' at least in relation to how Trumpener put it in the early 1990s. This problem cannot adequately be described as the perpetual reinforcement of European modernity—now in terms of the current politics of European integration—by means of the erasure of Romany memory from European canons and by making it impossible for the Roma to claim a representative space for their own histories and memories. Though the current promotion of a 'pan-European Roma problem of integration' seriously risks reinforcing persistent stereotypical Roma representations (van Baar, 2008b), current Romany activism and networking as well as recent scholarship on the Roma illustrate that Romany memorial practices and discourses are far from absent.

More generally and in line with the idea that we need to understand the "memorial-making process" itself (Young, 1993, pp. 8–15) as an endeavour to articulate representations of the Holocaust, we need to consider new exhibitions, debates, and even controversies about Romany memory as part of this process. It has been argued that "the real monument is not the stone object but the debate itself" (Carrier, 2005, p. 228). In this line of reasoning, to some extent memorials are always "dialogic" (Carrier, 2005). Even if memorials do not (yet) exist materially and even if the dialogue has not been based on consensus or reciprocity, the ongoing debates about the place of Romany memory in European cultures, societies, and histories actively shape and reshape Romany memories and identities, and contest and revitalize current Roma/non-Roma relationships.

Bibliography

Acković, Dragoljub (1995). *Roma Suffering in [the] Jasenovac Camp*. Belgrade: The Museum of the Victims of Genocide, Roma Culture Center.

Barany, Zoltan D. (2002). *The East European Gypsies. Regime Change, Marginality, and Ethnopolitics*. Cambridge: Cambridge University Press.

Bardi, Abby (2006). "The Gypsy as Trope in Victorian and Modern British Literature." *Romani Studies* 16, no. 1 (2006): 31–42.

Breger, Claudia (2004). "Understanding the 'Other'? Communication, History and Narration in Margriet de Moor's *Hertog van Egypte*" in *The Role of the Romanies: Images and Counter-Images of 'Gypsies'/Romanies in European Cultures*, eds. Saul, Nicholas and Susan Tebbutt. Liverpool: Liverpool University Press, pp. 131–44.

Busurca, Emil (2004). *Transnistria: The Forgotten Cemetery*, Documentary. Romania and the Netherlands: John Kok Productions, 56 min.

Carrier, Peter (2005). *Holocaust Monuments and National Memory Cultures in France and Germany since 1989*. Oxford: Berghahn.

Clendinnen, Inga (1999). *Reading the Holocaust*. Cambridge: Cambridge University Press.

Cooper, David (2001). "Béla Bartók and the Question of Race Purity in Music" in *Musical Constructions of Nationalism: Essays on the History of European Musical Culture 1800–1945*, eds. White, Harry and Michael Murphy. Cork: Cork University Press, pp. 16–32.

Danbakli, Marielle, ed. (2001). *Roma, Gypsies: Texts Issued by International Institutions*. Paris and Hatfield: Centre de recherches tsiganes and University of Hertfordshire Press.

Deleuze, Gilles and Felix Guattari (1986 [1975]). *Kafka: Toward a Minor Literature*. Minneapolis: University of Minnesota Press.

Deleuze, Gilles and Felix Guattari (2004 [1980]). *A Thousand Plateaus: Capitalism and Schizophrenia*. London: Continuum.

Dobreva, Nikolina (2007). "Constructing the 'Celluloid Gypsy': Tony Gatlif and Emir Kusturica's 'Gypsy Films' in the Context of the New Europe." *Romani Studies* 17, no. 2 (2007): 141–54.

Dulić, Tomislav (2006). "Mass Killing in the Independent State of Croatia, 1941–1945: a Case for Comparative Research." *Journal of Genocide Research* 8, no. 3 (2006): 255–81.

EP (1984). "Education for Children of Parents Who Have no Fixed Abode." *European Parliament Working Documents 1983–84*, 1-1522/83 (PE 87.789/fin) 12th March 1984.

Fabian, Johannes (1983). *Time and the Other: How Anthropology Makes Its Object*. New York: Columbia University Press.

Fings, Karola, Herbert Heuss, and Frank Sparing (1997). *From "Race Science" to the Camps. The Gypsies During the Second World War*. Vol. 1. Hatfield: University of Hertfordshire Press.

Finnan, Carmel (2004). "From Survival to Subversion: Strategies of Self-Representation in Selected Works by Mariella Mehr" in *The Role of the Romanies: Images and Counter-Images of 'Gypsies'/Romanies in European Cultures*, eds. Saul, Nicholas and Susan Tebbutt. Liverpool: Liverpool University Press, pp. 145–55.

Fonseca, Isabel (1995). *Bury Me Standing: The Gypsies and Their Journey*. London: Vintage.

Foucault, Michel (1998 [1971]). "Nietzsche, Genealogy, History" in *Aesthetics, Method, and Epistemology. Essential Works of Michel Foucault 1954–1984*, Vol. 2, ed. Faubion, James D. New York: The New Press, pp. 369–91.

Frigyesi, Judit (1998). *Béla Bartók and Turn-of-the-Century Budapest*. Berkeley: University of California Press.

Gay y Blasco, Paloma (2001). "'We don't Know Our Descent': How the Gitanos of Jarana Manage the Past." *Journal of the Royal Anthropological Institute* 7, no. 4 (2001): 631–47.

Gay y Blasco, Paloma and Dina Iordanova, eds. (2008). "Picturing 'Gypsies': Special Issue on Interdisciplinary Approaches to Roma Representation." *Third Text: Critical Perspectives on Contemporary Art and Culture* 22, no 3 (2008).

Gocić, Goran (2001). *The Cinema of Emir Kusturica: Notes from the Underground*. London: Wallflower Press.

Gotovitch, José (1998). "Verfolgung und Vernichtung Belgischer Sinti und Roma" in *Sinti und Roma im KL Auschwitz-Birkenau 1943–44. Vor dem Hintergrund ihrer Verfolgung unter der Naziherrschaft*, ed. Długoborski, Wacław. Oświęcim: Verlag Staatliches Museum Auschwitz-Birkenau, pp. 209–25.

Hancock, Ian (1987). *The Pariah Syndrome: An Account of Gypsy Slavery and Persecution*. Ann Arbor: Karome Publishers, Inc.

Hancock, Ian (1989). "Uniqueness, Gypsies, and Jews" in *The Impact of the Holocaust on the Contemporary World*, eds. Bauer, Yehuda *et al.* Oxford: Pergamon Press, pp. 2017–25.

Hancock, Ian (1996). "Responses to the Porrajmos: The Romani Holocaust" in *Is the Holocaust Unique? Perspectives on Comparative Genocide*, ed. Rosenbaum, Alan S. Oxford: Westview Press, pp. 39–64.

Hasdeu, Iulia (2008). "Imagining the Gypsy Woman: Representations of Roma in Romanian Museum." *Third Text: Critical Perspectives on Comtemporary Art and Culture* 22, no. 3 (2008): 347–57.

Hoskins, Andrew (2003). "Signs of the Holocaust: Exhibiting Memory in a Mediated Age." *Media, Culture & Society* 25, no. 1 (2003): 7–22.

Hubert, Marie-Christine (1999). "The Internment of Gypsies in France" in *In the Shadow of the Swastika. The Gypsies during the Second World War*. Vol. 2, ed. Kenrick, Donald. Hatfield: University of Hertfordshire Press, pp. 59–88.

Huyssen, Andreas (1995). *Twilight Memories: Marking Time in a Culture of Amnesia*. London: Routledge.

Huyssen, Andreas (2000). "Present Pasts: Media, Politics, Amnesia." *Public Culture* 12, no. 1 (2000): 21–38.

Imre, Anikó (2006). "Play in the Ghetto: Global Entertainment and the European 'Roma Problem'." *Third Text: Critical Perspectives on Contemporary Art and Culture* 20, no. 6 (2006): 659–70

Imre, Anikó (2007). "Hip Hop Nation and Gender Politics" in *Sonic Interventions*, eds. Mieszkowski, Sylvia, Joy Smith, and Marijke de Valck. Amsterdam: Rodopi Press, pp. 265–86.

Iordanova, Dina (2001). *Cinema of Flames: Balkan Film, Culture and the Media*. London: British Film Institute Publishing.

Kapralski, Slawomir (1997). "Identity Building and the Holocaust: Roma Political Nationalism." *Nationalities Papers* 25, no. 2 (1997): 269–83.

Kapralski, Slawomir (2004). "Ritual of Memory in Constructing the Modern Identity of Eastern European Romanies" in *The Role of the Romanies: Images and Counter-Images of 'Gypsies'/Romanies in European Cultures*, eds. Saul, Nicholas and Susan Tebbutt. Liverpool: Liverpool University Press, pp. 208–25.

Kelso, Michelle (1999). "Gypsy Deportations to Transnistria: Romania, 1942–1944" in *In the Shadow of the Swastika. The Gypsies during the Second World War*. Vol. 2, ed. Kenrick, Donald. Hatfield: University of Hertfordshire Press, pp. 95–129.

Kenrick, Donald and Grattan Puxon (1972). *The Destiny of Europe's Gypsies*. New York: Basic Books.

Kenrick, Donald and Grattan Puxon (1995). *Gypsies under the Swastika*. Hatfield: University of Hertfordshire Press.

Kenrick, Donald, ed. (1999). *In the Shadow of the Swastika. The Gypsies During the Second World War*. Vol. 2. Hatfield: University of Hertfordshire Press.

Kenrick, Donald, ed. (2006). *The Final Chapter. The Gypsies During the Second World War*. Vol. 3. Hatfield: University of Hertfordshire Press.

Lajosi, Krisztina (2008). *Opera and Nineteenth-Century Nation-Building: the (Re)sounding Voice of Nationalism*. Amsterdam: University of Amsterdam.

Lemon, Alaina (2000). *Between Two Fires: Gypsy Performance and Romani Memory from Pushkin to Postsocialism*. Durham: Duke University Press.

Lewy, Guenter (2000). *The Nazi Persecution of the Gypsies*. New York: Oxford University Press.

Linenthal, Edward (1995). *Preserving Memory. The Struggle to Create America's Holocaust Museum*. New York: Penguin.

Lucassen, Leo (1990). *"En men noemde hen zigeuners ..." De geschiedenis van Kaldarasch, Ursari, Lowara en Sinti in Nederland: 1750–1944* ("And they called them Gypsies ..." The history of Kaldarash, Ursari, Lowara, and Sinti in the Netherlands: 1750–1944). Amsterdam and The Hague: Stichting beheer IISG/SDU.

Malvinni, David (2004). *The Gypsy Caravan: From Real Roma to Imaginary Gypsy in Western Music and Film*. London: Routledge.

Margalit, Gilad (2002). *Germany and Its Gypsies: a Post-Auschwitz Ordeal*. Madison: The University of Wisconsin Press.

Peritore, Silvio and Frank Reuter (2006). "Die ständige Ausstellung zum Völkermord an den Sinti und Roma im Staatlichen Museum Auschwitz: Voraussetzungen, Konzeption und Realisierung" in *Die Kunst ist der Zerstörer des Schweigens. Formen künstlerischer Erinnerung an die nationalsozialistische Rassen- und Vernichtungspolitik in Osteuropa*, eds. Grüner, Frank, Urs Heftrich, and Heinz-Dietrich Löwe. Vienna: Böhlau Verlag, pp. 495–513.

Quintana, Bertha B. and Lois Gray Floyd (1972). *¡Qué gitano! Gypsies of Southern Spain*. New York: Holt, Rinehart, Winston.

Reinhartz, Dennis (2006). "The Genocide of the Yugoslav Gypsies" in *The Final Chapter. The Gypsies During the Second World War*. Vol. 3, ed. Kenrick, Donald. Hatfield: University of Hertfordshire Press, pp. 87–96.

Reuter, Frank and Silvio Peritore, eds. (2003). *The National Socialist Genocide of the Sinti and Roma. Catalogue of the Permanent Exhibition in the State Museum of Auschwitz.* Heidelberg: Documentary and Cultural Centre of German Sinti and Roma.

Rose, Romani (1987). *Bürgerrechte für Sinti und Roma. Das Buch zum Rasissmus in Deutschland.* Heidelberg: Zentralrat Deutscher Sinti und Roma.

Rose, Romani, ed. (1995). *The Nazi Genocide of the Sinti and Roma.* Heidelberg: Documentary and Cultural Centre of German Sinti and Roma.

Rosenhaft, Eve (2008). "Exchanging Glances: Ambivalence in Twentieth-Century Photographs of German Sinti." *Third Text: Critical Perspectives on Contemporary Art and Culture* 22, no. 3 (2008): 311–24.

Said, Edward (1978). *Orientalism.* New York: Vintage.

Seybold, Katrin and Melanie Spitta (1982). *Es ging Tag und Nacht, liebes Kind. Zigeuner (Sinti) in Auschwitz,* Documentary. Germany, 76 min.

Seybold, Katrin and Melanie Spitta (1987). *Das falsche Wort. Die 'Wiedergutmachung' an Zigeunern (Sinte) in Deutschland?,* Documentary. Germany, 83 min.

Simhandl, Katrin (2006). "'Western Gypsies and Travellers'—'Eastern Roma': the Creation of Political Objects by the Institutions of the European Union." *Nations and Nationalism* 12, no. 1 (2006): 97–115.

Sokolova, Věra (2008). *Cultural Politics of Ethnicity: Discourses on Roma in Communist Czechoslovakia.* Stuttgart: Ibidem Verlag.

Solms, Wilhelm and Daniel Strauss, eds. (1995). *"Zigeunerbilder" in der deutschsprachigen Literatur.* Heidelberg: Dokumentations- und Kulturzentrum Deutscher Sinti und Roma.

Stewart, Michael (2004). "Remembering without Commemoration: The Mnemonics and Politics of Holocaust Memories among European Roma." *Journal of the Royal Anthropological Institute* 10, no. 3 (2004): 561–82.

Tebbutt, Susan, ed. (1998). *Sinti and Roma: Gypsies in the German-speaking Society and Literature.* Oxford: Berghahn.

Tebbutt, Susan (2005). "Stolen Childhood: Austrian Romany Ceija Stojka and Her Past." *Holocaust Studies: A Journal of Culture and History* 11, no. 2 (2005): 38–61.

Tebbutt, Susan (2004). "Disproportional Representation: Romanies and European Art" in *The Role of the Romanies: Images and Counter-Images of 'Gypsies'/Romanies in European Cultures,* eds. Saul, Nicholas and Susan Tebbutt. Liverpool: Liverpool University Press, pp. 159–77.

Trumpener, Katie (1992). "The Time of the Gypsies: A 'People without History' in the Narratives of the West." *Critical Inquiry* 18 (Summer 1992): 843–84.

Trumpener, Katie (2000). "Béla Bartók and the Rise of Comparative Ethnomusicology: Nationalism, Race Purity, and the Legacy of the Austro-Hungarian Empire" in *Music and Racial Imagination,* eds. Radano, Ronald M. and Philip V. Bohlman. Chicago: University of Chicago Press.

Tucker, Dan, ed. (2004) *The Heroic Present: Life Among the Gypsies. The Photographs and Memoirs of Jan Yoors.* New York: The Monacelli Press.

van Baar, Huub (2005). *The Role of the Globalization of Holocaust Discourses in Processes of Romany Identity Formation.* Third Lecture in the Series *The Roma Holocaust in Europe.* 12 October. Bratislava: Office of the Council of Europe.

van Baar, Huub (2008a). "Scaling the Romany Grassroots: Europeanization and Transnational Networking" in *Roma-/Zigeunerkulturen in neuen Perspektiven—Romany/Gypsy Cultures in New Perspectives*, eds. Jacobs, Fabian and Johannes Ries. Leipzig: Leipziger Universitätsverlag, pp. 217–41.

van Baar, Huub (2008b). "The Way out of Amnesia? Europeanisation and the Recognition of the Roma's Past and Present." *Third Text: Critical Perspectives on Contemporary Art and Culture* 22, no. 3 (2008): 373–85.

van Baar, Huub (2010a). "Cultural Policy and the Governmentalization of Holocaust Remembrance in Europe: Romany Memory between Denial and Recognition." *International Journal of Cultural Policy* 16 (2010): forthcoming.

van Baar, Huub (2010b). "Memorial Work in Progress: 'Auschwitz' and the Struggle for Romany Holocaust Representation." *Cultural Politics* 16 (2010): forthcoming.

van Baar, Huub (2010c). "Romani Identity Formation and the Globalization of Holocaust Discourse" in *Representation Matters: (Re)Articulating Collective Identities in a Postcolonial World*, eds. Hoffmann, Anette and Esther Peeren. Amsterdam: Rodopi Press, pp. 115–32.

van de Port, Mattijs (1998). *Gypsies, Wars, and Other Instances of the Wild. Civilisation and Its Discontents in a Serbian Town*. Amsterdam: Amsterdam University Press.

Vermeersch, Peter (2008). "Exhibiting Multiculturalism: Politicised Representations of the Roma in Poland." *Third Text: Critical Perspectives on Contemporary Art and Culture* 22, no. 3 (2008): 387–96.

Willems, Wim (1997 [1995]). *In Search of the True Gypsy: From Enlightenment to Final Solution*. London: Frank Cass.

Yoors, Jan (1967). *The Gypsies*. New York: Simon and Schuster.

Yoors, Jan (1971). *Crossing*. Prospect Heights: Waveland Press.

Young, James (1993). *The Texture of Memory. Holocaust Memorials and Meaning*. New Haven: Yale University Press.

Zimmermann, Michael (1996). *Rassenutopie und Genozid: Die nationalsozialistische "Lösung der Zigeunerfrage"*. Hamburg: Christians Verlag.

Zimmermann, Michael, ed. (2007). *Zwischen Erziehung und Vernichtung: Zigeunerpolitik und Zigeunerforschung im Europa des 20. Jahrhunderts*. Stuttgart: Franz Steiner Verlag.

Michael Stewart

THE OTHER GENOCIDE

For me it is unbelievable that I am still alive. My survival has been a punishment. Again and again and again I have asked God: why was I left alive, I alone? They destroyed our whole life, the love, the families, the cohesion. We don't have families anymore. Everything is in tatters. They took everything. The trust in others, the openness and warm feelings, they are all destroyed. I don't even believe in myself any more. It was our faith in other people that they took from us, all the feelings from which that derives...

Maria R., Sterilised 1944, Interviewed Hamburg, 1989.

Between 1939 and 1945 in every country that was brought under Nazi rule, in every city, in every village, in every concentration camp, Gypsies, like Jews, were persecuted because of their birth. By the end of the war, two thirds of Germany's thirty thousand Gypsies, a greater proportion of Austrian, Czech and Croatian Gypsies and tens of thousands elsewhere, were dead. Of those who remained in Germany, many had been sterilised, others had been crippled through slave labour. Although it is still extremely hard to put precise figures on the total number of dead, it seems that at least 130,000 Gypsies and maybe many more were killed as a direct consequence of racial policies pursued by the German state and its various allies in Italy, Croatia and Romania in particular (Zimmermann, 1996, pp. 381–83).

Although the special facility at the Auschwitz death camp, the Gypsy Family Camp, *Zigeunerfamilienlager*, which constituted the largest single concentration of Gypsies created during the war, only operated from March 1943 till July 1944, genocidal initiatives directed at Gypsies were proposed (and in part enacted) from the first to the last days of the war. Three weeks after the outbreak of hostilities, on the 21st September, 1939, at a conference called by the head of the Security Police, Richard Heydrich, it was agreed that the 30,000 German Gypsies were to be deported to 'General Government in Poland.' This deportation did not in fact take place—but only for administrative reasons. Two years later, in the late autumn of 1941, the first transports of 'racial aliens' were sent from Austria to the occupied territories. 5,000 Austrian Gypsy citizens accompanied 20,000 Jews. With more than half of these Romany deportees being children, and crammed together in a few buildings in the centre of Lodz (Littmannstadt), typhus and other disease spread with such rapidity that even the Germans became alarmed—particularly after typhus brought down the German ghetto commandant, Eugenius Jansen (Dobroszycki, 1984, p. 96). It was in fact in response to the difficulties of managing the ghetto at Lodz that the decision was taken to experiment with mass gassing at a camp in the village of Chelmno (Kulmhof) some fifty kilometres northwest of the city. A special commando unit that had been operating in eastern Prussia, carrying out euthanasia killings among Germans, was brought over and the first Jews were killed there in December 1941. Five weeks later, in January 1942 4,400 Gypsies were taken from the ghetto. Even using the primitive instrument of carbon monoxide poisoning in specially adapted vans, the Germans were able to kill at a rate of one thousand victims a day. The liquidation of the Gypsy ghetto was completed with almost no one noticing (ZSL Ludwigsburg, 203 AR-Z 69/59, Bd. 1; Dobroszycki, 1984).

Three months later, on the eastern Front, formal instructions were given to the Wehrmacht and other fighting forces that Gypsies were to be treated 'as the Jews.' In this situation, the Gypsies may actually have been the worse off. Jews who were captured might be subject to selection—the Germans needed skilled slave labour. Gypsies, lacking formal education, were shot upon capture. Wherever the Germans went, Gypsies fell: in the Ukrainian forests where they had sought refuge with partisan units; on the Baltic coast, where 800 of the tiny Estonian Gypsy population of 850 were dead by 1944. In the Reich itself, towards the end of the war, some Gypsies were given the possibility of having themselves declared 'socially adjusted.' If they then 'consented' to sterilisation they would be exempted from the oppressive and often murderous regulation of their people. Hanjörg Riechert, who researched this very practice, estimated that 2,500 German Gypsies lost the ability to reproduce thus (Reichert, 1995, p. 135).

In the Romanian wartime fiefdom known as Transdnistria, alongside one hundred and fifty thousand Jews deported from Bessarabia, at least twenty five thousand 'nomadic' and 'asocial' Romanian Roma were sent to starve to death; our best evidence suggests that possibly 40% of the deported Roma died there (Varga, 2005). On the Reich's southern front, in Serbia, Gypsy 'hostages' were shot alongside Jews and partisans; in neighbouring Croatia, the Ustashe-run camp of Jasenovac became the graveyard for somewhere between 50 and 95% of the Croatian and Bosnian Gypsy populations (Reinhartz, 1999; Jasenovac, 1997; Ackovic, 1995).

In brief, despite profound differences in the motivation, scale and intensity of the persecutions of Gypsies and Jews, the Romany peoples were threatened with extinction—and, had the course of the war turned otherwise, without the slightest shadow of a doubt they, like Europe's Jews, would have disappeared.

And yet, the mass murder and sterilisation of the Sinte, Roma and Gypsies provides, perhaps, the locus classicus in the modern world of a genocidal catastrophe denied and cast into public oblivion. Despite the efforts of a number of historians and activists, the general European public remains almost totally unaware of the Nazi treatment of the Romany peoples and in no European country are these persecutions taught as a part of the national curriculum. One saga is particularly telling in its absurdity. In 1992, the German Federal Government agreed to construct a memorial to the Sinti, Roma and Gypsies of Europe to go alongside the national monument to the Jews. They had only conceded after years of campaigning and direct action by Romany organizations. Seventeen years later, in the summer of 2009, the agreed location remains an ugly building site in a copse at the edge of the Tiergarten opposite the Brandenburg Gate and diagonally opposite Peter Eisenman's Memorial to the Murdered Jews of Europe. After much debate about the site itself and, more fundamentally, the purpose and meaning of such a memorial, the construction itself has been delayed to the point that, at its opening, it is conceivable that no adult Romany survivors of World War Two will be alive.

In this short text I want to link the particular character of the Nazi persecution of the Roma and Sinte with the treatment the genocide received after the war and its fate in terms of historical memory. In doing so, I hope to explain why this catastrophe remains contested, how the killing of Gypsies differed from that of Jews and why is it important to put the case of the Gypsies in the context of "denial" or forgetting since this is one of the factors that helps explain the terrible treatment accorded this day to many Gypsy communities in Central and Eastern Europe.

After the Catastrophe

For years after the Second World War ended, many Gypsy victims of the Nazis campaigned, some of them to the end of their lives, for proper acknowledgement of what they had been through as well as some sort of monetary compensation for everything they had lost. In the majority of cases this was a fruitless endeavour. In every case it involved the humiliating discovery that the attitudes that had sent them to the concentration camps were alive, flourishing and had found new legitimacy (Margalit, 2002, pp. 83–142). Take the case of just one man whose story is by no means atypical.

Berhardt Reinhard, a Sinto, or German Gypsy, had a fairly typical war for a person of his background and age. He was one of many socially consolidated German Gypsy families who had deep historical roots in the country, Reich citizenship, and a strong sense of belonging to the German nation. His family, who had settled in the city of Kassel in the heart of Germany, and in the smaller town of Fulda to the south, had been well integrated into local German society, and his conscription into the army at the outbreak of war was never in question. However, his service in the *Wehrmacht* was terminated early in 1943 when all Gypsy recruits were expelled from the armed services on racial grounds (Lewy, 2000, pp. 95–97). Immediately transported to Auschwitz, he was then transferred to Sachsenhausen in 1944, before the liquidation of the Gypsy camp. From there he was sent to Ravensbruck where, like other Gypsies who were exempted from extermination, he was forcibly sterilised. On the 9th of

January, 1945, he was conscripted into a military 'suicide' unit—a *Sonderkommando* of the SS named the *Dirlewanger*, after the convicted paedophile who led it. Originally the *Dirlewanger* had offered ordinary criminals and 'asocials' an exchange: service in lieu of internment in a concentration camp. As the German army collapsed at the end of the war, political prisoners and sterilised Gypsies were offered the same deal. Reinhard was among the luckier recruits. Badly wounded in the foot a few weeks later, he survived to the war's end.

Four years later, in November 1949, Bernhardt Reinhard applied for compensation for 'bodily and mental injuries' suffered between March 1943 and April 1945. The first doctor he saw declared that his wound and various persecutions, including his forced sterilisation, reduced his ability to earn an income by 50%. Since the minimum rating for compensation stood at 25%, he was assured a pension. But that was not at all the view of the people who would have to foot the bill, the Kassel welfare office. They immediately questioned his right to a monthly pension. First they wanted to be persuaded that the grounds on which he had been sent to Auschwitz were racial and not behavioural. If he had been deported as an 'asocial' this would not count as 'political persecution' under the terms the Allies had set for the compensation procedures.

Janos Korpatsch—on the right of the three men, here photographed in 1904
when his family were held at the German/Dutch border for several weeks,
unable to cross the frontier—became the object of a veritable show trial in 1936
when he was accused of being the King of the German Gypsies
by the Nazi controlled police in Frankfurt. Copyright, R.H. Postma.

The Fulda police, who had effected the deportation, confirmed that Reinhard's deportation was 'without doubt' racial in character. Kassel town hall then came up with a new objection. They suggested that since the *Dirlewanger* was a 'parole unit' his service there was presumably for a 'common misdemeanour' committed while in Ravensbruck. Since common criminals—even if they had been worked to death's door as slave labour in a concentration camp—were not eligible for compensation, this was a way to query the state's liability for his foot wounds at least. The Kassel authorities suggested that, for establishing the extent of his claim to compensation, his period of 'loss of liberty' should end in December 1944, before conscription into the *Dirlewanger.*

For six years the argument went back and forth. Every time Reinhard received a supportive or sympathetic testimony from a doctor or other assessor, the Kassel welfare office found new quibbles with his application. In 1956, it seemed he was in a winning position when all parties agreed that he was suffering 30% loss of earning capacity as a result of his sterilisation. But the town council then pointed out that he had not originally asked to be compensated for this 'intervention.' They asked him to demonstrate that his foot wounds—for which they did now accept liability—were causing him a similar degree of incapacity.

In the delay caused by this manoeuvre, a new public health officer took over his case and set the whole procedure to naught. In his view, the age of the applicant at the time of sterilisation, 22 years old, made it "unlikely that his personal development would have been unfavourably influenced by this intervention." He sent Reinhard back for yet further examinations, this time in the clinic of a Prof. Dr. Villinger and a Professor Dr. Sophie Erhardt, two people who were, you might say, particularly well qualified to understand where their patient was coming from. In November 1957 Werner Villinger had not yet been exposed as one of the higher ranking doctors involved in the secret "T4 action," the euthanasia murders of over 100,000 people in mental hospitals between 1939 and 1941. Sophie Erhardt had also managed to avoid prosecution for her work in the Racial Hygiene Office of the Reich, determining which Gypsies were to be sterilised and which sent to Auschwitz. No surprise then that they examined this case with uncommon thoroughness; nor at their perverse conclusion. They found the patient mentally and physically sound and complained that no adequate hereditary or medical reasons had been recorded to justify a sterilisation in the first place.

This superficially sympathetic stance was merely a cover for a cunning piece of sophistry: since he was in good health as far as the effects of his sterilisation were concerned, with no 'morbid perturbations' or 'psycho-neurological impairment,' there were no grounds on which to compensate him! Eight years after his original application for material compensation, Bernhardt Reinhard was turned away, with a formal decision from the Regional authority, on the basis that he had retained over 75% of his earning potential.

Zigeunerkamp in het Zuidoosten van Friesland, September 1904

Fascination with the distinctive life-style of Roma and Gypsies
sat comfortably beside the kind of official harassment
that stopped them travelling freely.

The single positive aspect of this development was that his lawyer was, at last, entitled to challenge the administrative decision in the courts. The Regional Compensation Office sensed that their apparently heartless stance might need defending and wrote to the Judge saying that Reinhard's tireless battle for a pension was, from their perspective, entirely understandable. It was a psychic reaction to his circumstances. 'Specifically,' they thought he might be suffering from what they dubbed 'a pension neurosis.' Their considered view was that were Reinhard now to receive a pension this would only serve to tie him to his past, reminding him every month of the original trauma. Compensation could only worsen his condition. It was thus not cold heartedness but their 'duty of care,' so they reasoned, to refuse him the money he requested. Once again the court found against his main application—though this time he was awarded a one-off payment for 'mental and bodily suffering.'

Reinhard bravely rejected the proposed settlement. And so a few months later he found himself once again publicly humiliated, this time at the regional appeal court, the senior judge of which told him that he should not think of comparing himself to the seventeen-year-old childless, sterilised girl whom they had just compensated. His puberty had come to an end and he had had two children before 'the unfortunate operation'. The judge did not mention that one of these had died in Auschwitz. He refused to alter the lower court's decision.

A full twenty years after the end of the war this doggedly determined and endlessly patient Sinto man won what he had originally sought. A change to the Compensation Law in 1965, allowed many disputed Gypsy cases to be referred back to the courts, his included. In 1963, the *Bundesgerichtshof*, the highest court of the Federal Republic, had broadened the legal responsibility of the state to the Gypsy victims by overturning a highly restrictive definition of the racial persecution of the Gypsies. Until this decision the courts only acknowledged *racial* persecution from the date of the implementation of the Auschwitz Decree (January, 1943). Any actions against a Gypsy before this date were presumed by the courts to have been due to their individual 'common criminality' or 'asociality'. As the radical shift of the 1963 decision worked its way down the legal system, Reinhard was re-examined by a doctor who, for the first time since his original examination in 1949, saw his case in its plain human dimension.

This new doctor penned a furious report, implicitly denouncing his forebears' narrow-minded approach to both the client and the law. If Reinhard had no immediate physical symptoms from the sterilisation that reduced his capacity to work, the fact that he had lost the ability to reproduce and that his marriage had collapsed under the double burden of both his and his wife's sterilisation was very much the concern of the law. He was awarded a monthly pension, backdated to 1944. It took another twenty five years for the Federal courts to award the now 68-year-old Reinhard something that, had he not been a Gypsy, he would have received at the outset of his application, a period of 'therapeutic treatment' in a sanatorium.[1]

Rendering the Romany Victims Invisible

What do we learn from the progress of Bernhardt Reinhard's application through the compensation offices and the courts?

The American and British military administrations after the war wished publicly to recognise all victims of the Nazis and, as a moral and political gesture, to reward them with financial compensation to be taken from the coffers of the German state.[2] They then, however, made a fundamental interpretive error by restricting the definition of the victims to 'racial' and 'ideological' enemies. In so doing they tied the hands of the future (German) administration by denying compensation to those who had been interned for any kind of common crime. The logic appeared flawless. Why should rapists, thieves, drunks or murderers be treated as victims of the Nazis? But for the Gypsies the logic was fateful. 'Asociality' counted in both popular belief and the legal

1   Many of the documents from this case are reproduced in Mettbach and Behringer, 1999, pp. 94–114.

2   The Soviet administration was only willing to compensate victims of 'fascism' and active fighters against it. Racial enemies of the Nazis were declared 'passive' victims and denied compensation (Margalit, 2002, p. 87).

system as a common delict and thus most Gypsies whose lifestyle had been classified as 'asocial' by the Nazis were denied access to the compensation funds.

In this way the interim allied administration failed to acknowledge that the Nazi system of criminal justice worked in deeply discriminatory ways against members of ethnic minorities and other social outcastes. Many Gypsies had convictions for petty offences like begging, loitering, selling goods without a licence or even holding foreign currency and since Nazi justifications for interning Gypsies always referred to their criminal tendencies, the Allied definition of political or racial victim implied that every Gypsy would have to go through a special procedure to establish their *individual* eligibility. But even more basically, the Allies failed to understand that by 1940, if not earlier, the whole of criminal law had been poisoned and perverted by political considerations. Central to this perversion was the crucial notion of 'preventive justice,' by which people could be imprisoned before any crime had actually been committed. What this meant in effect was the politicisation of ordinary crime. And after the outbreak of war the very distinction between 'ordinary' and 'political' crime was lost as the former was seen and punished as a form of opposition to the regime (Gellately, 2001, p. 78).

Still from a wedding staged for Austrian Radio in the early 1930s.
Gypsies in Central Europe were believed to have a special capacity
for taking pleasure in celebration. Copyright: Gerhard Baumgartner

With these erroneous procedures in place, especially as power and authority were handed back to the Germans, the Gypsies were ever more systematically excluded from procedures for official recognition and compensation. A punctilious and thrifty local bureaucracy, who felt charged above all to conserve their limited resources, allied itself with the plain prejudice of others involved in cases like these. The presence at all levels of the state bureaucracy of officials who had been active partners in the Gypsies' persecution meant that Gypsies came up against almost exactly the same prejudices as they had under the Nazis. In several regions of post war Germany payments of any compensation to Gypsies were limited to those who could prove they had fixed accommodation and employment (Margalit, 2002, p. 98).

And so while few officials would have dared after 1945 to use the anti-Semitic language and imagery of the war years to suggest to Jewish applicants that it was their membership of "a parasitic community" that had "tried to achieve world domination" that had given rise their persecution, Gypsy supplicants did not benefit from the same restraint. From the end of the 1940s people like Reinhard were told that the 'admittedly combative measures' taken against them were their own fault. It was the Gypsy character type, their 'antisocial behaviour,' 'crime,' and 'wandering drive' that were the root of the problem. And it was not just open racists who reasoned thus. Many officials who had not been directly implicated in the persecution of the Gypsies felt that while Nazi policies had been a little harsh they lay within the standards acceptable in time of war.

Even more widely shared was an implicit ranking of the different groups of victims in which the Gypsies invariably came towards the bottom. As the full extent of the criminality of the Nazi regime was revealed for the first time in 1945, it was only natural that the sheer, overwhelming scale of the Holocaust should provide the standard measure for all the other crimes of the regime. Those persecuted for their religious faith like the Jehovah witnesses and some other Christians were likewise quickly recognised. The mentally sick, apparently an embarrassment to all concerned, were forgotten; homosexuals, so-called 'asocials,' communists even and Gypsies all had a hard time asserting the injustice of their persecutions.

Sophie Erhardt, the anthropologist who had been called as an expert witness in the Reinhard case and who had worked during and after the war on Gypsy specimens taken from prisoners, easily aligned her own, deeply ambivalent stance, with views like these. In 1963, in the context of a debate about general compensation for all the forcibly sterilised, she wrote to the finance ministry in these terms:

> What would people say if some asocial alcoholic, who from the point of view of hereditary science (*erbbiologisch*) was wrongly sterilised, should from now on be treated as the equal of all those who, as reputable citizens, were tortured for years on end in concentration camps simply because of their race, their

beliefs or the political convictions. A compensation provision for the sterilised would in many cases lead to a disavowal and ridicule of restitution among right thinking minds (*echten Gedankens*).[3]

This moral hierarchy was in some respects built into the institutional structure of the Federal Republic. The compensation offices, for instance, used Nazi anti-Semitic ideology and practice as their point of reference for defining 'political' persecution. And the Gypsies struggling for recognition found themselves trapped within this logic.

The Fog of Genocidal Planning

For Roma and Sinte seeking financial compensation as well as moral recognition, their interest, indeed their obligation has been to assert the identity of the Jewish and Gypsy persecutions. Between 1950 and 1985 a political, legal and intellectual campaign was fought for the Gypsies to be included as victims of the Nazis. All efforts were focused on proving the courts wrong but this meant that the terms of the whole debate were set by the legal context. Given the procedures of the judges, the most persuasive, perhaps the only way to win the argument was to trace the evolution of Nazi policy to the Gypsies in dated, signed decrees and orders. It was with the help of such documentary proof, that the start date for 'racial persecution' was pushed back from January 1943, when Himmler signed the Auschwitz decree that sent most German Gypsies to concentration camps, to an earlier decree of the same office dated December 1938.

It is essential to understand that the pernicious influence of this misapplied model had little or nothing to do with the personal histories or the political stance of the individuals involved. This much became clear in the 1980s when a new generation of lawyers, prosecutors and judges came to office. Many were ashamed by the failure to identify individual perpetrators or hold anyone accountable for the persecution and genocide of the Gypsies and were determined to try and set the historical and judicial record straight. In a number of German cities, long-abandoned investigations into employees of the Racial Hygiene and Population Research Offices were reopened.

But time and again these reached a similar dead end. In Hamburg an energetic public prosecutor investigated a certain Ruth Kellermann who had worked alongside Sophie Erhardt carrying out individual racial classifications of all the Gypsies living in Germany. The case never made it to court. The prosecutor published a statement, explaining that "as regards the Gypsies a clear and traceable chain of orders, analogous to the order for the 'Final Solution of the Jewish Question' is missing." Since the only other charges against Kellermann fell under the statute of limitations, there was no

---

3   Cited in Mettbach and Behringer, 1999, pp. 107–8, original Schäfer, 2000, p. 251.

case to be answered. Two years later a similar investigation led to a prosecution of one of the 'small fish,' a former Block leader in Auschwitz. At the end of a three-year long trial, SS Rottenführer, Ernst-August König, was sentenced to life imprisonment in 1991 on three counts of murder in the Gypsy Family Camp at Auschwitz-Birkenau. But the more serious charge that these murders as well as his participation in organising transport to the gas chambers were evidence of involvement in genocide was dismissed. The judges reasoned that since the court had not been presented with an *order* for the extermination of all Gypsies they could not accept that König's actions had been part of a broader plan.[4]

Beyond questions of interpretation of bureaucratic procedure, there was of course another reason to cling to this version of history: an account of the racial persecutions of the Nazi era that stressed the culpability of the Nazi elite and exonerated the ordinary population fitted nicely into the myth of post-war Germany that Nazi policy was never an expression of popular wishes but rather the imposition of a Party leadership who forced their ideas on an unwilling population. According to this convenient story, the actual work of persecution was seen through by the SS and not by ordinary Germans. This was at best a simplification and in many respects a plain fabrication. After the effective closure of thorough de-nazification proceedings in 1948, those bureaucrats and very town hall employees who, as we shall next see, had participated to one degree or another in discriminatory practices, persecutions or even outright genocide had a clear interest in claiming that the Nazi regime had never been an organic part of German society. Uncovering the true story of the Gypsy genocide would have put the spotlight on precisely those layers of the professions who had successfully managed to whitewash their past, as we shall now see.

Four Steps to Genocidal Catastrophe

In the official treatment of the Roma and Sinti after World War II we see how a more or less mythologised version of the Jewish Holocaust, as the outcome of an order from the Führer, misled the legal and other professionals when they came to consider other persecutions. But even were officials to have operated with a more realistic understanding of how the Final Solution came into being, the judges and investigators would have had great difficulty sustaining an equation of the Jewish and Romany genocides. Let me be clear. I do not wish to belittle the treatment or fate of the Sinte and Roma. The point is rather that 'the Gypsy problem' occupied a totally different place in Nazi ideology than that of 'the Jewish problem.' Likewise, the measures necessary to exclude a socially and economically marginal minority from German society were not the same as those required to remove a highly educated and culturally dominant elite.

---

4   For these cases see, ZSL Ludwigsburg, 414 AR 540/83, Bd. 4, pp. 233 and 799.

I stress here some fundamental differences and derive these from the history of public policy towards these two minorities in the half-century and more preceding the Nazi takeover. For the Jews the institution and consolidation of the modern nation-state meant—in fits and starts but ineluctably nonetheless—their emancipation and integration into European societies, Germany included: Jewish legal and civil equality in the German states that was established during the 1860s, the great movement out of the ghettos and into the cities from the 1870s on and above all their integration into banking, trade and the professions, all this marked their passage to full members of the national citizenry.

For the Gypsies, the same period saw a decline in their status and a reversal of a number of 'privileges' or 'protections' from which they had benefited in the early modern social order. Even if they had occupied a radically marginal and often impoverished socio-economic niche and had profoundly circumscribed political claims, in localities where they could demonstrate longstanding affiliation they were subject to the 'protection' (*Schutz*) of the *Herrschaft* and, as Thomas Fricke has brilliantly demonstrated, found a substantial degree of integration into the local social order. The end of the 19th and beginning of the 20th centuries saw a set of institutional moves the effect of which was to exclude many Gypsies from the new social and political protections of the modern German state. Traditionally well-integrated and tolerated as the providers of cheap labour, until the early 19th century the Gypsies had lived a kind of caste-existence, providing specialised services to the otherwise more or less socially isolated and economically insulated communities of farmers in early modern Germany, bringing news of the outside world and purchasable tokens of modernity with them. With the rise of a mass, increasingly urbanised, consumer society, as all kinds of tradesmen, commercial travellers included, were coming under state regulation, the Gypsies found themselves caught in a whole new set of administrative procedures. In country after country local authorities sought to determine who was a legitimate 'salesman' and who was merely 'a Gypsy' using their wanderer's status as a cover for supposedly shadier activities.

The task of distinguishing one from the other was handed on to the body which, till then, had had the most systematic dealings with the Gypsies—the police. To facilitate what was in effect surveillance work the police composed registers of legitimate tradesmen and illegitimate ones (Gypsies)—creating card registers and even, in some cases, books of descriptions to enable rapid identifications. In Munich in 1905 Alfred Dillman published his synoptic work, 'The Book of Gypsies' building on over one hundred years of police documentation, providing aliases, locales, occupations and identifying features of different 'clans.' From this time on the issuing of what were called '*Wandergewerbschein*' or travelling-tradesman permits became a central point of conflict between Gypsies and the local authorities responsible for regulating their activities.

The police were in the frontline of the persecution of Gypsies before and during the war devoting relatively enormous resources to a small minority. Source: Burgenländisches Landesarchiv. Anonymous police photographer, 1930s. Courtesy of Gerhard Baumgartner.

The second negative shift for the Gypsies was the transformation of the old duty of the local *Herr* to provide for his 'own' poor into a nationally imposed obligation on the local authority to provide various forms of support (*Fursorge* or *Schutz* as in '*Kinderschutz*') for the locally registered needy, which led to all kinds of efforts to define the boundaries of responsibility and to the exclusion of many Gypsies from such social support. As Andreas Wimmer has argued, the first moves towards creating what was later to become the welfare state went hand in hand with restrictions on immigration (on the import of new potentially welfare-dependent persons) and with efforts to cleanse the population of problematic 'elements': 'the logic of inclusion and exclusion' that he sees as central to the specific form of 'social closure' that is a national community (Wimmer, 2002, pp. 57–64). With the 'nationalisation of the regime of mobility' those beyond the borders became de facto out of the 'realm'. But that is not the end of the matter. Since integration and exclusion are articulated around notions of national citizenship, questions of ethnic attachment and the status of persons and groups as 'proper citizens' acquire novel force. And these lines are drawn within the state. With limited resources to distribute among the needy the local state even has an interest in such demarcation work.

Moreover, the terms in which the nationalist 'compromise' on social solidarity among citizens was justified included powerful notions of social improvement. If *Kinderschutz* were to be handed out to the socially and morally dubious classes then one had to be assured that its effect was moral improvement. There was no single European language in which such socio-moral reform was couched, but across the political spectrum from left to right biology, psychology and sociology mixed in various combinations. With the rise of early genetic science, the possibility emerged, on the horizon, of population improvement by regulation of demography. Just as pasteurisation had made milk safe to drink for the masses congregated in the cities, so population science offered to de-contaminate the nation's demographic profile. In Germany in particular, even more than Italy, France or the United States, notions of eugenics, 'racial hygiene' and the language of 'degeneration, decay and corruption' took deep root amongst many intellectuals Graphic and lurid imagery, implicating not just the clearly alien like Gypsies but the poor, the alcoholic and, brilliantly vague term, the 'asocial', spread in the years before the war, turning illness itself into a political concern (Frevert, 1984; Evans, 2001). Under the Nazis, this trend led to a situation where anyone who 'stood out' or 'came to the attention of the authorities' (the German term *äuffalig* is hard to render exactly) because of their idiosyncratic or irregular comportment, might be labelled asocial and carted off for correction.[5]

It was in the police force of the new nation state that these various trends came together in a particularly pernicious constellation. The police in Germany, as a national

---

5   See especially Kranz and Koller, 1941, pp. 160–62 for this loose definition of the 'socially unadaptable' (*gemeinschaftsunfahig*).

institution, had in fact come into being partly in response to the perceived threat posed by 'rootless,' 'wandering' and 'hard-to-identify' criminally-inclined social groups, the '*herrenloses Gesindel*' (hordes of masterless men) and among those the '*Zigeuner*' in particular. The very first 'police circulars' and list of wanted persons had been created at the end of the 18th century to help track down families of Gypsies, and the gradual centralisation of the German state and modernisation of police procedures had, if anything, intensified their professional interest in this area of work (Lucassen, 1996; Fricke, 1996).[6]

With the rise of modern policing came the first efforts at scientific criminology, many of which were, inevitably considering the overall intellectual climate, couched in more or less biological terms. It was not necessary to have signed up to the agenda of Cesare Lombroso's rococo pseudo-science, to adopt the apparently innocent idea that 'if the father is a loafer and thief so will be the son'.

The police were being asked to determine administratively who was and was not a Gypsy, just as welfare services were deciding who was and was not a worthy recipient of public charity (with a considerable overlap in the families being labelled deviant) and leading criminologists and detectives were adopting notions drawn from the ever-expanding field of 'criminal biology' to account for the phenomenon of the 'incorrigible' or 'habitual' criminal. It was to deal with such that the police developed the final ingredient in this devilish broth: the adoption of a program of preventive detention. On November 13, 1933 the Prussian Minister of the interior announced the introduction of a new status of detention, *polizeiliche Vorbeugungshaft*, preventive detention. Habitual and sex criminals could now be indefinitely detained in concentration camps to prevent them committing the crimes to which they were biologically driven. After Heinrich Himmler unified the German police and security apparatus under his command in 1936 the number of persons held in such custody rose dramatically. A few hundred were in camps at the end of 1935 but mass arrests in March 1937 and in December 1938 took the number to over 13,000. At least 2,000 of those arrested in 1938 were 'Gypsies'—taken away for their asocial and 'work-shy' lifestyles. (Wagner, 1996, pp. 255–98; Buchheim, 1966).

In fact, this kind of treatment of Gypsies, though in a far less intense and aggressive fashion, pre-dated the Nazi takeover of the police. Indeed before 1933 Gypsies were subject to special police measures reserved only for the Gypsies and those who lived like them. In 1926 the state legislature in Bavaria passed a law that aimed to drive Gypsies, travellers and the 'work shy' out of the country. Among its numerous repressive measures, one stands out: any Gypsy over the age of 16 who could not prove regular employment could be sentenced to up to two years labour in a work house.

---

6   It is no accident that at the creation of Interpol, the pursuit of Gypsy criminals was identified as one of the specific tasks that this form of transnational cooperation would permit.

This was punishment for a disposition, not an actual crime, and the sentence was renewable (Strauss, 1986). This was a model of the kind of preventive policing that the Nazi Reich's Police Administration (RKPA) was to adopt after the reorganisation of the police in 1936. Then, following the 'father to son' logic, once they had detained the son, the whole family and clan should follow: and thus the persecution of the Gypsies became what Henriette Asseo has called a 'familial genocide'—a persecution carried out through genealogical records and on family social structures.

The Decisive Role of the Municipal and the Local

There is one final ingredient—beyond their exclusion from the trading and craft niche, their exclusion from welfare and their inclusion amongst the biologically predisposed to crime—that was needed for the institutional encirclement of the Gypsies to become complete: the power of local conflicts to create apparently unstoppable desires for someone to 'sort things out'. After 1933, few ever thought to 'get rid of *the* Gypsies,' but the coming to power of a regime proclaiming national regeneration unleashed these great currents and in locality after locality officials began to work out ways to 'get rid of *these* Gypsies here.'

To understand the dynamic of the Gypsy persecution we have to turn to the activities of civil servants, the Mayors, town planners, welfare officers, policemen, university lecturers, members of scientific research institutes who dealt with Gypsies in the course of their normal work routine. It was in the offices of these academic and town hall racists, in the cells of the Frankfurt and Münich criminal police, on the plots of the compulsory municipal camps of the Ruhrland where Gypsy families were visited by racial scientists hunting for the gene of 'asocial behaviour,' in the university Departments of Anthropology and Racial Health, in the 'hereditary health' (sterilisation) clinics run throughout the Reich by the City Health Office and then in the various concentration and death camps that *local, individual* 'solutions to the Gypsy problem' were found. If we try and read all the local initiatives and approaches as the unfolding of some central plan, or the inevitable consequence of structural features of Nazi rule we can never make sense of what happened.

In the case of this despised, socially isolated minority at the bottom of the social scale, Nazi rule offered the chance to thousands of people, civil servants and party men in particular, but plenty of ordinary citizens as well, to turn their private agendas into state policy. The author of the most authoritative survey of the Jewish persecutions, Saul Friedlander, explains that the majority of Germans shied away from widespread violence against Jews, urging neither their expulsion from the Reich nor their physical annihilation. But in relation to the Gypsies and other marginal groups, public opinion lay not so far from Nazi policy. Public order, social reform, a return to a 'healthy community' of productive workers, the re-evaluation of the rural idyll of farmer and

his family in their *hof,* 'a national community without criminals'— these were popular slogans among the German electorate. In fact one wonders if the fact that Gypsy policy was not tainted by an association with Nazi fanaticism was precisely what enabled these orderly people to use the opportunities presented by National Socialism so enthusiastically.

Burgenland was the zone in Europe where the greatest percentage of Roma and Gypsies died in World War Two. Burgenlandisches Landesarchiv. Courtesy of Gerhard Baumgartner.

But while keen local bureaucrats, 'ordinary citizens' in every other respect, innovated and initiated, in Berlin, both Chancellery and Ministerial headquarters not only lagged behind but deliberately dragged their feet. During the 1930s and even into the war, officials in various ministries committed themselves to producing a 'Reich Gypsy Law' that would create a unified and consistent approach to the Gypsies and replace the incoherent old policy by which each district would expel as many Gypsies from its own territory as it could, leaving its neighbours to fend for themselves.[7] But nothing ever came of these promises.

It was at the interface of central inertia and local mobilisation of new state resources that Gypsy policy developed. If we take the early development of the Gypsy camps as an example of this process, we see that what began as slightly stricter versions of municipal camps for travellers metamorphosed gradually towards ethnic internment lager. In fact the appearance of continuity is deeply misleading, for the *Zigeunerlager* can only really be understood in the broader context of the entire 'camp system' that the Nazis were in the process of constructing.[8] Like the scores of miniature Concentration

---

7   See, for example, Dr. Zindel's letter to State Secretary Pfundner of 4th March, 1936 and his 'Thoughts on the design of a Reich Law for the Gypsies.' There we find promises of rapid new and specific proposals, but there is no further trace of these in ministerial papers. Bundesarchiv, Berlin R 18, R1501 5644, pp. 215–27.

8   See Newborn, 1993, especially, Vol. III.

and Labour Camps that sprung up in 1933, the municipal Gypsy camps had a characteristically ad hoc and local nature (Burleigh, 2000, p. 198–205). Above all, they had no legal basis whatsoever—not even by executive decree. In creating them each city council operated more or less as it saw fit using whatever Circular Instructions were in operation at the time. In Berlin, an instruction to establish a 'manhunt day' to track down Gypsy criminals provided the pretext.[9] In Hamburg, a year later, the Mayor turned to the Decree of December 14th on the Preventive Struggle against Crime, the provisions of which allowed closed camps for 'improvement,' through labour, or, helpfully, for 'sundry other purposes.'[10] Just as the legal basis of the camps was determined by unchecked local power, so, in the absence of any overarching Regulation, each camp developed its own system of regulations.

If the evolution of the

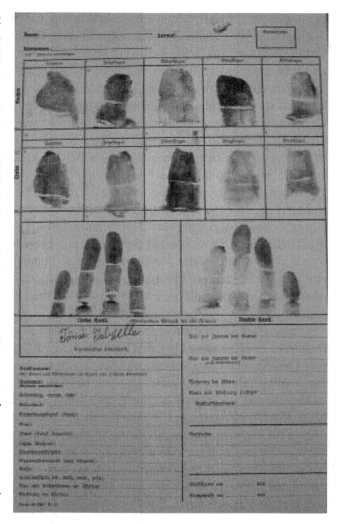

During and after WW1 many European Police forces started to issue special identification cards for 'Gpysies' or 'nomads' who were, supposedly 'hard to identify'. Later these registers were used by the Nazis to identify Gypises for deportation. Großwarasdorf/Veliki Boristof StadtArchiv. Courtesy of Gerhard Baumgartner.

9   In Frankfurt the same decree was used to justify the 'sedentarisation' of 'domestic' Gypsies.

10 "Grundlegender Erlass über die Vorbeugende Verbrechensbekämpfung durch die Polizei." Confidential, unpublished decree, circulated in the *Erlasssammlung* Nr. 15. Available at the Institut fur Zeitgeschichte, Munich.

camp order was not planned at the outset this does not mean it was determined entirely by chance. While a camp like Marzahn was set up in order to make Berlin *zigeunerfrei* for the foreign 'guests' at the Berlin Olympics almost no thought was given to how order would be maintained. Once in existence, by an almost ineluctable logic, regulations were introduced which governed an increasing number of the inmates' activities. Within a short period a camp superintendent and a police watch had been appointed: what was the point of forcing all the Gypsies to live in one place if not to control their activities and to reduce the threat they posed to the surrounding population? The coming and going of residents could be restricted to departure for work (eight to ten hours) or for shopping (a much more limited time allowed for those without work). To ensure the Gypsies obeyed these rules a register could be kept of all departures and arrivals. To enforce registration, punishment would be introduced for failure to present oneself. And what was the point of controlling the movement of the Gypsies if outsiders were allowed free entry?[11] As this ever-sharper residential and physical segregation of the Gypsies was implemented so blatant discriminatory measures were also introduced, followed by their gradual exclusion from the last remaining bastion where Gypsies had a place in German society, the school system. And little of this required decrees, laws or written orders.

Later when central orders were issued, as in the decisive Auschwitz decree of December 1942/January 1943, this itself can better be seen as the outcome of a struggle between different wings of the Reich Security apparatus created by Himmler's insistence that a small minority of 'pure' Gypsies be exempted from some of the regulations hitherto aimed at all Gypsies. The *Kripo*, convinced that matters were getting out of hand, used evidence from the racial hygienists to argue for the deportation of 'the rest' of the Gypsies, the so-called '*mischlinge*'. The most fateful decision as far as the German Sinte and Roma were concerned emerged, if this interpretation is correct, not as an effect of pure ideological or value commitment but from the way existing conditions, conceptual commitments and political struggles intertwined at a particular conjuncture (Zimmermann, 2007).

Prevention?

Why does any of this matter? Well, first because of the historical record and its impact on later generations. I have carried out research for over twenty years among Romany populations in the countries where these persecutions took place. Throughout this time I have been aware that the lack of recognition of their racial persecution and genocide undermines trust and fuels fear of new persecution. The descendants of victims look at the peoples among whom they live influenced by a knowledge that is rarely openly articulated. Day by day, this influence is hidden. It is not talked about in public. But the

---

11 For Marzahn, see Sparing, 1997.

sense of persecution is quietly transmitted from generation to generation. As part of my doctoral research I lived with Romany-speaking Gypsies in Hungary in the 1980s and I found that the Rom barely bothered to recall or discuss the distant past and their experiences of the war. There was not even a term in Romany for 'the holocaust.' An American Romany intellectual had coined the term *pharajmos*, the 'devouring', but none of the people I knew had ever heard of or used this word.[12] And yet they had not forgotten the war.

Shortly after I returned to England I discovered just how vividly the past lived on. Hungary was at this time going through a rapid political liberalisation, one consequence of which was that the police no longer repressed the small numbers of home-grown 'skinheads.' Groups of shaven young men toured the country playing their brand of rock music and painting racist graffiti wherever they went. Slogans like 'Gypsy Free Zone' appeared on bus stops and factory walls. And then something strange happened. Throughout the summer of 1988, a series of what the media called 'skinhead hysterias' swept the Romany communities of Hungary. The men and women amongst whom I had lived were caught up in one such collective panic attack in June 1988. One night on a wall facing the settlement where they lived someone had sprayed, 'we'll be back to get the stinking Gypsies.' A few days later an elderly Gypsy woman had seen a car full of skinheads pass through the main square, or maybe she had seen skinheads gathering there; the stories varied. On her return home the self-defence of the settlement was agreed. The twenty-eight Gypsy families living nearby moved at once into three houses in the centre of the settlement. At night, the men armed themselves with spades and pitchforks and kept watch. In other villages across the country similar incidents were taking place. And in every case, when interviewed, the Roma gave the same explanation: the fascists were coming back to kill them.[13] I have written this paper partly in response to such fears, maybe to help lay them to rest. There is little in the position of Roma in Europe to celebrate but a repeat of those persecutions seems, for the time being at least, unlikely.

There is also is a broader lesson that the Romany genocide can teach us that speaks beyond the particular case. If we accept that the Nazi persecution of the Gypsies does count as genocide then it may be necessary to rethink our understanding of the crime of genocide. Ever since Rafael Lemkin, the Polish-Jewish scholar who coined the term *genocide*, first wrote on this topic in 1943, the scholarly and legal tradition has assumed that this is a crime carried out with a 'special intent' and invariably involves the execution of a plan. This genocide, however, shows that it is possible to arrive at

---

12 In fact since the original term was *porrajmos* but because this also has an obscene meaning it has recently been rejected by most Hungarian Romany speakers who use the calqued term *Holocausto* or use a more appropriate Romany form, *sa madaripen*, 'the killing of everyone'. Both these have the advantage of being closer to common usage than the rather literary invention of '*porrajmos*.'

13 See e.g. Udvardy, 1998, p. 5; Hámor, 1998, p. 7.

The ambiguous status of Romany economic activity—as alms-seeking or begging for which the peasants then demanded domestic service in return—left the Roma with an indelible reputation as 'work-shy.' This folk notion played into Nazi plans to reform the folk community around notions of the productive citizen. After the war the Communist Parties took over a very similar ideological opposition to Romany economic strategies. Burgenlandisches Landesarchiv. Courtesy of Gerhard Baumgartner.

a genocidal solution of a social 'problem' without the political leadership or central authority of a state coming to an explicit decision or formulated 'intention' as the International Genocide Convention misleadingly has it.

This is by no means a purely academic matter. In 1993, a fellow anthropologist prophetically pointed out that the outside powers were misrecognising the policy of ethnic cleansing being pursued by Franjo Tudjman and Slobodan Milosevic in former Yugoslavia against the Bosnian Muslim population. At a conference held in December of that year, eighteen months before the massacre of Srebrenica, Cornelia Sorabji argued that a 'holocaust' model was hampering understanding of this new genocide. She suggested that in this case a 'franchise organisation' had been adopted by Serbian and Croat leaders. This made the ethnic cleansing appear anarchic and decentralised (Sorabji, 1995). Haphazardly using schools, factories, abandoned collective farms as their detention centres, the Bosnian Serb forces made it appear as if these were 'merely' improvising temporary solutions for holding and neutralising enemy combatants and their supporters.

But destandardisation and disorderliness did not imply a lack of organisation. Rather there was 'organisation of a different type in a different political, historical and cultural setting' (Sorabji, 1995, p. 86). One of the ex-inmates of Omarska camp in North-East Bosnia appeared astonished when asked whether the torture there was organised: 'Anyone could come there and do whatever they liked.' Or, as another man detained in the same camp explained, "Omarska camp was open for all those Serbian volunteers who had someone of 'their own' in it, some captive on whom they wanted to vent their rage."[14] I suspect that this model of genocide is in fact the historical norm and what one might call the 'Wannsee-Auschwitz model' the exception. Predictable outcomes may arise from a persecution that has plenty of regional variations, a variety of different routes to killing and even divergent ideological justifications for the crime.

Surveying the catalogue of 20th mass crimes from the Turkish killings of the Armenians in 1915, through the massacres of around one million persons in Bali in 1965, the thirty-six-year-long campaign against the Mayans in Guatemala, carried out under cover of an anti-insurgency war from 1960 to 1996, through to the horrors of Darfur today, where again a restrictive definition of genocide is allowing the Sudanese government to dispose of a troublesome minorities, we can discern a clear enough pattern.[15]

Every genocide at the moment it takes place appears to outsiders to be ambiguous and inherently implausible. The world turned the other way during World War II, preferring not to believe. It allowed the criminally incompetent to represent it in Bosnia in the form of a UN envoy whose hand-wringing and procrastination allowed the ethnic cleansers to turn his presence into one of their primary devices for pursuing a mass crime. It claimed not to have time to notice in Rwanda and, as I write, it is shamefacedly looking at its collective feet, denying that the slaughter in Darfur is properly speaking genocide and hoping no one will force it to take action against the criminal regime in Khartoum. It is only after the event that genocides appear with certainty and without ambiguity to have taken place. It is only in their aftermath that world leaders and the peoples of the world behind them vow that they must never happen again. It would be absurd to imagine that the research that underpins publications such as this will alter this profound disposition to incredulity and inaction in the face of such man-made catastrophes. The desire to disbelieve is as built into the individual psyche as it is into the structure of the present world order. But it may set the record straight for one group of victims and it should alter our understanding of the way mass murder occurs.

---

14   Cited Sorabji from Hukanovic, 1996, p. 56.

15   In fact, as a younger generation of German historians has demonstrated, the same argument applies to the development of the Holocaust. Focussing on the period before the Wannsee conference, Ulrich Herbert, Dieter Pohl and others have shown that the practical preparations and to some extent even the intellectual origins of the Final Solution lay less in plans conceived in Berlin than in the improvisations of commanders on the ground on the eastern Front and in the former Polish territory of the General Government. The fate of the Gypsies in this sense is not so different than that of the Jews before the meeting on the lake in Berlin (Herbert, 2000).

Bibliography

Ackovic, Dragoljub (1995). *Roma Suffering in Jasenovac Camp.* Belgrade: Museum of the Victims of Genocide, Roma Culture Center.

Buchheim, Hans (1966). "Die Aktion 'Arbeitscheu Reich'" in *Gutachten des Instituts für Zeitgeschichte* 2. Munich: Institut fur Zeitgeschichte, pp. 189–95.

Burleigh, Michael (2000). *The Third Reich: A New History.* London: Macmillan.

Dillman, Alfred (1905). *Zigeuner-Buch.* Munich: K.B. Staatsministeriums des Innern.

Dobroszycki, Lucjan, ed. (1984). *The Chronicle of the Lodz Ghetto, 1941–1944.* New Haven: Yale University Press, pp. 96, 181–94.

Evans, Richard (2001). "Social Outsiders in German History: from the Sixteenth Century to 1933" in *Social Outsiders in Nazi Germany,* eds. Gellately, Robert and Nathan Stolzfuls. Princeton: Princeton University Press, pp. 20–44.

Frevert, Ute (1984). *Krankheit als politisches Problem: Soziale Unterschichten in Preussen zwischen medizinischer Polizei und staatlicher Sozialversicherung.* Gottingen: Vandenhoek & Ruprecht.

Fricke, Thomas (1996). *Zigeuner im Zeitalter des Absolutismus. Bilanz einer einseitigen Überlieferung: eine sozialgeschichtliche Untersuchung anhand südwestdeutscher Quellen.* Pfaffenweiler: Centaurus-Verlagsgesellschaft.

Friedlander, Saul (1997). *Nazi Germany and the Jews 1. The Years of Persecution, 1933–1939.* London: Phoenix Giant.

Gellately, Robert (2001). *Backing Hitler: Consent and Coercion in Nazi Germany.* Oxford: Oxford University Press.

Hámor, Szilvia (1998). "Börfejűek pedig nincsenek..." (But there aren't any skinheads...), *Népszabadság,* 6 August 1998, p. 7.

Herbert, Ulrich (2000). *National Socialist Extermination Policies: Contemporary German Perspectives and Controversies.* Oxford: Berghahn Books.

Hukanovic, Rezak (1996) (1993). *The Tenth Circle of Hell: A Memoir of Life in the Death Camps of Bosnia.* New York: Basic Books.

Jasenovac, sistem ustaskih logora smrti... (1997). Beograd: IS «Strucna knj.» actes en serbe d'un colloque de 1996.

Kranz, Heinrich W. and Siegfried Koller (1939, 1941). *Die Gemeinschaftsunfahigen: Ein Beitrag zur wissenschaftlichen und praktischen Losung des sogenannten «Asozialenproblems»* 1–2. Giessen: Karl Christ.

Lewy, Guenter (2000). *The Nazi Persecution of the Gypsies.* Oxford: Oxford University Press.

Lucassen, Leo (1996). *Zigeuner. Die Geschichte eines polizeilichen Ordnungsbegriffs in Deutschland 1700–1945.* Cologne: Bohlau.

Margalit, Gilad (2002). *Germany and Its Gypsies: A Post-Auschwitz Ordeal.* University of Wisconsin Press.

Mettbach, Anna and Josef Behringer (1999). *"Wer wird die nachste sein?" Die Leidensgeschichte einer Sintezza, die Auschwitz uberlebte/ "Ich will doch nur die Gerchtigkeit" Wie den Sinti und Roma nach 1945 der Rechtsanspruch auf Entschadigung versagt wurde.* Frankfurt: Brandes & Apsel.

Newborn, Jud (1993). "'Work Makes Free': the Hidden Cultural Meanings of the Holocaust." Unpublished PhD thesis in Dept of Anthropology, University of Chicago. 3 vols.

Reichert, Hansjörg (1995). *Im Schatten von Auschwitz: Die Nationalsozialistische Sterilisationspolitik gegenuber Sinti und Roma.* Munster: Waxmann.

Reinhartz, Dennis (1999). "Unmarked Graves: the Destruction of the Yugoslav Roma in the Balkan Holocaust, 1941–1945." *Journal of Genocide Research* 1, no. 1 (1999): 81–9.

Schäfer, Wolfram (1998). "Flüchtlinge, Vertriebene und 'Neubürger' in Marburg um das Jahr 1950" in *Marburg in den Nachkriegsjahren.* Vol. 2: *Aufbruch zwischen Mangel und Verweigerung,* eds. Hafeneger, Benno and Wolfram Schäfer. Marburg: Rathaus Verlag, 2000.

Sorabji, Cornelia (1995). "A Very Modern War: Terror and Territory in Bosnia-Hercegovina" in *War, a Cruel Necessity?: The Bases of Institutionalized Violence,* ed. Hinde, Robert A. and Helen E. Watson. London: I. B. Tauris, pp. 80–95.

Sparing, Frank (1997). "The Gypsy Camps" in *From "Race Science" to the Camps: The Gypsies during the Second World War,* eds. Fings, Karola, Herbert Heuss and Frank Sparing. Hatfield: University of Hertfordshire Press, pp. 55–70.

Strauss, Eva (1986). "Die Zigeunerverfolgung in Bayern: 1855–1926." *Giessener Hefte für Tsiganologie* 3 (1986): 31–108.

Udvardy, János (1998). "Bőrfejű-hisztéria Borsodban" (Skinhead hysteria in Borsod county), *Népszava,* 21 July, 1998, p. 5.

Varga, Andrea and Nastasa Lucian, eds. (2005). *Tiganii din Romania (1919–1944).* Bucharest: Centrul de Resurse pentru Diversitate Etnoculturală.

Wagner, Patrick (1996). *Volksgemeinschaft ohne Verbrecher: Konzeptionen und Praxis der Kriminalpolizei in der Zeit der Weimarer Republik und des Nationalsozialismus.* Hamburg: Hans Christians.

Wetzell, Richard F. (2000). *Inventing the Criminal: A History of German Criminology 1880-1945.* Chapel Hill: University of North Carolina Press.

Wimmer, Andreas (2002). *Nationalist Exclusion and Ethnic Conflict: Shadows of Modernity.* Cambridge: Cambridge University Press.

Zimmermann, Michael (1996). *Rassenutopie und Genozid: Die Nationalsozialistische "Losung der Zigeunerfrage".* Hamburg: Hans Christians.

Zimmermann, Michael (2007). "Die Entscheidung fur ein Zigeunerlager in Auschwitz-Birkenau" in *Zwischen Erziehung und Vernichtung: Zigeunerpolitik und Zigeunerforschung im Europa des 20. Jahrhunderts,* ed. Zimmermann, Michael. (Beitrage der Geschichte der Deutschen Forschungsgemeinschaft, Band 3). Stuttgart: Franz Steiner, pp. 392–424.

Zentrale Stella der Landesjustiz (ZSL) Ludwigsburg, 203 AR-Z 69/59, Bd. 1.

Zentrale Stella der Landesjustiz (ZSL) Ludwigsburg, 414 AR 540/83, Bd. 4.

Zsuzsanna Vidra

"THE UNHIDDEN JEW"
Jewish Narratives in Romany Life—Stories

During the Second World War, Roma in Hungary were exposed to different forms of persecution. Historical research (Karsai, 1992) shows there was no all-embracing anti-Roma legislation issued at government level that aimed to destroy the whole Roma population. As a consequence, while in certain parts of Hungary Roma fell victims to the worst of persecutions—being deported to the concentration camps—, in other parts of the country their lives, at least, were not in danger. However, because of the enhanced xenophobic and anti-Roma climate that characterised the war period (Szita, 2004), even those who lived in regions immune from deportations had to face various types of abuse and maltreatment. That is to say, while they did not become actual victims, they were in every sense "potential victims". It is this element of "potentiality" that makes this group and their situation in the war period special. In this paper, I will focus on this latter field, which has received relatively little attention: narratives of Romany people whose communities escaped the deportations. I will argue that the Roma who did not suffer direct persecutions still experienced a kind of exclusion that resulted in a consciousness among the first and second generation Roma after the war that differed from that of the rest of society. The difference can be identified in narratives, at points where people of Romany origin talk about and remember Jews differently from the non-Roma.

The interviews on which I base my argument were conducted in the framework of a research project that aimed to reconstruct Romany ethnic identity through the analysis of various narratives and discourses.[1] I set out with the aim of making life story interviews with the members of a Romany community in a post-communist town in the North East of Hungary, a region that had been badly affected by the economic and social changes that followed the fall of the communist regime in 1989. As in all post-communist societies, the Roma as a social group were the worst affected by the negative consequences of the transition. The interest of my chosen locality lies in the fact that the social integration of Roma during communism, and then their massive downward social mobility after the changes, could be well observed in that town, which had been a show-case example of the communist type of industrialisation. The political intention to integrate the Roma was very closely related to the enhanced demand for manual labour in the growing heavy industry sector: the Roma were mobilised to take the unskilled manual jobs (Diósi, 1999). My original goal was to

---

1   Interviews were conducted in 2004 and 2005.

explore how individuals of Romany origin who benefited from the "generous" integration offer of the communist system lived through the radical downfall, what kind of social and ethnic identities they constructed for themselves in the communist and the post-communist era. It was to my great surprise that in their life narratives my interviewees told shorter or longer stories of Jews that they knew or heard about. In fact, this notable presence of the Jews in the narratives caught my attention and led me to explore the question in more details.

To account for this phenomenon, I found that the conclusions and methodological approaches of both the oral history tradition in Roma Holocaust research (Bársony and Daróczi, 2005; Katz, 2005) and the narrative studies developed to explore the remembering strategies of different generations of Germans after the Holocaust (Rosenthal, 1991; Rosenthal, 1998) should be used.

Firstly, to understand the importance of the oral history method in Roma Holocaust studies, it is worth outlining the most essential concerns in this field of study. Despite the very different historical paths and cultural contexts, the "othering" (labelling) of Jews and Roma went to some degree parallel[2] until it reached its tragic climax during the Second World War (Sonneman, 2002; Willems, 1997). The bumpy road that led to the recognition of "other victims" of the Holocaust, including the Roma, was paved with opposing arguments as to who counted as a victim, whether the same fate affected the two peoples and if the same term could be used to refer to the persecution of the Jews and of the Roma. By now, the argument has been more or less settled and Roma are acknowledged as having been victims of the Nazi persecutions (Margalit, 2002; Vidra, 2003).

Nonetheless, historiography still has a lot to explore and explain; in most countries there is very little Roma Holocaust-related research, and this is true of Hungary too. In fact, not only the scientific community but society as a whole is far from recognising the full significance of the Roma Holocaust. There have been, however, some very important contributions intended to address the burning issue of the almost completely forgotten persecution of the Roma in Hungary during the Second World War. One of the earliest works that addressed the topic using scientific methods is László Karsai's monograph (Karsai, 1992) which examines how the anti-Roma legislation of the pre-war period eventually led to the final persecutions. The historian relies on archival sources to account for the course of events. Other researchers argue that the "true story" can only be grasped through personal narratives since the fate of the Roma was much less systematically recorded than that of the Jews, and therefore it is sometimes only individual stories that can reveal the unfolding of the events. Hence the importance

---

2   Similar imagery was constructed about Jews and Gypsies in European societies that both have lingered on for centuries. The idea of diaspora people created the (eternal) vagrant as well as the dangerous foreigner/stranger who corrupts the soul and mind of the autochthon people. (See Willems, 1997, p. 9).

of the oral history approach. The first to conduct interviews with survivals were János Bársony and Ágnes Daróczy, as well as Katalin Katz, who published very important collections of the victims' testimonies as well as the Roma Press Centre publication entitled "Porrajmos. Roma Holocaust Survivors are Remembering" (Bernáth, 2000). Although information about the topic is scarce, it is known that the treatment of Roma often depended on the local authorities, who could decide what to do with "their Gypsies". That explains why, as has already been mentioned, there were regions where the entire Roma population fell victim to the deportations while in other regions where they were exempt from the worst forms of persecution (Bársony and Daróczi, 2005; Karsai, 1992; Katz, 2005; Szita, 2004; Vidra, 2003).

Secondly, the relevance of narrative studies on the Holocaust should be explained. As I have pointed out, amongst my Romany interviewees—members of both the war and the post-war generations—the "Jewish theme" came up spontaneously and naturally, in contrast to what is usually observed with (non-Romany) others, whose main narrative strategy is to gloss over the theme. Rosenthal calls this reticence or narrative silence about the victims. This is why my observation that the Roma I interviewed were not in the least reluctant to talk about the Jewish victims and Jews in general (on the contrary, they themselves mentioned them without any sort of prompting) led me to apply Rosenthal's model to my special case. This is bound to reveal the peculiarity of the "potential victim" Roma narratives.

Rosenthal distinguishes three major characteristics of life narratives, particularly when they are related to war or other traumatic experiences. These are: narrability, biographical and social function of remembering. The first one, narrability, refers to the *ability to remember*, more precisely remembering in an articulate way, that is to say, to be able to tell a story about our own experiences. One of the basic assumptions is that remembering requires a certain structure: we cannot remember chaos but only something that has a form. We remember sequential events and we remember them even more vividly and in a more organised manner if the events can be connected to specific places. The second important aspect of narrability is whether the experience we want to recall is one that we had to suffer *passively* or whether we could take an *active role* in the course of events. The third dimension is the extent to which the experience was traumatic. The last two, passivity and trauma, are related. The more passive we were and the more traumatic the experience was, the less we (want to) remember.

The second characteristic of life narratives is the biographical function of remembering. This means that the particular experience has a certain relevance to the person in making his or her life-story into a consistent, meaningful narrative. War experience, Rosenthal says, is a typical example of an event that has a very important biographical function.

The third element, the social function of remembering becomes important when the question of responsibility—either individual or collective—arises. Rosenthal mentions various strategies that are used to avoid facing the questions of "what I did or should or should not have done in the war, especially in relation to the Jews". One of the strategies is *reticence* about the theme of the Holocaust as well as the *avoidance* of mentioning the word "Jew". Typically while "remembering" the fate of the Jews during the war, a person using the "avoidance strategy" would say something like: "they disappeared" or "they went away" etc. They would never really say what actually happened to them. Also very often the Jews are *dehumanised* in these narratives, that is to say they do not have names or professions, etc. Another characteristic that Rosenthal found in these narratives was that Jews were sometimes made *responsible for their own fate*. The fourth strategy is *inversion*, the commutation of perpetrator and victim: "We were all victims of national socialism"—is a phrase often used by her interviewees. If someone feels that s/he too was a victim of the regime, s/he can avoid the question of responsibility. It is very important to bear in mind that the mechanisms at work in the social function of remembering are the ones that are handed down from one generation to the next. The grandparents' silence and other techniques of narration are equally present in their children's and grandchildren's life stories.

The Stories Told by Romany People: the Jew Gets Unhidden

I have chosen one interview with a woman of the war generation for a more detailed analysis and several other interviews with people belonging to the post-war generation to demonstrate how people of Romany origin use the "Jewish theme" in their life narratives. I will analyse the interviews by applying the three dimensions of life narratives developed by Rosenthal: narrability and the biographical and social functions of the narrative. First of all, I will select the most memorable phrases of the narratives that are connected to the Jewish theme. In this first part I follow the chronological order of the stories; in the next chapter I will analyse the stories using the above-mentioned three characteristics of life narratives.

Pre-war Period

At the very beginning of the interview my interviewee—an 80-year-old Romany woman—describes the district where she and her family lived before the war.[3] "We lived in Magyar Street. One Gypsy, one Hungarian and some Jews lived there as well.

---

3   I wanted to keep the anonymity of my interviewees and that is why I avoid using the name of the town. As regards the names of the people mentioned in the interviews, I replaced them with similar names so that their identity should not be revealed either. Street names I left intact since they are "typical names" that could be found almost in any town in Hungary.

(…) There was no problem about who was a Hungarian and who was a Gypsy." Later on, while still talking about her life before the war, she mentions that "György Vári had a shop there which used to belong to Goldmann, the Jew." Another link between her and her family and the Jews in the community before the war is also mentioned in the interview: "Men[4] were working for the baron and the rich Jew."

She is still talking about the pre-war period, describing her job (she worked as a maid and a cleaner) when she mentions a detail that interrupts the chronology of her story. She says: "I was walking with my mother towards the Király Hotel. It had a courtyard where the Jews were gathered. But that happened much later, I've left out something from the story." She tries to follow a very strict chronological order, however, the mere mention of the place itself evokes her memories of the ghetto, something that she did not mean to talk about at this point of the interview but only later, when she got to it in the story.

War Period

She starts talking about the war period by telling a long story in which the ghetto gets a meaning and it is revealed why she was emotionally touched by it.

The second time I was at my aunt's place the Jews were there, working in the field. Suddenly, I see someone and he calls me. He says: "Are you from 'O'?" It was Béla Weiss, he had a cinema in the village where they built the brewery later on. (...) "Are you going home, my dear", he asked. I said yes. He says, "Tell my mother that I'm alive and I'm doing fine!". So we came home and I asked my family where the Jews were. They were all closed up in that courtyard. "Don't go there!", said both my mother and father.—"If the soldier catches sight of you, he'll throw you in and they will take you as well!". But I couldn't relax. I told myself I had to tell his mother, it would please her. I knew his mother. We used to go to their cinema. It cost thirty fillers a ticket. I liked the cinema a lot. So I went there. The soldier was walking up and down. "How shall I do it, what should I do?" In fact there were a lot of Jews. Oh my God, so many of them closed up there! Fenced in with barbed wire. I think they could have escaped if they wanted to. I don't know why they didn't break out. I would have fled. So when the soldier was not looking I ran to the fence and I told the first person I saw behind the fence that he should tell Béla's mother that he was doing fine, working in "R". Then I ran away. So I did it. It was very risky, especially for a Gypsy. They could have thrown me in there. There were so many of them! I had to do it. My conscience made me do it. I promised so I had to do it.

---

4   She refers to Gypsy men. Street names I left intact since they are "typical names" that could be found almost in any town in Hungary.

There is another episode that she mentions in relation to the ghetto and the Jews, which explains why she was so emotional about the subject, besides the fact that risking her life would have been enough to make her emotional. "I was very angry with Mr. Balogh, the butcher. He told me: 'They've taken away the Jews and now it's your turn, Gypsies!'" Then she continues the story: "They were taken away, very few came back. They didn't come back. They were burnt."

Chronologically an interesting episode follows: "Very few came back. The ones who did come back have died or gone either to Budapest or to Israel. No Jews left here. Only a few. I don't even know any of them. Although there used to be a lot. Oh my God, a lot. But we were afraid of them. Because they killed that girl, for her blood. Eszter.[5] I know it's not true, but we can still hear it. And in my childhood my mother used to tell me: "Don't go to the Jews to make up the fire because they'll kill you, they need your Christian blood!" Yes, I am Roman Catholic." After describing the ghetto scene so vividly and talking about the destiny of the Jews she mentions the ancient blood libel argument that is related to anti-Judaism. It will be worth accounting for this important detail in the analyses of the narrative.

Post-war Period

For my first interviewee, the "Jewish theme" ends more or less with the war. When asked about post-war memories of the Jews, she keeps referring back to the pre-war period and laments at the fact that so few came back. I have already mentioned that the model incorporates not only the war- but also the post-war generations' narrative analysis. That is to say, it is possible to reach conclusions regarding the mechanisms of intergenerational transfer of attitudes and narrative modes. Now, I will illustrate the way in which the Jews are typically referred to using extracts from interviews with Romany people born after the war.

> *We were sitting around the fire after the pig-killing and slowly someone took up his violin or accordion and started to play music and drink, and then they would go to the Jewish shop to buy a few pitchers of wine. He would give us the wine for free,[6] we did not even have to ask for it. (Mr. H.)*

---

5   My interviewee refers to the infamous Tiszaeszlár blood libel that stirred emotions in Hungary in 1882. A 14-year-old Christian peasant girl named Eszter Solymosi was a servant in the home of a Jewish family in Tiszaeszlár. One day she did not return from her duty. Rumour was quickly spread that the girl had become a victim of Jewish religious fanaticism who needed Christian blood for the preparations of the upcoming Passover. Some political agitators instigated the public against the Jews, resulting in a number of violent acts and pogroms.

6   This actually means on credit.

*There were lots of Jews there, in my district. There was this little man with
the moustache, he was of Jewish origin. Then there was this man called
Ernő. There were a lot of them. Then a motor-mechanic, we could go and
rent electric household equipment from them, a vacuum cleaner, a washing
machine, a spin drier, and so on. Also a sportsman lived there, too. So there
were a lot of Jews there. (Mr. F.)*

*I remember there was a Jewish man called Ernő Braun who had horses and
he always called me to go and help him. So we did and helped to put tiles and
bricks on the cart. He would always give us some money; that was my pocket
money. I watered his horses and washed them. (Mr. V.)*

Analyses: the Jew Gets Narrated

Firstly I will analyse in detail the interview with the war-generation woman and then
the accounts of the post-war generation interviewees, relying on the three dimensions
(narrability, biographical and social function) of the narrative analysis model.

War-Generation

As I pointed out narrability has the following three important characteristics: the story
has a form which is most often manifest in the chronology; the events can be more
easily evoked if the person was active and if the event was not too traumatic.

My interviewee insists on the chronological order. Rosenthal observed that places
make stories easier to remember. The interviewed woman was moving around a lot
during the war and she could easily connect her experiences to these different places.
She was also very active throughout, it was her own decision to risk her life to pass the
message to Béla's mother. The traumatising experience for her was when the butcher
threatened her. At this point becoming a victim became a real possibility. As long
as she could make decisions by herself (approaching the ghetto), she could think of
herself as a brave person. Even her parents advised her not to go there and warned that
she could be taken away as well. This explains why she was so convinced that the Jews
could have broken out from the ghetto if they wanted to: because she was an active
agent in her story.

The potential victim's perspective at one point almost becomes a victim's perspective
when the interviewee is threatened. Very interestingly, when she is intimidated by the
butcher, so when she is made a victim in a narrative sense, she defends herself in a
narrative way by taking an active role. She says: "I wished he would die, and he did a
bit later." Since she never became a real victim but remained a potential one, she could
keep her active role. In her narrative she killed her aggressor with her words.

As I mentioned, in her chronology after very meticulously describing the events
related to the Jews and her connection to these events, she came up—unexpectedly—

with the blood libel argument at the end of the story. One explanation could be that at this point of her narrative she was emotionally deeply moved: this is suggested by many details in the interview. All the horrors she had been describing in the narrative suddenly evoked in her another horrific memory: the image of the Jew who kills Christian girls for their blood, something she used to be threatened with as a child. So the horror that she saw (Jews gathered in the ghetto), the horror that she knew was connected to it ("They were burnt") and the actual horror that she had to go through (risking her life) finally made her remember another horror: the blood libel. It is fear that links these elements of the narrative, fear so great that the chronology was turned upside down. Up to this point of the narrative she had carefully kept to her chronology; then suddenly she went back in time, to her childhood, when she had been scared with the blood libel story. The repulsion she felt over the destiny of the Jews—that they were burnt, something that was unimaginable and unbelievable for her—evoked in her another memory of repulsion—killing for blood, which she also knew that was unimaginable and unbelievable: "It is not true!"—she said.

The second dimension of the narrative is its biographical function. Events that do not fit in with everyday routine, such as war-time, have to be somehow integrated into a person's life narrative; he or she has to make sense of them so that his or her life becomes and remains a coherent, meaningful story. For my interviewee, what had to be interpreted and integrated into her life narrative was the fact that she was on various occasions a potential victim, for example as a Gypsy girl threatened with "being taken away". This explains why she was not reluctant to talk about Jews: the experience she had with them during the war had a relevance to her own life and as a consequence to her life narrative.

The social function of the narrative in Rosenthal's research refers to the different strategies employed to avoid the fate of the Jews during the war. The first strategy is *reticence* over the Holocaust and the Jews. Rosenthal says that her interviewees avoided even mentioning the word "Jew". Nothing related to Jews is part of their life narrative. They "do not remember" them, either from before the war, or during the war. My findings differed from the typical non-Roma narratives[7]: in my research I found that Jews and their fate during and after the war appeared as part of the interviewees' life narrative. My first interviewee remembers them from both before and during the war. It is obvious that the two elements of her story mentioned above, risking her life while approaching the ghetto and being threatened by the butcher, made her emotionally involved in these events. Her experience of having her life threatened may explain why her narrative is different from the majority social group narratives.

---

7   My control group was the non-Romany habitants of the same community with whom I also conducted life story interviews. These interviewees would never mention anything about Jews in the town.

Apart from the fact that that Jews are part of her life narrative, the most significant difference between these narratives is the mention of what had finally happened to the Jews. Rosenthal underlines in her study that most often the fate of the Jews is expressed as "They disappeared" without actually saying what really happened. The potential victim's strategy is different. My interviewee says overtly what the others probably also know but would not say: "They did not come back. They were burnt."

The strategy of *dehumanisation* also serves to cover up reality. Jews have no names, no identity. Rosenthal says that in Germany the process of the psychological elimination of the Jews, that is to say depriving them of all human characteristics, started in the decade before the war. In my interview there are several episodes that illustrate that for this woman the dehumanisation strategy was not an option. She mentioned the names of Jews who were deported and said that they were killed. Not mentioning the names of murdered people is usually part of the dehumanisation strategy. Someone we pretend not to know or someone who does not have any human characteristics recognisable for us (names, for example) helps us disregard their existence as well as their deaths. The deportations were more real to this woman than to "ordinary Hungarians". Probably that is why she does not feel ashamed and does not use the narrative strategy of dehumanisation.

Making Jews responsible for their own fate was found in the narratives of members of the majority social group. In my interpretation this is the false rationalising strategy of the social function of the narrative. Rationalising, because it tries to articulate an answer to the troubling question of "why and how it happened". False, because it obviously gives an explanation that is not only untrue but irrational as well. Anti-Semitic arguments are used to support this strategy, such as the claim that the Germans would never have done that if they hadn't been given orders by people who were behind the scenes, the capitalists of the world (Rosenthal, 1998).

My interviewee also uses this strategy. At the end of the story when she talks about the Jews she mentions the blood libel argument. As we have seen, one possible reason why she came up with this at the end of the narrative is that her emotional involvement in the story and in its narration evokes in her the horrors of her youth, when children were terrified by stories of Jews killing them for their Christian blood. However, another interpretation of this could be that she felt the urge to seek an explanation for all the dreadful things that had happened to the Jews. According to the "making the Jew responsible" strategy they had to be killed or they would have killed us. Although rationally she denies this—"It is not true!"—the fact that in her narrative it stands at the end of the Jewish story implies that unconsciously she did seek an explanation and this was the only one she could come up with. She was unconsciously looking for an explanation and finally found an irrational one in her subconscious.

The function of her irrational anti-Judaism is analogous with the anti-Semitic reasoning used by the people interviewed by Rosenthal. Given my interviewee's social status it is more likely that anti-Judaism was at work, passed on by priests and by common superstition, than political and ideological anti-Semitism.

The *inversion strategy*, exchanging victims and perpetrators, is very common: we also suffered a lot, we are victims as well. My interviewee's memory of how the butcher threatened her right after she had mentioned the Jews, might be interpreted as treating herself as another victim.

Each person's suffering is real and is the only real suffering for him or her. No one can be reproached for mentioning, remembering and weeping over his or her suffering. The suffering of the other or the others is something one can only imagine and can only "feel" if one is empathic enough. Therefore, the meaning of the narrative strategy of inversion can only be understood in the context of the whole narrative and bearing in mind that it actually has a purpose—a social function. The social function, as I have pointed out, is that not remembering the Jews, depriving them of human characteristics, making them responsible for their fate and exchanging them with perpetrators all serve to avoid admitting individual responsibility for the events. Mentioning one's own suffering without mentioning the suffering of the other is part of this strategy. And mentioning it and at the same time using all the other three strategies indicates that the social function is being satisfied. In my interviewee's case the social function of the narrative is much weaker than in the other examples. She does not use the dehumanisation strategy. But she uses the other two narrative strategies: inversion and making the victims responsible. However in her case, the latter two strategies do have a different meaning. When making the victims responsible for their own fate she uses an anti-Judaic argument and not an anti-Semitic one, which she herself doubts. As for the inversion strategy, she really was a potential victim: it is only by chance that in this particular community Romany people were not taken away and killed. Nevertheless, the butcher's comment shows that the potential within the majority population to make them into real victims was there.

Post-war Generation

So far, I have been focusing on a narrative from the pre-war and the war periods. To study the intergenerational transfer of the narrative modes, it is the social function of the narrative that is of relevance. Thus, by examining the typical features of the "Jewish theme" in post-war personal accounts, we can enrich our findings regarding the differences between the "non-victim" and the "potential victim" narratives by integrating the intergenerational transfer aspect.

To arrive at a meaningful interpretation of the stories of the post-war generation interviewees, the explanatory categories should be applied in reverse order. The reason for this is that the transfer of narratives (and the emotive elements underpinning the narratives) from one generation to the other is best detected in the social function aspect. Narrability and the biographical function imply direct personal involvement in the events evoked during the narration whereas the social function can be understood as a reflection of the consequences of personal or collective actions or non-actions in the course of events.

The Romany interviewees tell stories of their experiences with their Jewish neighbours from the post-war period.[8] As a matter of fact, the "Jewish theme" comes up spontaneously in the narratives. This is all the more important as the "Jewish theme" was erased from the consciousness of the post-war generation as a consequence of the failure to collectively come to terms with the fate of the Jewish population during the war and to account for the responsibility of the Hungarian state and people in the events. The narratives of my Romany interviewees mirror a different consciousness, one that is not reluctant to mention Jews. We could thus conclude that the *social function* of the narrative is somehow differently constructed in the case of the Roma than in that of the non-Roma; neither avoidance nor dehumanisation is at work. It is equally true of the *biographical function* and the *narrability* of the stories. The presence of the theme in the narratives reflects the fact that interactions and relationships with the Jews were relevant in several ways to the lives of these people. As for the narrability of the theme, the relationships and interactions with Jews are located in specific places (the shop, the neighbours' house, etc.) which structure and prompt memory so that the story becomes tellable.

Concluding Remarks

The initial observation on which this study is based is that my interviewees of Romany origin have narratives which diverge from the "mainstream narrative" when talking about Jews. In my interpretation this phenomenon is indicative of their "potential victim" status during the war. The use of both the oral history method and the explanatory narrative analysis model enabled me to show that a different "collective consciousness" and historical recollection originating from the "potential victim" situation generates a different narrative pattern whose most important characteristics is the conspicuous presence of the Jewish theme among people belonging to both the war and the post-war generations. The majority of the narrative techniques observed among non-Roma narrators were absent. I also concluded that transfer of narrative modes did indeed take place. In contrast to the narratives of the post-war majority society, my Romany interviewees born after 1945 openly and spontaneously shared stories about their Jewish neighbours without using any narrative techniques to hide or avoid mentioning the ethnic origin of the people in question.

As to the factors that might explain the differences in narratives, the wider social context should also be taken into account. In my opinion the "potential victim"

---

8   Most of these stories refer to the 1950s, the childhood period of the interviewees.

situation in itself cannot provide a comprehensive answer. It can account for some of the differences arising from the generally enhanced fear that most of the Roma experienced during the war. However, to reach a more inclusive answer, it is not enough to rely on this factor alone: we must consider another one, too: the social status of Roma before and after the war.

In this respect, two factors seem to explain why mentioning the Jews seems to be natural and self-evident in Roma narratives but not in non-Roma narratives. One is that the Roma had been on the margins of the society both physically and symbolically. We have statistics which show in the pre-war period 80% of the Roma lived in segregated Gypsy settlements on the outskirts of towns and villages (Stewart, 1994) and only a very small proportion of them had proper school education or jobs before the Second World War. For example, the data show that in that period 50% of Roma children had no schooling at all (Kemény, 2000); in other words, their ideological indoctrination was not 'institutionalised'. As a result, although they shared to some extent the popular images of the Jews, they were exempt from the political anti-Semitism that prevailed at that time. They were 'social and discursive outcasts' from society.

The other explanation is that after the war the new regime's policy with regard to the Holocaust was to hush up what had happened. As a result two or three generations grew up without taking account of the Holocaust (Kovács, 2003). The Roma started to be socially integrated into Hungarian society during the communist period, very slowly and not very successfully, but at least to a much greater extent then ever before. Their social integration also allowed them enter 'our national discourses'. Nevertheless, their historical consciousness was their own and was very different form that of the majority society. They kept family narratives of persecutions that sometimes intersected with those of the Jews. In other words, two generations of the majority society were socialised in such a way that nothing was mentioned about the Jews and their history in general or about what had happened to them in this particular community. The Roma, however, because they had different memories and because this kind of socialisation started later for them, had fewer of the unconscious obstacles that prevented the majority society from talking about Jews.

Bibliography

Bársony, János and Ágnes Daróczi, eds. (2005). *Pharrajimos. Romák sorsa a holocaust idején I–II* (Pharrajimos. The fate of Roma during the Holocaust). Budapest: L'Harmattan Kiadó.

Bernáth, Gábor, ed. (2000). *Porrajmos. Roma Holocaust túlélők emlékeznek* (Porrajmos. Roma Holocaust survivors remember). Budapest: Roma Sajtóközpont.

Diósi, Ágnes (1999). "A cigányság ügye a demokratikus ellenzék történetében. Interjú Havas Gáborral" (The Roma issue in the history of the democratic opposition. Interview with Gábor Havas). *Esély* 11, no. 6 (1999): 83–99.

Karsai, László (1992). *A cigánykérdés Magyarországon 1919–1945. Út a cigány Holocausthoz* (The Gypsy question in Hungary, 1919–1945. The path to the Gypsy Holocaust) (Budapest: Cserépfalvi Könyvkiadó.

Katz, Katalin (2005). *Visszafojtott emlékezet. A magyarországi romák holokauszttörténetéhez* (Supressed rememberance. The history of the Holocaust of the Hungarian Roma). Budapest: Pont Kiadó.

Kemény, István, ed. (2000). *A magyarországi romák* (Roma of Hungary. Budapest: Press Publica.

Kovács, Mónika (2003). "Holokauszt oktatás Magyarországon" (Teaching the Holocaust in Hungary). *Regio* 14, no. 2 (February 2003): 88–106.

Margalit, Gilad (2002). "On Ethnic Essence and the Notion of German Victimization: Martin Walser and Asta Scheib's Armer Nanosh and the Jew within the Gypsy." *German Politics and Society* 20, no. 3 (March 2002): 15–39.

Rosenthal, Gabriele (1991). "German War Memories: Narrability and the Biographical and Social Functions of Remembering." *Oral History* 19, no. 2 (1991): 34–41.

Rosenthal, Gabriele. ed. (1998). *The Holocaust in Three Generations: Families of Victims and Perpetrators of the Nazi Regime*. London: Cassell.

Sonneman, Toby F (2002). *Shared Sorrows*. Hertfordshire: University of Hertfordshire Press.

Stewart, Michael Sinclair (1994). *Daltestvérek. Az oláh cigány identitás és közösség továbbélése a szocialista Magyarországon* (Time of the Gypsies. The survival of the vlach Gypsy identity and community in the socialist Hungary). Budapest: T-Twins, MTA, and Max Weber Alapítvány.

Szita, Szabolcs (2004). "A romák kirekesztése és deportálása. A cigány holokauszt kutatásáról." (The exclusion and deportation of the Roma. On Gypsy Holocaust research) *História* 24, no. 2–3 (2004): 61–64.

Vidra, Zsuzsanna (2003). "Public Discourses on the Roma Holocaust: A Case Study from Hungary" in *Open Minds. Europe in Global World—Blending Differences*, eds. Gawronska-Nowak, Bogna, Justyna Grochowalska, Jaroslaw Jura, and Grzegorz Walerysiak. Lodz: University of Lodz.

Willems, Wim (1997 [1995]). *In Search of the True Gypsy: From Enlightenment to Final Solution*. London: Frank Cass.

Contemporary Manifestations

Giovanni Picker

NOMADS' LAND?
Political Cultures and Nationalist Stances vis-à-vis Roma in Italy[1]

In May, 2008 Italian Prime Minister Silvio Berlusconi signed a decree declaring the "state of emergency in relation to settlements of communities of nomads."[2] Within nine days an ordinance was issued by the government ordering identification (including fingerprints) of people "also of minor age" living in the "nomad camps."[3] Five weeks later this decree was condemned by a European Parliament resolution stating that "collecting fingerprints of Roma [...] would clearly constitute an act of direct discrimination based on race and ethnic origin."[4] Nevertheless, the Italian government continued collecting personal data, and in July 27, 2008 the Minister of Interior Roberto Maroni gave a justificatory speech to the Parliament which led to numerous heated criticisms. Maroni's explicit rhetorical rationale was that the emergency status' salutory goal was to give identity to those living in the nomad camps who lacked ID cards. His clear concern during the speech was to work around the potential accusation of racism by stressing that "in the ordinance we never speak about Roma, but only about nomad camps. Therefore, this is not an ethnicity-based measure, but one which deals with a *de facto* situation [*situazione di fatto*], meaning the unauthorised nomad camps."[5]

---

1   I presented a previous version of this paper at the 2009 ASEN conference at LSE. I wish to thank the organisers and the participants of the panel on 'Minorities and the Mediterranean' for their helpful questions. I am also grateful to Arnold Ross and Andrea Kirchnopf for their insightful comments.

2   The text of the decree is available at http://www.poslazio.it/opencms/export/sites/default/ sociale/social/resourceGalleries/docs/decreti_e_regolamenti/D.P.C.M._21_05_2008.pdf [accessed January 2010]. The excerpt quoted is my translation.

3   The text of the ordinance is available at http://www.governo.it/GovernoInforma/Dossier/ Campi_nomadi/ordinanza_campania.pdf [accessed January 2010]. For an overview of the living conditions in the nomad camps, see Brunello, 1996 and ERRC, 2000; about their everyday implications on predicaments concerning legal status and access to citizenship rights, see Sigona and Monasta, 2006.

4   The European Parliament resolution is available at http://www.europarl.europa.eu/ sides/getDoc.do?pubRef=-//EP//TEXT+TA+P6-TA-2008-0361+0+DOC+XML+V0//EN [accessed January 2010].

5   The text of the Minister's speech is available at http://www.camera.it/_dati/leg16/lavori/ stenbic/36/2008/0723/s030.html [accessed January 2010]. The excerpt quoted is my translation. On the Minister's reasons for going on collecting data, see also: *La Repubblica*, 2008.

This series of events in spring and summer 2008 is part of everyday national politics vis-à-vis Roma in contemporary Italy; ever since the Berlusconi election of 2008 the government seems to have been carrying out a consistent "boundary-making process separating 'us' from 'them' according to principles that contrast with the hotchpotch of identities in pre-modern empires" (Wimmer, 2002, p. 52). Frequent forced evictions, political rhetoric blaming Roma for creating insecurity, and intolerance in political speeches, characterise the political discourse (Loy, 2009; Tavani, 2005).[6] Due to its relevance and its rather grave character, this discourse merits close-up critical attention, shedding light on its major elements.

The four major topics in such discourse are almost identical to the main themes in Maroni's speech, namely: 1. Deviance: Roma are said to be dangerous, and often criminals; 2. Nomadism: Roma are said to be vagrants, and for this reason hardly able to adapt to a modern sedentary way of life; 3. Security and legality: Roma are a threat for urban and national security, and the citizenry must be protected in everyday life with substantial policy measures; 4. Necessity of social policies and assistance coordinated between national and local authorities: Roma need to be assisted by social policies which can guarantee social integration in order to prevent deviance from spreading amongst them.

This policy is part of a deep-rooted xenophobic tradition against Roma in Italy (Colacicchi, 2008; Piasere, 2005) but contains two key novelties which make an analysis of its constitutive elements rather difficult. First, this was one of the first occasions when a usually locality-based issue, i.e. the "Gypsy problem" (Sigona, 2005) became a national issue, paving the way for nationalist measures. Second, those four major issues cannot be easily identified as belonging to a particular political culture, being neither clearly centre-Left or centre-Right-wing. It is crucial therefore to begin to recognise that this is not simply another instance of a typical Right-wing exclusionary idiom regarding social integration and multiculturalism, features traditionally associated with Left-wing politics. I therefore wish to raise here the rather obvious question: in which analytical context should the Italian authorities' measures be heuristically located?

When we focus on the unwinding of current nationalist policies vis-à-vis Roma, two sub-text issues can be detected that might explain its popular consensus. Since the early 1990s there has been in the public sphere an anti-immigration sentiment, largely rooted in fear of the stranger and fuelled by moral panic around petty crime and insecurity (Dal Lago, 1999; Maneri, 2001; Migione and Quassoli, 2002; Mura, 1995; Petrillo, 1999). A further sub-text is a rather long legacy of prejudices against Roma, filled with mythological tropes such as "the wild nomad" (Piasere, 2006) or "the kidnapper Gypsy woman" (Tosi Cambini, 2008), part of a world-wide narrative

---

6   For a detailed description of the governmental measures vis-à-vis Roma since 2006 see
     ERRC *et al*. For a legal point of view, see Trucco, 2008.

(Hancock, 1997). Moreover, a recent study shows that Italians in their negative opinions about Roma rank only just above the Czechs, who have the most racist opinions in Europe (Vitale and Claps, 2010).

Attention to this problematic intersection between anti-immigration sentiments and the anti-Roma legacy in Italian policies has been only partially analysed. Però (Però, 1999) explored the practices of the local municipality in Bologna in confining a group of Roma refugees in a camp close to a dog pound at the very edge of the town, and the rhetoric of tolerance and reception with which the operation was carried out. Piasere (Piasere, 2006) attempted to scrutinise the constitutive elements of the xenophobic discourse vis-à-vis Roma in Italy, examining how in the politically conservative context of Verona in 2005 people were mobilised against Roma settlements; the study of the prejudicial role played by the images of the "wild nomad Gypsy", so widespread in music (in Bizet's Carmen, for example) and other domains is worthwhile.

Moreover, Sigona (Sigona, 2003) showed how the assumption of nomadism underpinning regional policies was used to label Roma fleeing the 1990s Kosovo as nomads and "keep them as 'enemies', not 'strangers'" (Sigona, 2003, p. 76), secluding them into camps. Saitta (Saitta, 2008) found a similar pattern in the management of Roma by Sicilian local authorities, describing how criminal policies, when fuelled by the Berlusconi government's anti-Roma stance, prevent the implementation of long-term measures targeted at social integration. Finally, Vitale (Vitale, 2009) comparatively accounted for the demagogy of Italian policy makers in putting forward arguments in favour of the evictions and confinement of Roma as advantageous practices without any evidence. It is done also by exploiting the already-existing stereotypes on Roma.

From these studies we learn about three major tendencies in recent Italian institutional behaviour toward Roma. First, immigration seems to be the basic background against which those policies are carried out; second, the labelling of subjects against whom policies are targeted seems to be a key prerequisite, important decisions being made on the basis of an abstract image (e.g. nomad–nomad camps) rather than the mere material social conditions of those subjects; third, it seems that both Left- and Right-wing parties carry out exclusionary practices vis-à-vis Roma. The main analytical concern of those studies is the outcomes of policies and practices; however, it is rare to find analyses which link material living conditions of Roma with the forms of knowledge and the political culture that underlie Italian policies and institutional practices vis-à-vis Roma. Under which social conditions has the current nationalist xenophobic political stance vis-à-vis Roma in Italy emerged, and in which political culture does it find its main references?

To answer this question, in this article I shall carry out a comparative analysis of the public discourse in which the boundary-making process has been occurring over the last twenty years in two cities: one centre-Left wing migration context, Florence, and one centre-Right wing, traditionally non-migration context: Pescara.

I shall organise the comparison of these cities around two independent variables, namely the local public discourse and institutional practices with regard to Roma, and the arguments put forward by local Romani grassroots associations struggling for social rights and recognition. Instead of carrying out a thick description, which would require a narrow focus on the present-day situation, I will discuss the main results of the historical part of my ethnographic research. My standpoint is the anthropological relevance of understanding nationalist xenophobia against Roma in Italy and beyond, acknowledging the importance of alternative voices coming from Roma themselves. I will show that the current nationalist idiom consists of two overlapping discourses, namely the discourse of social integration and the discourse of deviance, and that they are both predicated upon the hazy category of "nomads".

Historical and Theoretical Framework

The best method by which to begin to dissect the constitutive elements of the nationalist boundary-making process concerning Roma in Italy is to view the events of 2008 from a distance. This means asking a basically naïve question: How was it possible for the Italian government to mask (or be unable to recognise) the racist stance behind the 2008 decree ordering the forced identification of people living in the nomad camps? One possible explanation comes from Wimmer's (Wimmer, 2002) understanding of nationalism as a natural product of modernity: "nationalist and ethnic politics are not just a by-product of modern state formation or of industrialization; rather modernity itself rests on a basis of ethnic and nationalist principles" (Wimmer, 2002, p. 4). According to the author, nationalism is a twofold process of politicisation of ethnicity and social closure. The politicisation of ethnicity implies a political emphasis on ethnic boundaries: "Each step towards integration reinforces the political importance of ethno-national categories. It brings forth new categories of people declared aliens and excluded from the realms of the nation. The emergence of national identities is closely associated with that of 'ethnic minorities' (Williams, 1989)" (Wimmer, 2002, p. 62). Given the functional and symbolic role of classification suggested in previously mentioned studies it is possible to recognise that the cover-all label of "nomads" is a key issue in policies vis-à-vis Roma. The idiom of nomadism is particularly powerful because it captures both a cultural and a social specificity. The former allows authorities to rhetorically organise the difference between "us" and "them" according to a distinctive way of life; the latter allows them to legitimise the implementation of measures designed to turn an exotic behaviour into a socially adaptable one. Therefore the idiom of nomadism simultaneously serves the interests of both social exclusion and integration, and for this reason it can be used to mask differentialist and discriminatory rhetoric and practices.

Social closure, the other side of the nationalist process, can be seen as having five dimensions, namely: 1. Politics—excluding foreign rulers; 2. Military—excluding mercenaries; 3. Social security—excluding immigrants; 4. Culture and Identity—excluding ethnic and religious minorities; 5. Law—excluding aliens. According to the Italian government's mainstream discourse Roma fall under three of these dimensions: social security (as immigrants); culture and identity (as ethnic particularity), and law (as aliens and deviants). While the first two dimensions are traditionally bound up with a conservative and explicitly exclusionary right-wing political tradition, the importance of the guarantees that underpin the rule of law is more commonly the concern of Left-wing progressive political culture. Apparently, a new recipe mixing traditionally conservative and progressive idiom offered a fruitful strategy for the government to justify its racist policies.

In the context of the new immigration towards Europe nationalism, far from being embedded in race-based exclusionary arguments, has been predicated upon a radicalisation of the understanding of "culture" (Taguieff, 1988; Stolcke, 1995). In particular, "culture" is seen by nationalist politicians as a force capable of merging individuals into homogeneous essential entities, theorising incommensurability between "cultures". More generally, this political rhetoric contextualizes culture "within a political process of contestation on the power to define key concepts" (Wright, 1998, p. 14). This phenomenon has been named "cultural fundamentalism" (Stolcke, 1995, p. 8) and "cultural essentialism" (Grillo, 2003), designating a characteristic orientation of the New Right in Europe.

However, in the Italian context, Però (Però, 2005; Però, 2007) analysed the turn from a class-based to a culture-based definition of migrants put forward by the Left in Italy and across Europe immediately after the collapse of the Communist regimes. He pointed to the discrepancies between the inclusionary rhetoric and the exclusionary practices of the Italian Left vis-à-vis migrants in the 1990s. Moreover, Stacul (Stacul, 2006), elaborating on the insights of Holmes (Holmes, 2000) has focused on the emergence of "integralism" in the Italian context as drawing authority: "from a broad range of collective practices that implicate family, language groups, religious communities, occupational statuses, social classes, etc. They create political orientations that defy easy categorisation, because they recombine ideologies such as nationalism, conservatism, liberalism, as well as populism with their identity politics, and are both 'Left' and 'Right'" (Stacul, 2006, p. 165).

This theoretical vision of interpenetrating institutions and biography informs the following empirical study, uncovering the way the boundary-making process vis-à-vis Roma has been occurring in two very different local settings. In the conclusion I will extend this argument about the anthropological relevance of understanding the idiom of exclusion of Roma to the national level and even beyond the borders of Italy.

Left-wing Florence

Since 1970, the year in which the Italian Regions as political bodies were officially created, Tuscany has been ruled continuously by Left-wing parties and coalitions. Since the end of World War II there has always been a dominant Left-wing political culture involving mass participation and self-conscious class struggle (Pratt, 2003). Between 1988 and 2000 the regional council issued three laws exclusively concerning Roma; at first these involved the construction of nomad camps, but later shifted to foreseeing alternative housing solutions. Since 2000 Amalipe Romano, a Romani grassroots association, has been actively struggling for cultural recognition and social rights.

From above

In the autumn of 1987 a roadblock was organised by some of the inhabitants of Castello, a neighbourhood on the outskirts of Florence. The protest was against about a hundred people who were driving around without a fixed place to stay, just living in damaged caravans (Colacicchi, 1996). On October 13, 1987, the local authorities ordered "the transfer of those nomads to an open-air area owned by the local council located in Olmatello Street, at the very edge of the city."[7] A few months later the us/them idiom was concretised when the municipality began to enclose the area with a thick, high permanent wall, and caravans and containers started to appear inside. This was the first nomad camp in town and it remains in operation today. The Olmatello camp was built up within the framework of the law entitled "Interventions for the protection [*tutela*] of Romani ethnie [*etnia rom*]". The law was proposed by a regional councillor, Giancarlo Niccolai, who gave a speech at the Regional council meeting, explicitly referring to the "protection of nomads" as an ethnic and linguistic minority whose needs are currently absent from both the national and the regional legal agenda. According to Niccolai the problems of the "nomads" are the following: "[1] We see, also in big cities like Florence, informal camps without essential services such as water or hygienic utilities, with repercussions for the health conditions of the inhabitants. [2] In addition to these disadvantages, difficulties caused by the lack of work are also present, [3] illiteracy as a consequence of the lack of education [...] situation represents a risk for young people and their behaviour, which is sometimes at the margin of the legal framework."[8]

---

7   Municipality of Florence, ordinance 2631, issued on October 13, 1987. The excerpt quoted is my translation.

8   Regione Toscana, 1987, p. 1 (my translation).

Further, he states the goals of the law: 1. To promote the implementation of the camps [*campi sosta*] for sedentary people [*sedentatizzati*] and transit areas [*aree di transito*], and set up health and social services for the guests who are staying. 2. To safeguard the positive values of the nomadic culture and in particular the typical arts and crafts, through: ad hoc initiatives aimed at the development and production of handmade products; financial support for the creation of handmade work activities within the camp; school education for children below eighteen years old and the struggle to vanquish illiteracy.[9]

After defining the problems of the Roma and confirming the intention to solve them, Niccolai concluded his speech by alluding to "the civic tradition which has always characterised Tuscany,"[10] underlining the importance of "reception" (*accoglienza*) as a distinctive value of this tradition. This boundary-making between us/Tuscans and them/nomads is closely echoed in a comparable account that occurred six months later in a similar institutional context. In order to improve the text of the law, in October 1987 a regional council commission had a consultation with some civil society organisations who were experienced in the field, having been dealing with problems involving "nomads". One of the consultants criticised the text of the law for not underlining the difference between "our" sedentary culture and "their" way of life: "One of the fundamental dimensions of the Romani way of life is a nomadic style. It is important to state this, also because [...] there are [in the text of the law] some elements in favour of those who decide to stop being nomadic, and in this way, disregarding those who are still nomads. The latter do not lead a nomadic way of life merely because they haven't reached a higher degree of maturity, but because the nomadic way of life belongs to their fundamental dimension."[11]

Discussing this remark, the president of the commission states: "This law is a product of our culture, and it could not be otherwise. Thus, we start from this point in order to reflect on something we discussed today, because the fact that it is a product of our own culture does not mean that it should overwhelm other cultures which are currently in our region."[12]

The impact of the law is outstanding, as in 1995, when the second law was approved,[13] there were approximately one thousand people living in the camps. This second law, entitled "Interventions for Roma and Sinti peoples", was discussed and

---

9   Regione Toscana, 1987, p. 2 (my translation).

10 Rossa, 1995, p. 43 (my translation).

11 Consiglio Regionale della Toscana, 1987, p. 14 (my translation).

12 Consiglio Regionale della Toscana, 1987, p. 28 (my translation).

13 Text of the 75/1995 law is available at http://www.rete.toscana.it/ius/ns-leggi/?MIval=
    pagina_2&ANNO=1995&TESTO=NIENTE&TITOLO=NIENTE&MATERIA=
    0&ANNO1=1995&NUMERO=73&YEAR=1995 [accessed January 2010].

designed on the basis of dedicated empirical investigations carried out at that time by an influential think tank.[14] An essential finding of their research was that Roma in Florence were in fact not nomads, shifting the focus of debate, and eventually changing the interpretation of camps from places of transit to places of permanent residence, creating in this way the necessity to provide only housing solutions which would suit the "Gypsy culture" (*cultura zingara*). Concomitant with this reorganisation of perceptions and policy practices, periodical and continuous interfering checks by the police were imposed, with demands for conformity to community standards, including hygienic checks, twenty-four-hour guards, and other such initiatives (Rossa, 1995).[15]

The Florentine media discourse of that period was mainly focused on the increased number of Roma fleeing the Yugoslav conflicts and settling in the Florentine camps. In particular, local committees of citizens protesting against the presence of the camps were a recurrent and predominant topic in the local press (see for instance: *L'unità di Firenze*, 1994). Interestingly, at that time the idiom deployed in newspapers to define the presence of Roma and the reasons for the necessity of evicting them from the municipal territory was very close to that used in the first two regional laws. After the two laws targeted at social integration were introduced and legitimated the idiom used to frame Roma in Tuscany by the regional council, committees of intolerant citizens began to exploit the idiom to exclude Roma. While the law said "they are different, therefore their culture should be protected", the committee could simply seem to be citing it in their own terms, saying "they are different, therefore they should either adapt to our rules or leave our land". Both cases are examples of a "culturalist" stance, "which stresses that the culture to which I am said or claim to belong defines my essence. Cultures (static, finite and bounded ethnolinguistic blocs labelled 'French', 'Nuer' and so on) determine individual and collective identities, and the subject's place in social and political schemas" (Grillo, 2003, p. 160).

This culturalist stance is reflected in the third regional law, in which Roma are framed as cultural subjects and (partially) nomads.[16] Although apparently more humane than its predecessors in eliciting successful social integration measures,

---

14 Fondazione Michelucci. (Reported in Marcetti, Mori and Solimano, 1993.)

15 In this limited space I cannot provide an in-depth analysis of the second law, for which see Picker, 2009, chapter 4.

16 Art. 1 states: "This law dictates the norms for the protection of Romani identity and cultural development with the aim of facilitating communication between cultures in order to guarantee the right to nomadism, to worship, to stop and to settle down, as well as access to social, healthcare, education and pedagogical services". The text of the 2/2000 law is available at http://www.rete.toscana.it/ius/ns-leggi/?MIval=pagina_2&ANNO =1988&TESTO=NIENTE&TITOLO=NIENTE&MATERIA=512&ANNO1=2007& NUMERO=2&YEAR=2000 [accessed January 2010].

by encouraging the participation of Roma (Scioscia, 2009), the third law in practice reproduces the idiom of culture and reception which was initiated by the first and then perpetuated by the second law.

From below

How did Romani migrants face the culturalist idiom? Often with the support of Florentine grassroots associations: since the early 1990s various Romani groups have raised their voices struggling for social rights and recognition, often profiting from the opportunities to advise local authorities. One of the most influential associations is the newer Amalipe Romano, founded in 2000 and still active. In the beginning Amalipe did not reproduce the culturalist idiom, preferring to openly denounce the unbearable material and hygienic conditions of the nomad camps. In 2000 the association sent a letter to the prefect of Florence openly declaring: "Above all, we ask for a definitive solution to the phenomena of the nomad camp, death-trap lagers", explaining that "some families came to Florence, which is a city of art and culture, known world-wide for its museums, its statues, monuments and libraries. But these are not the reasons why Roma came here, they came here to save their lives and those of their sons and grandparents."

These kinds of arguments were common in the early 2000s. However, in 2005 the association began to focus on the promotion of "Romani culture", taking a stance which was implicitly similar to the "Gypsy culture" described in the Michelucci research (Marcetti, Mori and Solimano, 1993). The politics of Amalipe then became less antagonistic, proposing cultural events such as dances, collective dinners with traditional food and most visibly giving a renewed importance to displaying the Romani flag and playing the anthem. Hence, although primarily concerned about the conditions of radical exclusion of Roma living in camps, Amalipe has gradually chosen a strategy positioning itself close to the culturalist idiom promulgated in the regional laws.

Centre-Right Wing Pescara

In Pescara, the Christian Democrats (DC) have been in power for almost fifty years through 2003, promoting a dominant conservative political culture inspired by Catholicism, ruling the municipality from 1956 to 1992, and from 1993 to 2003. Although Abruzzo is home to one of the few Italian Romani communities in Italy (see Manna, 1990) and to one of the local sections of an important national association, Opera Nomadi, both at the regional and at the urban level in Pescara the authorities have almost never addressed Roma, and in this vacuum of political discourse the local media have largely shaped public opinion about Roma.[17] I will now discuss the dominant idiom with which Roma have been framed in the press.

---

17   947 Roma living in Pescara hold Italian citizenship (Guarnieri and Dicati, 2005, p. 17).

From above

Stories about Roma in the local press mainly concern events in the third district, particularly the outlying neighbourhood of Rancitelli where the majority of Roma live. It is taken for granted that this is essentially a dangerous, crime-ridden "no-go" area. Over the last twenty years, accounts concerning Zingari (the local expression, of which the closest translation is Gypsies) in the local media fall into two distinct periods. The first was from the mid-1990s to 2000, when Rancitelli emerged as an area to be avoided, partly because of the strong presence of Romani migrants from the Kosovo war living in temporary housing. Secondly, from 2000 to the present, when Rancitelli is definitely portrayed as an almost totally different context compared to the civilised remainder of the urban territory. A constant element in both periods is the word 'nomads', which is used as often as 'Zingari'.

During the earlier period, reports in the press mention four actors and three main themes, The actors are 1. Zingari; 2. the State, i.e. police forces; 3. Inhabitants of Rancitelli, and 4. Civil Society, a Romani (4x) and a non-Romani (4y) grassroots associations: Opera Nomadi and Romano Prahl respectively; and the main themes are: A) Humanitarian emergency, due to the presence of potential refugees; B) Cultural and social integration, and C) Criminal activities carried out by both migrant and non-migrant Roma. The following is a schematic representation of the intersections between themes and actors:

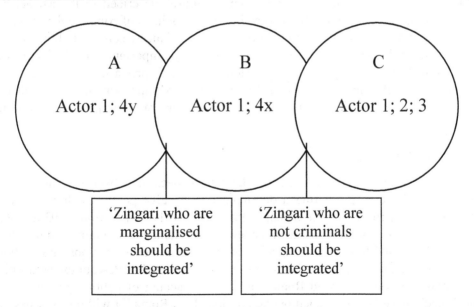

The mid/late 1990s press discourse on Zingari in Pescara. Actors: 1. Zingari; 2. State (police); 3. Inhabitants of Rancitelli; 4. Civil society (4x Romani, 4y non-Romani grassroots associations). Themes: A. Humanitarian emergency; B. Cultural and social integration.; C. Crime.

It is immediately apparent from a survey of the news coverage that the crime theme involves the largest number of actors. The other side of this pattern is that the State and the inhabitants of the neighbourhood share the opinion that crime is so widespread in Rancitelli because of the presence of Zingari. In this context, Kosovar Romani migrants are seen in two different ways: on the one hand, as victims of their own country and therefore in need of humanitarian help (theme A); and on the other hand, they are perceived as the causes of a general condition of decay [*degrado*], involving crime (theme C) that characterises Rancitelli. The two intersections provide rich-in-detail material for an analysis of Romani grassroots discourses, and I will come back to this. Since 2000, at the end of the humanitarian emergency, the main themes have been B and C, and the ways in which they intersect with one another can be heuristically shown by looking at a particular media case which took place in 2000.

In early July a local newspaper reported an initiative by Opera Nomadi, which was organising a big Gypsy party in via Lago di Capestrano for September of that year (*Il Messaggero*, 2000). The announced event became an occasion for the inhabitants of the neighbourhood to articulate their unhappiness about the presence of Zingari (*Il Centro*, 2000b). One of the inhabitants complains about the name used in the local public discourse to define its neighbourhood: "Why don't we stop calling the entire neighbourhood Rancitelli, criminalising it, when it is all about two streets?" (*Il Centro*, 2000a). The two streets the inhabitant is talking about are clearly via Lago di Capestrano and via Lago di Borgiano, the social housing area considered to be the most run down [*degradata*]. In line with the media position, the main argument put forward by the inhabitants of Rancitelli is that tension is already too high in their neighbourhood, that people have been listening to Zingari for too long a time! Zingari are seen by their neighbours exclusively as a problem of public order, and a party— although it would be a peaceful occasion, with songs and "typical" dances—would still belong to the "Gypsy culture" and would thus be dangerous.

Clearly, the idiom of deviance is substantiated by a culturalist stance, wherein Zingari are ultimately seen as radically different from the majority of the population. Since this is a feeling or a shared perception in the public discourse, and not a premise of public policy, it might be hardly recognisable as part of a nationalist process. However, it seems to be close to the reality of nationalism insofar as it helps to perpetuate the boundary-making in everyday life. Central to this process is the idiom of nomadism, as Zingari and nomadi are entirely overlapping categories, which are still nowadays routinely used both in everyday conversation and in the media discourse as ways of addressing a cultural difference.

From below

During the discussions about the "Gypsy party", despite the resistance to their planned event, Romani activists of Opera Nomadi continued to speak of cultural and social integration, claiming that their gathering would have a positive impact on the Rancitelli neighbourhood and favour the social integration of Roma (*Il Centro*, 2000c). The basic idea of Opera Nomadi was that once people become acquainted with "Romani culture" everyone would benefit, and that such an understanding would help to prevent those Zingari who might commit crimes or lead a deviant life style from doing so. Generally speaking, "cultural mediation" [*mediazione culturale*] is the main activity of Opera Nomadi, and the school is the core institution where it can be implemented as a practical goal.

Cultural mediation was the ultimate inspiration of the proposal for a regional law. Without being heard by urban and regional authorities, in 1998 Opera Nomadi proposed a regional law entitled "intervention for the Romani and Sinti people." Echoing many of the Italian regional laws for Roma which had mushroomed during the 1980s, the proposed law aimed to "protect ethnic and cultural identity and to facilitate progressive integration in all the social areas of the Regional community, respecting communication between cultures and, mutual knowledge and living together" (Guarnieri, 1998, p. 113).

This brand of multiculturalism reiterates the message that the association has constantly put forward since the early 1970s: a point that was made also during the first period when Opera Nomadi argued that "Zingari who are not criminals should be integrated" (see the figure, the intersection between theme B and C). The world view of the association at that time partially reflected the media discourse about crime; stressing that social deviance was indeed a phenomenon among Zingari, it also insisted that those who were not involved in it should be integrated through a process of cultural mediation. Opera Nomadi's voice is therefore partly assimilated to the media discourse insofar as it does not explicitly challenge the discourse on deviance; but it is also partly different in two principal ways: first, its priority is social integration through education and cultural recognition, and second, although the translation of its name is "Nomad's work", activists fully recognise the absence of nomadism among Roma in Pescara and generally do not use this category.

Conclusion. Political Cultures and Overlapping Culturalist Idioms

The research question I addressed in this introduction was the following: under which social conditions has the current nationalist xenophobic political culture vis-à-vis Roma in Italy emerged, and in which political culture does it find its main ideal references? Following Wimmer's generalisation (Wimmer, 2002) that contemporary nationalism is a twofold process of politicisation of ethnicity and social closure, during my investigation I became progressively convinced that both of these elements can be found in the two Italian localities visited, though with partial differences according to their own political culture.

Taken into account that the legal status of Roma living in the two localities is different, it is worth trying to understand similarities and differences in the idioms with which Roma are being addressed. In the Tuscan and Florentine context traces of the traditionally Left-wing idiom of social integration can be found among the authorities. This idiom is exclusively based on a culturalist conception of Roma, assuming their complete otherness in relation to the local Tuscan tradition, which partly explains the persistence up to the present of nomad camps on the outskirts. This also affects the "politics from below" carried out by Amalipe Romano, which in recent years has gradually been adopting a peculiar culturalist idiom, although primarily concerned with issues of radical social exclusion. On the other hand, the case of Pescara reveals a relatively homogeneous public discourse on Roma, or Zingari, embedded in a conservative Right-wing political culture. This discourse is almost exclusively about high crime rates in the outlying neighbourhood of Rancitelli. Indeed, in Pescara as in Florence this discourse is carried on within a strongly culturalist conception of Romani social life.

The distinctions drawn in my case studies of the two regions is not clear-cut. I showed that in Florence there was an overlapping idiom of social deviance, leading local authorities after 1995 to tighten their control over what was happening in the nomad camps. In Pescara, while the idiom of social integration was mainly absent, it was not completely alien to reports in the media.

The main element that both cases share is the idiom of nomadism as the most powerful rhetorical tool in the discussion of any problematic issues concerning Roma. This can also be identified in the current national politics vis-à-vis Roma. Having traced the two main cultural roots of this idiom, and the related representations of Roma that each of them imply, it is now possible to assert that the current government's xenophobic policies are rooted in a long tradition of culturalist assumptions about Roma; and that this enables it to reproduce a historically decontextualized and culturally static knowledge of Romani social life. This exacerbation of ethnic and cultural difference on the basis of fear of insecurity was expressed in the speech condemned by the European parliament; it took elements from both Left-wing and Right-wing rhetoric, each with a long history and rooted in precise local contexts, into account.

Nowadays xenophobic political campaigns vis-à-vis Roma are happening throughout Europe (Sigona, 2009). If we wish to understand the social conditions under which the logic and rhetoric of such campaigns became possible, it is perhaps necessary to examine situated forms of "modern" racism and analyse them anthropologically.

Bibliography

Brunello, Piero, ed. (1996). *L'urbanistica del disprezzo. Campi nomadi e società italiana* (Urbanism of defiance. Nomad camps and Italian society). Rome: Manifestolibri.

Il Centro (2000a). "La rabbia di cittadini e volontari. 'Stanchi delle chiacchiere'. La polemica: da anni si parla di questi problemi" (The citizens' and volunteers' anger. "We are tired of empty talk". The argument: we have been discussing these problems for years). 25 July 2000

Il Centro (2000b). "'Non vogliamo la festa dei Rom'. Rancitelli in rivolta: assemblea al Ghibli e incontro con il sindaco" ("We don't want the Romani party". Rancitelli protests: assembly at the Ghibli centre and meeting with the mayor). 2 August 2000.

Il Centro (2000c). "Guarnieri difende l'iniziativa. 'E' la cultura dell'incontro'" (Guarnieri defends the initiative. "This is the culture of meeting"). 2 August 2000.

Colacicchi, Piero (1996). "Rom a Firenze" (Roma in Florence) in *L'urbanistica del disprezzo. Campi rom e società italiana* (The urban scorn. Roma camp and Italian society), ed. Brunello, Piero. Rome: Manifestolibri.

Colacicchi, Piero (2008). "Ethnic Profiling and Discrimination against Roma in Italy: New Developments in a Deep-Rooted Tradition." *Roma rights* 2 (2008): 35–44.

Consiglio Regionale della Toscana, ed. (1987). *Consultazione della IV commissione sulla proposta di legge n. 175: Interventi per la tutela dell'etnia rom* (Consultation of the fourth commission about the proposition of law 175: Intervention for the protection of Romani ethnie). Florence: Regione Toscana. Typescript.

Dal Lago, Alessandro (1999). *Non-persone. L'esclusione dei migranti in una società globale* (Non-persons. The esclusion of migrants in a global society). Milan: Feltrinelli.

ERRC (European Roma Right Centre) (2000). "Campland. Racial Segregation of Roma in Italy." Available at http://www.errc.org/db/00/0F/m0000000F.pdf [accessed January 2010].

ERRC (European Roma Right Centre) *et al.* (2009). "Security a la italiana. Fingerprinting, Extreme Violence and Harrassment of Roma in Italy." Available at http://www.errc.org/db/04/28/m00000428.pdfv [accessed January 2010].

Grillo, Ralph D. (2003). "Cultural Essentialism and Cultural Anxiety." *Anthropological Theory* 3, no.2 (2003): 57–73.

Guarnieri, Nazzareno (1998). *La minoranza etnico-linguisica Rom abruzzesi. La mediazione culturale dalla follia dell'assimilazione alla corretta integrazione sociale* (The ethnic-linguistic Roma minority of Abruzzo. Cultural mediation from the madness of assimilation to correct social integration). Silvi Marina: Opera Nomadi Sezione Abruzzo.

Guarnieri, Nazzareno and Maria Grazia Dicati (2005). *Minoranza etnica Rom: reciprocità e integrazione culturale* (The Roma ethnic minority: reciprocity and cultural integration). Pescara: Media Edizioni.

Hancock, Ian (1997). "Roma: Myth and Reality." Available at http://www.geocities.com/~Patrin/mythandreality.htm [accessed January 2010].

Holmes, Douglas R. (2000). *Integral Europe. Fast-capitalism, Multiculturalism, Neofascism.* Princeton and Oxford: Princeton University Press.

Loy, Gianni (2009). "Violino Tzigano. La condizione dei rom in Italia tra stereotipi e diritti negati" (Gypsy violin. The condition of Roma in Italy between stereotypes and denied rights) in *Rom e Sinti in Italia. Tra stereotipi e diritti negati* (Roma and Sinti in Italy between stereotypes and denied rights), eds. Loy, Ginni and Roberto Cherchi. Rome: Ediesse, pp. 13–50.

Maneri, Marcello (2001). "Il panico morale come dispositivo di trasformazione dell'insicurezza" (Moral panic as a transformational device). *Rassegna Italiana di Sociologia* 42, no. 1 (2001): 5–40.

Manna, Francesca (1990). "I Rom abruzzesi di Pescara" (The Abruzzo Roma of Pescara). *Etudes et documents Balkaniques et Mediterranéens* 15 (1990): 88–95.

Marcetti, Corrado, Tiziana Mori and Nicola Solimano, eds. (1993). *Zingari in Toscana. Una ricerca della fondazione Michelucci. 1992–1993* (Gypsies in Tuscany. Research conducted by the Michelucci Foundation). Florence: Angelo Pontecorboli editore.

Il Messaggero Edizione di Pescara (2000). "Grande kermesse gitana in via Lago di Capestrano. Musica, balli e canti dall'11 al 16 settembre nell'ambito del giubileo degli zingari organizzato dall'Opera Nomadi" (Big Gypsy celebration in Lago di Capestrano Street. Music, dances and songs from the 11th to the 16th of September, in order to celebrate the Gypsy jubilee which is organised by Opera Nomadi). 6 July 2000.

Migione, Enzo and Fabio Quassoli 2002). "La sindrome sicuritaria" (The securitarian syndrome). *La rivista del Manifesto* 30 (July–August 2002). Available at http://www.larivistadelmanifesto.it/php3/ric_view.php3?page=/archivio/30/30A20020711.html&word=problema [accessed January 2010].

Mura, Loredana (1995). "Italy. Enduring a General Crisis" in *New Xenophobia in Europe*, eds. Baumgartl, Bernd and Adrian Favell. London, the Hague, and Boston: Kluwer Law International, 206–17.

Però, Davide (1999). "Next to the Dog Pound: Institutional Discourses and Practices about Rom Refugees in Left-wing Bologna." *Modern Italy* 4, no. 2 (1999): 207–24.

Però, Davide (2005). "The European Left and the New Immigrations: the Case of Italy" in *Crossing European Boundaries: beyond Conventional Geographical Categories*, eds. Stacul, Jaro, Christina Moutsou, and Helen Kopnina. New York and Oxford: Berghahan Books, pp. 64–80.

Però, Davide (2007). *Inclusionary Rhetoric/Exclusionary Practices. Left-wing Politics and Migrants in Italy.* New York and London: Berghahn Books.

Petrillo, Agostino (1999). "Italy: Farewell to the Bel Paese?" in *The European Union and Migrant Labour*, eds. Dale, Gareth and Mike Cole. Oxford: Berg.

Piasere, Leonardo (2005). *Popoli delle discariche. Saggi di antropologia zingara* (Peoples of the dumps. Essays in Gypsy anthropology). Rome: Cisu.

Piasere, Leonardo (2006). "Che cos'è un campo nomadi?" (What is a nomad camp?). *Achab. Rivista di antropologia* 8, no. 6 (2006): 8–16.

Picker, Giovanni (2009). *Romani/Gypsy Groupings in the Making. A Comparative Study of Ethnicity and Citizenship between 'Eastern' and 'Western' Europe. The Cases of Florence, Cluj-Napoca and Pescara.* Unpublished PhD diss., University of Milan-Bicocca.

Pratt, Jeff (2003). *Class, Nation and Identity. The Anthropology of Political Movements.* London: Pluto.

Regione Toscana (1987). *Proposta di legge 175 concernente Interventi per la tutela dell'etnia "rom".* (Proposal for law 175 concerning Intervention for the protection of the Romani ethnie). Florence: Regione Toscana. Typescript.

La Repubblica (2008). "Maroni: 'Avanti con impronte e censimenti nei campi nomadi'" (Let us go on with fingerprints and censuses in nomad camps). Available at http://www.repubblica. it/2008/07/sezioni/cronaca/sicurezza-politica-11/maroni-piano-nomadi/maroni-piano-nomadi.html [accessed January 2010]. 16 July 2008.

Rossa, Silvia (1995). "Regione e Comuni di fronte al problema degli Zingari in Toscana" (The region and the municipalities facing the Gypsy problem in Tuscany). Unpublished MA thesis, Faculty of Political Science, University of Florence.

Saitta, Pietro (2008). "Immigrant Roma in Sicily: The Role of the Informal Economy in Producing Social Advancement." *Social Science Research Network.* Available at http:// papers.ssrn.com/sol3/papers.cfm?abstract_id=1322153 [accessed January 2010].

Scioscia, Milena (2009). "L'integrazione fra politiche. Immaginare il futuro tra memoria e presente" (Integration between policies. Imagining the future between memory and the present) in *Politiche possibili. Abitare le città con i rom e i sinti* (Possible policies. Inhabiting cities with Roma and Sinti), ed. Vitale, Tommaso. Rome: Carocci.

Sigona, Nando (2003). "How Can a 'Nomad' be a 'Refugee'? Kosovo Roma and Labelling Policy in Italy." *Sociology* 37, no. 1 (2003): 69–79.

Sigona, Nando (2005). "Locating 'The Gypsy Problem'. The Roma in Italy: Stereotyping, Labelling and 'Nomad Camps'." *Journal of Ethnic and Migration Studies* 31, no. 4 (2005): 741–56.

Sigona, Nando and Lorenzo Monasta (2006). *Cittadinanze imperfette. Rapporto sulla discriminazione razziale di rom e sinti in Italia* (Imperfect citizenships. Report on the racial discrimination of Roma and Sinti in Italy). Santa Maria Capua Vetere and Cesena: Edizioni Spartaco.

Sigona, Nando (2009). "I rom nell'Europa neoliberale: antiziganismo, povertà e i limiti dell'etnopolitica" (Roma in neoliberal Europe: anti-Gypsyism, poverty and the limits of ethnopolitics) in *Razzismo democratico. La persecuzione degli stranieri in Europa* (Democratic racism. The persecution of strangers in Europe), ed. Palidda, Salvatore. Milan: Agenzia X, pp. 54–65.

Stacul, Jaro (2006). "Neo-nationalism or Neo-localism? Integralist Political Engagements in Italy at the Turn of the Millennium" in *Neo-nationalism in Europe and beyond. Perspectives from Social Anthropology,* eds. Banks, Marcus and André Gingrich. New York: Berghahn Books, pp. 162–76.

Stolcke, Verena (1995). "Talking Culture: New Boundaries, New Rhetorics of Exclusion in Europe." *Current Anthropology* 36, no. 1 (1995): 1–24.

Taguieff, Pierre-André (1988). *La Force du préjugé. Essai sur le racisme et ses doubles* (The force of prejudice. Essay on racism and its doubles). Paris: La Découvert.

Tavani, Claudia (2005). "Keeping the Criminality Myth Alive: Stigmatisation of Roma through the Italian Media." *Roma Rights* no. 1 (2005): 45–50.

Tosi Cambini, Sabrina (2008). *La zingara rapitrice. Racconti, denunce, sentenze* (The kidnapper Gypsy woman. Tales, complaints, verdicts). Rome: CISU.

Trucco, Lorenzo (2008). "Legal and Policy Developments in the Condition of Migrants and Roma in Italy." *Roma Rights* 2 (2008): 31–34. Available at http://www.errc.org/db/03/B7/m000003B7.pdf [accessed January 2010].

L'unità Edizione di Firenze (1994). "Oggi la Marcia antinomadi" (Today the anti-nomad demonstration). 6 September 1994.

Vitale, Tommaso (2009). "Sociologia dos Conflitos Locais contra os Rom e os Sinti em Itália. Pluralidade de contextos e variedade de instrumentos políticos" (Sociology of local conflicts against Roma and Sinti in Italy. Plurality of contexts and variety of political instruments). *Cidades. Comunidades e Territórios* no. 19 (2009): 65–80.

Vitale, Tommaso and Enrico Claps (2010). "Not Always the Same Old Story: Spatial Segregation and Feelings of Dislike towards Roma and Sinti in Large Cities and Medium-size Towns in Italy" in *Multi-Disciplinary Approaches To Romany Studies. Selected Papers From Participants of Central European University's Summer Courses 2007–2009*, eds. Stewart, Michael and Márton Rövid. Budapest: CEU Summer University, pp. 228–253.

Williams, Brackette F. (1989). "A Class Act: Anthropology and the Race to Nation across Ethnic Terrain." *Annual Review of Anthropology* 18 (1989): 401–44.

Wimmer, Andreas (2002). *Nationalist Exclusion and Ethnic Conflicts. Shadows of Modernity.* Cambridge, UK: Cambridge University Press.

Wright, Susan (1998). "The Politicization of 'Culture'." *Anthropology Today* 14, no. 1 (1998): 14.

Tommaso Vitale and *Enrico Claps*

NOT ALWAYS THE SAME OLD STORY:
Spatial Segregation and Feelings of Dislike towards Roma and Sinti in Large Cities and Medium-size Towns in Italy[1]

The scientific literature on the dynamics of public opinion and racism as a whole has neglected the spread of anti-Gypsy feeling (Morning, 2009). Only recently, with the Europeanization of the Roma Movements' claims, have official data from public opinion research made it possible to reach any empirically-based conclusions on the spread of anti-Gypsy prejudice in Europe. The availability of these data has not yet been fully exploited, and at the same time their use, albeit only partial, has not been critically worked out. On the other hand we know that the use of opinion polls within the public sphere cannot be ignored, because of the resulting reification of the prejudice and the effects on the objectified ethnic category. This will be the focus of discussion for this chapter, which will introduce unpublished analysis and focus on the Italian situation, showing how pragmatic reflection on the use of data may make it possible to tackle the main risks that these investigations entail. We will also be careful not to ignore the political relevance taken on by the research, even if, no doubt, this will have contradictory effects as well.

Italy, Europe: Prejudice and Reification

"How would you feel if you knew your neighbour was a Roma?" is the question which a year ago, between February and March, Eurostat asked 26,746 citizens of the 27 States of the European Union, 1,046 of whom were in Italy. It is a question typically asked in studies on prejudice and xenophobia. It is a subject that requires respondents to think starting for themselves, to deal with their own feelings, and the intention is to measure feelings of *comfort*—using an English word—towards a specific group. The result is an index that enables us to arrange countries in an ordinal scale from 1 to 10, where the highest scores belong to States in which the majority of the citizens feel comfortable with "Gypsy" groups[2]. Poland, Sweden and France occupy the top positions, while Italy and the Czech Republic are at the bottom end. Within the Italian sample, only 14% feel

---

1 Translated by Chiara Ka'huê Cattaneo.

2 The word 'Gypsy' should not to be taken as an offensive term, but as a general category including a large variety of very different groups: Roma, Caminanti, Manouches, Sinti and so on.

completely comfortable with the thought of having a 'Gypsy' neighbour, and only 5% declare that they have a personal relationship with at least one Roma or a Sinti.

Analysing the data from the 1999 World Value Survey, it rapidly becomes clear that in that year the degree of hostility towards "Gypsy" groups in Italy was far higher than in any other European country (see. graph no. 1).

Graph no. 1. Percentage of people
declaring that they would not want a Roma or Sinti as a neighbour[3]

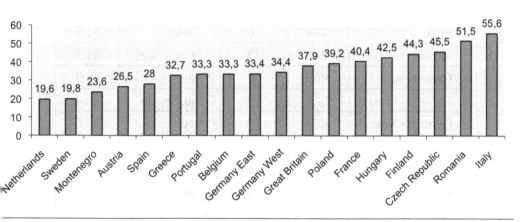

Source: World Value Survey. Data collected in 1999, except for Czech Republic and Hungary (1998), Finland (2000) and Montenegro (2001). Our elaboration.

While it may be presumed that in the last decade in Italy the degree of hostility towards the 'Gypsies' has increased in a quicker and more intense way than in the other nations, we do not possess reliable data that would allow us to compare these tendencies in detail. We can, however, start by considering the relative position of Italy compared to the other European countries. In order to better describe the relationship among European countries, we have developed an ordered scale of anti-Gypsyism, comparing data from different comparative sources. The data of the different years taken into consideration must not be compared directly with each other. Such an exercise allows us only to compare the relative ranking of the different countries on a scale of anti-Gypsyism. The diachronic comparison allows us to observe that Italy is always fairly firmly at the top of the scale, even though it is overtaken by the Czech Republic (and Romania goes down the scale of declared hostility to levels much more similar to those of Greece, slightly higher than Spain).

---

3   Bear in mind that the question in the WVS questionnaire was "On this list are various groups of people. Could you please sort out any that you would not like to have as neighbours? Jews, Arabs, Asians, Gypsies, etc..."

Table no. 1. Scale of anti-Gypsy hostility in European Countries, 1999–2008

1999			2008	
Italy	55.6	1	Czech Republic	78.5
Romania	51.5	2	Italy	70.8
Czech Republic	45.5	3	Germany East	56.4
Finland	44.3	4	Austria	55.9
Hungary	42.5	5	Hungary	55.6
France	40.4	6	Finland	51.9
Poland	39.2	7	Germany West	51.5
Great Britain	37.9	8	Portugal	48.9
Germany West	34.4	9	Great Britain	46.4
Germany East	33.4	10	Greece	45.5
Portugal	33.3	11	Romania	43.5
Belgium	33.3	12	Spain	37.3
Greece	32.7	13	Belgium	36.6
Spain	28.0	14	France	35.5
Austria	26.5	15	Netherlands	34.4
Sweden	19.8	16	Sweden	34.2
Netherlands	19.6	17	Poland	28.4

Source: World Value Survey 1999, except for the Czech Republic and Hungary (1998) and Finland (2000); Eurobarometer 2008 69.1 code SI233. Our elaboration.[4]

On the other hand, in Italy, hostility towards 'Gypsies' has been growing steadily over the last decade: it has risen by 22 percentage points. The WVS data do not allow us to compare growth tendencies in all the Countries, because not many nations have kept the question: nevertheless they allow us to compare the dynamics of hostility in two countries particularly relevant for our purposes. First of all with Spain, often associated with Italy in terms of a number of structural characteristics (Migliavacca, 2008), but with remarkably different political dynamics, cohabitation policies and

---

4   In both the surveys the question was the same, but the way of answering differs: in WVS survey hostility towards Roma people had to be explicitly stated, while in the Eurobarometer questionnaire respondents were asked to give a score of hostility from 1 to 10, allowing also the possibility of not answering or of responding "don't know" (in this case, in order to produce an ordinal scale we have dichotomized the answers).

relations with minorities. Here the hostility has increased by only 8 percentage points in six years, giving an increase equal to a quarter of that in Italy one. In the second place, with Romania, a nation with which Italy entertains delicate diplomatic relations concerning the Roma issue, and often depicted in the Italian neoliberal press as a locus of strong anti-Gypsy hostilities. Among the States analysed by us, it was certainly the one with the highest level of hostility at the end of the 1990s, but the level has not increased in the first years of the third millennium: instead, it has fallen slightly (see graph no. 2).

Graph no. 2. Change in hostility towards Gypsy groups 1999–2005.
Difference in the percentages of people who declare
they would not want Roma or Sinti as neighbours.

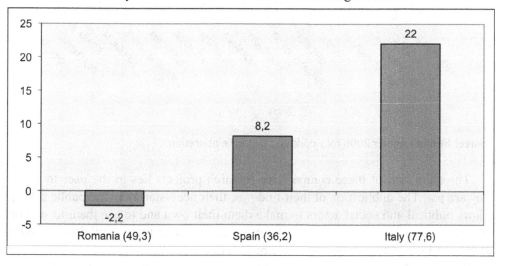

Source: World Value Survey 1999 and 2005. Our elaboration.
On the y-axis the difference in the percentage between 2005 and 1999 of those declaring they would not want a Gypsy as a neighbour. On the x-axis in brackets the 2005 percentage.

On the other hand, in Italy hostility towards Gypsy groups is so strong that even considering only those who declare that they "do not to have any problem with neighbours from other ethnic groups," this group contains a higher percentage than in other countries of people who do not welcome the presence of Roma and Sinti.

As a matter of fact, what emerges in many countries is a strong correlation between the declared absence of prejudice or tensions regarding neighbours belonging to other ethnic groups and the absence of anti-Gypsy attitudes (see table no. 2). In the Italian case the correlation is dramatically lower. Here, even among those declaring themselves anti-racist and open to multiethnic cohabitation, over 60% declare that they do not want any Roma or Sinti in their neighbourhood. This percentage is more than double the average of the other countries taken into consideration in the present paper.

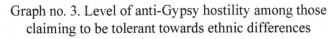

Graph no. 3. Level of anti-Gypsy hostility among those claiming to be tolerant towards ethnic differences

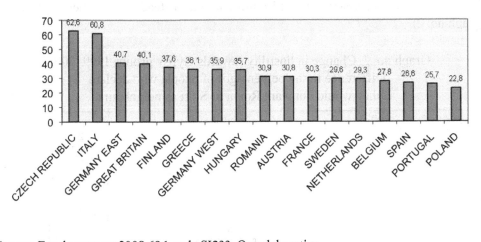

Source: Eurobarometer 2008 69.1 code SI233. Our elaboration.

The main risk of these comparative research projects lies in the uses to which they are put. The publication of their findings, their accessibility in the public sphere, allows political and social actors to make them their own and to use them to support their activities. There is no way to maintain control over the potential use of data, whereas it is possible to reflect on their potential use.

First of all, comparative investigations at European level allow us to better historicize and contextualize the dynamics of prejudice. Publishing the data of a single country may actually have very strong naturalising effects. In Italy, for example, through a public-opinion poll on a probabilistic-representative sample of the population (Vitale, Claps, and Arrigoni, 2009), we have estimated that the increase in the hostility towards Roma and Sinti has reached a disconcerting level, at which only 6.7% of Italian *gagi* (the non-Roma population) declare that they do not feel any hostility towards these groups. The trend of hostility has pushed the Roma into a terrifying social hostility zone. Such a piece of data, on its own, has a powerful reifying effect: if the vast majority of the population feels this way, may there not be objective (or natural, in other words) grounds? The reasons for hostility are thus automatically sought in the object of prejudice (its alleged behaviours, its alleged homogeneous culture, incompatible with the dominant culture) and not in the political dynamics that has caused the hostility to emerge and spread.

Table no. 2. Cross-tabs of anti-Gypsy hostility
and hostility towards ethnicities different from one's own

Nation		Do not want Roma as neighbours	Are not bothered by Roma neighbours
Belgium	xenophobe	77.60	22.40
	not xenophobe	27.80	72.20
Germany West	xenophobe	94.10	5.90
	not xenophobe	35.90	64.10
Germany East	xenophobe	91.20	8.80
	not xenophobe	40.70	59.30
Greece	xenophobe	82.80	17.20
	not xenophobe	36.10	63.90
Spain	xenophobe	82.80	17.20
	not xenophobe	26.60	73.40
Finland	xenophobe	91.00	9.00
	not xenophobe	37.60	62.40
France	xenophobe	86.40	13.60
	not xenophobe	30.30	69.70
Italy	xenophobe	89.70	10.30
	not xenophobe	60.80	39.20
Netherlands	xenophobe	79.60	20.40
	not xenophobe	29.30	70.70
Austria	xenophobe	91.70	8.30
	not xenophobe	30.80	69.20
Portugal	xenophobe	85.30	14.70
	not xenophobe	25.70	74.30
Sweden	xenophobe	92.40	7.60
	not xenophobe	29.60	70.40
Great Britain	xenophobe	83.50	16.50
	not xenophobe	40.10	59.90
Czech Republic	xenophobe	96.50	3.50
	not xenophobe	62.60	37.40
Hungary	xenophobe	91.50	8.50
	not xenophobe	35.70	64.30
Poland	xenophobe	84.60	15.40
	not xenophobe	22.80	77.20
Romania	xenophobe	89.50	10.50
	not xenophobe	30.90	69.10

Source: Eurobarometer 2008 69.1 code SI233. Our elaboration.
Xenophobes: people declaring that they are not comfortable with neighbours of other ethnic groups. Not-xenophobes: people who are comfortable with neighbours of different ethnic origins.

Even comparing this piece of data with the one related to prejudice towards foreigners in Italy, although it does bring up some interesting elements, does not help from this point of view, because it reinforces the same logic of ascribing responsibility to the objectified category, moreover hinting that Roma and Sinti are immigrants, ignoring a centuries-old history of residence in all the urban and rural areas of the Italian peninsula. The negative effects of removing the historical memory are extremely dangerous (Asséo, 2005).

Quite differently, comparison with other European countries, in particular with the countries considered relatively similar to Italy as far as government traditions, social models and types of industrialisation are concerned, may produce a preliminary effect of putting things into perspective, leading people to wonder what gave rise to the spread of such strong prejudice precisely in Italy. It has a first effect of contextualisation.

Long Term Stereotypes on Roma and Sinti Behaviour and Imperatives of Contextualisation

We have already discussed elsewhere how even the anthropological and social sciences have partially contributed to a homogeneous and a historical representation of Gypsy groups in Italy, with powerful decontextualisation effects in the public discourse, including anti-racist discourse, in Italy (Vitale, 2009b). Two additional remarks need to be made before we can proceed. First of all, presenting data aggregated on a national basis tends to hide the effects of drawing averages between very diverse dynamics operating at regional and local level. With reference to Italy, for example, the region of residence constitutes quite a strong factor affecting the likelihood of an individual 'falling' into racist prejudice.

Overall, there is the risk of obtaining 'plain' representations of what happens within a nation state neglecting structuring dynamics; that is to say that hostility towards Roma, even though it has some peaks spread out across the whole national territory, is characterised by extremely local mobilisations. This is of course part of the dynamics of moral panic, which always starts from the aversion towards a group *located* in a very confined local context, whose behaviours are stigmatised, and generalised to the identified population as a whole (Maneri, 2001). These mobilisations are never 'spontaneous': they are indeed mobilisations, that is to say, collective actions, organised by 'entrepreneurs', in which the actors involved raise local problems and make them public, interacting with authorities and public policies and pursuing one or more shared objectives. There are subjects which initiate deliberate action, finding resources which they place at the disposal of whoever wants to organise and support a mobilisation. Often and not by chance, when referring to mobilisations, we talk about political or moral entrepreneurs.

The feeling of hostility is never the automatic consequence of confrontation between socially and culturally different groups, as Tajfel has clearly shown (Tajfel, 1984), but is always the result of a political and moral construction: the analytical observation of the presence of entrepreneurs of mobilisation, like the careful observation of the tools used to manage the presence of Gypsy groups (Vitale, 2009a) is important because it allows one not to presume that anti-Gypsy prejudice manifests itself in hostile actions directly, and without any mediation.

But what does anti-Gypsy prejudice consist of? We know that in Italy it is structured in the constitution of the State-nation and the tightening of borders between the nineteenth and twentieth centuries. We do not know its contents in detail, though. This is why we have conducted qualitative research to try to specify its components. Let us now examine them very briefly, before going back to the main theme of our argument, which is related to how to present the research results without producing effects that fuel new forms of discrimination.

We conducted in-depth interviews to gather people's emotional reactions and deep feelings, by showing them photographs and video clips, and asking them to complete cartoon stories previously prepared by us.[5] Undoubtedly the most frequent reason for stigmatisation and intolerance towards Roma people is their alleged 'inclination' to theft, considered a cultural trait. Moreover, a link with 'blood' emerges: it is not their living conditions that push the Roma towards deviant behaviours but their 'nature'. It is worth noting that prejudice does not have a purely automatic dimension: people are thoughtful and they place the effects of reification reproduced by their representations within a chain of cause and effect. One specific form of the tendency to steal is the 'abduction' of children. Already back in the '50s in Italy there was a widespread rumour according which Gypsies abducted Italian children in order to make them beg. We know very well that a negative action performed by a member of another group is interpreted according to the principle of individual responsibility, whereas similar actions performed by members of one's own group of origin are ascribed to context, adversity, chance and another external factors (Mazzara, 1997) and we therefore observe a different emotional response depending on the socio-cultural 'home' of the wilful subject: the deviant behaviour (of, for example, a child beggar) tends to be justified if it is performed by a member of the group one belongs to (stirring emotions such as compassion or astonishment, conveying more understanding and a more sympathetic approach), whereas when Roma are involved the same behaviour is ascribed to natural characteristics—according to an unjust equivalence between culture and nature (giving rise to negative emotions)—and it is also considered to comply with the prejudicial expectations of society.[6]

---

5   The authors wish to thank Stefano Arcagni, who realised the interviews (Marradi, 2005).

6   Let us not forget that stereotypes are more effective as the idea that all individuals of the target group possess certain characteristics equally becomes stronger and stronger within society (Mazzara, 1997).

Nomadism too, considered in general a trait peculiar to 'Gypsy culture' (please note the singular), contributes to this ambivalence. But the ambivalence is considerably reduced, and in the in-depth interviews we did not find any significant traces of something that a few years ago still had a certain relevance: the fascination with the 'children of the wind', sensual, knowledgeable about the secrets of magic. The Roma are the objects of what Boltanski (Boltanski, 1999) defines *unanimous indignation*, meaning the kind of indignation that identifies the offender immediately and demands punishment,[7] the accusation accompanying indignation may be interpreted as a verbal trial fuelled by the voices and the judgement of the street (being therefore prejudicial), and it targets a homogeneous subject.

Beyond each stereotypical representation of Roma people, what is worth stressing is that it seems as if a significant lack of emotional control towards them emerges: when dealing with Roma people, all inhibiting factors seem to vanish. Prejudices shape emotions: contempt and hatred,[8] always appearing in combination with resentment, are the forms taken on by a feeling of rage and a sense of hostility towards a group considered objectively inferior. The result of this contempt is represented by the desire to physically eliminate this *"minority of the worst"* (Elias, 1965), given their uselessness and their 'bestiality'. These strongly negative emotions are linked to a disgust that also becomes a refusal to have any contact with them.

Qualitative research based on in-depth interviews is extremely important because it allows us to truly grasp the content of certain prejudices and their emotional overtones. It does not, however, enable us to say anything about how widespread they are, either in terms of extension or with reference to the prevailing common social characteristics among those showing different positions and feelings. Research of this kind may easily run the risk of leading once again to a homogeneous and undifferentiated interpretation of the reactions towards Gypsy groups. The construction of the sample has no relevance, because the logic of qualitative research pursues an aim of saturation rather than a circumscribed question (in our case, the relationship between stereotypes and emotional expression), and not a representative logic of (Small, 2009). There is therefore a risk of delivering data that may once again be moulded in a deterministic fashion by political actors who, in this case, will finally obtain a repertory of sophisticated topics to use in their attempts to mobilise consensus and to fuel renewed anti-Gypsy feelings.

Setting up sample-based investigations which also permit multi-varied analysis does not solve all the problems raised by our knowledge of this field, but it does enable us to improve the situation by putting those problems into perspective.

---

7   Indignant people make up a united crowd which, encountering no opposition, restricts the scope of the inquiry and passes straight to action (Boltanski, 1999).

8   Contempt is a result of the idea that the other person is inferior, hate derives from the idea that the other person is evil (Elster, 1999, p. 28).

The Social Basis of Anti-Gypsyism

From a panel research project conducted in June 2007 it emerged that in Italy Roma and Sinti are perceived as a single people, and an unpleasant one: 81% of respondents considered them not very or not at all pleasant, while only 39% expressed such a harsh opinion of migrants as a whole.[9] Leaving out the 'don't knows', only 6.7% found them pleasant, a significantly smaller percentage than had been found only 8 years earlier, in October '99. Another point worth noting: our data show that the higher the level of education, the stronger the liking for foreigners, except for Romanians and above all for Roma and Sinti people. Indeed, the higher the level of education, the stronger the dislike of Roma and Sinti: while 71% of respondents with 5th grade education have no sympathy for these groups, the percentage soars to 90% among those with a university degree. Finally, the feeling of dislike is equally distributed across self-ascribed political affiliations, with almost no difference between those considering themselves to be of right and centre-right political views (88%) and those belonging to the left (86%).

The resulting representations are almost never positive, but they immediately relate, and as a first response, on one hand to images and feelings of hostility (for 47%), and on the other hand to an idea of marginalisation and poverty (35%). The image of the 'Gypsy' tends to coincide with that of the 'thief' (according to 92% of our sample), of someone living in a closed group (87%), living *out of a personal choice* in camps on the outskirts of the city's (83%), and who in many case exploits children (92%). At the same time there are also some more positive opinions: 65% of the sample admits—and it is an important admission—they are marginalised people, among the most discriminated-against, suffering under living conditions which they have not chosen. Around 73% tend to consider Roma and Sinti as having a great sense of freedom (in this faintly recalling the cinema stereotype of the children of the wind) and as extremely united communities (85%). They are also credited with a 'positive' imagination, even alongside negative opinions, especially in the case of retired people (73%), those living in North-eastern Italy (74%) and those claiming to be left-wing (71%). The most radically hostile positions and those which show no openness at all are dominant among those less informed, i.e. the ones who know less about Roma groups, either some basic data.

The trends indicated by these results find additional confirmation in the most recent Eurobarometer data, although these were collected from a numerically smaller sample compared to the research that we conducted in 2007. The new data nevertheless shed some light on certain tendencies to change following the wave of criminalisation of Roma that has taken place between the two research projects.

---

9   The authors wish to thank Paola Arrigoni, who coordinated the research, and the ISPO research centre, which supported it. Statistical information on the sample and on the research itself can be downloaded from the CEU Press website.

Table no. 3. Cross-tabs. Socio-demographic variables, political and value aspects of sympathy towards Gypsy groups on the feeling of sympathy, on opinion regarding the possibility of coexistence and on preference for integrative policies (2007)

	Sympathy for Gypsy groups	Coexistence with Gypsy groups is considered possible	Integrative social policies should be preferred
Age			
18-29 years	7.40	32.60	19.80
30-39 years	4.70	27.80	14.00
40-49 years	6.00	27.00	14.90
50-59 years	8.70	34.70	23.00
60 and over	4.20	29.30	10.10
Total	5.80	30.00	15.30
Education			
Degree	4.40	34.60	25.40
High school	7.40	32.20	19.00
8th grade	5.60	26.00	13.30
None or primary education only	5.00	31.30	11.10
Total	5.80	30.00	15.40
Social-professional category			
Bourgeoisie	8.40	35.10	21.90
Upper middle class	7.20	25.40	18.80
Middle class	5.90	29.60	15.90
Worker	5.80	27.60	16.30
Unemployed	2.30	27.80	17.30
Student	9.30	39.40	18.60
Housewife	7.00	24.60	16.30
Retired	3.20	33.30	7.60
Total	5.90	30.00	15.30
Attendance at mass			
Never	4.50	29.90	15.30
1 or 2 times a year	9.00	29.00	13.40
Several times a year	6.80	29.70	12.20
1\3 times a month	6.20	25.60	15.00
Every week	5.50	34.60	16.10
Total	6.50	30.20	14.50

	Sympathy for Gypsy groups	Coexistence with Gypsy groups is considered possible	Integrative social policies should be preferred
Political self-identification			
Left	5.50	29.80	15.90
Centre-Left	8.90	39.80	18.30
Centre	7.20	25.70	12.50
Centre-right	6.00	25.90	13.40
Right	5.10	24.50	15.20
Total	6.90	29.70	14.90
Interested in politics			
Very much	9.30	48.80	20.90
Quite	3.30	29.80	21.10
A little	3.90	26.50	12.60
Not at all	9.00	27.00	13.70
Don't know	8.70	34.60	4.80
Total	6.20	28.80	14.30
Geographical macro-area			
North-West	7.70	27.90	13.30
North-East	5.00	31.40	12.00
Centre	5.10	27.00	14.00
South	6.20	37.10	19.40
Islands	3.80	26.70	21.00
Total	5.80	30.00	15.30
Urban dimension			
Less than 5,000 inhabitants	5.50	38.40	13.20
Between 5,001 and 20,000	7.20	31.50	12.40
Between 20,001 and 50,000	7.00	27.20	21.60
Between 50,001 and 100,000	4.40	26.10	15.30
Above 100,000	4.60	27.20	16.10
Total	5.90	30.00	15.30

Source: ISPO 2007. N= 2.171. Our elaboration.

Percentages of row. The column "Sympathy for Gypsy groups" is an index merging the answers "very much" and "quite" to the question "We do not like everybody in the same way. I ask you now to state your degree of sympathy towards other groups". The column "Coexistence with Gypsy groups is considered possible" is an index merging the answers "yes, for sure" and "probably yes" to the question "Can the Roma, the Gypsies, coexist with us?" The column "Integrative social policies should be preferred" is an index of those who completed the statement "The condition of Gypsies in Italy could improve if…" choosing as the first of three possible answers "…they could live in healthier and more proper housing", or "…they were offered more opportunities of getting a regular job", or "…their children attended compulsory schools".

Table no. 4. Social profile of anti-Gypsyism in Italy (2008)

	Do not want Roma as neighbours	Are not bothered by Roma neighbours
Gender		
Male	71.50	28.50
Female	70.40	29.60
Total	70.80	29.20
Age		
15-24	68.90	31.10
25-39	65.30	34.70
40-54	71.40	28.60
55+	76.60	23.40
Total	70.80	29.20
Years of education		
15-	81.70	18.30
16-19	71.50	28.50
20+	56.00	44.00
Still studying	61.10	38.90
Total	71.00	29.00
Employment		
Students	61.10	38.90
Managers	61.40	38.60
Unemployed	62.10	37.90
Self-employed	69.40	30.60
House person	69.60	30.40
Other white collar	70.00	30.00
Manual worker	75.10	24.90
Retired	80.20	19.80
Total	70.80	29.20

	Do not want Roma as neighbours	Are not bothered by Roma neighbours
Political orientation		
Left	66.70	33.30
Centre-Left	64.20	35.80
Centre	71.00	29.00
Centre-Right	61.70	38.30
Right	91.20	(only 8 cases) 8.8
Refusal	74.50	25.50
Don't Know	72.80	27.20
	70.80	29.20
Religion		
Atheist, agnostic, non-believer	67.10	32.90
Religion stated	71.10	28.90
Total	70.80	29.20
Has Roma friends		
Yes	66.00	34.00
No	71.00	29.00
Total	70.80	29.20
Comfortable with neighbours of different ethnic origins		
No	89.70	10.30
Yes	60.80	39.20
Total	70.50	29.50

Source: Eurobarometer 2008 69.1 code SI233. Our elaboration.

Extreme ignorance of the Roma world and a negative, hostile image of them leads the *gagi* to perceive coexistence with Roma as very problematic. As far as the issue of coexistence is concerned, we can outline three segments of public opinion: 1) the first, consisting of 30% of respondents, is *possibilist*, and tends to consider *gagi* as co-responsible for the present situation; 2) the second segment, including 36%, is *worried*, tending to think that the two cultures are difficult to reconcile, but does not ascribe specific responsibilities to Roma and Sinti; 3) the third, up to 34%, thinks coexistence is impossible and that the 'Gypsies' are responsible for this.

Destruction on a Roma settlement within an industrial building
Milan 19 November 2009

1. The *Gagi* Who Think It is Possible to Live with Roma People

When presenting our results, we deemed it important to highlight the character of the most possibilistic subjects, in order to show that there are pockets of consensus which could easily be strengthened by putting forward social policies and not demagogic actions of the 'clearing out and segregation' kind (Vitale, 2009c). In order to better understand the 30% of people who declared that coexistence with Gypsy groups was possible, we traced their valour and socio-demographic profile with some cross-tabs (see table no. 3), later checking potential spurious relations through logistic regression (see table no. 5). Let us therefore focus only on the significant variables in the model. First of all, the cohort of people in their fifties (50–59 years) proves to be significant: they are still working, many of them have experienced internal migration, they lived through the cycle of workers' and students' protests between '68 an '77 and, most of all, they still retain memories of a phase during which local relations with Gypsy groups were *also* positive and marked by exchanges and economic complementarity. Not going to Mass, or not going very often, has quite a strong negative impact, suggesting that places where the parish as such congregates are contexts in which even though a feeling of sympathy for Gypsies is not promoted, there is nevertheless an atmosphere open to the possibility of good urban coexistence of all social groups, even those most stigmatised (see also table no. 3). A political leaning towards the centre-left proves to be significant, clear of all the other variables, with a powerful effect: it is worth reflecting on the fact that the "odds" of the possibility of coexisting with Gypsy groups of those claiming to hold centre-left ideas are almost double the "odds" of those claiming to be 'left-wing' (who are traditionally hostile to groups perceived as unproductive and sub-proletarian). Living in a small village has a positive impact compared to living in a little town, whereas living in a medium-size city has a negative effect. Among people living in Southern Italy, the percentage of those who believe coexistence is possible is absolutely higher than in all other Regions (see table no. 3), proving that Roma people in Southern Italy are better rooted in urban and rural areas; it emerges therefore that living in the North-West, in the Centre and on the Islands has a negative effect.

2. Coexistence and Social Policies

When asked to put forward some proposals to improve Roma and Sinti conditions in Italy today, more than half of the Italians (57%) first suggest either that Roma people should abide by the laws (32%) or that they should cease begging, stop relying too heavily on welfare, and should behave in a more pragmatic and active manner (24%). In other words, these are suggestions which identify the Roma and Sinti themselves as the main cause of their own condition of exclusion. For this last segment, victim and tormentor coincide, and the 'Gypsies' are responsible for their own dreadful conditions: *"if they respected the rules and got down to it, they would come out of it."* This is why we define this segment as *"dominant"*, domination being definable precisely in relation to the mechanism of assigning guilt to the victims themselves (Boltanski, 2008).

We have worked out an index related to those who feel that it would be important to favour *first of all* social policies favouring coexistence, that is to say active policies of employment or policies of school integration or of improvements in housing conditions. Around 15% of the population falls into this category, that is, almost three times as many as the extremely limited circle of those showing feelings of sympathy, but only half as many as those who think that coexistence is possible. This group has very interesting characteristics (see table no. 3). The age distribution follows the same trend as the group sympathising with Gypsies (higher levels among young and retired people), while as far as the level of education is concerned, there is a different profile, following

Table no. 5. Logistic regression. Socio-demographic variables, political and value aspects of opinion regarding the possibility of coexisting with Gypsy groups

	B	Sig.	Exp(B)
50–59 years	0.623	0.013**	1.864
Never attending Mass	-0.535	0.049**	0.586
Attending Mass many times a year	-0.51	0.037**	0.6
Centre-left	0.661	0.017**	1.936
Size of urban centre < 5.000	0.497	0.026**	1.643
Size of urban centre 50,001–100,000	-1.644	0**	0.193
North-West	-0.723	0.005**	0.485
Centre	-0.943	0.001**	0.389
Islands	-0.887	0.002**	0.412
Constant	-0.312	0.537	0.732

Source: ISPO 2007. Our elaboration. ** Sig. ≥ 0.05; N = 1.025; R^2 of Nagelkerke 0.168; Log. Likelihood 1.028.541.
The dichotomous dependent variable is obtained by merging the answers "certainly yes" and "probably yes" versus "certainly not" and "probably not" to the question "Can the Roma, the Gypsies live together with us?" In the table are listed only the significant variables, but in model also included other variables related to gender, the cohorts of age (reference category: 40-49), level of education title, social-professional category, frequency of the attendance at Mass (reference category: every week), political self-identification (reference category: left), interest in politics, size of urban centre (reference category: between 5,001 and 20,000 inhabitants), geographical macro-area (reference category: North-East).

a clear linear and positive relation: as the level of education rises, the agreement with social policies favouring integration increases (this agreement is 14 percentage points higher among degree-holders than among people with only primary education); the relation is spurious of course, given the well-known effects of age. The same linear trend may be observed in relation to social stratification and interest in politics. In the South and on the Islands, even though there are higher levels of intolerance, there are nevertheless higher percentages support for the primacy of social policies, far higher than in the other Regions, which is probably due to a stronger tendency to expect the state to play an active role in supplying public policies and services. Even living in a small to medium city of between 20,000 and 50,000 inhabitants, in which the local authorities are usually more responsible and capable of adopting a consequential logic in tackling problems, leads to an increased percentage of people who would expect social policies to favour integration.

A public demonstration against a Roma settlement eviction in Segrate (Milan), 16 February 2010
Placards saying:
"If you evict me, I do not fade away";
"State has to guarantee aid and accommodation";
"Each eviction costs 100.000 Euros."

However, analysing not only the first answer, but also the others, we come across more constructive and articulated solutions, that take into consideration the opportunity to implementing initiatives of public responsibility and politics for integration in schools and workplaces. Examining the whole range of answers given regarding possible solutions (and not only the first answers), three different positions emerge on what could be done: 32% of the *gagi* suggest as preferred solutions both that Roma should abide by the law and that "they should do something" (corresponding to a more closed behaviour). Mirror-like, another 30% of *gagi* suggest only policies of inclusion and public responsibility (in general they are the same people who show more open behaviour). Finally, 38% fall between the two positions, suggesting mixed solutions, that is to say respect of the law by the Roma but also more structured and active policies by Italian institutions.

The Voice of Italian Roma and Sinti Leaders

The data in question could be subjected to other forms of analysis, including even *cluster analysis* to explain the *gagi*'s behaviour in relation to the problem of civil coexistence with Roma and Sinti, which would outline a synthesis typology (Vitale, Claps, and Arrigoni, 2009). But we are not interested in going beyond this point. The aim of the previous section was to account for the possibility of differentiating the analysis of prejudice, and to highlight also the characteristics of those rejecting repressive and xenophobic solutions, an analysis that, as we have seen, also presents some unexpected elements which we feel could have a positive impact on the public sphere, should they be circulated.

This did not seem enough for us, however, and that is why, after having elaborated the data presented here, we asked some Roma and Sinti opinion leaders to comment both on the stereotypical images the gagi have of them, and on the main prejudices that, according to them, Roma and Sinti have towards *gagi*.[10] What emerged is an impressive and deeply felt confrontation that has shed light, despite the differences, on a mirror-like view of prejudice.

1. On the *Gagi*'s Prejudices

The Roma and Sinti we interviewed tend to group prejudices towards their communities in three areas: 1) prejudices they perceive as not responding to reality: 'they kidnap children, they're nomads, they don't want to work, they're dirty'; 2) prejudices that may refer to individual and not to widespread behaviours: 'they exploit children, they break the law'; 3) prejudices fuelled by more or less widespread behaviours: 'they don't send their children to school, they steal, they beg'.

Let us start with the first group of prejudices, those considered to be 'false'.

"They kidnap children": despite a number of research projects which show that in fact this is untrue, the interviews single out this prejudice as the one which weighs most heavily on Sinti people's everyday life. A real mark of shame, continuously reiterated by the media: "... after they arrested that woman, accused of having 'stolen

---

10   Between July and September 2007 we interviewed 12 people (8 male and 4 female), the majority with Italian citizenship (9 out of 11), who are or have been active in the fields of social mediation, politics, culture and health, almost all of them involved in associations committed to safeguarding of Roma and Sinti rights. Here we report excerpts from their interviews in italics.

a child', the witnesses admitted they weren't sure about it and that actually they are extremely afraid of Roma people. It was a collective hallucination."[11]

"They're nomads": according to the interviewees, this is a prejudice with notable consequences, which can lead to support and justification for the idea of the 'nomad camp' as an appropriate policy acceptable to the recipients themselves.

"They're dirty": in the interviews the prejudice is criticised because of the superficial way in which situations are judged, with people unjustly attributing to a culture what should rather be associated with the conditions of some nomad camps and shantytowns. Roma and Sinti are quite obsessed with hygiene and even in the most devastated camps, the dwellings are kept in good order and cleaned with great care.

A Roma settlement within a former industrial skeleton
Milan, 21 November 2009

"They don't want to work": according to the Roma and Sinti, such a statement cannot be proven, because it is extremely difficult for them to have any opportunity to work. Besides, the fact that they don't prioritise work in the way that the majority society does, is in no way equal to the statement "they don't want to work". On the contrary, they can recount endless tales of great efforts and investment being made just to be able to work.

In relation to this second area, according to our interviewees the prejudice about the 'exploitation of children by criminal conspiracies' cannot be applied to the majority of the communities. It is rather the result of episodes linked to organised crime and cannot be considered the norm. To explain their statements, the majority of the interviewees trace a parallel with very common clichés, such as the notion that "all Italians are members of the mafia".

Finally, the third area relates to prejudices that have some grounds in reality.

11　For an in-depth discussion of this episode, see Mannoia, 2008.

"They don't send their children to school": our interviewees make a distinction in this regard between those who consider schools as *gagi* institutions, where Roma children are uncomfortable and experience feelings of inferiority, and the majority who understand and value the potential of education and suffer because of the barriers to access: the unsustainable costs, the distance between schools and the places where they live, the discriminatory behaviour of the institutions, the relocations which keep them constantly on the move: "what can we say of the Roma coming from the East, educated over forty years ago, who would want to send their children to school?"

"They steal": according to our interviewees this prejudice is true but cannot be generalised to the whole population: "stealing, this is true, for pity's sake! Everyone knows it's like this and we cannot hide reality: but only some steal, not everybody, and only because they really are forced to do it". According to the interviewees, this is the most controversial problem, one which can only be solved through specific long-term policies, not merely repressive ones, but also allowing different options, contributing to the possibility for these communities to escape from marginalisation and segregation.

2. On the Political Solutions to Coproject with Roma

Roma and Sinti identify different issues at stake, closely interlinked, and they can also suggest some ways out.

Dwelling. The so-called 'nomad camps' are considered the tangible expression of discrimination, degraded places where Roma and Sinti do not like to live: "Gagi cannot imagine the situation Roma people live in: I'd want a gagè to live in a camp, even only for one week, so that he could understand that reality better; gagi go to reality shows like Celebrities Island for two months, whereas Roma live all their lives in the same conditions and never complain". And again: "they are an administrative invention", that is to say "they have not been planned together with Roma people, there has been no interaction, they tried to concentrate the phenomenon to obtain greater social control over the issue of nomads". There is no doubt that everybody considers them as contexts which create and fuel marginalisation and exclusion: "Vicious circles of misery. What can a nomad camp bring?" "It's not easy to find a job because you may even have a fair skin but your documents state that you live in a camp". As the issue of dwelling is intimately linked to that of anti-Gypsyism and exclusion, many consider getting out of the camps as the priority problem to be solved through specific accommodation policies, bearing in mind the heterogeneities of the different Roma and Sinti: from micro-areas to council estates.

Working. In the short-medium term policies of vocational training may be promoted, besides policies aimed at reviving traditional skills, involving them in the projects and leaving behind dependence on welfare: "for example, the role of the commercial agent would suit a Roma perfectly because even if he depends on a firm, and therefore works under a boss, the profession of the commercial agent involves relationships, the freedom to move around and dealing with others: a characteristic of the 'Gypsy' spirit." With great clarity: "welfare dependency is not acceptable and you cannot consider Roma as subjects who can only perform craft-based activities, and are not capable of aspiring to a profession... let's say, being a doctor. Abroad it is pretty well normal". Many also ask for "reserved jobs in the civil service, whereas we are systematically pushed away from the civil service".

Studying. For all the interviewees education is the key to the future emancipation of new Roma and Sinti generations. Today "only 30% of Roma and Sinti children in Italy are enrolled in primary school, and even they do not attend". What prevents even the children coming from groups who have been educated for decades (for example the Roma coming from Eastern European Countries) from going to school are the costs of books and of transportation and the discriminatory behaviour of educational institutions: "in Rome there are schools that don't accept Roma children and they are proud not to have them, and in some others they let them in through a different entrance to the one used by gagi children". Employing cultural mediators would be extremely useful.

Participating. An element stressed with great emphasis by all the *opinion leaders* interviewed is that *gagi* cannot speak in the name of the Roma: Roma and Sinti themselves ought to do it: "Without our active participation in social, cultural and political life, there will never be cultural integration". They develop an articulated reflection on the reasons of the historic weakness of Roma activism, with a tendency to delegate it to associations who have acted in their name, even with positive results, but which today should support and not substitute: "now the time has come to support the capacity for participation within all the different groups".

Being citizens. Urgent issues have to be tackled at the national legislative and political level, starting from the tragic cases of statelessness: people who may have lived in Italy for years, who have children and grandchildren here, but who administratively do not exist (just as their children and grandchildren do not exist): "in the sense that they have not been recognised in their countries of origin, they speak only Italian and Romanès and they have no documents". The civil code should also be amended where it deals with the attribution of residence: there are people born in the camps who have not been declared residents "because living in a camp, even if it's official and owned by the town hall, did not give them the right to residence". The official camps are not, in fact, dwellings, but transition areas, and they cannot be considered as the first residence of a person. Finally, "we are the only minority not recognised in Italy by the law on minorities".

Facing each other. To reverse the trend towards discrimination, they believe greater interaction and reciprocal knowledge are needed: this would mean creating chances to meet, providing information and training in schools, carrying out campaigns against discrimination on the model of the 'Dosta!' (Enough!) public awareness campaign promoted by the Council of Europe: "...so that Roma culture may emerge and thus become known, so as to demolish the prevailing cultural 'vision' (the misery, the marginality), mistaken because it is partial, and replace it with events of Gypsy art (music, painting, sculpture, performing arts) but also with social, cultural and gastronomic meetings". They also ask for more affective application of the legal instruments that already exist, in particular in the field of ethnic and racist discrimination. Finally, they also call for a stronger deontology by the media, in order to deliver more accurate information where they are concerned.

Beyond Logical Blindness: the Researcher's Responsibility

One of the main problems characterising the public discourse on Roma and Sinti is the pervasiveness of certain rhetorical constructions with the resulting effects of making them inferior and reproducing stereotypes. One of the most pervasive and at the same time most powerful is usually called 'logical blindness', or 'restriction' (Guillaumin, 1995). Despite these being clearly relational dynamics, the media and political actors systematically name only one of the parties involved, only one of the poles of the reaction. Thus, for example, we hear about the 'Gypsy problem', or the 'nomad emergency' as if the Gypsies were nomads and in any case a single and homogeneous group, but most of all, in the sense we are discussing here, as if the issue concerned only the Gypsies (whether they cause the problem or suffer from it), and we hear nothing about the relationship between "Gypsy" groups and other social groups.

Besides, the presentation of research results, be they qualitative or quantitative, often runs the risk of worsening the logical blindness. When we talk about Roma or Sinti, we tend to render them more exotic, describing their strange habits and considering their culture as fixed. Otherwise we talk about the *gagi*'s opinions of them, showing that Roma constitute a problem. The relation between the groups hardly filters into the public sphere. Thus research, even projects which strive to better contextualise the dynamics of public opinion, systematically fall into an error of restriction. Research into the dynamics of public opinion sheds light on the results of hostility, which may be used in ways that are completely at odds with denunciatory or emancipatory intentions of the researchers themselves. Such research can easily be used to justify the reasons for exclusion and discrimination, and to provide more solid arguments supporting favour of markedly anti-Gypsy initiatives.[12]

Considering this potential misuse of the research, those presenting their results can either choose to remain indifferent or, on the contrary, reflect in critical terms

---

12 In reflecting on issues of this kind, we were deeply influenced by Thévenot (Thévenot 2007) on the difference among regimes of action and on the 'tyranny' exercised by the most public regime on the more intimate one: different regimes have different grammars.

on the potential uses of their work (Boltanski, 2009). No solution is obvious or definitive. Certainly the historicisation of explanations may help to avoid the effects of objectification and naturalisation of the data. But historical comparative explanations are sometimes ignored in favour of numerical data, which thus end up appearing as independent truths in the public sphere, ready to be used without reference to the explanations that accompany them. The results of qualitative in-depth research can be accompanied by their quantitative contextualisation. The comparative presentation of data can be useful, in turn, to provide context, just as can a more refined analysis which breaks down people's feelings according to social and geographical categories. Overall, though, these ways of presenting the data run the risk of remaining locked into the vice of logical opacity which creates and nurtures so much racism (Alietti and Padovan, 2000).

The solution we have adopted in presenting the results of our research, from 2007 till the present day, has been to try to give value to a *relational configuration* in presenting the data. The Roma's voice is rarely assumed a priori, either in policies implemented at local level or in projects run by *gagi* activists of associations supporting Roma people. In the modalities that we identified, we have not found it worthwhile to compare by adding the opinion of Roma and Sinti to that of the *gagi*, as if they were two different people whose different opinions needed to be stressed. What we thought would be useful was to present to the Italian public (both at conferences organised by the Ministry of Home Affairs and in widely distributed magazines) not the qualitative and quantitative data on the representations of Roma and Sinti, *but what some Roma and Sinti think of these data.* Thus we have tried to give greater weight not to the opinions of a homogeneous group on certain issues, but to the opinions of some Roma and Sinti leaders on the data gathered and summarised by us. Thus it was they who decided by themselves how to comment on the most widespread opinions and how to contextualise them and put them in perspective.

We do not, of course, believe that this is an 'exportable' solution, or one with a generalisable value. It is a temporary and case-specific solution that we have adopted for the presentation of our research to the Italian public in the last few years. A weak solution, overall, given the small size of the sample selected and the cost of the operation. We know that the differences of opinion between *gagi* and Roma and Sinti that we have identified may be exaggerated by the difference in the means of research we have adopted. Moreover, even though we asked them to tell us not only their own point of view but more in general the diffused point of view of the community they belong to, we are not so naïve as to ignore the real *bias* that this represents.

However, what seems worthwhile is the idea of taking into consideration the voice of the Roma and Sinti about what concerns them, even on the hardest and most hostile opinions about them. A voice that is not only interesting in itself, but also a potential resource to reflect on the potential use of research and to keep a close watch on the automatic mechanisms of logical blindness. Because in the end the value of research lies not only in what is being written but also in the use that is made of it. Which clearly does not leave us without worries.

Bibliography

Alietti, Alfredo and Dario Padovan (2000). *Sociologia del razzismo* (Sociology of the racism). Rome: Carocci.

Asséo, Henriette (2005). "L'avènement politique des Roms (Tsiganes) et le génocide. La construction mémorielle en Allemagne et en France." *Le Temps des Médias*, no. 5 (Autumn 2005): 78–91.

Boltanski, Luc (1999). *Distant Suffering: Morality, Media and Politics*. Cambridge: Cambridge University Press.

Boltanski, Luc (2008). *Rendre la réalité inacceptable* (Make reality unacceptable). Paris: Demopolis.

Boltanski, Luc (2009). *De la critique. Precis de sociologie de l'emancipation*. Paris: Gallimard.

Elias, Norbert and John L. Scotson (1965). *The Established and the Outsiders: A Sociological Enquiry into Community Problems*. London: Sage Publications.

Elster, Jon (1999). *Strong Feelings: Emotion, Addiction, and Human Behavior*. Cambridge: The MIT Press.

Guillaumin, Colette (1995). "The Specific Characteristics of Racist Ideology" in *Racism, Sexism Power and Ideology*, ed. Guillaumin Colette. London: Routledge, pp. 29–60.

Maneri, Marcello (2001). "Il panico morale come dispositivo di trasformazione dell'insicurezza" (Moral panic as a transformational device of insecurity). *Rassegna Italiana di Sociologia*, no. 1 (March 2001): 5–40.

Mannoia, Michele (2008). "Come si costruisce il pregiudizio: la leggenda delle Zingare rapitrici" (How the prejudice is constructed: the legend of Gypsy women's kidnapping) in *Crocevia e trincea. La Sicilia come frontiera mediterranea* (Crossroads and trench. Sicily as border of the Mediterranean), ed. Pirrone, Marco. Rome: XL Editions, pp. 111–28.

Marradi, Alberto (2005). *Raccontar storie. Un nuovo metodo per indagare sui valori* (Telling stories: a new method to inquiry about values). Rome: Carocci.

Mazzara, Bruno M. (1997) *Stereotipi e pregiudizi* (Stereotypes and prejudices). Bologna: il Mulino.

Migliavacca, Mauro (2008). *Famiglie e lavoro* (Family and work). Milano: Bruno Mondatori.

Morning, Ann (2009). "Toward a Sociology of Racial Conceptualization for the 21st Century." *Social Forces* 87, no. 3 (2009): 1167–92.

Piasere, Leonardo (1991). *Popoli delle discariche* (People of the dumps). Rome: CISU.

Small, Mario Luis (2009). "'How Many Cases do I Need?' On Science and the Logic of Case Selection in Field-Based Research." *Ethnography* 10, no. 1 (2009): 5–38.

Tajfel, Henri (1984). *Social Groups and Identities*. London: Routledge.

Thévenot, Laurent (2007). "The Plurality of Cognitive Formats and Engagements: Moving between the Familiar and the Public." *European Journal of Social Theory* 10, no. 3 (2007): 409–23.

Vitale, Tommaso (2009a). "Comuni (in)differenti: i "nomadi" come "problema pubblico" nelle città italiane" ((In)different municipalities: the "nomads" as a "public problem" in Italian cities) in *Rom e sinti. Storia e cronaca di ordinaria discriminazione* (Roma and Sinti. History and chronicle of ordinary discrimination), eds. Cherchi, Roberto and Gianni Loy. Rome: Ediesse, pp. 215–42.

Vitale, Tommaso (2009b). "Da sempre perseguitati? Effetti di irreversibilità della credenza nella continuità storica dell'antiziganismo" (From time immemorial persecuted? Non-reversibility effects of the belief in historical continuity of anti-Gypsyism). *Zapruder. Rivista di storia della conflittualità sociale*, no 19 (June 2009): 47–61.

Vitale, Tommaso (2009c). "Politique des évictions. Une approche pragmatique" (Eviction policies: a pragmatic approach) in *Les approches pragmatiques de l'action publique* (Pragmatic approaches to public policies), eds. Cantelli, Fabrizio, Luca Pattaroni, Marta Roca, and Joan Stavo-Debauge. Bruxelles: P.I.E. Peter Lang, pp. 71–92.

Vitale, Tommaso, Enrico Claps, and Paola Arrigoni (2009). "Regards croisés. Antitsiganisme et possibilité du vivre ensemble, Roms et gadjés, en Italie." *Etudes Tsiganes*, no. 35 (May 2009): 80–103.

Romany Responses

Marcelo Frediani

THE WEB AGAINST DISCRIMINATION?
Internet and Gypsies/Travellers Activism in Britain

Information and Communication Technologies (ICTs) have become a particularly important object of research and deserve increased attention from researchers in the social sciences. In fact the use of these technologies world-wide affects all areas of social life and has acquired growing importance especially in our European and North-American societies, and within the framework of the labour market and economic life. ICTs have become essential tools and ICT skills are considered core life skills which have also become fundamental in various aspects of social and political life. Moreover, the use of cell phones, the internet, chats, blogs, multi-media, e-learning, CD-ROMs and Cyberspace has become an inevitable part of everyday life in our societies. The social transformations linked to the use of these technologies are undeniable and the pace of change is staggering. ICTs evolve continually and society also adapts and changes, in a continuous cycle. As Castells notes: "We know that technology does not determine society: it is society. Society shapes technology according to the needs, values, and interests of people who use the technology. Furthermore, ICTs are particularly sensitive to the effects of social uses of technology itself" (Castells and Cardoso, 2006, p. 3).

The transformations in society linked to the use of the internet have been the object of many studies over the last fifteen years (cf. Castells and Cardoso, 2006; Miller and Slater, 2003). The internet is widely considered an empowering instrument and Castells (Castells, 2001) recognizes that it has an enormous capacity to liberate dominated groups. However, he is also aware of its ability to marginalise and exclude those who do not have access to it. The question of access brings us to the issue of the digital divide and marginalised minorities. How are groups living on the edge of mainstream society using ICTs? And are the needs and values of marginalised minorities also shaping technology?

There are many studies on the digital divide and minorities (cf. for example Mehra, Merkel, and Bishop, 2004; Miller and Slater, 2003), but it appears that Gypsies, Roma and Travellers[1] are vastly underrepresented (Furey, 2006; Marks, 2010). Nevertheless, even if little is known about the impact of ICTs on Travellers, a quick search reveals the massive presence of Travellers' organisations in the web. In this paper, I propose to examine the impact of the latest technological developments on Gypsies and Travellers and their lifestyle.

---

1   The terms Gypsy/Traveller or Traveller to refer to the whole nomadic community in the UK.

This paper is based on intensive "virtual ethnography": two years following dedicated Traveller websites (see some examples in the bibliography); as well as Yahoo groups, YouTube and Facebook groups. Moreover, I have been in constant contact with Traveller representatives and have conducted in-depth interviews both face-to-face and via email. My ethnographic fieldwork took place in England (Oxfordshire area and Saint Albans) during four months in 2007–2008 and two more months in 2009. In this article I especially focus on the use of the Internet by Travellers' associations in their political and educational activities to illustrate how the internet is being used as a tool which helps Travellers maintain their nomadic lifestyle, decrease their isolation and promote contacts with the sedentary community as well as with other Travellers. It will present a few examples showing how these technologies are being used politically to support their lifestyle, to gain recognition of their rights and to make life on the road more viable. We will especially focus on how the internet has been used to lobby for law reforms, showing that the internet can be used for protest but also that it can play a role in democratising political debate, even for this minority which has a limited access to ICTs. We will also explore educational projects that have been launched to increase the uptake of this technology within this population group.

Who Are the Gypsies, Roma and Travellers in the United Kingdom?

A brief description and some basic facts concerning this community are necessary to understand the legal and the social issues related to these groups more clearly. The present day Gypsy, Roma and Traveller population of England and Wales can be divided into five main groups, each with its own cultural heritage and identity. The community is composed of the Romanies or Romany-Chals of England and Wales, which is the largest group and numbers 63,000, including house-dwelling families. The Kalès of North Wales, some 1,000 persons. The Irish Travellers are estimated to be around 19,000. Scottish Travellers are estimated to be 20,000 living in Scotland and in England (Kenrick and Clark, 1999, p. 21). And finally, after the 1960s we witness the arrival of New Travellers, estimated to be between 2,000–15,000 persons in the 90s. Precise figures for Gypsies and Travellers are difficult to establish as their numbers are not recorded at present in census records (London Gypsy and Traveller Unit, 2009). There are said to be 90–120,000 nomadic Gypsies, Roma and Travellers but according to some there are as many as 200,000 people of Gypsy and Traveller ancestry living in housing. It is worth remembering that Gypsies and Irish and Scottish Travellers[2],

---

2   This last group was recognised as an ethnic group only in 2008 after a long court case. Scottish Travellers do not consider themselves as Roma, nor do they claim Indian origin. In fact, their non Indian origin had always been used against them to justify all kinds of discrimination. After 2008, they were given the same rights under the Race Relations Act (1976) against racist discrimination as Irish Travellers and English Gypsies. I would like to thank Judith Okely for providing this information the day after the court reached its decision.

this latter group only after 2008, are recognised ethnic groups for the purposes of the Race Relations Act (1976), identified as having a shared culture, language and beliefs. Travellers living in housing are not the object of this study; the issue is how mobility and a traditional lifestyle are affected by ICTs. In July 2004 the government counted 15,014 caravans in England and Wales. Most (10,777) are on council-run or legal private sites. Just over a quarter are on unauthorised sites (1,855) or roadside verges (2,409) (London Gypsy and Traveller Unit, 2009). It is this issue of sites and parking which has been causing friction between Travellers and the rest of society since the beginning of the 90s and which has led to a campaign which benefited from the internet.

The Struggle to Change a Law: Gypsy/Travellers[3] Organisations in the Web

At present the Gypsy/Traveller population in the UK includes New Travellers who are of diverse ethnic origin. It is important to mention that the emergence of this group in the social environment of nomadic communities in the UK has had an impact on the life of these traditional communities.

Defined as Hippies in the 70s and New Age Travellers in the 80s, they fled sedentary life and began squatting buildings and land and living nomadically. New Travellers sometimes parked in stopping places and encampments/sites reserved for Gypsies. Moreover, New Travellers received copious media attention, especially because of the squatting, the raves and festivals and the convoys of vehicles roaming around the country to music festivals (Stonehenge and Glastonbury being the most important). At the end of the day it was the whole nomadic population that came under the spotlight and a wave of panic swept the countryside, fomented by the tabloid press. This atmosphere of anti-nomadic sentiment is one of the reasons that led to the passing of the Criminal Justice and Public Order Act in 1994 (CJPOA 94). This law, among other things, made trespassing a criminal offence. Many researchers agree that the difficult relations between local authorities and "traditional" Travellers worsened after this law was passed because of the authorities' tendency to confuse New Travellers with Gypsies (see Hawes and Perez, 1996; Acton, 1997).

It was in 1994 that some New Travellers created the organisation called Friends Families & Travellers as a reaction to this law and with the objective of protecting the whole Traveller community. Their mission statement reads:

> Friends Families & Travellers (FFT) was established in response to the 1994 Criminal Justice & Public Order Act ... FFT grew from an informal support group and network helping to deal with crises faced primarily by

---

3 In this paper, we are using the term Gypsy/Traveller or Traveller to refer to the whole nomadic community in the UK.

New Travellers as and when they arose, to a formal advice, information and training organization providing a wide range of services to all Travellers nation wide—whether traditional or new, settled or on the road... The overall objective of the organization is to work towards a more equitable society where everyone has the right to travel and to stop without constant fear of persecution because of their lifestyle.

Nowadays, according to the FFT report of 2003–2004, the services of FFT are being used by the whole community, but mainly by Gypsies (46%) and Irish Travellers (35%).

Legal issues became the centre of activist lobbying and FFT joined the Gypsy & Traveller Law Reform Coalition (G&TLRC) which was created in 2002. It is an alliance of Romany Gypsy, Irish Traveller and New Traveller campaign groups "committed to raising the social inclusion of these and other Traveller communities. A primary aim is to lobby the government to introduce a statutory duty to provide or facilitate a broad range of Traveller accommodation in accordance with the aims and principles of the Traveller Law Reform Bill drafted by the Traveller Law Research Unit of Cardiff University." (Mission Statement)

I have chosen the most representative organisations to provide examples of how the internet underpins political action. Since 1994, these organisations work with Travellers and for Travellers, they do traditional outreach work visiting the sites, but also offer advice through help lines and office visits. Nowadays, the internet has become another ally. During these years much of their work centred on the infamous CJPOA 94, giving legal explanations to Travellers and offering advice about how to obtain the legalisation of their sites and planning permission. They were also informed of what to do when threatened with eviction, which became easier and hence more frequent with this law. The CJPOA 94 relieved councils of the duty to provide authorised sites for Travellers, with the aim of promoting private sites. The results were disastrous: a wave of evictions with Travellers not knowing where to go and unable to obtain planning permission when they applied. (90% refusals compared to 20% for the sedentary population.) The Coalition actively lobbied ministers in both houses and central government directly to bring about law reform for Travellers and successfully set up an All Party Parliamentary Group on Traveller Law reform which requires cross party support and representation. The internet has made it possible to e-petition parliamentarians (an example of the letter is available on the website) and to inform both Travellers and the general public of the implications of the laws and the reasons for change. The organisations' sites offer a wealth of information which is readily available for Travellers, researchers and legislators. Together with the consultations carried out during the visits and during conferences, the internet made the voice of Travellers stronger and played a role in reform. Travellers could now learn about their rights through the associations' web sites and wide-ranging consultations took place between the Traveller representatives to draft a law (Traveller Law Reform Bill). This coalition made itself heard in the press and with the government. The Housing Act 2004 indeed imposes a new duty on councils to assess Traveller accommodation needs and there is a New Planning Circular (Circular 1/2006) which replaces circular 1/94. The G&TLRC disbanded in April 2006 but FFT, the Gypsy council, the Irish Traveller movement and the London Gypsy and Traveller Unit wanted to establish a way of continuing the valuable work on law reform achieved by the Coalition and so agreed to set up the Traveller Law Reform Project. This project will keep up the aims of G&TLRC; namely, to bring about positive changes in the law in relation to the rights and needs of all the Gypsy and Traveller communities and to monitor the implementation of current legislation which is in part a response to campaigning in recent years. The network created throughout the country has found an ally in the internet which will continue to be used. It is indeed only the beginning and the organisations are trying to foster the use of ICTs among the general Gypsy and Traveller population.

Though the internet and specialist websites are recognised as a valuable tool for lobbying and awareness campaigns, for a nomadic group such as Gypsies, ICTs are especially useful as a resource—a place to find vital information wherever you are, even if you are far from the organisations' offices. The FFT website indeed offers practical help as well as being a forum for the exchange of stories and ideas. The site offers safety tips against fires, advice in case of discrimination and harassment and the organisation continues to offer advice on the new law. The details and the implications of the law are explained in clear and understandable language. FFT also requests reports on the extent to which Councils fulfil their duty to provide sites, thus being able to follow up cases. The importance of this issue should not be underestimated—30% of the Traveller community lives on unauthorised sites, which is inconvenient not only for them but for the housed population as well. Solving the problem would reduce tensions within the community, and if proper information is provided online as well, it becomes easier to ensure that rights are respected. It also becomes easier to report violations of these rights. The organisations' web sites also ask for reports on cases of racism or even biased press reports and act promptly to redress the situation.

FFT realises that ICTs play a fundamental role in today's society and in particular it recognises that internet technology could make Travellers' lives easier, that it can support their lifestyle—and making their lifestyle viable is a political act against sedentarism as a norm. E-learning tools could be invaluable to families who are not settled and can also help improve literacy—but there is still the digital divide. There is general awareness of the need for educational tools and training both for the Traveller population and the teaching community; which brings us to the next section of this paper.

Internet Use and the Education of Gypsies and Travellers: Supporting a Culture

The problem of the digital divide in the case of Gypsies and Travellers is compounded by other factors besides the usual poverty and non-literacy or semi-literacy that characterise other minority groups—namely nomadism and the physical conditions under which Gypsies and Travellers live, whether in authorized or unauthorized encampments. Travellers' sites have poor access to services and amenities and obviously to computers and the internet, which may lead to doubts about the impact of ICTs on Travellers. Moreover, Trevor Philips, the chair of the Commission for Racial Equality, said that discrimination against Gypsies and Travellers appears to be the last "respectable" form of racism (McCluskey and Lloyd, 2005) and this widespread discrimination means that even access to an internet café can be a source of tension and unease.

During an interview with Lucy Beckett (Head of Advice Service for the education of Travellers (ASET), Oxfordshire), she underlined that in matters pertaining to the education of Gypsies and Travellers in the UK, one has to keep in mind that the main issue to tackle is how this community is dealing with discrimination. According to this educator, we have to consider that the central issue is not an economic one; the main problem is the discrimination and the racism that Travellers suffer "everywhere in Europe". Their coping strategy entails avoiding close contact "with mainstream society" (Gorgio society). This observation is important to establish the perspective from which to consider work with the Gypsy/Traveller community.

Lucy Beckett, like many other educators, believes in the importance of education as the solution to many of the difficulties Travellers encounter. Before tackling issues concerning ICTs, she states that we have to start with the basics, namely literacy. She (and, according to her, the whole Traveller community) doesn't believe in home education (which in any case is quite difficult for Roma-Gypsies—as opposed to New Travellers—to provide). In general, home education is used to avoid the integration of Traveller children in the school system and contact with the others. As we know, Roma-Gypsies are not completely against primary education. Nevertheless, for the educational service the challenge is finding a strategy which makes it possible to reach these communities. Lucy Beckett states that her Service after all these years "has become a reference in the field." Any project concerning education has to go through them, especially because they have managed to acquire the trust of the Travelling community in the Oxford area and also at institutional level. They have a team of 12 teachers visiting the six county council permanent Travellers sites and a number of unauthorized encampments across Oxfordshire. Moreover, the Oxford Advice Service for the education of Travellers is using e-education instruments such as the E-lamp 4 system (cf. Marks, 2010).

Our interviews allow us to consider the field from another point of view and especially to understand the obstacles that discrimination and nomadism raise in the application of educational methods to Roma-Gypsies (it is also interesting to compare this with the situation of New Travellers in Britain, who are much better able to deal with mainstream society since it is where they originate from).

One of the main difficulties concerning these groups from an educational point of view is precisely their travelling lifestyle. How can you follow children who never stay for long in the same place? ASET managed to convince families to send their children to school at least twice a week initially and then to send them three times a week. In general, fathers are reluctant to send the boys to school for long periods and prefer them to work (they buy and sell cars, are blacksmiths and do some mechanical engineering too). The school itself was against accepting these children for only two days a week, requiring them to attend full time. Lucy Beckett explained to the school head that "it is two days or nothing, what is better?" and the school reluctantly gave in. She exemplifies the non-flexibility of institutions in meeting Travellers' needs with the fact that some schools send Traveller children back home when their uniforms do not correspond to the norm, because they are incomplete, dirty, crumpled or missing a button.

The examples that will be provided in this paper are intended to give an idea of the effect the internet has already had, and especially of the potential that remains to be exploited. But first of all it is important to provide some background information to explain the full implications of e-learning for Gypsy/Travellers. As stated by "The Commission for Racial Equality" (in its "Gypsies and Travellers: CRE Strategy 2004–2007"), this group still has problems of non-literacy and access to schools in the UK. It is difficult to evaluate the situation precisely: recently Gypsies/Traveller groups have been included in school censuses, but research, and data collected by Traveller support services, suggests that the census statistics gathered so far are a considerable underestimate of the existing difficulties. However, research findings suggest widespread low attendance, significant "underachievement" and disproportionately "high levels of disciplinary exclusion". By Key Stage 3, it is estimated that only 15–20% of Traveller pupils are registered or regularly attend school (Commission for Racial Equality, 2004). Save the Children recently estimated that 10,000 Gypsy/Traveller children in England are not attending school (SCF 2001 quote in Bhopal, 2004), while Kendall and Derrington (Derrington and Kendall, 2004) note that according to official estimates only Traveller children aged 11–16 were enrolled in secondary schools. Moreover, "counting" Gypsies/Travellers is a sensitive issue in itself. Families who do not wish to self identify will not be counted. Some children may feel safer in school if they can conceal their identity.

It is clear, however, that many Gypsies/Travellers in Britain do not participate fully in state education, particularly at secondary level, with the result that many have difficulties with literacy and lack qualifications, all of which may limit their participation in, and promote exclusion from, wider society (Derrington and Kendall, 2004; Padfield and Jordan, 2004). Mobility in the lifestyle of some families is only one factor that contributes to difficulties in attending and achieving results at school. Even more critical may be their perception of schools as unsupportive of their community, their values and their lifestyles (Lloyd and Stead, 2001; Derrington and Kendall, 2004).

Many Gypsy/Traveller parents fear that wholesale integration into regular schooling from 5 to 16 years of age might lead to their children increasingly adopting the values and habits of the wider peer group and consequently attributing less value to their own Traveller culture.[4] There are persistent worries about cultural dilution though views about schooling within Gypsies and Traveller communities are diverse: some are fearful of the experiences their children will have in school while many others express strong support for the basic numeracy and literacy skills offered by primary schools (Lloyd and Stead, 2001; Lloyd, Stead, and Jordan et. al., 1999; Bhopal, 2004). Nevertheless, they remain sceptical about the relevance of much else that is on offer particularly, for older children and young adults. Gypsies and Traveller communities often have high regard for family-based learning (McCluskey and Lloyd, 2005, pp. 7–9). Considering the issues from this point of view, e-learning tools become very important in the education of this community, not only because of the flexibility they offer to nomadic groups, but also in the sense that each family can control the content of the education of their children. Developing e-learning in this context may represent a way of respecting diversity and resisting assimilation. There are various projects going on in this field and the Travellers organisations' Websites propose a number of solutions for families involved in home-education (e.g. CyberPilot project, E-Lamp projects and Travellers' School Charity e-learning Bus). The Traveller School Charity Bus travelled around sites physically bringing educational material; it continues to do so but the material has changed and there are more opportunities for exchange. Now the material is online and has a wider audience—though as Tammy Furey, the webmaster from FFT, found out with the CyberPilot project, it is still necessary to "get out there" and visit communities, projects and sites.

The FFT CyberPilot project is especially concerned with community, identity and self-esteem. The website is for the young and wishes to promote Traveller goals and values while educating society to accept a diverse culture. Tammy states: "The technology can also enable young people to participate in ways and from places that would otherwise not be possible... the website has been used to inspire young people

---

4   According to an ICT Gypsy teacher (living and working in the Saint Albans area) whom I met through Norbert McCabe (Head of Gypsy Section. Hertfordshire County Council), one of the first questions that Gypsy/Travellers parents ask an educator about the internet is about how to secure their computer against potentially "polluting" websites. Derrington and Kendall, 2004.

to create material and go on the internet" (Furey, 2006). This is an online community for Young People and the website is intended to strengthen identity and enable self expression. The CyberPilot website has a movie section, an art gallery, Roma football, an advice section, stories, poems, links, games, other Traveller projects, outreach materials and an extensive adult section. This website is a building block which will certainly lead to interesting developments in the near future. The site is used regularly and every year since the project began the number of Registered Young People taking part has increased by at least 50% with the final year doubling the figures of year three (Furey, 2006).

The project has already helped to create other websites. Gypsies and Travellers are new to the internet, in a certain sense, and field studies are lacking to evaluate the impact of ICT on their lifestyles. The organisations realise that they need a "hands-on" approach to bring the technology and experience that this community needs. Tammy says of the digital divide "it can be used to reference either a difference in skills, or a difference in ownership or access to technology. Young Gypsy Travellers are unusual in this country, as they experience both types of divide... this means that many educational and job opportunities might be closed to them in the future" (Furey, 2006). But she also states, mentioning technology developments such as free wireless signals, as well as free online word processing and other programs, that the digital divide can be overcome and "the systems that are evolving will truly serve the Gypsy and Traveller population, giving greater access to services, education and creating greater networking opportunities" (Furey, 2006).

The E-Lamp projects (E-Learning and Mobility Project) should also be mentioned because of the technology provided to support e-learning which makes it possible (with outreach and training) to overcome the problems linked to mobility. Ken Marks was responsible for the main fieldwork in these projects. All of the projects have been concerned with the use of ICTs to enhance distance learning provision for mobile Traveller children who do not have access to normal schooling. The project explores the use of laptops and data-cards to enhance the distance learning support already offered to Traveller children by their winter 'base-schools' and through traditional work packs. Access to the Internet was provided via the data card devices (which link to mobile telephone networks). Obviously this was a pilot project, so we cannot state that the use of ICTs is widespread, simply that interesting experiments are going on, which offer valuable opportunities, perhaps even beyond the initial scope.

There are a series of e-lamp projects and the e-lamp2 is especially interesting as an applied project for the primary sector during the travelling season (summer). The project makes it possible for the children to exchange e-mails with their teachers and schools, to exchange some of their work electronically (allowing it to be checked and feedback given relatively quickly, along with new tasks), and enables them to access recommended websites and pursue projects (cf. Marks, 2010).

By early 2006 approximately 100 Traveller pupils were using laptops and data cards. These developments are only just beginning and the project concentrates on maintaining the children in school in a certain sense, even though it is "virtually". The children are integrated into the normal school circuit. It is worth mentioning this project because the potential of these technologies is enormous—if not having a landline is no longer an obstacle then Travellers can also opt for home education, and of course they can access Travellers' websites and their community wherever they happen to be in the country. In general, there is the potential to enjoy greater freedom (Marks, 2010). In September 2008, a total of some 600 young participants, and about half of the families now involved travel away from school for less than 6 weeks during term-time (see Marks, 2009). It remains to be seen if and how this potential is being exploited and whether there will be an exponential growth of ICT skills amongst Travellers.

The importance of involving the adults in the educational process is fundamental, so that the whole community is committed to their children's progress. But what kind of strategies need to be employed in order to involve adults? Many Gypsies are interested in obtaining computer skills in order to solve very practical problems. For example, during one interview a Gypsy girl mentioned the use of computers and their importance for preparing her driving test. I also met a group of middle age women organizing a class with teachers from ASET, Oxford to learn basic IT skills.

During our visits to an English Traveller's site, we were able to confirm that some Gypsy/Traveller families have a telephone, a computer and internet access at home. The father in one family owns a forge. He apparently uses internet and email for his work. The mother can read and write and helps her husband with the administrative side of the company (she also helps their little son with his reading exercises). She notes, for example, that the older girl has excellent computer skills. She tells us she is good at finding things on the Web and already uses the mobile phone to send messages. The mother uses the web for different purposes and mentions Google and sites such as e-bay and YouTube. During this visit she also received a package of sheets, apparently bought through some commercial website (sheets decorated with teddy-bears, nothing specifically Traveller). Talking about the supposed North Indian origins of Travellers, she quotes the web and says: "you can find all that in the internet!" According to the teacher from ASET, this lady is very proud of her Gypsy origins and even shows us her family album ("This was me grandmother and her sister—a very bad woman", "this was me grand uncle—me kid look like him", etc.—which was a wonderful opportunity to talk about Kinship!).

For Lucy Beckett (ASET, Oxfordshire) it is obvious that if Travellers do not acquire IT skills it will be another element contributing to their marginalisation. "Travellers are going to be even more excluded—social and digital divide". As Castells says, "the issue is not how to reach the network society as a self-proclaimed superior stage of human development. The issue is to recognize the contours of our new historical terrain, meaning the world we live in. Only then it will be possible to identify the means by which specific societies in specific contexts can pursue their goals and realize their values by using the new opportunities generated by the most extraordinary technological revolution in humankind, the one transforming our capacities of communication and enabling to modify the codes of life, that is the one giving us the tools to actually master our own condition, with all the potentially destructive or creative implications of this capacity" (Castells and Cardoso, 2006, pp. 5–6).

Final Considerations

My purpose in this paper is neither to warn against the use of these new tools by these communities nor to herald the beginning of a brave new world. It is important to remember that this new technology is not enough to change society: it is necessary for technical innovation to meet social and community expectations and needs. Nevertheless, many researchers believe that the Internet represents a new opportunity for minorities to overcome difficult life situations. Matthew Ciolek provides a concise summary of the uses and the usefulness of the internet for minorities, stating that "members of a minority, as well as its supporters and allies, whether in the home country or abroad, can use the Internet to: intensively liaise and network amongst themselves and with other friendly groups; document their culture, language, history and achievements; inform and educate the neutral sections of public opinion about their plight and grievances. Such networked information, like all internets' information is available both locally and globally" (Ciolek, 2004).

Judith Okely told me that during her fieldwork in the '70s, a pub owner was seriously annoyed to hear his phone ringing late into the night with people calling for some second-hand car company. In fact, it was common for Gypsies to give the telephone number of a pub as a contact number for personal and professional reasons. By the mid 90s several Travellers were already using cell telephones both for work and personal contacts. The increasing flexibility of the labour market and the use of temporary agencies mean that the Internet and cell phones play a fundamental role in finding a job. In precarious living conditions these new instruments offer more opportunities to this population group. In particular, New Travellers, who generally have more formal education than traditional Travellers, exploited this potential to support their lifestyle. Mobile phones meant they could be called for a short-term job or could inform Travellers of a possible stopping site or of an eviction taking place. Now Travellers need not worry about finding a reference address and thanks to this technology the pub owners of Britain can sleep serenely all night.

Travellers' organisations rely on the Internet for the myriad reasons we have seen. Their sites provide information on legal issues, health issues and bullying and also represent a political will to create a community with a recognised identity. The sites also work as forums for the direct exchange of information and stories between Travellers. According to a personal email message from Steve Staines, founder of FFT, the use of ICT is increasing in the traditional Traveller community. He recently met a couple of Irish Travellers living in Ireland who operated a road-surfacing firm and used ICTs—e-mail and web address. So, as he says and as I saw during my visits, "things do move on". Moreover, ICTs and the internet are being used to promote educational opportunities for children and their parents who are "on the road". By offering educational tools on the road and through e-learning materials it becomes possible to receive an education even without having to participate in mainstream schools, though the introduction of ICTs may be targeted to maintaining the children in school, as the e-lamp project shows. ICTs and the internet make it possible to act and react in society and enable this group to participate in the political life of society. It gives them a voice in mainstream society while maintaining and promoting their life style.

People are still marginalised, but what they are trying to do is to use these new technologies to disseminate information about their culture to public opinion and policymakers. Through the educational projects they are also trying to revive their culture and keep it alive so that history and stories are not lost and children can also find out about their roots. This is not, however, a backward-looking approach but a forward-looking one, to guarantee the future of this group, its traditions and its lifestyle. They are using the technology to defend their rights and to spread the knowledge of these rights both around the country and internationally. The Traveller law Reform Bill is a model which inspires others as well and the coalition will continue its work. The internet may make it easier for them to foster their community and to pursue their goals and values.

Judith Okely stated in 1983 that "those who confront the prevailing order, be it in small ways, those who demonstrate alternative possibilities in economic spheres, in ways of being and thinking, those who appear as powerful symbols, must, it seems, be contained and controlled... since a travelling people are seen to defy the State's demand for a 'fixed abode', they are seen as both lawless and fascinating" (cf. Okely, 1983, p. 2). How are these alternative ways of thinking and being affected by the internet? Have perceptions changed in the general population and is the Traveller identity reinforced or weakened by ICTs? How have their means of subsistence been affected? Is life easier for Travellers now, after the internet revolution? For us it is interesting to try to understand how these marginalised groups are taking possession of these technologies and how they are adapting these instruments that are at the core of capitalist society to resist assimilation and the disintegration of their autonomous identity. The internet can be and is being used to spread the sense of community and belonging that some groups had lost. In this globalised world can ICTs help minority groups become fully recognized and respected members of society or are they merely instruments for uniformity and conformism? It is difficult at this stage to generalise about Travellers and ICTs and we have more questions than answers for the moment. At present, it is predominantly organisations that are using the internet, yet they are working hard to encourage the spread of IT skills and we are seeing the first signs of change.

Bibliography

Acton, Thomas Alan, ed. (1997). *Gypsy Politics and Travellers Identity.* Hatfield: University of Hertfordshire Press.

Advisory Service for Squatters. Available at http://www.squatter.org.uk [accessed 23 February 2010]

Bhopal, Kalwant (2004). "Gypsy Travellers and Education: Changing Needs and Changing Perceptions." *British Journal of Educational Studies,* 52, no. 1 (2004): 47–64.

Castells, Manuel (2001). *The Internet Galaxy.* Oxford: Oxford University Press.

Castells, Manuel and Gustavo Cardoso, eds. (2006). *The Network Society: From Knowledge to Policy.* Washington D.C.: John Hopkins Center for Transatlantic Relations.

Ciolek, T. Matthew (2004). "2001. Internet and Minorities" in *The Encyclopedia of World's Minorities,* ed. Skutsch, Carl. Independence, K.Y.: Taylor & Francis –Routledge. Available at www.ciolek.com/PAPERS/minorities2001.html.

Commission for Racial Equality, ed. (2004). *Gypsies and Travellers: CRE Strategy 2004–2007.* London: Commission for Racial Equality.

Derrington, Chris and Sally Kendall (2003). *Gypsy Travellers in English Secondary Schools; a Longitudinal Study* (Stoke on Trent: Trentham Books.

Derrington, Chris and Sally Kendall (2004). *Traveller Pupils' Perceptions on Language and Learning.* Paper presented at SATEAL conference, General Teaching Council, Edinburgh.

Frediani, Marcelo (2006). "La législation concernant les New Travellers en Grande Bretagne: Nomadisme et identité aux marges de la légalité." *Études Tsiganes* 26, no. 3 (2006).

Frediani, Marcelo (2009). *Sur les routes. Le phénomène des New Travellers.* Paris: Éditions Imago.

Friends, Families and Travellers. "CyberPilot Project." Available at http://www.gypsy-traveller.org/cyberpilots/Projects/index.htm [accessed 22 January 2010].

Friends, Families and Travellers. Working on Behalf of All Gypsies and Travellers Regardless of Ethnicity, Culture or Background. Available at http://www.Gypsy-traveller.org/ [accessed 23 February 2010].

Furey, Tammy (2006). "Does Every Child Matter?" NATT Conference, London.

Gypsy Roma Traveller Achievement Service in Leeds—GRTAS. "The Gypsy Council." Available at http://www.grtleeds.co.uk/information/GypsyCouncil.html [accessed 24 February 2010].

Hawes, Derek and Barbara *Perez* (1996). *The Gypsy and the State: the Ethnic Cleansing of British Society.* Bristol: Policy Press.

Hine, Christine (2003). *Virtual Ethnography.* London: Sage Publications.

Kenrick, Donald and Colin Clark (1999). *Moving On: The Gypsies and Travellers of Britain.* Hatfield: University of Hertfordshire Press.

Lloyd, Gwynedd and Joan Stead (2001). "'The boys and girls not calling me names and the teachers to believe me'. Name calling and the experiences of Travellers in school." *Children and Society,* 15 (2001): 361–74.

Lloyd, Gwynedd, Joan Stead, and Betty Jordan (with C. Norris and M. Miller) (1999). *Travellers at School; The Experience of Parents, Pupils and Teachers.* Edinburgh: Moray House.

London Gypsy and Traveller Unit (2009). "The Gypsy and Traveller Law Reform Project" [accessed 23 February 2010]. Available at http://www.travellerslaw.org.uk.

Marks, Ken (2009). *Using ICT to Support distance learning for Traveller Children.* A report on the progress of strand 'A' of the E-LAMP initiative Phase 5. Department for Children, Schools and Families. National Associations of Teachers of Travellers and other professionals.

Marks, Ken (2010). "E-learning and Mobility Project." Available at http://www.shef.ac.uk/content/1/c6/02/73/58/elamp.doc.

McCluskey, Gillean and Gwynedd Lloyd (2005). *Schooling and Gypsies/Travellers— a Complex and Challenging Relationship.* Paper submitted to BERJ. Edinburgh: University of Edinburgh.

Mehra, Bharat, Cecelia Merkel, and Ann P. Bishop (2004). "The Internet for Empowerment of Minority and Marginalized Users." *New Media Society* 6 (2004): 781–802.

Miller, Daniel and Don Slater (2003). *The Internet. An Ethnographic Approach.* Oxford and New York: Berg.

Morris, Rachel. *Cardiff Law School.* Available at http://www.cf.ac.uk/claws/tlru/ [accessed 23 February 2010].

Okely, Judith M (1983). *The Traveller-Gypsies.* Cambridge: Cambridge University Press.

Padfield, Pauline and Elizabeth Jordan (2004). "Education at the Margins; Outsiders and the Mainstream" in *Scottish Education; Post-Devolution,* eds. Bryce, Tom G.K. and Walter M. Humes. Edinburgh: Edinburgh University Press.

Rua Design. *Pavee Point. Promoting Travellers' Human Rights.* Available at www.paveepoint.ie [accessed 22 January 2010].

Travellers' Times. Available at http://www.travellerstimes.org.uk/ [accessed 23 February 2010].

Johannes Ries

ROMANY/GYPSY CHURCH OR PEOPLE OF GOD?
The Dynamics of Pentecostal Mission
and Romany/Gypsy Ethnicity Management

One day, Karli and I visited the site where the Pentecostal congregation of the Transylvanian village of Trăbeş was constructing a radio station.[1] Karli, the Saxon (German) leader of the multiethnic congregation, started to chat with the Romany/Gypsy[2] converts who had been hired as construction workers. During the conversation one of the Roma, who had only recently started to attend the Pentecostal services, suddenly confessed that he had once stolen something from Karli's farm house. Radiant with happiness because of this spontaneous confession of sin, Karli hugged him and rejoiced: "It is all forgiven, brother, everything is forgiven. Praise the Lord!" In Transylvania, such a scene in which a 'proud Saxon' and a 'dirty Gypsy' dramatically transgress ethnic boundaries, embrace each other to become (spiritual) brothers, can hardly be imagined outside the evangelical context.

In the 1950s the Pentecostal movement identified Roma as a target for their global mission. And in fact, over the last decades, it has been very successful in 'saving' souls among the transnational minority. Nevertheless, Romany/Gypsy Studies in general have practically ignored the cultural dynamics which are produced by the conversion of Roma/Gypsies to Pentecostalism. It is only recently that some lucid studies on Romany/Gypsy Pentecostalism have been published.[3] Interestingly, they seem to come to different, even contradicting conclusions in their analysis of the impact of Pentecostalism on Romany/Gypsy ethnicity.

---

1   This paper is based on fieldwork in Transylvania between 2002 and 2004, which was carried out for my PhD-project at Leipzig University (c.f. Ries, 2007). The name of the village and all other names of persons or organisations have been replaced by pseudonyms. The project was kindly financed by a grant from the *Studienstiftung des deutschen Volkes*. Parts of this text were presented at the international conference on 'Religious Conversion after Socialism' at the Max Planck Institute for Social Anthropology in Halle/Saale (7–8 April 2005) in a different form. I am grateful to Annegret Ries for her comments on this text.

2   In the heterogeneous field of self-representation and foreign perception there are different discourses about the adequate designation of the transnational minority. I use the dual terms *Rom/Gypsy* (noun sg.), *Roma/Gypsies* (noun pl.), *Romany/Gypsy* (adj.) in order to consciously transport this tension.

3   For an overview of the scientific studies on Romany/Gypsy Pentecostalism c.f. Ries, 2007, Chapter 1.

Some scholars interpret Romany/Gypsy Pentecostalism as a reformulation of Romany/Gypsy ethnicity. For example, Acton sees the *Gypsy Evangelical Church* as an 'autonomous movement' (Acton, 1979, p. 14) which reinforces the separation between Roma/Gypsies and Gaže (i.e. non-Roma/Gypsies) by telling its members "that they can be better Gypsies for being Christian—and better Christians for being Gypsies" (Acton, 1979, p. 13). Similarly, Gay y Blasco states that in Madrid the demarcation of Evangelical Gitanos from the Gaže is intensified by a "double Gitano/Payo-convert/ non-convert axis" (Gay y Blasco, 1999, p. 162). I would like to call this interpretation the *Romany/Gypsy church argument*.

In contrast, other researchers (many of them studying Eastern European Romany/ Gypsy groups) argue that conversion offers the possibility to overcome all ethnic boundaries between Roma/Gypsies and Gaže. For example, Fosztó and Anăstăsoaie state that the Romanian Pentecostal church takes "no account of ethnic or national divisions". Moreover, the authors interpret Romany/Gypsy conversion as a general "strategy aimed at social integration" (Fosztó, 2001, p. 361). Slavkova reports from Bulgaria that for most Romany/Gypsy converts the new religious self-definition as believers is even more important than traditional kinship ties (Slavkova, 2003, p. 174). I would like to call this assumption the *transethnic congregation argument*.

In this paper I will demonstrate that these arguments, which at first sight seem to contradict each other, do in fact correspond because Pentecostalism configured both as a monoethnic Romany/Gypsy church and as a transethnic congregation promises the successful evangelisation of Roma/Gypsies. I will introduce the case of the Transylvanian village of Trăbeş, in which a Pentecostal congregation tries to use the transethnic congregation model to proselytise the two resident Romany/Gypsy groups. The case shows that this missionary strategy fits in with the aims of the Ţigani ('Gypsies') who are trying to assimilate to Romanian society; but it also demonstrates that for the Corturari ('tent-Gypsies') the Romany/Gypsy church model would be more successful, because they set great store by ethnic exclusivity. I conclude that the success of Pentecostal missionary strategies depends very largely on the local setting and on the cultural profile of the targeted Romany/Gypsy groups.

Pentecostal Romany/Gypsy Mission

In contrast to ethnic religions (such as for example Judaism), Christianity is a universal religion which tries to mobilise disciples irrespective of their ethnic affiliation. But in Transylvania the different Christian denominations do not meet the universalistic claims of Christian theology. De facto they are used as religious 'ethnic markers' (Barth, 1969) and thereby function as quasi-ethnic religions. In Transylvanian logic, a Lutheran Protestant *is* Saxon, while a Romanian *has to be* orthodox. In general, Roma/ Gypsies formally join the church of the Romanians. Neo-evangelical denominations such as Pentecostalism invade the marked out territories of Transylvanian ethnic Christianities and import a denomination that is not occupied by any specific ethnic group.

The situation in Trăbeş confirms the national trend: there is a deserted Lutheran church which belonged to the Saxons, who left the village after 1989, and an orthodox one for Romanians. Both of the Romany/Gypsy groups settled in the village call themselves orthodox, but most Ţigani and Corturari do not attend Sunday services. Since the beginning of the 1980s Trăbeş has hosted another Christian church: a Pentecostal congregation. After the peaceful revolution, more and more Trăbeşian Romanians and Ţigani joined the converts' congregation, and today more than 120 of the villagers (half of them Ţigani) have received baptism. The congregation is led by Karli and a fellow Saxon, both of whom are financed by two German missionary organisations. Actually, the village of Trăbeş serves as the Romanian outpost of the Bethany Mission and supervises a wide network of Pentecostal congregations all over Romania. Every year, several conferences and meetings take place in the village, during which German evangelists educate the congregation leaders. Additionally, the second Saxon congregation leader, Michael, is the organiser of the Romanian Romany/Gypsy Mission, which is affiliated to and supported by the German Romany/Gypsy Mission. He travels constantly all over Romania in order to look after Romany/Gypsy converts in many multi- and monoethnic congregations and to evangelise Roma/Gypsies from different subgroups of the heterogeneous Romanian Romany/Gypsy spectrum.

The Trăbeşian converts, even the missionary and his Romany/Gypsy disciples, are convinced of the concept of transethnicity. "Bye bye. The old life will die now. There will be no more Romanians, no more Gypsies or Saxons... You'll rise as new men. Hallelujah, this is the new society!" With these words a German evangelist prepared Trăbeşian Roma/Gypsies and Romanians for their baptism. The Trăbeşian Pentecostal congregation fundamentally focuses on ethnic inclusion. But such multiethnicity does not mean that the converts dedicate themselves to interethnicity. The transethnic discourse does not mediate *between* different ethnic groups but argues *beyond* all ethnic ascription.

The Saxon Michael is married to Speranţa, a Romanian, and they are not the only ethnically mixed couple in Trăbeş. There are several Romanians who met a Ţigan in the congregation, fell in love and got married. For the converts it makes no difference which ethnic group bride and groom belong to—as long as they are both converts. Even if these couples are stigmatised in the secular world, they do not suffer any sanctions in their religious community. On the contrary, they are supported by many sermons which time and again preach the discourse of transethnicity. Here, for example, is part of the sermon which Carol—a Ţigan whose nephew is married to a Romanian—delivered one Sunday to of his fellow converts:

We are all very different. Here in this hall are sitting different races, different nations and different cultures. Brothers and sisters, we are all *very* different. One of us might be a musician, another a mathematician or a doctor. Here are sitting poor and rich, strong and weak, thick and thin... We are all *very* different. But what connects us? There is something in us, which is common to all of us and which unites us: the desire to be with the Lord. And this desire makes us all equal.

Carol represents the theology of transethnicity in simple phrases. The subject of his talk is the individuality of every man. For the converts, ethnicity is only one of many patterns which differentiate one individual from all others. They are convinced that every man receives specific talents from God and ethnic affiliation is only one such gift. At the same time, Carol's sermon reduces every human being to his or her basic relationship to God and thereby levels all secular ascriptions.

Another Sunday, Michael gave a sermon and supported the same discourse by insisting on the 'spiritual poverty' of every man:

Those of us who have read the gospel have understood that we have been nothing. And then came Jesus Christ, Hallelujah, and with God, man is no longer nothing. We are nothing without the help of the Lord, this is our personal poverty—we have to understand this. And we can only reach spiritual wealth by capitulation before God. Oh, we have to bend our knees before God and say: Lord, take me into your hands, I am yours. Brothers and sisters, we are poor in ourselves, but we are endlessly rich in God! Amen!

This sermon transcends more than the financial status of man. Moreover, it refers to the mere nothingness of all sinners and by doing so endows all ethnic groups with the same value. It sets the rich Romanian landlord on equal terms with the poor Ţigan fruit picker and generates equality between all converts. In Pentecostal cosmology ethnic differences blur and are expelled to the world of the non-converts. But in fact, a new frontier replaces ethnic boundaries: in a cosmological dichotomisation mankind is divided into the secular world (non-converted sinners who are lost in the clutches of Satan) and the sacred world (faithful, saved souls who belong to the people of God). Ethnic differentiation is reconfigured as theological differentiation. The secular Roma/Gypsy is reborn as a sacred child of God.

Nevertheless, there are several Pentecostal congregations in which the transethnic discourse is challenged by the idea of a Romany/Gypsy church. Recently some Romanian Romany/Gypsy congregations split off from the Pentecostal umbrella organisation Pentecostal Cult (which the Trăbeşian converts and the Bethany Mission officially do not belong to) and founded the Romany Union led by Roma/Gypsies. Some of the congregations financed by the Bethany Mission are now discussing whether they should join this new association of Pentecostal Roma/Gypsies. An extract from a debate between Michael and a Romany/Gypsy elder from a Rudar settlement in Southern Romania shows how the Trăbeşian missionary has to argue against the reinstallation of ethnic boundaries:

> *The Rudar elder*: Michael, you know that there has been some controversy between our leader and the pastor of the [Pentecostal] Cult. Tell us: Is our congregation with Bethany or is it with the Cult? And what about the *Romany Union*?
>
> *Michael*: Such things don't matter. No organization can lead you to heaven, only Jesus Christ. Pentecostal Cult, Bethany, Romany Union—these are only secular names. For us, these names don't count. We are believers without names. The only name that matters is the name of Jesus Christ. We are neither working for Bethany or the Cult nor for the Gypsies alone, but for Jesus. In some parishes we collaborate with the Cult, in others we don't. I never told you that you have to split off from the Cult in order to receive money from Bethany. There are many of your kindred who are in need of the Lord. But I don't want you to create a Rudar [Romany] island here. There is no difference between Gypsies and Romanians. My soul is bleeding when you want to split off. It was not good to establish a Gypsy cult [Romany Union]. Our wish is that you live together with the Romanians as if they were your kith and kin.

These words demonstrate how on the national level both contradicting Pentecostal mission concepts—transethnic congregation and Romany/Gypsy church—are transformed into social praxis. But it also shows that on a local level the congregation must decide on one of them. Otherwise it runs the risk of schism.

Conversion and Romany/Gypsy Ethnicity Management

Aurari, Băieşi, Căldărari, Ciurari, Gabori, Lăutari…, there are many different Romany/Gypsy groups in Romania, all of which differ significantly in their cultural profiles and relationships with other ethnic groups. Logically, they react to the Pentecostal missionary concept in different ways. I will now go on to show that in Trăbeş Pentecostalism with its transethnic claims is very attractive for the Ţigani—many of whom actually convert. Conversely, the Corturari, who generally do not convert, would prefer Pentecostalism in the form of a monoethnic Romany/Gypsy church—if at all. This can be explained by the different strategies of ethnicity management the Corturari and the Ţigani use in the village. They represent themselves in very different forms towards the Romanians: the Corturari set great store by cultural exclusivity while the Ţigani try to assimilate to the Romanians.

The Corturari ('Tent-Gypsies') were nomads until they settled down in the western part of the village in the early 1960s; they still practise their prestigious craft as coppersmiths. Men and women can be recognized by their own 'traditional' costume and speak a specific Romany/Gypsy dialect. Indigenous institutions such as a special purity complex (*mahrime*), their own legal court (*kris*) or the informal position of the Romany/Gypsy leader (*rom baro*), as well as strict endogamy and the strong authority of kinship are very important pillars of Corturar ethnic identity. Today many Corturari lead relatively prosperous lives, carrying on of their vital business at an international level. This cultural profile ensures that the Corturari are visible for all others as a clearly demarcated ethnic group. They are proud of their 'own culture' and actively display it.

In contrast, the Țigani ('Gypsies') have been living in the southern Gypsy quarter (*țigănie*) of the village for centuries, cheek by jowl with the peasant society. In the wake of post-socialism most of the Țigani lost their jobs in factories or on collective farms, so that today they try to earn a living as indebted day labourers for the Romanian peasants. Most Țigani are on welfare and many of them beg in order to survive. No Țigan speaks Romany or wears a 'traditional' costume. 'Culturally', the Țigani try to adjust themselves to Romanian society but they differ significantly in terms of their low standard of living and poverty. Passively, they are driven out of Romanian society.

How do the Romanians react to these two different manifestations of Romany/Gypsy ethnicity? In general, Roma/Gypsies are subjected to a wide range of stereotypes which show them in a very bad light. But apart from abstract stereotypes the Romanians in the village of Trăbeș carefully distinguish between Corturari and Țigani. They show far more tolerance for the former than for the latter. Even if the Romanians recognize the 'cultural' differences of the Corturari, they credit this Romany/Gypsy group with some of their own values For example, the Corturari are said neither to beg nor to steal, to be friendly and obliging, and to act reciprocally, just to mention a few positive stereotypes. In contrast, the Țigani are seen as beggars and thieves, stupid day labourers, responsible for their own misery. Because of their 'cultural' assimilation, the Țigani are said to have no 'culture of their own' while the Corturari are seen as an instance of conservativism and 'tradition'. For rural Transylvania, 'culture' is a key element for the definition of an ethnic group. And in the eyes of the Romanians (as well as for the Saxons and Corturari) the 'cultural' demarcation between the different ethnic groups is one of the most important features of a well-ordered multiethnic society. Consequently, to the Romanians the Corturari appear as welcome foreign friends whereas the Țigani radiate subversive danger as internal enemies.

As I have mentioned above, religious denomination can function as an important ethnic marker. By converting to Pentecostalism, Roma/Gypsies take over a denomination which they can use as a strategy to manage their ethnicity. How could the Trăbeșian Corturari use Pentecostalism for their representation towards the Romanians? They do not need to compensate for negative stigmatisation since their 'cultural' performance is already tolerated by the Romanians. What is worse: for the

Corturari an adoption of the transethnic discourse would lead to unification with other ethnic groups; it would undermine their claim to ethnic exclusivity. If the Trăbeşian converts preached the discourse of an exclusive Romany/Gypsy church instead of the inclusive transethnic discourse, they would be supporting Corturar ethnic exclusivity. Probably, they would then achieve far more success in 'saving souls' among the Corturari.

For the Ţigani the situation is different. They want to 'culturally' assimilate but they are not accepted by the Romanians. In the Pentecostal congregation they find equal rights and the ability to actively share their concerns with Romanians. Furthermore, conversion allows the Ţigani to replace their negative ethnic stigma with new religious stereotypes. In fact, the Romanians positively acknowledge the success of the Pentecostal Romany/Gypsy mission in 'taming' the Roma/Gypsies, whom they perceive as 'undomesticated'. They note with approval that Ţigan converts do not steal, drink or smoke, but dress neatly and behave politely. In the eyes of the Romanians, Pentecostalist asceticism—so to speak—balances Gypsy excesses. Thus, for the Ţigani the burden of being a member of a sectarian Christian fundamentalist group is easier to carry than the bitter Gypsy stigma. Naturally, Ţigani converts remain Ţigani in the secular world; but they have found a reference group into which they can escape from all worldly stereotypes. For the Ţigani, conversion and taking over the transethnic discourse becomes an important strategy of partial inclusion.

In fact, the Ţigani in Trăbeş suffer double stigmatisation, for they are stigmatised not only by Romanians but also by other Roma/Gypsies like the Corturari. Even if the Romanian Romany/Gypsy spectrum is highly heterogeneous, there are certain criteria—such as craft, costume, language or wealth—which place the different Romany/Gypsy subgroups on an internal ladder of prestige. On this ladder, the Corturari enjoy a high position and look down on most of the other Romany/Gypsy groups in the region. They are acknowledged as authentic, 'true Gypsies': *rom* (Romany: men). On the contrary, the Ţigani can only occupy the lowest step of this internal ladder of prestige; they are seen as half-breeds: *kherutne* (Romany: house-occupants).

I would say that one of the main reasons why the Corturari do not convert is the simple fact that the Ţigani have locally 'occupied' Pentecostalism. For the Corturari, who perceive themselves as 'true' *rom*, the Trăbeşian congregation is 'contaminated' by low class *kherutne*. The converts' invitation to get 'mixed up with' with the Ţigani is an insult in terms of the Corturari wish for ethnic purity and 'traditional' authenticity. For the Corturari, conversion would imply a serious loss of credibility and prestige within the internal Romany/Gypsy hierarchy. Again, I would argue that a Pentecostal mission would be much more successful within the Corturar community if it presented itself as a Romany/Gypsy church and concentrated on the maintenance of specific Romany/Gypsy 'cultural' traits.

With regard to the interior differentiation of the Transylvanian Romany/Gypsy spectrum, the Pentecostal mission in its Trăbeşian transethnic configuration is again much more attractive for the Ţigani. Through conversion they replace their self-definition as Roma/Gypsies by a self-definition as children of God. With this shift, they not only escape their low *kherutne*-position in the internal Romany/Gypsy hierarchy: they leave the whole system of classification behind. They now follow discourses of acknowledgement that are completely different to those of the Corturari. They take over the Pentecostal dichotomised cosmology in which they can position themselves as a saved people of God above all Corturari unbelievers. Moreover, their 'cultural' intermingling with Gaže (which the Corturari sternly reject as an aberration from 'true' *rom*-ness) is positively valued in the converts' theology of transethnicity.

Conclusions

It should now be clear why the Saxon Karli embraced the Ţigan who had once stolen from him. Naturally, the open arms were those of a missionary who was trying to save a new soul and wished to ensure the Ţigan's complete conversion. But these arms would never have been spread if the Saxon had not been a member of the people of God, a dedicated follower of Pentecostalism as a transethnic congregation.

As the case discussed has shown, Pentecostal missionary work produces vivid dynamics in the field of Romany/Gypsy cultures. Roma/Gypsies can use Pentecostalism as a strategy for successful ethnicity management in relation to the Gažo majority. For some groups like the Ţigani conversion to a transethnic congregation can become an important means of social inclusion. Others, such as the Corturari, might use the new Romany/Gypsy church to express their ethnic exclusiveness. Even if the Pentecostal mission is financed and controlled by western organisations and tries to implant uniform concepts, it is nevertheless dependent on the local setting and the people involved. The worldwide success of Pentecostal mission may be rooted in the fact that the new discourses and social practices it introduces are not yet fixed or occupied by hegemonic groups. Pentecostalism as a new religious movement is therefore extremely flexible and adaptable to the specific needs and aims of marginal groups.

Conversion causes significant changes in the social field and it is the task of science to document and interpret these modifications. The subjects of our study would probably have a different explanation, one that is beyond rational argument. A converted believer knows that the cause of all change is God. However, it is more than doubtful whether the agnostic tools of science are sufficient to explain that power.

Bibliography

Acton, Thomas (1979). "The Gypsy Evangelical Church" in *Ecumenical Exercise*, Vol. V, ed. Cranford, Stephen. Geneva: World Council of Churches.

Barth, Fredrik (1969). "Introduction" in *Ethnic Groups and Boundaries*, ed. Barth, Fredrik. London: George Allen and Unwin.

Fosztó, László and Marian-Viorel Anăstăsoaie (2001). "Romania: Representations, Public Policies and Political Projects" in *Between Past and Future*, ed. Guy, Will. Hatfield: University of Hertfordshire Press.

Gay y Blasco, Paloma (1999). *Gypsies in Madrid: Sex, Gender and the Performance of Identity.* Oxford and New York: Berg.

Ries, Johannes (2007). *Welten Wanderer. Über die kulturelle Souveränität siebenbürgischer Zigeuner und den Einfluß des Pfingstchristentums.* Würzburg: Ergon.

Slavkova, Magdalena (2003). "Roma Pastors in Bulgaria as the Leaders for Roma Protestant Communities" in *Roma Religious Culture*, ed. Dordevic, Dragoljub B. Niš: PUNTA.

Hana Synková

CLAIMING LEGITIMACY IN/OF A ROMANY NGO

In public imagery and in many social science texts Roma[1] are described as people "outside (official) institutions". While research done in more impoverished settings often confirms this image and shows acute power differences, exclusion, resistance and complex negotiations between Roma and institutions, the case study of the Czech NGO sector challenges this simplification. Changes after 1989 brought the possibility to associate and to create civic organisations. This new option was explored by many and Roma themselves, according to the Government Council for National Minorities, founded more than 400 organisations.[2] My research was done in one such organisation which I will call "Amaro" ("Ours"),[3] where I have worked as a volunteer since 2005. Amaro is mainly a social service organisation: it provides field social work, runs a work and counselling programme, is occasionally involved in antidiscrimination campaigns and works with children. It presents itself as a "Romany NGO" and most of its clients are of Romany origin. I am not interested in exploring any "specific way that Roma manage institutions"; I focus rather on how an institution with such a label can survive and how it is shaped by internal conflicts and external pressures.

Organisations can hardly be studied as objects. An NGO is always a constant discussion about what an NGO "should be" and people inside organisations often have different views on what an organisation is and means. Together with William Fisher I conceive of organisations as "flows of ideas, knowledge, funding and people" (Fisher, 1997, p. 441), as processes that are influenced by people involved in the organisation and the networks of knowledge they have access to. Dorothea Hilhorst aptly called these processes NGO-ing (Hilhorst, 2003, p. 5)—"doing" an NGO. NGO-ing is further

---

1   The term "Roma" is used in the Czech political and NGO discourse as a general term to designate several different groups of Roma (Slovak, which is the most numerous, Hungarian, Czech/Moravian and Vlach) and a few Sinti families living in the Czech Republic. In this text, the "Romaniness" of organisations is explored as a label that is created and formed in the context of the Czech NGO sector. Part of the construction of this label is usually the act of identification of an organisational representative as a "Rom".

2   Government Council for National Minorities. "Romská národnostní menšina" (Romani national minority). Available at http://www.vlada.cz/cz/pracovni-a-poradni-organy-vlady/rnm/mensiny/romska-narodnostni-mensina-16149/ [accessed 10 January 2010]. This does not mean, however, that all the registered organisations are active.

3   Other fieldwork-related names of people and organisations used in this text are also pseudonyms.

influenced by the reasons why one wishes to start an organisation, by legislation that regulates the functioning of organisations, by politics and the particular characteristics of the local nongovernmental sector. In the Czech Republic, people who start "Romany" organisations are frequently relatively well educated, have a certain knowledge of institutions,[4] are from more powerful, business-minded backgrounds and grew up in mixed or activist families. Organisations can definitely function as one of the possible mobility channels for those who are already skilled. Other Roma figure as the "clients" and "target groups" of such organisations, they are subjects of legitimation claims by these organisations, which often build on a "Roma should help Roma" principle. Still, Romany organisations form only a small portion of all the organisations that have Roma among their target groups.

Hilhorst presents an NGO as a "claim-bearing label", which provides a credible explanation about how a particular organization is doing good for the development of others (Hilhorst, 2003, p. 7). The claims made by NGOs and their reasons for obtaining funding are thus largely moral. One of the worst things that can happen to an NGO is that it is no longer successful in making such a claim, because others no longer trust it. That is why focus on the production of legitimation is crucial. The following paper is thus devoted to looking at how legitimation is done in the case of Amaro.

Legitimating Amaro

When Anna Šťastná, a middle aged woman, started the organisation in 2001 while still employed by a local municipality as a social worker, she did not take the issue of legitimation very seriously. There were just Roma that needed help and this was "a fact" that required action. The founding of a civic organisation does not require much investment. Three people have to subscribe to a mission statement that gets registered at the Ministry of the Interior. In the case of Amaro, not much energy was put into the preparation of the mission statement—the founding papers were partly copied from another Romany organisation. Examples of mission statements are widely available on the Internet and it is a common practice in the whole NGO sector for such texts just to get reworked and adapted. In general, during the first years of Amaro, texts were not very important. Later on, the goal of the organisation was articulated on its web pages in a little more detail: "to help people, mostly members of the Romany national minority, and strengthen the versatile progress of this minority". The "minority and progress" terminology started to be used widely.

Each organisation develops its survival strategies with the help of some kind of public relations. One of the possibilities that Amaro can obviously draw on is the strategy of using the "Romany" label as a form of resource. My concept of strategies

---

4   The first generation of founders were often former army employees, party members, dissidents and cultural events organisers.

was influenced by Michael Herzfeld's suggestion that one should see strategies behind essentialist claims: "essentialism is always the one thing it claims not to be: it is a strategy..." (Herzfeld, 1997, p. 165). Many anthropologists writing on Romany topics (Williams, 1982; Stewart, 1997; Gay y Blasco, 1999; or Okely, 1983) have described how people can manipulate the presentation of Romany identity and how some of these manipulations contribute to survival strategies. Their work, however, focused mainly on less institutionalised settings. Organisations today can reinvent strategies to serve the image of the organisation, to bring resources to it and to get access to some networks of legitimacy provided by local or international actors, who search for "Romany representatives". Organisations can employ certain strategies of essentialism.

In 2005, when I came to Amaro, Romaniness was praised even as a sort of qualification that makes people in the organisation ideally suited for social work with Roma. According to Anna, Roma are more suitable to this type of work, because they know the environment and inspire trust. Moreover it sends a good message to the "majority": "It is time, and I acknowledge that, that our people should get educated, they should resolve their problems themselves, because then the majority society sees it. When we are not able to defend ourselves, when we can't orientate in the current situation, how then can we go one step further? It does not work." Anna is not the only one who holds the view that Roma should be active in working with "their own" people. She is in contact with other activists, leaders and officials who make similar claims, so "strategic Romaniness" has formed a network that cuts across NGOs and government offices. NGOs are thus not directly opposed to governments and municipalities; the label does not correspond to the reality of funding channelled mainly through ministries, to the regulation of social services and to social networking. It is quite common to get a post in state structures after working in the NGO sector, and people move from one sector to the other.

Another legitimation Anna used when describing the reasons for helping was that "we are doing it for our children", the metaphorized children being the future of all the Roma in the Czech Republic. Some Romany women, more often older ones, use the "care discourse" as legitimation for their NGO work and activism.[5] Such legitimation is understandable both to Roma and non-Roma, who look on women as responsible for their families and hence their communities. Organisations, Amaro included, frequently direct one of their first projects at children, since working with them seems to be more publicly appreciated. Small municipal grants for free-time activities are also more easily accessible than complex social work schemes.

The Romany label can be used even when a significant number of employees are not Roma, but it seems to be associated with the image of a Romany leader as the head of an organisation. When I joined Amaro, apart from Anna there were four young

---

5   As was also described by Pulkrábková, 2009.

female university students and graduates working partly for free, two of whom were said to come from more or less distant mixed marriages, and finally Anna's son, who was employed as a social worker.

By volunteering I quickly became an active participant in strategic Romaniness. The first task I was assigned was e-mailing potential sponsors. This looked like an ideal opportunity to explore organisational discourse used for external presentation; no one just told me what it should look like and there were no written instructions. However, I had to produce something so I started to write: "We are a Romany organisation (Should I use Romany, won't it stigmatise the organisation? No, better use "Amaro"—you can tell from the name that it is Romany anyway). Amaro is an organisation that helps (No, another word...), that works with people in 'difficult life situation' (At least, that's what I found written in web pages)." I had started to create an organisational image, although I was not used to this kind of discourse and had all sorts of doubts about what I was doing. Only later on did I recognise that "learning by doing" is an important part of many people's idea about what Amaro "means", this form of learning being of course equally necessitated by the circumstances of a young, small organisation dependent on volunteer work. It could be also illustrated by the discussion I had before deciding to volunteer: "What does a volunteer do here?" Anna: "Everything. Everyone is doing everything; we are only just beginning to specialise." Neither the texts nor the positions described on the Amaro web pages meant much when looking at the everyday organisational practice. Nevertheless, the idea that specialisation was something coming or something desirable was already present.

While I was doing this work, the idea of a more neutral presence in the organisation became "unsustainable"—I suddenly noticed that I was promoting work standards for volunteers, sorting hundreds of documents in a computer into well-arranged folders, creating an address book or starting to write up an application for a certificate of socio-legal protection of children (if an organisation wants to work with children and be considered trustworthy, it should "definitely" have one of these). Organisations grow and bureaucratise and Amaro became a ground for observing these processes. Together with other employees I encountered disciplinary mechanisms of the state that require certain standards from organisations and I caught myself applying my own internalised norms about how an organisation should function. The way to proceed with my research then was by exploring these contradictions, reflecting on my position and looking at how people working in the organisation were negotiating different pressures.

Professionalization

Not many non-Romany-led organisations are part of Amaro networks. The Czech NGO sector is quite competitive and organisations are not only in competition over resources, but also over the best legitimation strategies. Some of these organisations have started to be more careful about the use of ethnic labels, trying to counter public stereotypes which say that the only people that are helped, "problematic" or poor, are Roma. Discussion centred as well on what one should call emergent enclaves of substandard living conditions, where people recognised as Roma form a significant part of the population. Ethnicizing the image of "ghettos" was considered dangerous in that it supported the stereotypical image and obscured the social mechanisms that create such places. "Social exclusion" gradually became a term widely used to explain these localities; it appeared as a category in grant schemes, and an introduction of the concept has been supported by European institutions as well. Recently there has been another move towards "social inclusion" or even "social cohesion" discourse. Many Romany activists on the other hand feared that by concentrating on "social problems" the Roma would be erased from the picture or even reduced to a social problem, which reminded them of the rhetoric of the previous socialist state, where "Gypsiness" was a negative feature that the state wished to get rid of.

This discussion affected organisational strategies as well. Some social scientists connected to the NGO sector and doing government-funded research recommended: "abandoning the misleading category of 'Romany' ('Pro-Romany') organisations and supporting projects based on their quality... and not on the 'ethnicity' of organisations" (Hirt and Jakoubek, 2004, p. 23). The issue of quality and professionalism should be the only category on the basis of which the founders decide. The accusation of amateurism became almost as serious a weapon as the accusation of non-transparency, which is one of the most effective de-legitimating strategies based on the idea of NGOs as accountable subjects. During an interview, the leader of the social work programme in a non-Romany organisation connected the word "amateur" with the old non-professional times: "We have raised quality [...] before, there were two people working here, one of them an amateur. The amateur left and we have taken in, because there was a demand for it, two professionals." There is a clear discursive strategy to claim professionalism and thus quality, which makes an organisation special and trustworthy. Another new trend is to use the "demand for service" business rhetoric.

To present such a division in strategies as the division between "Romany" and "non-Romany" organisations would be misleading. All the organisations function in a legislative and institutional environment that pushes them in certain directions and towards certain changes of strategies. Their NGO-ing has to deal with similar pressures.

In the summer of 2006, money from European Social Fund grants initiated the biggest change in Amaro. The fact of getting so-called "European money" had the potential to transform the organisation profoundly. Amaro moved from one small room subleased from another Romany organisation to a handsome four-room office and began to recruit new employees needed for recently approved projects. Instead of a handful of employees there were soon forty-three. At this time, another of Anna's sons, Viktor and his long-time friend joined the organisation in the posts of work programme (and later on executive) director and financial director. For some time already they had been doing volunteer work in Amaro, supported the organisation financially, provided their personal computers for the office and offered free driving services. During this period of growth, a mix of both Romany and non-Romany people from associated organisations, Anna's circle of friends as well as "complete strangers" came aboard.

With the change of scale from a small organisation largely based on volunteer work to a professional body, the tasks were becoming much more difficult and specialised: a lot of writing, managing the projects and finances, developing new control systems and coordinating the employees. Less experienced people were learning, but sometimes not quickly enough. Compared to the former situation of everyone doing multiple tasks, helping each other and holding positions mainly on paper, for external PR purposes, the roles solidified and people started to have more strictly defined responsibilities. More funding brings institutionalisation and the institutionalisation reconfigures hierarchies, decision-making procedures, legitimation strategies and even the self-images of employees.

Other pressures to professionalize are significant as well. Donors have moved away from the Czech Republic, heading further East, and the use of funds is no longer as open-ended as it was during the first years after the revolution. Competition for grants increased. Money from European Structural Funds is channelled through state ministries which increases the NGOs' dependence on state structures. Some Amaro employees commented on the situation: "the grant applications that were 'winning' a few years ago, would now fall below the line of projects acceptable for funding". There is a demand for people who can "write well" (applications) and their status is growing, as they are the ones who understand the complex application procedures.

The social services law of 2006 added to the pressure. It makes higher education a pre-requisite for the post of social worker. This move was criticised by some Romany organisations that felt it was discriminatory, given the background of their employees. Organisations have to have so-called standards of quality of social work, which must be written down and implemented. Standards can be checked by an inspection and an organisation could be forbidden to work if it fails to meet them. This whole process creates a new kind of desirable subject—a controllable expert worker, who can provide social services wherever the state and the NGO sector needs him.

Because of these pressures, Amaro has gradually gone for both the PR of professionalism and social exclusion reasoning in its grant applications, while not completely abandoning the Romany label. The composition of its employees, however, presents some challenges. It has to think strategically about who will represent the organisation at which event, because not all the employees are equally skilled in all the legitimation strategies. When personal talk is needed and Romany stylisation is acceptable, Anna deals with it; when there is a need for professional presentation skills, for instance using PowerPoint, one of the employees with a university background in social work prepares it. What actually happened several times was that Anna and Viktor used a PowerPoint presentation written by their colleagues. What I experienced in one university conference was an interesting mismatch between what was shown on the slides and what Anna was saying. Behind her on the screen there were slides talking in de-ethnicized terms about social exclusion and long-term methods used by the organisation, while Anna was presenting a case of immediate assistance provided for poor Roma by Amaro.

Tensions Inside

The organisation might look more or less homogeneous from the outside (and this is a wish of most organisations), but looking inside, tensions are present. The pressure to formalise and projectize meant that the organisation had to stop taking on people who would ideally "learn by doing", instead, there was a need for people who would already be fully qualified for the job. This strategy was also forced by the funding being more and more dependent on the professional capacities of organisations and the fact that it was linked with "providing services" and not activism. New employees come with their ideas about what an organisation is and how it should function. These ideas were formed by university curricula and by previous working experience in other organisations, where they became used to certain standards of work. Anna's representation is sometimes categorised as "improper" because of being unprofessional, and when it is successful, the success is more often attributed to "her personal charm and charisma" and her persuasive skills.

Grant applications are frequently written by university-educated people, who are at the same time non-Roma. Before and throughout the writing process they consult with other colleagues, who agree on the general goal of the application and contribute suggestions about what should be "written down"; the financial director might help with the budget. The power to write and the power of writing are however visible and a successful application is also considered to be an individual achievement with authorship—"my grant". "Writing employees" thus frequently serve as "translators" when the language of goals and strategies has to be implemented. Norman Long (Long, 1999) has described that the moment several discourses meet, the interface is born. In the case of Amaro the interface exists not only when the organisation talks to some external actors, but has appeared inside as well. The organisation needs internal mediators and translators between different ways of representation, which takes a lot of energy. When I was writing for the organisation and contacting potential sponsors and people in power I often became a kind of secretary of Anna's. She was convinced that her writing "did not look good" because of the style and potential grammatical mistakes and that she needed someone who would use the right words well. NGOs have become dependent on a lot of credibility-producing writing and Amaro needed writing that looked credible. Anna preferred to get the writing job done by someone else and to concentrate on meetings and representation.

To withstand the professionalizing pressure, some people had to leave Amaro. The position of less well-educated employees was weakened as they were not the ones with the right kind of expertise. Viktor changed his position from being an executive director and work programme director to the less demanding position of managing the production and sale of products made by client's work programme. He calls the period of changes the "rebirth" of an organisation and commented that he is now "glad not to be in the management", because of the huge stress connected with these positions—he was responsible not only for the organisation but for the job security of two other members of his family. On the other hand, he evaluated the chance to "trust each other naturally" in the former organisational setting very positively. He is proud to have gained experience and to have had the opportunity to try such a position.

The possibility to create self-employment possibilities for other people in an NGO is quite an attractive and a logical one, given that finding a job is a hard task. The employment of family members has sometimes been criticised by other organisations (Romany and non-Romany alike) trying to delegitimate their competitors. Anna is aware of the dilemma and danger of such employment to the legitimation process. I discovered how troubling she finds it only after I made a mistake when I was setting up a meeting, calling the head of one organisation that was in a latent conflict with Amaro to say that Anna's son was coming to the meeting. I got told off: I should just have said his name and position. When he came to the meeting neatly dressed in a suit and with a well-bred dog at his side, he presented himself as an executive director and gave the other director his name-card. The process of NGO-ing thus needs constant attention to the art of presentation to outside actors and practice in a sort of code-switching.

Peter Pels, in a book edited by Marilyn Strathern: *Audit cultures,* writes (Pels, 2000, p. 164) about "impression management", which also involves the researcher. During my research I had to learn how this impression management works for Amaro and to think carefully about its presentation. Organisational anthropologists have had some difficulty in writing about organisational processes and strategies given the relative proximity of the field and power differences among actors. Laura Nader

(Nader, 1999 [1969]), p 303) notices that: "To say that kula-ring participants don't perform in practice what they say they do has very different consequences from saying that a government agency is not living up to its standards." When David Mosse (Mosse, 2005) wrote an insider study about the development policies and practices of the United Kingdom Department for International Development, showing how projects are constructed as "unrealistic" causal models oriented upwards to justify the allocation of resources, how project discourses condition certain coalitions both inside and outside the organisation, how texts are produced as results of these power struggles and expertise is often made only after the intervention serving as a legitimating and validating device, many of his former colleagues sent complaints to his university ethics committee, to the Association of Social Anthropologists and to his publisher. What Mosse succeeded in doing was to disclose organisations and their projects as sites of social and institutional reproduction producing authoritative and coherent frameworks of interpretation and meaning of practice, which are embraced by a certain "interpretive community" that supports them and determines their success or failure. Because of these strong presentation mechanisms and interpretive communities, disclosing "the social" behind organisations might become uncomfortable both for a researcher and for an organisation.

"The social" behind organisations seems to be delegitimated by the ideology of professionalism that likes to see private links invisible in the first place and public and private sphere isolated.[6] If the claim of NGOs is moral, it is trying to appeal to some kind of public moral "common sense". Weber, of course (Weber, 1978, p. 957), has established the private/public division as one of the defining features of bureaucracy and it is used as well in a definition of corruption as a process when this boundary is "corrupt", when it does not divide clearly and there are blurred areas of opaqueness. The word "amateur", interestingly, also has a private connotation. Amateurs are people deeply involved in something, but not necessarily in the most effective way. I have noticed, however, a certain difference in the construction of the acceptability of private relationships. The fact that some Romany organisations had "families" inside was mentioned much more often than the fact that non-Romany organisations are also full of lovers, spouses, friends and sometimes parents and children. To explain this by the sheer percentage of such organisations and a work of stereotypical dominant discourse does not seem to cover the whole picture.

Just before Christmas of 2009, I attended a party held by a non-Romany NGO, Humanitas. There were a number of my former fellow-students holding positions in Humanitas, in NGOs networked with Humanitas, in government offices, and research

---

6   Except in cases where the personal story of a leader is at the foundation of an organisational narrative, e.g. the cases of some organisations created by hardworking businessmen, ethical celebrities and famous activists. These biographies then represent the moral legitimacy of organisations.

and development agencies. These people were part of my own social network of friends and at the same time professionals. Humanitas was once started by a group of friends/colleagues, but it seems its private networks are less visible. New employees at Amaro are also encouraging their professional friends to apply for newly opened positions and these people get into the organisation. The presence of these new friends is explained through the fact that they know, understand and trust each other—in very much the same way as Viktor explained working in the "old" Amaro, the construction of trust thus not being so different. The "new professional elite" finds kinship relationships definitely more illegitimate than friendship relationships, maybe precisely because of the fact that it often builds organisations from these (professional) friendships. Whatever private link we take, however, it appears that professionalism has a capacity to neutralise the critique of private links and solidify the boundary between private and public—quality professionals are less scrutinised. On the contrary, those relationships which cannot be legitimated via the need to have professionals around seem more inappropriate.

Conclusion

The changes in the Czech NGO sector are strikingly similar to the descriptions in other studies of transformation. Lisa Markowitz and Karen Tice (Markowitz and Tice, 2001, p. 6) describe scaling up women organisations in the Americas in this way: "...differences in roles among organisation members construct different constituencies or stakeholders within the organisation, and these groups often clash in ways that mimic power inequalities in the larger social order. These dynamics relate directly to the sort of institutional facelift involved in formalisation. Dealing with broader publics requires individuals with certain capacities, typically consonant with privileged class background and higher levels of education." If the organisation wants to survive in this environment, it is thus pushed to take this direction. Amaro has still some preference for hiring Roma, but now selects the better educated ones, if these show up and succeed during the selection procedure. A young woman with an MA was recently hired as a leader of a new children's club. There are even some cases of social-work related organisations where the founders left altogether or are no longer so active, being replaced by more educated non-Roma and Roma.

The Romaniness as an organisational image and strategic essentialism still brings some benefits as the search for "representatives" continues, but there is an increasing expectation of its "professional" presentation. No wonder that the recent hit among younger activists is a professional advocacy group. The case of Amaro shows that organisations usually combine different strategies to access resources and the success of these organisations is based more on knowing how to use the right strategy at the right time, how to diversify resources and how to "socialise well" into the world of professional and personal networks. It is possible to create new categories and ways of NGO-ing, but the power structures do not allow endless mutation. As the concepts of controlling actors prescribe certain forms of practices in NGOs and delegitimate others, organisations have to negotiate with these norms and actors and invest heavily in the successful management of their image of effectiveness and transparency. Recent developments in Amaro combine Romaniness and professionalism, as professionalism has finally turned out to be the more powerful strategy, supported by networks of governmentality. The art of the flexible use of strategies and of adapting the image and structure of an organisation to the concepts of controlling actors are fundamental for the survival of any organisation. Amaro is now posing as a professional Romany organisation: the success story.

Bibliography

Fisher, William F. (1997). *"Doing Good? The Politics and Antipolitics of NGO Practices."* *Annual Review of Anthropology* 26 (1997): 439–64.

Gay y Blasco, Paloma (1999). *Gypsies in Madrid: Sex, Gender and the Performance of Identity.* Oxford: Berg.

Government Council for National Minorities (2006). "Romská národnostní menšina" (Romany national minority). Available at http://www.vlada.cz/cz/pracovni-a-poradni-organy-vlady/rnm/mensiny/romska-narodnostni-mensina-16149/ [accessed 10 January 2010].

Herzfeld, Michael (1997). *Cultural Intimacy: Social Poetics in the Nation-State.* New York: Routledge.

Hilhorst, Dorothea (2003). *The Real World of NGOs: Discourses, Diversity, and Development.* London: Zed Books.

Hirt, Tomáš. and Marek Jakoubek, eds. (2004). *Souhrnná zpráva o realizaci výzkumného projektu HS 108/03 "Dlouhodobý stacionární terénní výzkum sociálně vyloučených romských komunit" realizovaného Katedrou antropologie FHS ZČU v Plzni* (General report about the research project HS 108/03 "Long-term stationary field research of socially excluded Romany communities" conducted by Department of Anthropology, Faculty of Humanities, University of West Bohemia in Pilsen). Available at http://www.mpsv.cz/files/clanky/1727/zprava.pdf [accessed 10 January 2010].

Long, Norman (1999). "The Multiple Optic of Interface Analysis" in *UNESCO Background Paper on Interface Analysis.* Paris: UNESCO.

Markowitz, Lisa and Karen Tice (2001). *The Precarious Balance of Scaling Up: Women's Organizations in the Americas.* East Lansing, M.I.: Michigan State University.

Mosse, David (2005). *Cultivating Development: An Ethnography of Aid Policy and Practice.* London: Pluto Press.

Nader, Laura (1999 [1969]). "Up the Anthropologist: Perspectives Gained from Studying Up" in *Reinventing Anthropology*, ed. Hymes, Dell. New York: Pantheon Books.

Okely, Judith (1983). *The Traveller Gypsies.* Cambridge: Cambridge University Press.

Pels, Peter (2000). "The Trickster's Dilemma: Ethics and the Technologies of the Anthropological Self" in *Audit Cultures: Anthropological Studies in Accountability, Ethics and the Academy*, ed. Strathern, Marilyn. London and New York: Routledge.

Pulkrábková, Kateřina (2009). "Rámování reprezentace romských žen v české společnosti" (Framing of representation of Romany women in the Czech society). *Socioweb, sociological webzin.* Prague: Institute of Sociology of the Academy of Sciences of the Czech Republic, November 2009. Available at http://www.socioweb.cz/index. php?disp=temata&shw=324&lst=120 [accessed 10 January 2010].

Stewart, Michael (1997). *The Time of the Gypsies.* Boulder, CO.: Westview Press.

Weber, Max (1978). *Economy and Society: an Outline of Interpretive Sociology*, eds. Roth, Guenter and Claus Wittich. Berkeley: University of California Press.

Williams, Patrick (1982). "The Invisibility of the Kalderash of Paris: Some Aspects of the Economic Activity and Settlement Patterns of the Kalderash Rom of the Paris Suburbs." *Urban Anthropology* 11, no. 3–4 (1982): 315–344.

SHORT BIOGRAPHIES OF THE CONTRIBUTORS

Huub van Baar

Huub van Baar is a PhD candidate at the Amsterdam School for Cultural Analysis (ASCA) at the University of Amsterdam, the Netherlands. His current work focuses on past and current forms of Romani minority governance in Europe and the ways in which these forms relate to different conceptions of Europe and its minorities. His PhD thesis is entitled *The European Roma: Governmentality, Representation, and Memory* (forthcoming, 2010).

Stefan Benedik

Stefan Benedik studied history with a focus on gender history in Graz and Prague. He is currently fellow of the Institute for History, and a PhD student of the "Multidisciplinary gender studies" doctoral programme, both at the University of Graz, Austria. He is former fellow of the Research-Focus on Migration at the Centre for Cultural Studies (Graz) ("Migration-Gender-Identities" Project), and of the Ludwig-Boltzmann-Institute for social and cultural history. He is a member of the "shifting Romipen" trans-disciplinary research team. His doctoral research is on gendered structures in the creation of ethnicities in Central European Romani migrations.

Enrico Claps

Enrico Claps is a Ph.D. student in "Urban and Local European Studies" at the State University of Milan-Bicocca, Italy, where he is a teaching fellow in "Local Development". His main research interests include both qualitative and quantitative research methods, economic sociology and local development studies. He has also published extensively on civil society and political participation. On discrimination issues he has recently published an article in the French Journal *Etudes Tsiganes* ("Regards croisés. Antitsiganisme et possibilité du vivre ensemble, Roms et gadjés, en Italie," with T. Vitale and P. Arrigoni).

Judit Durst

Judit Durst is a sociologist. She currently holds a Bolyai Postdoctoral Research Fellowship of the Hungarian Academy of Science at the Corvinus University, Budapest, Hungary. She is also an honorary research fellow at the Anthropology Department of UCL, London, UK. She was a faculty member of the Marie Curie Roma course at the CEU Summer University, 2007-2009. Her main research interests are ethnic relations, poverty, reproductive decision-making and anthropological demography.

Marcelo Frediani

Marcelo Frediani is a socio-anthropologist with an MA in philosophy and a PhD in social sciences (Anthropology) from the University of Louvain, Belgium. He has worked as a therapist in psychiatrics and taught sociology of social movements and political anthropology at Paris University-Vincenne. He has had a life-long interest in alternative communities and new modes of socialisation. His work on *New Travellers in England* was published by Imago in Paris in 2009.

Yasar Abu Ghosh

Yasar Abu Ghosh, PhD. has studied ethnology at Charles University in Prague and social anthropology at EHESS in Paris. His has conducted fieldwork in South Bohemia on the survival strategies of Roma and is working on a book based on this research with the working title *Escaping Gypsyness*. His current research focuses on questions of governmentality and citizenship, drawing on an historic-cum-ethnographic investigation of the placement of Romani children in children's homes, a policy intensified in the 1970's but never abandoned after 1990. He is Assistant Professor and Head of the Department of Anthropology at Charles University.

Kata Horváth

Kata Horvath is a cultural anthropologist. She is a PhD student in cultural studies at the University of Pécs and a researcher in the Káva Cultural Group, a Hungarian association which runs community theatre, theatre in education and other drama pedagogy programs. Coeditor of the of *Theatre and Pedagogy* volumes and of *AnBlokk* journal. Her main focuses of interest are: race-, queer- and performance-studies, fieldwork and arts-based methodologies, and Gypsyness in Hungary.

Cecília Kovai

Cecília Kovai graduated in Hungarian language and literature and Cultural Anthropology at the Faculty of Arts and Social Sciences of Eötvös Loránd University (ELTE), Budapest. She is PhD candidate in the Doctoral Program of Cultural Studies at the University of Pécs. Her research interests are Romany studies, gender studies, mainly using a performative approach. As a cultural anthropologist she has been working with Roma since 2000. She did three months of fieldwork in a Roma group living in a small settlement of Eastern Hungary. Since then she has conducted further field research within the same community as well as in other settlements.

Katalin Kovalcsik

Katalin Kovalcsik is an ethnomusicologist, musicologist and senior researcher at the Institute of Musicology of the Hungarian Academy of Sciences. Her main field is the musical culture and the music-making of Romani communities, the forming of the Romani stage folklore in the 1980s (as her PhD dissertation), the creation of Romani ball-room music in the 1990s, popular genres played by Roma, minority-majority musical connections in the rural environment. She is the editor of the Institute's bilingual book series "Gypsy Folk Music in Europe". She has published eight books of her own (partly with co-authors) and more articles. She has given university lectures on Romani music making in Pécs and also on Romani and Boyash languages and ethnomusicology in Budapest.

Judith Okely

Judith Okely is Emeritus Professor, Hull University, Deputy Director of IGS and Research Associate, School of Anthropology, Oxford University. She studied at the Sorbonne, Oxford and Cambridge. She has also held permanent posts at Durham, Essex and Edinburgh Universities. Her publications include *The Traveller Gypsies* (1983), *Simone de Beauvoir: a re-reading* (1986), *Anthropology and Autobiography* (1993) (co-ed.), *Own or Other Culture* (1996), *Identity and Networks* (co-ed.) (2007) and *Knowing how to Know* (co-ed.) (2008). She is working on a book 'Anthropological Practice' (Berg). This draws on dialogues with over 20 anthropologists who have conducted fieldwork around the world. It challenges formulaic, positivistic methods but reveals consistent practices as suggested in her recent debate with George Marcus in Social Anthropology.

Alexey Pamporov

Alexey Pamporov holds an MA in Social and Cultural Anthropology (2001) and a PhD in Sociology (2005). He is a Research Associate in the Institute of Sociology at the Bulgarian Academy of Sciences and a Head of the Research Unit of the Open Society Institute – Sofia. He teaches courses on Romany Everyday Culture in the Anthropology Department of the New Bulgarian University and History and Culture of Roma people in the Culture Studies Department of Sofia University. The latter programme was developed with a Course Development Competition grant from the Curriculum Research Centre of the Central European University – Budapest (2006).

Giovanni Picker

Giovanni Picker obtained his Ph.D. in Sociology in 2009 from the University of Milan-Bicocca. He is currently a researcher at the FIERI research institute in Turin, working on migration and public policy in Italy from an anthropological perspective. He is also a teaching assistant in Political Sociology of Europe in the Cultural Anthropology MA curriculum, University of Milan-Bicocca. His research focuses on the intersection of EU integration, ethnicity and citizenship in the case of Romani groupings in Italy and Romania, and covers the last twenty years. His interests are particularly centred around urban life and the contemporary city.

Johannes Ries

Johannes Ries studied Cultural Anthropology and the Study of Religion in Leipzig. In 2007 he participated in the CEU Summer University Course entitled *Multi-Disciplinary and Cross-National Approaches to Romany Studies – a Model for Europe*. His PhD in Cultural Anthropology at Leipzig University focuses on Transylvanian Romani/Gypsy cultures and the impact of organized Pentecostal missionary work. Together with colleagues he founded the *Forum Tsiganologische Forschung*. After teaching Cultural Anthropology and Romani/Gypsy Studies at Leipzig University Johannes Ries is currently working as an organisational anthropologist and consultant in Weinstadt/Stuttgart. His research interests include: Romani/Gypsy cultures, Anthropology of the Sacred and Business Anthropology.

Hana Synková

Hana Synková is a lecturer in anthropology at the University of Pardubice, Charles University and of the J. A. Komenský University in Prague. She is doing research into the strategies of NGOs that work with Roma in the Czech Republic for her PhD at the Institute of Ethnology at Charles University. She conducted research on the construction of borders and Romani migration from Slovakia and has been involved in the ongoing reform of so-called "multicultural education" in the Czech educational system. She is a co-founder and editorial board member of *Cargo – Journal for Social/ Cultural Anthropology,* the first anthropological journal in the Czech Republic.

Michael Stewart

Michael Stewart is a Senior Lecturer in Anthropology at the University College of London and a Recurrent Visiting Professor at Central European University. He has been directing the Romany Studies Summer Course programmes at CEU for over 10 years. In his 1998 publication, *The Time of the Gypsies,* Dr. Stewart reflects on the survival of the Gypsies through the socialist period in Hungary and their refusal to assimilate into the majority population. A second book, *Lilies of the Field* (a volume co-edited with Sophie Day of Goldsmiths College and Akis Papataxiarchis of the University of the Aegean), focuses on marginal people who live for the moment. Lilies presents an ambitious theoretical comparison of peoples across the globe who share some of the Gypsies' attitudes to time and history.

Zsuzsanna Vidra

Zsuzsanna Vidra is a Research Fellow at the Research Institute of Ethnic and National Minorities of the Hungarian Academy of Sciences. She holds a PhD in Sociology from the École des Hautes Études en Sciences Sociales, Paris, an MA in Sociology from Eötvös Loránd University, Budapest and an MA in Nationalism Studies from the Central European University, Budapest. She lectures at several universities in Hungary (Eötvös Loránd University, Pécs University). Her main areas of research include the construction of national and ethnic identities; labour market strategies of Roma communities; poverty and ethnicity; educational inequalities; the construction of "otherness" and the media. She has worked as a researcher on several European Union-funded projects.

Tommaso Vitale

Tommaso Vitale is Assistant Professor of Urban Sociology at the Department of Sociology, Sciences Po. Paris. Member of the Centre d'études européennes, he is the scientific director of the biannual master "Governing the Large Metropolis". His main research interests are in the fields of Comparative Urban Sociology, and in Urban Politics, where he has published books and articles on conflicts and urban change, on spatial segregation, on social service planning and on local governance of industrial restructuring. He is involved in the Milan network of Roma Associations and Advocacy Groups, providing consultancy and training for activists. He has edited the Italian books *Possible Policies. Living in the Cities with Roma* (2009) and *Roma and Public Policies* (2008).